ONE WOMAN'S PASSION FOR PEACE AND FREEDOM

Syracuse Studies on Peace and Conflict Resolution

HARRIET HYMAN ALONSO, CHARLES CHATFIELD, AND LOUIS KRIESBERG
Series Editors

Mildred Scott Olmsted, 1984. *Courtesy of Swarthmore College Peace Collection.*

ONE WOMAN'S PASSION FOR PEACE AND FREEDOM

THE LIFE OF MILDRED SCOTT OLMSTED

MARGARET HOPE BACON

SYRACUSE UNIVERSITY PRESS

First Edition 1993

93 94 95 96 97 98 99   6 5 4 3 2 1

The paper used in this publication meets the minimum requirements
of American National Standard for Information Sciences—Permanence
of Paper for Printed Library Materials, ANSI Z39.48-1984. ∞™

Library of Congress Cataloging-in-Publication Data

Bacon, Margaret Hope.
   One woman's passion for peace and freedom : the life of Mildred
Scott Olmsted / Margaret Hope Bacon. — 1st ed.
      p.   cm. — (Syracuse studies on peace and conflict resolution)
   Includes bibliographical references and index.
   ISBN 0-8156-0270-7 (alk. paper)
      1. Olmsted, Mildred Scott, 1890–1990.   2. Pacifists—United
States—Biography.   3. Women and peace—History—20th century.
I. Title.   II. Series.
JX1962.O56B33   1992
327.1′72′092—dc20
   [B]   92-13755

Manufactured in the United States of America

CONTENTS

MARGARET HOPE BACON worked for twenty-two years for the American Friends Service Committee and is a past president of the Friends Historical Association. She has authored numerous books, among them *The Quiet Rebels: The Story of Quakers in America*, *Valiant Friend, the Life of Lucretia Mott*, and *Mothers of Feminism: The Story of Quaker Women in America*. In 1981 she was awarded an honorary doctorate in humane letters from Swarthmore College.

ILLUSTRATIONS

ACKNOWLEDGMENTS

Jane Addams often said that the Women's International League for Peace and Freedom was based on pooled intelligence. In writing a biography of Mildred Scott Olmsted I found myself also writing the story of the WILPF through many decades, and in this task I had the benefit of the pooled intelligence of many women.

I must start by acknowledging the support given to me by the Jane Addams Peace Association, its executive secretary, Ruth Chalmers, and its former president, Barbara Sprogell Jacobson. Barbara Jacobson, a niece of Mildred Olmsted, and her husband Sol Jacobson, were helpful in many ways. Many current officers and members of the WILPF, including Jane Midgley, Anne Ivey, Kay Camp, Phyllis Rubin, Regene Silver, and Mary Zupernick, aided me throughout the project.

Most of the research for this book was done in the Swarthmore College Peace Collection. To its curator, Wendy Chmielewski, and its staff, Barbara Addison, Eleanor Barr, Mary Ellen Clark, Kate Myer, Marty Shane, and Wilma Mosholder, I owe a great debt of gratitude for their unfailing courtesy and helpfulness.

To J. William Frost, curator of the Friends Historical Library of Swarthmore College, to Wendy Chmielewski, to Regene Silver, and to Kay Whitlock I am deeply grateful for their willingness to read and comment on the manuscript in process.

Persons with whom I had conversations or interviews include: Enid Burke; William Burke; Ari Breckenridge; Edwin Bronner; Elise Boulding; Kay Camp; Stephen G. Cary; Ruth Chalmers; Margaret S. Clews; Marian Dockhorn; Robert Dockhorn; Polly

Fine; Robert Folwell; Anne Ivey; Betty Jacob; Barbara Sprogell Jacobson; Sol Jacobson; Roberta James; Anna Harvey Jones; Roberta Kramer; Jane Midgley; Joe Miller; Melva Mueller; Anthony Olmsted; Isabel Olmsted; Kenneth Olmsted; Marcy Olmsted; Patricia Olmsted; George Oye; Grace Potts; Phyllis Rubin; Jane Rittenhouse Smiley; Adele Saul; Robert Sayre; Roger Scattergood; Doris Schamleffer; Regene Silver; Marian Smith; Edward Snyder; Nancy Webster; Kay Whitlock; Mary Zupernick.

Finally, I must thank friends such as Lady Borton and Dorothy Kurz for their encouragement to stick with the book, and my husband, S. Allen Bacon, for his unswerving support.

INTRODUCTION

THE TWENTIETH CENTURY, now drawing to a close, has seen
two major world wars, the proliferation of scores of smaller wars
all over the globe, and the frightening development of nuclear
weapons of mass destruction. It has also seen the growth of a
worldwide reaction against war as a method of settling disputes,
and the development of an international peace movement of growing sophistication and strength.

An important role in that peace movement has been played
by the Women's International League for Peace and Freedom, begun in 1915 when women from twelve nations came together with
the ambitious goal of helping to arbitrate an end to World War I.
Of the peace organizations operating today, the WILPF is the oldest. In the more than seventy-five years since its birth, it has
spread until it now encompasses twenty-three nations. Plagued by
small numbers, great distances, constant financial crises, many
leadership struggles, attacks from the right and from the left, the
WILPF has persevered. The only international women's peace organization for many years, it has nurtured other such groups into
being, both at home and abroad.

The founders of the WILPF had been drawn from the suffrage
movement and can be considered early feminists. In common with
many other American women's groups, the WILPF dropped its
feminism during the 1920s and only began to recover it in the
1970s. Many of its members today are older women who are not
accustomed to a feminist analysis. Yet aspects of its work through
the years, in building networks of women's friendship across inter-

national boundaries, and in knitting together coalitions of women working on common issues, are illustrations of current feminist theory.

As interest in women's history has quickened in the past two decades, many scholars have begun to look at the WILPF as a case study to determine whether women have made in the past or can make in the future a unique contribution in the peace movement. And when they sought someone to interview in this quest almost all of them ended up in the company of a white-haired woman from Philadelphia, Mildred Scott Olmsted, who had begun work with the WILPF in 1921 and had known all the earlier pioneers.

Mildred Olmsted had become a pacifist in the aftermath of World War I, when she worked with the American Friends Service Committee in the battle-ravaged villages of France, and later in starving Germany. She had pioneered an exchange with the women of the USSR that began in 1931, and she had gone into Hitler's Germany in 1934 and into Austria in 1936 to look into the situation of WILPF women. During the antiwar struggle preceding World War II she had played a leading role in the creation of coalitions, and during that war she had led an effort to prevent the draft from being extended to others, including women. She fought vigorously for civil liberties during the Joseph McCarthy era and became an activist in civil rights and in the anti-Vietnam War action in the 1960s. For a whole generation, she symbolized a lifelong struggle for peace and justice.

Mildred Olmsted was gracious with all her callers, but they soon discovered that she was interested not in reminiscing about the past, as are many older persons, but rather in examining the past for what it might teach us about the present and the future. It was necessary to take the long view, she told them and the many audiences that she was asked to address. If one did, the prevalent pessimism of the last decade of the twentieth century would quickly be dispelled. Instead, one can count scores of victories. She remembered the day when the United States refused to belong to the League of Nations. Now the United States belongs to the United Nations and attempts, however imperfectly, to work in accord with the UN in international disputes. She remembered when there were only a small number of conscientious objectors to

World War I, and most were jailed or beaten up in army camps. Today the principle of the right of conscientious objection has been upheld by the Supreme Court and built into our legal system, and during the Vietnam War, when the draft was last in effect, the number of objectors was close to 100,000. She remembered a tiny peace movement in which the members all knew each other and were reviled by the general public. Today the peace movement is international in scope and is represented by a plethora of organizations. The development of such groups as Lawyers for Social Responsibility and Physicians for Social Responsibility made her feel that the movement had now spread beyond the lunatic fringe and into the respectable elements of society that had once so scorned her and her colleagues for their involvement. She was delighted by the development of such new groups to advance the study of peace as the Consortium for Peace Studies, and the Peace Academy in Washington. To her mind the peace movement had come of age and would soon have a far greater impact on American foreign policy.

Look at the other changes she had seen in her lifetime, she liked to tell audiences. Suffrage for women! The end of child labor! The gains of the civil rights movement! The birth of environmental concern! The legalization of birth control! So many, many issues for which she had fought, and won. She could hardly wait each morning to read the paper, she said, to find out what new proof there was of progress for the human race. Inevitably her optimism would lift the spirits of her listeners. At the end, she always spoke to standing ovations.

Many people began to feel that it would be important to preserve Mildred Olmsted's optimism, and her adventurous life story, for generations to come. Biographies of WILPF's founder, Jane Addams, and its longtime international executive secretary, Emily Greene Balch, both Nobel Peace Prize winners, had contributed to an understanding of the women's peace movement in the past, but Addams died in 1935 and Balch, who died in 1967, was not active in her later years. Recent books on the peace movement in the United States had slighted the contribution of women. Because I had written several biographies of reformers, among them that of a nineteenth-century woman peace activist,

Lucretia Mott, and a twentieth-century scholar involved in the peace movement, Henry J. Cadbury, I was frequently approached by people with the suggestion that I interview Mildred Olmsted, with a view to a possible book. Through my work for the American Friends Service Committee, and my membership in such organizations as the American Civil Liberties Union and the National Committee for a Sane Nuclear Policy (SANE), I had known Mildred Olmsted for many years as a frequent figure at banquets, giving and receiving awards, and an eloquent platform speaker at rallies and marches. As the women's movement developed in the 1960s and 1970s she was particularly sought after as a role model for a strong and independent woman, as well as a link to the past. The fact that she once worked with Jane Addams and other leaders of the women's movement in the 1920s attracted historians and journalists by the score. But each interviewed her about only one segment of her life. I decided that if the life of this inspiring and important woman was to be preserved properly I had better begin with a series of interviews right away. I was drawn to the project by the fact that she had entered the peace movement in the year I was born, and that her life would provide me with a review of my experience in the fields of reform.

Mildred Olmsted was almost ninety-seven when I made this decision. I went weekly for many weeks in the fall of 1987 and the spring of 1988 to her home in Rose Valley, a suburb of Philadelphia. Thunderbird Lodge is an old barn converted into two large studios for former artist owners, with a large added living wing. Here Mildred Olmsted lived in some style with a housekeeper, a gardener, and a handyman in attendance. She always had breakfast brought to her on a tray while she was still in bed, in a large bedroom suggesting her opulent tastes, with furniture of black and silver, many mirrors, and a small chest of drawers to house her collection of jewelry, gathered from all over the world. Guests were served lunch in the dining room lined with gold leaf, on elegant china and linen. There was always a color scheme; Mildred Olmsted loved to match colors, and her housekeeper enjoyed this too. When Mildred was alone, her dinner was served on a tray in front of her television set, where she kept up with the news of the day.

Many people understandably had the impression that Mildred Olmsted was wealthy. Once, before I came to know her well, I was asked by a women's organization to approach her for a generous donation. She laughed. Later I came to know that she had always had to scrimp and save in order to live in the manner to which she wished to become accustomed. Although her closets were jammed with dresses, most of them had been acquired at thrift shops and had been made wearable by her talent at mending. When a banquet was given in her honor just before her ninety-sixth birthday, her older sister, Adele Saul, had told her that she could not wear a sleeveless gown. Dutifully she rummaged in the closets until she found a beautiful blue silk with sleeves and a relatively high neck. "There was a small torn spot but I fixed it so that it wouldn't show," she told her niece, Barbara. Everyone found her radiantly beautiful that night. Mildred Olmsted had not been a beauty as a young woman, but she had grown lovely to look at in her old age, her snowy white hair piled on top of her head, high cheekbones, pink cheeks, a hawklike nose, and piercing blue eyes. There was something regal about her manner, and people often said she might have been a duchess.

Mildred Olmsted was very proud of her house, but when I began to visit her, it had a somewhat shabby, neglected air. Most of the furniture had been bought at auction many years ago. There had been little money for upkeep or even for regular heavy cleaning. Piles of papers and books were everywhere. Peace posters from various campaigns hung about, some fading. Despite the efforts of her part-time gardener, the garden, which was the very center of Mildred Olmsted's life, often seemed to need a good weeding or pruning.

As I became a regular member of this household, I discovered that Mildred Olmsted lived on a very small income. The rental from the two studio apartments barely covered the cost of heating them. The housekeeper earned room and board for herself and a son. What she paid the rest of "the staff" I never learned, but it cannot have been very much. Mildred Olmsted was always famous for being extremely careful with money.

Other things surprised me. Mildred Olmsted was known throughout the Philadelphia area as well as in many parts of the country as a staunch liberal, in the best sense of that abused word, a valiant foe of racial and religious intolerance. Yet when I talked with her I discovered that she was very conscious of class distinctions, very proud of her prerevolutionary ancestors, very oriented toward the upper-middle-class world to which her father, Henry Scott, had long ago aspired. That world had been white Anglo-Saxon Protestant to the core, and though Mildred Olmsted had worked with women of many ethnic backgrounds and faiths and considered herself and was widely thought to be entirely without prejudice, some remnants of her childhood grounding in an all-WASP society were evident in her letters and our interviews.

Mildred Olmsted was eager to have her biography written and had saved all her letters and papers, going back to early childhood, with a future biographer in mind. Her husband's papers she had also saved. She presented me with boxes and boxes of these letters and papers, some of them mildewed and mice-nibbled from long storage, and I began to sort and read them at the same time I started a series of taped interviews. I also began to interview WILPF colleagues, especially those who had worked with Mildred Olmsted in the 1930s, 1940s, and 1950s, family members, members of her local Friends Meeting, men and women who had worked with her in the peace movement. I also began reading her correspondence for WILPF in the Swarthmore College Peace Collection and tracing her through the minutes of the various WILPF boards and committees on which she served, through publications of WILPF, and through the letters she wrote to WILPF branches for twenty years, a project that ultimately occupied more than a year of my time.

I soon began to discover that the story Mildred Olmsted was telling me and other interviewers, the story with which she charmed audiences and won admiration everywhere, differed in substantial ways from the story that began to unfold from the letters and other sources I consulted. This should not have been surprising; many historians have discovered that autobiography is a good part fiction. Most people remember selectively. Some leave out all the bad memories and concentrate on the good; others make themselves miserable by reversing this process. Mildred Olmsted remembered only the victories, and these she had embellished considerably as she told them over and over, with dramatic flair. Those who knew her well sometimes called her Sarah Bernhardt. In some cases she had forgotten the very existence of men and women who opposed her. Even when I would show her in writing the evidence of such opposition, she continued not to remember it.

Because she seemed so youthful and vigorous, it was hard to remember that she was ninety-seven. Her memory seemed good to me in certain respects, but she had been repeating the same story so many times that it was hard to deflect her from the course of her narrative. Reading the transcripts of oral interviews made in the 1960s and 1970s I saw that her mind then had been more subtle, able to remember important details and deal with ambiguities. I came to realize that some memories were permanently lost and that I would have to accept the fact that I would never be able to know the answers to some pressing questions.

In addition, I soon learned from Mildred that she felt herself to be composed of four different personalities. I am not a psychologist, and I am not prepared to state that Mildred suffered from multiple personality disorder, but the experts whom I consulted felt that this sounded likely. Such persons are prone to be ignorant of whole aspects of their past because the surviving personality did not experience them.

After the first five or six sessions, our interviews became something of a dialogue. She would tell me her version of the story of her life, and I would raise questions and objections, and ask for clarifications, based on my reading of her papers or the results of interviews with others. In a strange way, I became better acquainted with some aspects of her past than she was. Once or twice she asked me whatever had become of one of her college friends. At first I was afraid to question her story, but she encouraged me to do so. "Go ahead, challenge me!" she said. And no matter how damaging my evidence was to her version of events, she would listen and say she was going to think it over. Not surprisingly, however, she soon forgot the questions I had raised and returned to her original version of the story.

As I went on with my research, I began to discover that there were elements of tragedy as well as triumph in her past. The triangular relationship she maintained between herself, her husband, and a dear and lifelong friend, Ruth, caused pain to all three. The Olmsted marriage itself had been tumultuous, involving three separations, although it ultimately endured for fifty-five years. One son had committed suicide, and Mildred Olmsted herself told me that her relationships with her two living children were not close, and they did not remember much maternal warmth in their childhoods. Some of the women I interviewed who had worked with her in WILPF admired and loved her very much; others felt bruised by her. In the WILPF records there was evidence that Mildred Olmsted had often been a controversial figure.

Mildred Olmsted's personal life and her relationships were a good deal more complicated than any I had previously dealt with in writing biography. Yet behind each book has been a quest to discover how the personal and the political interact in the person of a reformer. I did not see how I could write the biography without dealing with the personal trauma. In addition, Mildred Olmsted herself wanted me to write the whole story. She told me at great length about her personal life, and she gave me the letters to read that revealed the problems in her marriage. I wondered at first why she did this, but I came in time to see that her sense of a divided self, with which she lived for so long, demanded some final summing up and synthesizing.

Mildred Olmsted's personal story was important to tell, I concluded, because many of her problems grew out of her place in the evolving history of women. She represented a generation that had to struggle against deeply ingrained concepts of gender role in order to achieve autonomy. It was a form of pioneering that was bound to create some pain, but that made it more possible for me and many in my generation to combine the roles of homemaker and career woman, and that has led to the further liberation of our daughters.

For too long reformers in general, and women in particular, have been viewed with a double standard. They have been expected to achieve notable changes in the world, and at the same time to lead exemplary private lives. In the case of a woman, the question of whether she was a good wife and mother is always raised. Rarely is the parallel question, was he a good husband and father, asked about men. But those who create progress in society often draw their fire and enthusiasm from dealing with inner conflicts. In Mildred Olmsted's case, a passionate commitment to personal freedom, projected upon the world scene, made her a battler for peace and justice everywhere. Her story, I concluded, matters very much to us all.

*O*NE *W*OMAN'S *P*ASSION FOR *P*EACE AND *F*REEDOM

1

A Troubled Childhood

*M*ILDRED SCOTT WAS BORN on 5 December 1890, the second of three daughters of Henry J. and Adele Brebant Scott. Henry Scott had wanted a son and never hid from Mildred his disappointment in her gender. Adele Scott was wrapped up in her first daughter, Edna Adele, born three years earlier, a child of extraordinary beauty and grace. A second daughter, and a plainer one, was probably disappointing to her also. Mildred closely resembled her father, with a Roman nose, a cleft chin, piercing blue eyes under straight brows. While he was a handsome man, and she became in later years a handsome woman, she regarded herself as a child as quite plain. One of her earliest memories was being fitted for a new dress and asked to look in the mirror. "How do you like it?" her mother asked. "The dress is fine," Mildred answered, "but I hate the face."[1]

The sense of being an unloved ugly duckling dominated her childhood. When she was very young she had a high fever, which caused her mother to cut off her hair. This made her feel "more like a boy than ever," she remembered. Experiencing little closeness with her mother, she turned to her father, whom she both admired and resented, and sought to model herself after him. In return, she wanted his love. "You love Adele better than me," she once accused him. "You always prefer the first child," he answered matter of factly. This wounded her, and it came as a shock to discover later that he cared for her and Adele, not because of their intrinsic selves, but because they were his children.[2]

Henry J. Scott was a trial lawyer and for some years an assist-

3

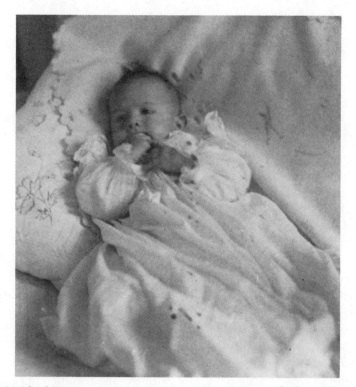

1. Mildred Marian Scott at three months. *Courtesy of Olmsted Papers.*

ant district attorney in the city of Philadelphia. The youngest of five children of John Holmes and Harriet Maull Scott, he grew up in South Philadelphia and studied law at the University of Pennsylvania. The Scotts were proud of their prerevolutionary American roots, their faithfulness to the Baptist church, and their commitment to the work ethic. John Scott was a carpenter, but his children all moved into the middle class, and Henry developed a decided taste for elegance.

It may have been this taste that drew him originally to Adele Brebant Hamrick, the gay and social daughter of an importer, Charles Hamrick, a widower who lived with his five children in fashionable North Philadelphia. The Hamricks were more social and more intellectual than the Scotts, a cut above them socially, according to Mildred. They also prided themselves on old American roots and on lifelong adherence to the Baptist church, although they were not particularly religious.

Adele Hamrick's mother had died when Adele was seventeen, and Adele had taken over running the household, playing the role of the steady one, while her more beautiful and spirited sister, Laura, was a social butterfly. But Adele too had an active social life, going to weddings and parties, and spending a week at a time visiting friends in the suburbs. She liked to dance, to play the piano, and to take part in card games. It was during one of these suburban interludes, when she served as a bridesmaid at a wedding in Moylan, that she met and fell in love with Henry Scott.

It was never a good marriage, according to Adele Saul and Mildred Olmsted, although it started out as a love affair. Aside from social life, the two had little in common; Henry soon fell out of love and treated his wife with little respect. He had a strongly Victorian view of his role as husband, and later as father. He believed himself always to be right and supported his position with a series of moral aphorisms. If his pronouncements were ever questioned by either his wife or his children he would order them to obey "because I said so" and would consider the matter closed.

Money was the root of much of the trouble in the Scott household. Henry Scott handled all the money, upbraided his wife over household bills, and kept her ignorant of the state of their finances. He would sometimes order Adele to persuade the butcher or the grocer to invest in a Henry Scott enterprise if he wanted to continue to do business with the household. He also occasionally asked his wife to ingratiate herself with his clients. Once he demanded that she board an older woman who was important to his practice. Adele resented these intrusions into her household sphere but was powerless to rebel. Her resistance was passive; she spent too much money. Both Adele and Mildred remembered scenes between their parents when the monthly bill from Wanamakers came to the house.

Henry Scott also regulated Adele's social life. Although she was a profoundly social person, he told her whom she might and might not see. He once refused her permission to have lunch with a man, even though the man was an old friend of the family and had played a part in their wedding. Adele Scott could not fight her argumentative husband, but she developed deep and lasting resentments that further poisoned the atmosphere of the family.

Before one condemns Henry Scott, it is important to remember that he was acting out of the conventional wisdom and mores of his day. The concept that man must be master of his own household was reinforced by church and state. The spheres of men and women were strictly separated, and Henry saw it as his duty to protect his wife and daughters from the tough man's world he inhabited. The other side of his need for absolute control was his sense of duty in providing well for this family. He always believed in sending the children to the best schools, and he took his wife and daughters on expensive vacations each summer he was able.

To earn money to support his family thus in proper style, Henry Scott believed that in addition to the practice of the law, at which one could earn a modest living, it was necessary to undertake other financial ventures. Sometime after his marriage, while he was still under thirty and living with the Hamricks in North Philadelphia, he bought a large tract of land in Glenolden, a farming area about halfway between Philadelphia and Chester. The tract surrounded an old farmhouse, dating back to colonial times, with a lookout for Indians and a secret passage to the river. Scott envisioned the development of a prosperous suburban area here. He divided his land into lots, built several houses, and began to invite his friends and relations to move out to the country. His brothers-in-law, Oliver and Winfield Hamrick, each bought a house at the beginning. Confident that his fortune was already made, Scott lavished attention on the house he built for himself and his family on a five-acre lot. In each room the woodwork was of a different wood—one mahogany, one oak, one maple, and so forth—and the library was stocked with fine books with tooled leather covers. The Scotts moved into the house in October 1890, and it was here that Mildred was born in December. Only a few months later, when Adele had taken her two daughters to visit her sister Laura, now Laura Biddle, in Wilkes-Barre, the house caught fire and burned to the ground. Henry Scott described to his daughter Adele his sense of utter helplessness as fire ate the books of his new library, page by page.[3]

Henry Scott next moved his family to one of the houses he had built on speculation. It was nearby, on Scott Avenue. Though not large, the house was ample for the Scotts. It had a large porch, a central hall, and four rooms downstairs; a parlor and kitchen on one side and a living room and dining room on the other. There were three bedrooms and a bathroom on the second floor, and maids' quarters on the third. The maids were not allowed to use the family bathroom but had a toilet in the basement.

Next to the house was a vacant lot, which Mildred remembered as full of daisies in summer, and a dirt road leading down to a little creek that wandered through the property, where you could dip up tadpoles and find squashed persimmons on the ground in the fall. A lonely child, Mildred turned to nature for solace, developing a love that would last a lifetime. She noticed that when adults walked in her meadow or along the stream they seemed entirely ruthless, trampling down the flowers or muddying the waters. Anger, never far below the surface, flamed in her against these transgressions.

She loved animals from an early age. Henry Scott did not allow the children to have pets, but Adele and Mildred managed to salvage some Easter chicks and raise them to be pullets. Mildred used to feed them and became quite attached to them. One of the chickens finally got so large that Henry Scott decided that they would eat him. Mildred tried to defend her pet and, when he was nevertheless brought to the dining table on a platter, refused to share the meal, but in vain. Her father insisted until she chewed a few bitter mouthfuls.

Some years later, Henry Scott was given two fox terriers by a client. Not knowing quite how to dispose of them, he gave them to Adele and Mildred. But it was too late; they were more his dogs than theirs and a nuisance to boot, getting into the sewer pipes at night and barking their heads off.

Mildred by this time had developed a passion for horses. She asked for wooden or brass horses rather than dolls for Christmas, and she began saving up her money for a real pony. William Scott, her uncle, always gave each niece a ten-dollar gold piece for Christmas, and by saving these and other windfalls she eventually had ninety dollars toward the pony. With her father's help, she

2. Mildred Scott, 20 April 1894, age three years, four months. *Courtesy of Olmsted Papers.*

placed this money in a bank. But the bank failed, and Henry Scott would not make up the loss to his younger daughter. "She has to learn what the world is really like," he said, when reproached for his hardheartedness.[4]

Hearing of her loss, a friend of her mother who lived in Springfield, Massachusetts, and had come to pay a visit said he had a horse named Mildred, and he thought it really ought to belong to Mildred Scott. Mildred was terribly excited, and when the family paid a return visit to Springfield she met her horse and thought the mare was beautiful. But as the Scotts were preparing to leave for home, the owner said he thought the horse had better stay in Springfield, and Mildred, with a burning sense of injustice, realized that she had been trifled with. She felt physically sick for days afterward. Her distrust of adults, and particularly of men, grew.

The only person Mildred felt she could rely on completely was her older sister, Adele, who was kinder to Mildred than either of her parents. She could believe Adele when she could not believe her mother, Mildred remembered. Adele always seemed to have friends, and Mildred often tagged after the older girls on their adventures. Once Adele and a girl called Kay Wilson decided to run away to Philadelphia, and took Mildred with them, pulling her in a little cart along the railroad until they came to a trestle over a river. They were part way across when they realized that they would not be able to escape if a train came along, and they hastily turned back.

Yet Adele, Mildred discovered early, did not need her as she needed Adele. Although affectionate, Adele was always aloof, self-contained, and modest despite the amount of attention heaped upon her. While Mildred told her big sister everything, Adele did not confide in Mildred. Mildred must have felt some envy and anger toward this paragon, though it was well buried by the time she reached school age. She had a memory of throwing a shoe at her older sister and thinking, as the shoe flew through the air, "What if it hits her and kills her and I'll be to blame?" She determined to overcome her temper and to learn to rule her emotions.[5]

"He that ruleth his spirit is better than he who taketh a city," Henry Scott was fond of saying. Mildred had many battles with her father but soon learned that it only made matters much worse if she lost her volatile temper. Keeping her feelings hidden became her goal at an early age. She struggled to learn rigid self-control, giving herself exercises to improve her ability to govern her emotions. She experimented with ordering her favorite food on the rare occasions when the family ate in a restaurant and then refusing to eat it when it was served. She forced herself to stand all the way to town on the bouncing trolley, though seats were available, balancing herself without holding on. She stood at the top of the stairs at the Glenolden house and let herself fall just to see what would happen. She was not hurt, and her parents were bewildered by the fall.

One day she decided to risk punishment. Normally her mother disciplined her daughters by spanking them with a clothes brush. Otherwise the girls might be reported to their father when he came home from work in the city. On this day, to her father's routine question, "Have you been a good girl?" she answered, "No." Henry Scott sent her to her room and joined her some time later, bewildered. "Your mother says you have been a very good girl." "I just wanted to see what would happen," Mildred said.[6]

She was intensely curious in this period, as she remembered it, wanting to know the why of everything. Her incessant questions drove her parents to distraction, and her father's routine answer, "Because I said so," was not satisfactory to her. She continued to make experiments on herself. Since she had two eyes and two ears and two nostrils, why not two mouths, she reasoned. She wondered if it would be possible to say two words at one time, using different sides of her mouth, and tried to experiment by holding her lips together in the middle.

When Mildred was five years and four months old, her mother gave birth to a stillborn son. The parents named him Earl and brought his two sisters to see him, lying white and still on the bed. Mildred must have experienced a tangle of emotions; here at long last was the son for whom her parents had yearned, and yet he was dead. Was this her fault? Was she now more than ever destined to fill the role she had begun to assume as hers, to make up to her father for not being born a son? But she remembered nothing more than the fact of the event. The effort at self-mastery, born of her struggles with her father and her sense of being rejected by both parents, eventually cut her off from access to her deepest feelings. Denial became habitual.

Three years later, in 1899, a third daughter, Marian, was born. She was a "blue baby" in the parlance of the day, suffering from insufficient oxygen at birth. As a result she was somewhat mentally retarded and always in poor health. Adele Scott was fiercely protective of this child and lavished affection on her.

Friends and relatives asked Mildred if she had a broken nose. Mildred did not know what they meant and felt to see if her nose was in fact broken. But she remembered feeling no jealousy. She was nine and had long ago decided her mother was not a very important member of the household. It was her father, whom she loved but could not trust, whose attention mattered.

Not surprisingly, she began to think it would be more fun to be a boy than a girl. She knew little of boys at first except for her two first cousins, Forrester Scott and Dale Barton, whom she saw at holiday time. The Scotts were not a close family, but they got together over the holidays, observing an unshakable pattern: Thanksgiving at Uncle John Scott's in West Philadelphia, Christmas Eve at Grandmother Scott's house on Farragut Street, Christmas dinner at Uncle Will's on Springfield Avenue, New Year's dinner at Henry Scott's in Glenolden. On Christmas Eve they were served nonalcoholic punch and fruitcake by Aunt Harriet Scott, who lived with her mother; on the other occasions they were fed a long and boring dinner of fourteen courses. Four of the cousins— Adele, Mildred, Forrester, and Dale—slipped away, while Florence and Ada, Uncle Will's girls, were much more dutiful and sat at the table while their elders worked their way stiffly through the meal. Inevitably the four truants got into some form of mischief. Once they dropped water bags from the third floor. Another time they took turns sampling Uncle Will's toilet water until they had used up a whole bottle. Despite watering the bottle, they were caught and punished.

The Scotts also got together during the summer, when Henry Scott would take his family to the Strathaven Inn, near Swarthmore, Pennsylvania, for a summer vacation, joined by Uncle Will, who would come along to deliver the Fourth of July oration, and the rest of the family. Here again the cousins would get into mischief. Since she was the youngest, Mildred was frequently the butt of the boys' roughhousing. They would twist her arm to see how long she could go without crying out. If she cried, the elders would intervene, and the game would be over. This was another incentive for Mildred to practice self-control.

Mildred had little to do with Florence and Ada Scott, her girl cousins. Both were confined to the female role of being passive and good, and Ada was frequently ill. Florence had learned to play the piano to entertain the company, something girls were supposed to do. Mildred was sure she would never play such a role, but she liked to hear Florence's playing and would creep into the parlor to listen.

Aunt Harriet, or "Aunty," was a pathetic figure in the Scott family. As the eldest daughter, she had been designated to stay home and take care of her mother. After the elder Mrs. Scott died, she was to come to live with Henry and Adele Scott, despite Adele's strong objections. Mildred felt for the indignity of Aunty's situation. Later, she wrote to her frequently and tried to make life a little easier for her. But Aunty was another reason that Mildred was determined not to be trapped in the female role.

In addition to enjoying her boy cousins, Mildred discovered that the conversation of men was far more interesting to her than that of women. When her parents entertained dinner guests and the women withdrew to Adele Scott's room to attend to their toilets and to gossip, Mildred thought their conversation was insipid. Instead, she tried to find ways to hang around the dining room where her father and his men guests lingered, enjoying their cigars and brandy. Once she hid under the folds of snowy damask on the dining room table in order to listen to their talk of politics and the law and the real world from which she was so sheltered.

Having given up on producing a son, Henry Scott decided that Mildred was the one of his children to be trained to follow him into the law. Beautiful Adele would surely marry well and happily; Marian was destined to be at home with her mother. Only Mildred was smart enough and assertive enough to be a lawyer. Although Mildred had been betrayed before by her father's broken promises, she trusted this one. Some day, she thought, she would have something to contribute to the interesting talk of the men, and perhaps they would let her enter in.

The other men in Mildred's life were her Hamrick relations. Grandfather Charles Hamrick, a distinguished and dapper gentleman, was interested in his granddaughters and the world they would inherit in the upcoming twentieth century. "Someday," he predicted, "you will be able to go to the wall and speak to someone in the next block." Charles and his three sons, Oliver, Winfield, and Harry, were interested in jewelry, fine china, and fabrics, and Adele Scott often bought jewelry and other imported articles from them for her home.[7]

She had to do this somewhat surreptitiously. Henry Scott had apparently quarreled with his father-in-law and brothers-in-law, perhaps over the financing of the Glenolden property, for he avoided them as much as possible. Adele invited them to visit during the day, when Henry was at work in his small law office in the city. They came frequently, for they were fond of their sister. Oliver and Win were bachelors; Harry was unhappily married. When Mildred was about eight, Uncle Oliver shocked and upset her by kissing her passionately and sticking his tongue deep into her mouth. Mildred reported the episode to her mother, who told Henry Scott. Henry ordered that this uncle was not to set foot in the house again, but after a while Adele permitted him to come, although thereafter he kept his distance from Mildred.

When it was time for school, the Scotts enrolled Adele in a small private school kept in the second floor of a household in the neighborhood. Mrs. Wilson, who must have had some background in education, taught the children reading, writing, arithmetic, and music for the first three grades. Adele was popular at this school, as she always seemed to be. After completing third grade, she was sent to a local Catholic convent, the Holy Child Jesus, much to the horror of Aunty, who was sure the nuns were going to convert her. In fact, Adele felt that she received a good education at the convent and was helped to get rid of some of the raw anti-Catholic prejudice that was endemic in her Protestant middle-class background. Too young to go to the school, Mildred sometimes accompanied Adele there to Saturday morning classes, and she felt she too learned to be more sympathetic to the nuns they sometimes saw walking together, their black robes swishing, on the streets of Philadelphia.

Mildred followed Adele to the Wilson school but made no friends there. At six she felt herself to be both unimportant and unlovable. But she was quick and did well in all her studies except singing. In the Wilson home, the piano was on the first floor, the school on the second. When it was time for singing, the teacher asked one child to go downstairs, strike a note on the piano, and carry it, by singing it, back to the group. Mildred tried and tried but was unable to carry the note. This led to a further sense of insecurity; until she was a junior in college she was inhibited about her speaking voice.

At the same time that she entered the Wilson school, Mildred started playing the piano. Both girls were offered lessons, but Adele did not keep hers up. Mildred liked piano and did well, though typically she argued with her teacher, wanting to experiment with and change the arrangements she was given to practice.

She was looking forward to following Adele to the convent, but by the time she was ready for the change her father decided to move his family back into Philadelphia. Glenolden was not developing as he had hoped; the path of upper-middle-class suburban expansion was much more along the Main Line, as the railway route to Paoli was named. The few families he had persuaded to move to Glenolden had moved away. He was faced each January with a huge sum due on his original investment in the land and little in the way of sales and rentals to offset it. At the same time, his own one-man law practice was not flourishing. He decided to seek a job as an assistant district attorney for the city of Philadelphia. This required a move to the city in the year 1899.

The Scotts first rented a house at 843 South Forty-eighth Street, around the corner from Uncle Will Scott's. This house faced east, and the backyard looked out upon a working farm, perhaps one of the last within the city limits. The city was growing rapidly, and West Philadelphia was the frontier. After about a year, the Scotts bought the other half of Uncle Will's double house and lived in it for over twenty years. Number 4708 Springfield Avenue was a substantial three-story brick-and-stone house in the Victorian style, somewhat larger than the house they had inhabited at Glenolden.

Years later Mildred's husband was to comment that her father had scarred her twice, by making her fearful of sex and by moving her to the city. The fear of sex, of having her body invaded and used by another person, was with her all her life, to the extent that she resented nursing her baby. Her Victorian father warned both of his daughters against the wiles of men and insisted that they be chaperoned at all times, but Adele grew up to overcome the fear he instilled, and Mildred did not. Just what happened to make the difference was never entirely clear to me, though I thought it must have contributed to Mildred's ambivalence about growing up to be a woman.

Her resentment of the move to the city, which was also with her all her life, was on the other hand clear enough. Having loved the country, and having often found balm for her wounded spirit in the meadows or down by the creek, she found the change a painful trauma. She hated the cement sidewalks, the noisy street-cars and drays, the houses packed together all around the block, the lack of vista. While they lived on Forty-eighth Street she at least had the farmyard to look at, but now her only relief from the city was the long backyard, separated from the neighboring yard by a low metal fence. This bit of green meant so much to her that she offered to help her father garden it. Except for an occasional rabbit, she was allowed no pets. Instead she nurtured her plants with loving care.

Even in this she was thwarted, because Uncle Will and other neighbors insisted that plants should not be allowed to grow higher than the top of the fence and thus obstruct the view of the other gardens. Mildred was always trying to get around this rule, starting such plants as small lilac bushes. Inevitably, when they got as high as the fence, she would be told to remove them, or her father would come and dig them up, perhaps to be planted at Glenolden or one of his other properties.

School was another shock. Henry Scott placed his older daughter in Regents Academy, a small private neighborhood school, at Forty-ninth and Regent. But it was expensive, and because Mildred was the better student of the two, he thought she could go to the local public school for at least a few years. A large public school had just been opened at Forty-sixth Street, and Mildred was enrolled in the fall. She entered dutifully but was bewildered by the big classes and her noisy classmates and felt she never knew what the teachers were talking about. In her anxiety, she got sick in the classroom and had to be escorted home by a neighbor boy with a note asking the Scotts to keep her at home until she was well enough to attend.

Realizing that she was not going to adjust to public school,

Henry Scott transferred Mildred to Regents Academy. Here she blossomed, finding that she enjoyed learning. She did well and after several weeks made friends with a girl her age, Frances Anderson. Frances was the first real friend Mildred had ever had. The two were inseparable, in and out of each other's houses, spending overnights and weekends together. Then Frances's mother told her she must break off with Mildred and have other friends. Whether she saw something in the intensity of the relationship that disturbed her, or whether, as Mildred later surmised, she was ambitious for her daughter to make friends with someone higher on the social scale than the daughter of an assistant district attorney, one can only speculate. But for Mildred it was a crushing blow, one in a long series of disappointments, confirming her bitter faith that one must rely on no one but one's self.

Adele as usual had made a circle of friends. Her mother was wrapped up in Marian, now a toddler. Even her father seemed to take Marian's part. When Marian wanted to pick up one of Mildred's precious rabbits, though she didn't know how to hold it properly, he insisted that Mildred give way to her younger sister.

Mildred found some solace in attending Sunday school in the nearby Baptist church, where Uncle Will was a deacon. Though both her parents were formally Baptists, they were not much interested in religion and did not attend church, but they saw to it that both Adele and Mildred went regularly. Both girls were baptized, and Mildred became a class leader. She entered into a period of conventional religiosity, praying and reading the Bible, which lasted well into her college years. She never lost her habit of questioning authority, however. She recalled in later life saying that she couldn't see that there was any difference between being sprinkled or immersed with water in baptism. "It really doesn't matter what you think," the pastor told her.[8]

Even in the city she found after a while that it was possible to search out natural beauty. From the house on Springfield Avenue she could hike to Bartram's Gardens, a colonial house and forty-acre botanical garden dedicated to the memory of John Bartram, the great naturalist. It has many flowering fruit trees and in the spring is a breathtaking scene. As often as she could, Mildred visited the gardens. In the summer was the annual trip to Strathaven Inn in Swarthmore and often as well a visit to Harvey's Lake near Wilkes-Barre, in the anthracite region of Pennsylvania. Laura Hamrick Biddle, Mildred's maternal aunt, had a cabin on this lake, and here Mildred and Adele learned to swim and to boat. They made their first trip by train without their parents one summer to spend two weeks with Aunt Laura. The lake was beautiful and cool after steamy Philadelphia, and Aunt Laura was a jolly person to visit. She was extremely sociable, liking to play poker and later bridge, and had many interesting visitors. She somewhat dominated her wealthy husband, much to Mildred's surprise, who had thought men were always the dominant ones. There were also three Biddle cousins, two boys and a girl. The boys were older, but Dorothy, who was the same age as Adele and very pretty, became close to the Scott family.

Sometime after the move to the city, Henry Scott bought a houseboat, the *Novelette,* which he kept moored off Beach Haven, at the Jersey shore. Weekends at the beach became a pleasant respite from Philadelphia heat. Mildred loved the sand, the gentle surf, the sparkle of sun on water. Sometimes she read; at other times she liked to go sailing or fishing with her father.

Reading was a source of escape and inspiration to Mildred throughout this period. Her father had amassed a good library to take the place of the one that had burned, and she went through volumes of Charles Dickens, Sir Walter Scott, James Fenimore Cooper, Louisa May Alcott, the Brontës, and other classics. When she ran out of books to read at home, she joined the local public library and loaded up with new books every Saturday. She was bothered by the puritan sense that she ought to be working rather than reading, but she kept on, in good light or bad, until she felt it had affected her eyes.

The single interest she had in common with her mother was clothes. There was a sewing room on the third floor of the house on Springfield Avenue, and once a week a seamstress came and worked on a dress for one or another of the Scott women. If Mildred needed a dress she could go up to the fourth floor or the attic, where her mother kept drawers full of fabrics, pick out a material and a pattern she liked, and ask the seamstress to fit it for her. Both Adele and Mildred learned to do some of the sewing and finishing as well as embroidery. Mildred loved nice fabrics and vibrant colors and developed an interest in style. Sitting in her mother's bedroom, sketching or sewing with Adele and her mother and perhaps an aunt or cousin, was the closest approach Mildred made to playing the role of a typical Victorian young lady.

Adele Scott was a very good cook, but most of the time she had several maids, usually Irish, working for her, and she entered the kitchen only on the maids' night off. The girls were not encouraged to hang around in the kitchen and bother the servants, and they grew up not knowing how to cook. Mildred was so determined never to play her mother's role that she decided periodically that she would never learn to cook, no matter what.

With this ambivalence about being female, Mildred resented fiercely the changes that were happening to her body as adolescence approached. Although her mother attempted to prepare her for menstruation, she was angry about it. Why were women subject to this form of periodic enslavement to their bodies? Particularly those who never wanted children? She was sure that she would never marry, for that would be placing herself in the same humiliating position as her mother, dominated and unimportant. In fact she wanted never to grow up at all but to remain young like Peter Pan and avoid all these difficult questions. She sometimes thought of herself as Peter Pan, a secret she shared with her most intimate friend after she graduated from college.

By now there were fresh grounds for humiliation for her mother. After the birth of Marian, Henry Scott decided he wanted no more children, and he no longer shared his wife's bed. Instead he undertook a series of flirtations. He went on vacations by himself and often found new women friends in this fashion. Adele, always close to her mother, knew about these activities and was very protective. Mildred was less aware of exactly what was going on, perhaps because of her growing habit of denial, but she had a sense that it was somehow her responsibility to keep her parents from quarreling.

It was at this time of adolescence, she told me and other interviewers, that she began to think of herself as having four separate selves, each with its own name and gender. Joseph was the efficient manager; Jeremiah, the philosopher of long vision; Jane, the athlete and humorist; and Judy, the artist and dreamer and lover. In the course of her long life the names she gave these different personas changed: Jonathan became the one who took the long view. She was never submerged in these different person-alities—she, Mildred, felt herself to be in charge at all times—but she recognized when one or another of the selves was dominat-ing her behavior.[9]

The development of multiple personalities in adolescence is often a symptom of some form of abuse in childhood—often phys-ical, sometimes sexual, sometimes emotional deprivation. It is im-possible to know exactly what happened to Mildred as a child to cause this rupture of the developing self. At ninety-seven she could not dredge up any buried memories, and the record of her brief excursion into psychoanalysis is lost. What we do know is that she had grown up with a strong sense that no one loved her, and that she had somehow failed her parents by being born the wrong sex. She had a sense of inner wildness which she described vividly in an undated letter probably written when she was in her late twenties:

> She is a queer person, this I of mine and leads me into strange doings when I let her have her way, as of late. Do you suppose she is to be trusted or is she just a whimsical body who is stirring up trouble for me, her master? and shall I ever again really be her master?
>
> For all she is so happy and carefree, so content to live in the present she troubles me for she takes me down to a sub-terranean sea within me which I have ignored for so long that I had almost—but not quite—forgot that it is there. I have ignored it, I have kept away from it, I have built a strong floor over it and lived above it and away from it. I have shut my ears to its sounds and crushed its existence out of my consciousness—for I feared the power which I so vaguely felt.
>
> As a child, I knew something of its intensity in the violent outbursts of temper, and in my wild hatred of injustice in others, of impotence to right it in myself, in the bitter keen-ness of even small disappointments which left me fairly sick for days.[10]

Against this subterranean sea, she built a set of controls so strong that they served to insulate her most of the time from her own feelings. The four personas she developed at this time may have helped with the insulating but they also gave her endless trouble, leading her this way and that and bewildering those who sought to be close to her. When she was in her thirties, she said, they became more muted; nevertheless, they never entirely left her. In her nineties she was still talking about the self that took the long view. The male selves tended to be dominant; as a result she often felt more like a boy than a girl.

Mildred's body reflected some of her ambivalence. Her voice and her stance were somewhat masculine, but her figure was feminine, curved and full-breasted. She was of average height and slender build and had feminine hands and feet. Her pictures from her high school days show her to be straight-browed and serious, but there is a suggestion of sweetness about her chin and lips.

In the fall of 1903, when she was just short of thirteen and in the beginning of this adolescent turmoil, Mildred Scott entered the seventh grade at Friends Central School at Fifteenth and Race, one of several excellent private schools run by the Society of Friends in the Philadelphia area. Adele had entered the seventh grade the year before, enrolling in the general course. Mildred, however, embarked on a college preparatory program.

She was prepared to be lonely, as she had been most of her school life. Many of the girls at Friends Central had been together for years. Cliques had formed, despite the best efforts of the teachers, and there were evidently small secret societies of a transient nature, as there were at other Quaker schools at that time. Mildred had so well learned to hide her feelings that she must have appeared self confident and disdainful, when she was longing for a little human warmth. No one dared reach out to her.

At first she spent her recess period at Friends Central alone, sitting out in the brick patio behind the school, trying not to appear lonely. As usual, Adele was popular and had little time to comfort her sister. Mildred passed several lonely weeks in this fashion. One day she decided to see if she could balance herself standing on a low rail fence around the inner garden. As she stretched out her arms to steady herself a girl ran out of the building and offered her a hand. Gertrude Rhoads became her friend that day and remained so for more than seventy years.

Gertrude was the daughter of a Philadelphia lawyer and lived in Oak Lane. She was an open, warm girl, always rather religious, and she offered Mildred uncomplicated friendship. Soon the two girls were often together, spending nights at each other's houses and sharing adventures. Gertrude's father was far more permissive than Henry Scott and far more supportive. He was always urging Mildred and Gertrude to try new things. Once they decided to see if they could stay awake all night, sitting on the Rhoads's front porch. The parents gave their permission, but the girls finally found it too boring and exhausting and went to bed.

The Society of Friends had a long tradition of offering girls and boys equal educational opportunities. The classes were taught separately at this time, but the girls had the same curriculum as the boys, including astronomy, botany, chemistry, geology, zoology, Latin, and Greek, subjects often reserved for boys in other institutions. Mildred remembered "eating up" the sciences, which answered some of the many questions she had asked herself for years. There were also sports, which Mildred found she enjoyed and excelled in. She was on the gymnastics team for three years and the basketball team in her senior year.

One of her favorite subjects was English composition, which was a required course every year at Friends Central. Mildred excelled in writing skills and by her senior year was sure she was going to be a writer, as well as perhaps a lawyer. Dr. John Carver, who taught English, encouraged her to write short stories, which were much admired by her classmates. At least one was published in the school magazine. Her themes were tragic, emphasizing loneliness and loss. One of the stories that survives concerns a ragged street boy who is befriended by a young woman who lives in a house he was trying to rob. Under her influence the little thief goes straight but is finally disillusioned when he learns she is marrying. In another, a girl has to give up her acting career to take care of her mother. Mildred also wrote briefer word pictures: likening the life of a city to that of the ocean, or describing a little ragamuffin boy of the streets with an infectious smile. Although derivative, the writing is crisp and sometimes moving.

Another skill she developed while at Friends Central was that of debating. There were classes in rhetoric in the sophomore and junior years, and Mildred's love of arguing found its first outlet. She remembered that her teacher in seventh grade, whom she did not like, once spoke on woman's suffrage and why she was for it. Mildred decided to marshal the arguments against woman's suffrage and presented them to the class.

This same teacher once tried to punish her for insubordination by telling her to stand in the corner. Mildred said she was willing to be punished since she thought she deserved it, but she was too old to be told to do such a childish thing. Her parents would not ask it of her. She was then sent to the principal, who thought Mildred's objections to standing in the corner were logical and excused her from that class for the rest of the year.

Mildred's habit of resisting whatever she thought unreasonable or unjust got her into trouble with some of the school rules. Once she took a piece of chocolate cake into the weekly Quaker meeting for worship that all the students were required to attend every Wednesday. A teacher saw her and ordered her to stop eating. She put the cake down, but it began to melt, so she decided she had better finish it. When the teacher saw her disobeying a second time he sent her to the principal. "Why did you do it?" he asked. "I thought it was better to eat it than to have it spill all over the meeting floor," Mildred replied. He said he thought this was reasonable and gave her only a light punishment.[11]

By the time she was ready to graduate, she had made a name for argumentativeness. In the yearbook of Friends Central for 1908, the verse next to her picture spoke of this ability: "In arguing she owned her skill / For even though vanquished, she argued still."[12]

As she grew older Mildred realized that she was quite different from the other girls at Friends Central. All her peers seemed to be becoming interested in boys, and some of them developed crushes on particular ones. Mildred realized that boys interested her not at all. On the other hand, she discovered that she liked to dance and to go to parties. When she was fifteen, her Aunt Mildred Barton, whose husband was an admiral at Annapolis, invited her to come down for a whirlwind week with the cadets. Adele

3. Mildred Scott at graduation from Friends Central, June 1908. *Courtesy of Olmsted Papers.*

had gone the year before, at seventeen, and had taken the place by storm. The cadets voted to place her picture in their yearbook, and Admiral Husband E. Kimmel, later of Pearl Harbor fame, was one of her escorts. Mildred was really too young for this debut, but by putting her hair up and her skirts down she was able to pass muster. She too was given a whirl by the midshipmen, but she knew perfectly well that they were interested in her only because she was the admiral's niece, and she came home as uninterested in boys as ever.

For Adele it was different. When she was only seventeen she met and fell in love with Maurice Bower Saul, a distant cousin through the Hamrick line. Maurice was a lawyer, a large, energetic, whirlwind of a man who carried all before him. His brother, Walter Biddle Saul, had first spotted Adele when he visited Henry Scott's office on Washington Square and decided to ask if he might call at the house on Springfield Avenue. Given permission, he began to visit Adele frequently. Hearing Walter's glowing accounts of Adele's grace and beauty, Maurice asked if he might come along on one of the visits. Soon the two brothers were both enamored of Adele. Walter finally asked Maurice how serious he was, and when Maurice said, "Very serious," Walter decided to withdraw rather than jeopardize his relationship with his brother.[13]

With the field to himself, Maurice Saul began to pepper Adele with attentions. According to Mildred, her parents became worried about how to protect this young high school girl from the tempest Maurice was creating and urged her to go away to college. Adele's memory, when I interviewed her, was that she had always intended to go to college and was not influenced by Maurice's attentions. She had not, however, taken the classical, or college preparatory, course at Friends Central, so when she decided to go to Smith College in Northampton, Massachusetts, she needed tutoring. Maurice of course eagerly volunteered to be the tutor.

Always wanting to get closer to Adele, Mildred may have resented this eager suitor who absorbed her sister's time and thought. But she liked Maurice as a companion and an accomplice in taking care of Adele. He had some of the same driving energy as her own father, to which she responded. When Adele finally left for college, Maurice and his brother, Walter, decided to take Mildred in hand, saying that she was much too naive and needed an education before she too went to Smith. They escorted her to the theater and got her books to read. While she enjoyed the attention, it did not change her mind about the male sex in general and her determination never to marry.

In 1907, following Adele's graduation, Henry Scott decided to take her and Mildred on a western camping trip. He had met a woman on his travels who had a ranch near Yellowstone National Park and had invited him to visit. Loyal to her mother, Adele was bothered by the situation, but Mildred seemed unaware that anything was amiss, writing her mother, "We were wishing you were here but all agree you could not enjoy it." Whereas previously the girls had always ridden sidesaddle, here they had western ponies and western saddles and rode all day long. Their hostess arranged for them to attend rodeos and a cowboy dance, where Mildred was struck by a sign she always remembered, "Gentlemen are asked to leave their guns outside." Later they joined a party for a week's trip into the Rockies, camping out every night under the stars and riding up through snow fields. Mildred kept a journal in the form of letters home to her mother, in which she described rather well the snow, the wildflowers, the melting streams, the stars. After the trek was over, Henry Scott took his two daughters on to the West Coast, then home by train in easy stages. Mildred's clothes were rumpled and needed mending, she wrote her mother, but her spirits were high. She had found a new love, camping. [14]

One of the great outcomes of the trip, Mildred thought, was that she and Adele were now closer than ever. But with Adele off to Smith, she felt lonesome in the fall. Gertrude Rhoads had another close friend with whom she was spending a lot of time. Maurice was rushing off periodically to Smith to see Adele, and when he was home he went to call on Adele's friend and Mildred's classmate, Dorothy Vodges, which Mildred felt was disloyal. She poured out her feelings in a letter to her sister. Adele wrote back immediately to comfort Mildred:

> I know you are different from the other girls, but you are much better, and I don't want you to be like them. And Mildred, you always have me and I always have you, and that, honey, is something, a great deal in fact . . . I think you will like college very much and I have already told Mademoiselle that if nothing unforeseen happens I would like this room next year for you and me, and I have wished so many times you were here this year, and we could take some grand long walks together. [15]

Mildred wrote back to say that things were better now, the crowd was more friendly, and she and Gertrude more intimate. Her mother was coming to depend upon her a little more. "I ought to be very happy and I want to try to be for there is everything to make me so. I want to make the most of my time for somehow I don't believe it will last so very long and someday I shall look back to it and say that was the happiest time of my life." [16]

Thus, insecure but adventurous, Mildred prepared herself for the next chapter in her life, Smith College.

2

"Educated Gentlewomen"

ℱOUNDED IN 1875, Smith College in Northampton, Massachusetts, was thirty-three years old when Mildred Scott entered in the fall of 1908. Like its sister colleges, Vassar, Wellesley, Mt. Holyoke, Bryn Mawr, Barnard, and Radcliffe, its aim was to offer young women a superior education, equal to that obtainable in the best men's colleges. But Smith also wanted to turn out "educated gentlewomen." It chaperoned its young women, insisted on dress codes, urged daily chapel attendance. Smith women were expected to learn to entertain gracefully, to wear white gloves on the appropriate occasions, to have impeccable table manners, and to make polite table conversation.

The twin goals Smith had for its graduates reflected the ambivalence of the view of educated women of the day. On the one hand, women were invited to set their sights high and to try to achieve whatever men could achieve. On the other, it was understood that the majority of them would become wives and mothers. They were prepared to be the mates of prominent men, able to hold their own in conversation, to supervise properly the education of their children, to play a volunteer role in the community.

There was also still a strong expectation that an unmarried daughter ought to return to the family fold and keep her mother company until and unless she got married. Mildred's mother wrote a somewhat plaintive letter to her college daughters, saying that "sometimes when I am here alone and need your companionship I wonder why it is I am denied your company." Though she convinced herself that it was all for the best, she looked forward to their return. In the years immediately after graduation, the letters Mildred received from her college friends were full of the struggle they experienced between wanting to get on with a profession, or at least with interests outside the home, and their deep sense of duty to be their mother's companion. Many seemed immobilized and depressed as a result of the conflict.[1]

Even the feminists of the day did little to help college women clarify their goals. The suffrage movement, now at a high point, emphasized the need for women to vote not only for the sake of fairness but because as wives and mothers they had something to contribute to the social good. The concept of combining marriage with career was new and rarely practiced. Women who chose careers, primarily in social work or education, generally expected to forgo marriage.

Mildred Scott came to Smith looking forward to more education and a career, sure that she would never marry. She somehow expected her classmates to be like her. Instead it was her first and lasting impression that they were predominantly conservative, interested in playing the conventional role of proper young ladies who would devote themselves to their families until it was time for marriage. They talked about "celebs" and sports and boys, but none of the things Mildred was interested in. She felt out of place, an ugly duckling among cygnets.

Although Adele had once promised to room with her, she had apparently decided against this arrangement when Mildred arrived on campus. Instead, Adele had found another roommate and had moved to Haven House, on the north side of the campus. For Mildred, she arranged for a room in a house for twelve first-year students at 36 Green Street. Here Mildred arrived on a late September day, her wardrobe trunk carefully packed with college clothes, a bright smile hiding her insecurity. Would she be liked? Would she find anyone she could trust?

At first prospects seemed gloomy. A number of the other women at the house on Green Street came from New England and had known each other previously. Table conversation seemed to her uninteresting. When the topic of woman's suffrage came up, Mildred was its only vocal advocate. As a result, the housemother, whom Mildred described as "prim and prissy," took to introducing

4. Mildred Scott at graduation from Smith College, June 1912. *Courtesy of Olmsted Papers.*

Mildred as "our little suffragette" whenever company came. It made a lasting impression. At the age of ninety-seven she decided not to go to her seventy-fifth Smith College reunion because she still remembered and resented that label.

Woman's suffrage in fact was not very popular at Smith at this time. The faculty did not permit a suffrage club to be organized on campus until 1913, and then under strict conditions: it was to be for education and discussion only, it was to be open to both pro- and antisuffragists, to have no outside affiliations, and to invite no speakers without the advice and consent of the president. In October 1909, when Emmeline Pankhurst spoke at city hall in Northampton, those women faculty members who attended expressed their disapproval by the tilt of their chins, according to a classmate of Mildred Scott. At about the same time, a woman speaker invited by the college to address the students lamented the new feminist ideals, which led, she said, to selfishness and shallowness and abused "that regal word 'ought.'"[2]

Mildred Scott reacted to the label of "suffragette" by attending the woman's suffrage meetings held in town. "I don't see how anyone could disagree," she wrote in her diary. Later, joining the Current Events Club, she was able to organize a debate on the issue by seeking out antisuffragists from among the student body. As a result, as she ruefully remembered, an antisuffrage group was formed. Once, she also recalled, she was at a Harvard commencement when a woman chained herself to the gate, fastened the chain with a padlock, and threw away the key. The event had a profound impression on her, making her less willing than ever to conform to the conservative values of Smith.[3]

Her rebellion expressed itself in many ways. She never liked to obey rules unless she understood them and agreed with them. At one point when she was living in a college dormitory she asked if she might paper her room in blue and brown, paying for the work herself. "The next girl who comes along might not like it," she was told. "If she doesn't like it then she can change it," Mildred argued, to no avail. She also wanted to put up a hammock in the backyard and was told that if she were permitted to do so, all the other women would want one too. "Why don't you wait and see if everybody else does?" Mildred argued. She did not get her hammock. Because there were strict rules against smoking, she decided to try cigarettes, going out into the woods to smoke. She found she liked it, and was a secret smoker throughout her college years.[4]

After a year at Smith she wrote a secret paper entitled, "Why I Am Not Like Other Girls." The others did not express opinions unless wholly conventional, did not resent anything, did not share confidences, did not defend people of whom others disapproved. "In short, not to have any strong spirit or personality was their goal," she wrote. They did not like abstract questions, had no perspective, judged quickly, went to extremes, disapproved of what they could not understand. They were sensible when alone, but "in the air" when in a crowd. They were prejudiced against woman's suffrage but had no arguments against it, "submit unquestionably to all rules whether reasonable or unreasonable—disapprove of those who do not. . . . Can see only one side of a question, close to narrow mindedness." They followed each other like sheep, lacked ambition for anything but popularity, were generous, sympathetic, and willing to help each other, but only in superficial ways. "In short, they are the world in miniature, kindhearted but narrow minded," she wrote. "The above observations are made after one year's experience with twelve girls, from one college and one class. Further experience will doubtless cause many not only modifications but complete reversals."[5]

Cut off from her housemates by these feelings of estrangement, Mildred Scott spent several lonely weeks. Then she was considerably surprised to be befriended by one of the most popular women in the group. Gwen Lowe was involved with a much older man who wanted to marry her. Her family did not approve, and Gwen was constantly in a state of crisis over the matter. She chose Mildred as a confidante for these troubles, and Mildred was glad to be turned to for advice. It was not a two-way relationship, but it gave Mildred for a while the emotional anchor she needed.

If feeling comfortable at the house on Green Street came slowly, Mildred Scott moved with speed and delight into her course work. She wanted to take as much English as possible and signed up for three courses as well as for history and math. She also went on with Latin and German, which she had been studying at Friends Central, and continued to practice the piano.

Her favorite teacher that first year was Everett Kimball, who taught English history. He raised the question of the relative merits of the parliamentary versus the American system, a discussion that Mildred Scott found very stimulating. She continued to take courses from Kimball throughout her college years but became impatient that it was always either British or American history. What about the rest of the world, especially the world east of Suez, she queried? What about Africa? Or China? But the college had no one equipped to teach such subjects at the time, so she remained frustrated. The history courses helped her to make an important decision, however; she would be a participant in history, not a spectator.

English also was a source of disappointment. The teachers at

Friends Central had been enthusiastic about Mildred Scott's writing, but at Smith the standards were evidently higher, and Mildred's themes came back with such comments as, "needs coherence," "improbable," "stilted," and "unclear." Her grades in English themes both semesters of her first year were Cs. It was a comedown, but Mildred Scott resolved to do better and continued to consider herself a budding writer.

Athletics were an important outlet to her. As soon as she was eligible she went out for field hockey and eventually made the team and earned a letter. She and some friends also organized a baseball game but were told that young ladies did not play baseball. Mildred did not want to be a young lady; at home in the dorm she loved to challenge the other girls to pillow fights and roughhousing. "Roughhoused" was a regular entry in her diary. She also liked to slip off to the library and read. Mostly, though, she was busy throughout her college years racing from chapel to class to the gym to the library, to see her teachers, to the village and back. A lifelong habit of keeping busy, of jamming too many obligations into too tight a schedule, was established.

She saw little of Adele Scott, and the old longing to be closer to her sister asserted itself. She was glad when Christmas vacation came and they traveled home together, and again when the long summer vacation stretched ahead. That summer Henry Scott took his family to Lake Temagami in northern Ontario. Maurice Saul came along to be near his beloved, and Mildred Scott was appointed chaperone to make sure the two lovers were never alone. She and Maurice fell into a pattern of together taking care of Adele, a role that delighted her.

During that first summer Mildred Scott corresponded frequently with Gwen Lowe, whom she now called Bobbie. Gwen was still having problems with her older man, and Mildred urged her to come and visit. "I must see you and talk to you. If I wanted you before, I want you ten times as much now, Bobbie, You must come, you can't possibly stay there, you must come to me, for I love you and am waiting for you."[6]

The tone of the letter would seem excessive to modern ears, but this is the language in which Mildred Scott and many of her friends wrote to each other. "I want you so badly. I feel sometimes

I can't be separated from you so long," wrote Trudy Rhoads, Mildred's friend from Friends Central, from Wellesley. The relationship between Mildred and Gwen had in fact grown deeper, and Mildred felt that she had at last found a friend she could trust. In the fall, they moved together into a small house at 13 Belmont Street with many of the other women from the Green Street house. They had no sooner gotten settled, however, than Gwen was invited to spend her junior and senior years in a socially prestigious invitational house elsewhere on campus. Mildred was not included in the invitation. Gwen agonized over leaving "Scottie," but in the end the lure of the invitation was too strong, and she succumbed.[7]

Mildred told Gwen she must go, but she felt betrayed. Typically, she was at great pains not to show her feelings. "People don't think I care," she wrote triumphantly in her diary, but she felt this disappointment as keenly as she had the loss of Frances Anderson as a friend. She continued to room with Gwen for the balance of the year, but it was not the same. The next fall, she moved into Tyler House where she shared a room with Mildred Norton, of Buffalo. The two Mildreds had very little in common. Mildred Norton, "Norty" as she was called, was exceedingly conservative. Once when they were going to Edwards Church, across the street from College Hall, she became upset because Mildred refused to wear a hat. "If they don't want me without a hat, they don't want me, and I'm going to see what happens," Mildred said. Of course nothing happened, although Norty remained uncomfortable. Despite these conflicts, however, the two got along well enough on a personal level and remained roommates the rest of their time at Smith.[8]

During her second year at college, Mildred Scott branched out into the study of physics. She loved science because it explained so much about the universe, and she determined to take as many hours as possible. Since she was also specializing in history and taking a lot of language, this meant that she was building up more academic credits than she needed, but she told the registrar she didn't care and was willing to do the work. Her grades were not outstanding, mainly Bs and Cs, but she was not particularly interested in grades and worked hard when she was interested and when she believed the course requirements were reasonable.

It was during this sophomore year that she took the first of a number of courses in elocution, which she would need to be a courtroom lawyer. She still felt inhibited about her voice, remembering the experience of being unable to carry a note when she was at the Wilson school in Glenolden. In the elocution course the students were sometimes asked to sing or to project their voices from their diaphragms. Mildred Scott was terrified of being called on and always answered that she was not prepared, when the teacher, Mary Curtis, asked her to perform. One day Professor Curtis called her into her office and tested her voice. "Why, there's not a thing the matter with your voice, you could fill an auditorium," the teacher told her. "Would you feel happier if I did not call on you until you gave me a sign that you are ready?" Mildred agreed and eventually got her courage up to speak before the group. In later years she looked back on this event as a turning point and was always grateful to the teacher who had liberated her.[9]

Despite some discouragement from her teachers, she had kept on with her writing and the ambition of becoming a writer. In her junior year she had an English course with Jeannette Lee, whom she found stimulating and challenging. However, another teacher, Mary Augusta Jordan, chose to read aloud and criticize a paper of Mildred's before the whole class. Of course it was done anonymously, but Mildred felt the teacher ridiculed her paper—"tore it to pieces," in her words. Mildred was crushed, although with typical fairmindedness she thought the teacher was correct in at least some of the criticism. She went to see Professor Jordan the next day to talk over her faults. Whatever was said in that interview, Mildred came away with the feeling that she was really not much good as a writer after all. The best she could hope to do was to write clear reports.

She was doing well at the piano, and her teacher suggested that she consider a career as a musician. She had good hands as well as excellent technique. But the world of knowledge that was opening up to Mildred seemed to her too vast to stick to anything as single-minded as music. She decided to go on learning as much as she could, while still preparing for the law.

In that same junior year she was introduced to the study of

evolution in a course on zoology. She found that evolution answered many of the questions she had puzzled over for years and felt she hardly needed to take notes, the information was so fascinating to her. The concept of biological evolution seemed to give a scientific base to the belief in human evolution, that human society was on an upward path, spiraling toward an improved social condition. This idea was basic to the Progressive Era, as the decade before 1914 came to be called, and shaped the thought of liberals in her generation. Mildred Scott never came to question it. Asked at the age of ninety-eight what she believed in, she said simply, "I believe in history," meaning that she still perceived history as leading inevitably to progress.[10]

She was, however, beginning to question the simple and fundamental religion she had learned from the Baptist church. A course in comparative religion helped to liberate her, as she saw it later. Religion had been a help to her during her adolescence, but now she was beginning to feel that she had outgrown that need, although she continued to use religious language until well into her twenties. Instead she was excited about the concept of human evolution and the possibility of playing a role in the shaping of history.

The education of the Smith women was enhanced by a series of public lectures. John Dewey came to the college twice to talk on pragmatism; Florence Kelley of the Consumers' League spoke on enlisting young women in the campaign against sweatshops and tenements. In October 1910, when a new college president, Marion LeRoy Burton, was inaugurated, Mary Woolley of Mt. Holyoke, Jane Addams of Hull House, and Julia Ward Howe of Civil War fame received honorary degrees along with six other outstanding women. Both Ernestine Schumann-Heink and Sergei Rachmaninoff gave concerts. Ellen Terry, the actress, performed and spoke to the women of Smith about her career. Vida Scudder, a Smith graduate then teaching at Wellesley and working at a social settlement, Dennison House, in Boston, told the Smith women that a social revolution was coming. "I will never see it but you will," she said, electrifying Mildred Scott.[11]

Some of these outstanding women were of course unmarried and provided the Smith women with an alternative role model to the wife-and-mother ideal. So did unmarried faculty women. Occasionally, a lecture would be scheduled on "Vocational Opportunities for College Educated Women." But the message the college gave its students was clearly mixed. The president and the majority of faculty members were male; the *College Monthly* was full of notices of the engagements and marriages of alumnae.

Mildred Scott's strong feelings against matrimony did not abate and made her feel more isolated as time went on. She wrote about it in her diary in February 1910.

> First time I have ever told anyone and I don't know why I did it now and to Norty. She has always been crazy about someone. I never have, she always has wanted to marry & nothing more. I never have, except in a very impersonal way—it would be binding and narrowing and then, the man! Since I have been very young I have felt that I am being fitted for something. I don't know what. This is probably all imagination and very foolish, I know, so I rarely think about it—in the end I shall probably be a nice settled comfortable married lady though the very thought makes me excited and rebellious and I lose my head, though I am learning to keep quiet. I shall probably suffer a great deal someday but everything is in God's hands and He is always with me and I can stand it, and I am different from most people, it seems, and influence them. [12]

In the fall of her junior year, Mildred Scott moved into Tyler House on the Smith College campus. The women at Tyler were to stay together for two years and become a closely knit group. They liked to have Sunday morning breakfast together in the house, to chat and invite guests. Mildred had chosen to room with Norty, but at Tyler she made a new and lasting friendship. Ruth Mellor, who came from Plymouth, Massachusetts, was the youngest of four children. Albert was the oldest, and well loved by his parents as their only son. Then came the twins, Edna and Louise, wrapped up in each other. Ruth was very close to her father and modeled herself after him, but she felt herself to be isolated in the family and had some of the same loneliness as a child that Mildred had experienced. This loneliness was intensified when her father died

5. Mildred Scott with her mother, Adele Scott, her sister Marian Scott, and her sister Adele Saul, at the time of her college graduation, 1912. *Courtesy of Olmsted Papers.*

suddenly during her senior year. "Passionate friendships spring from starved childhoods like pent up oil from the ground," Mildred once wrote to Ruth in analyzing the attraction between them.[13]

At the time of their meeting Ruth Mellor was a tall, warm, friendly young woman who could ride, play tennis, drive an automobile, swim, and climb mountains. Like Mildred, she was a rebel against the conventionality of their classmates and housemates and had little use for men. She also thought of her Tyler roommate as conventional, and although she and Dorothy Faunce got along well, they had little in common.

Ruth Mellor came from a well-to-do family and had brought her own horse to campus. It was the horse that first attracted Mildred Scott. Ruth was generous about sharing it, and the early entries in Mildred's journal speak of riding on Brownie, or of their rides together. The two young women took to escaping campus, going for hikes and picnics, which the Smith women called "bacon bats," to get away from campus when the atmosphere at Tyler House seemed oppressive.

Almost sixty years later, Mildred wrote Ruth to describe the origins of their friendship:

> Looking back on it I can see what attracted me to you first; it was your horse! I adored horses and a girl with or on a horse stood out instantly. So I inquired your name and interests and you, sensing my interest in Brownie, undoubtedly asked me occasionally to ride with you and suggested that I could borrow him sometimes. I never did but the possibility brought up by that generous gesture of yours brought near to fulfillment, it seemed somehow, that long, long delayed wish, even from early childhood for a pony of my own.
>
> The second thing which followed from our treks on those rides together was the realization that you were willing to be unconventional too, to go for walks in the rain or otherwise run off from the girls in "our crowd" at Tyler House whose ideas and attitudes so often smothered me and made me rise in rebellion which I didn't want to show. But you were more popular with them than I and more accustomed to living with a crowd. I wonder what attracted you to me?[14]

Despite this new friendship, Mildred Scott was still exchanging letters and visits with Trudy Rhoads and still considered her her best friend. But nobody mattered as much as Adele; throughout the journal are wistful references to catching a glimpse of her sister or going to her room only to find her out. She was still comparing herself to her older sister, always with a touch of envy; in one diary entry she wrote that she was surprised to be told that the women liked her better than they did Adele. She knew in her heart, however, that this was not true.

Adele Scott continued to be preoccupied with Maurice Saul. He blew into campus periodically, bringing huge bouquets of flowers, and took Adele and all her friends out to dinner. The other women were enchanted and kept asking when Maurice would come next. Mildred of course was invited to participate in these whirlwind visits. Maurice wanted to marry Adele, but her parents insisted that she first graduate from college. The date was finally set for October 1911.

In June 1911 Mildred Scott served as a junior usher for her sister's graduation. Then she went home to keep house for her father, while Maurice took Adele, her mother, the aunt who had raised him, Aunt Tillie, and Adele's cousin Dorothy Biddle for a premarital trip to Europe. They cruised the Mediterranean, then traveled in Switzerland, sending ecstatic letters home about the mountains and the coolness. Mildred meanwhile wrestled with trying to manage the kitchen, since the cook her mother had hired had quit. Henry Scott kept telling her he needed only very simple food, but Mildred burned the potatoes and overcooked the vegetables and served the meat half-raw. Aunt Harriet Scott, who lived around the corner, dropped by periodically to check on how Mildred was getting along and began to bring casseroles to the house, sure that her youngest brother was not getting properly fed.

Mildred Scott may have hoped to get closer to her father during this summer alone with him. She had taken up pistol shooting the summer before in order to shoot with him, and he had bought her a pistol, which she kept for years and sold only when she decided that it was unbecoming for a pacifist to own one. Whenever he took her down to the shore she liked to join him in fishing. She continued to admire him and model herself after him, although she felt that she could never trust him.

She must have reminded him during this time of her intention to follow him into the legal profession, for he told her now that he had changed his mind about that; he did not want her to become a lawyer after all and would not pay for any further education. The law, he said, was really not a good place for a woman. "All the interesting part of the law is in court, and you are at a great disadvantage being a woman." Mildred tried to argue, but it was hopeless, as it always was when Henry Scott had made up his mind.[15]

This must have been a crushing blow, but Mildred Scott did not remember it as such. Instead, she began to wonder how she was to continue her education, for the four years at Smith were clearly not enough, she thought.

Toward the end of this difficult summer, Henry Scott, who had a case in Atlantic City, moved down to live on the *Novelette* and told Mildred that it would be all right for her to visit her Aunt Laura at Harvey Lake. Since her own daughter, Dorothy, was traveling with Maurice and Adele, Aunt Laura may have exerted herself to give Mildred a good time. It was probably this summer that an anonymous jingle was written to Mildred:

> I hate the men, said Mildred Scott
> But that was yesterday, I wot
> For many, many things she's learned
> Wilkes-Barre's quite the fussers place
> The men like moths attend her grace
> The men like moths around a flame
> In hundreds to her feet, they came
> "I hate the men," was soon forgot
> By pretty little Mildred Scott. [16]

But however much Mildred Scott liked attention and enjoyed dancing, she had not changed her mind about men or marriage. Returning to Smith that fall, she decided to redeem herself in her father's eyes by learning to cook, and she enrolled in a cooking class at a neighborhood center in the village. The class was predominantly attended by engaged women and was called the Diamond Ring class. When Mildred said she was not engaged, had no intention of ever marrying, and was taking the class only because she wanted to rectify her lack of cooking ability, she was teased. Perhaps for that reason, she did not learn particularly well, although there was a Scott family legend about the lemon meringue pie she once made. Eventually she lost her cookbook and felt she forgot what few skills she had acquired.

Adele was getting married on 30 October, and Mildred took a week off from school to help prepare for the wedding. It was a formal affair, with bridesmaids and ushers, and took place at the Baptist church on Springfield Avenue to which the Scotts belonged. There were parties and fittings before the wedding and

6. Henry Scott, Mildred's father, 1908. *Courtesy of Olmsted Papers.*

endless excitement as the wedding presents began to arrive at
4708 Springfield. The young couple were moving immediately
into a new house at Rose Valley, an interesting intentional community near Media, and many of the presents went to furnish this
establishment. Maurice's boss, John Johnson, sent Adele a check
for $500, an unheard-of amount. After the wedding the Scotts
entertained twenty-five for dinner, and Mildred danced with one
of the ushers. But she was glad to leave for Smith again.

Aside from the cooking course, she was enjoying her senior
year, taking astronomy, which she loved, as well as English, history, and sociology. The sociology course, taught by Frederick

Roman, was oriented toward social work. Students were assigned families in the village whom they were to visit—Mildred drew a Greek family—and they also visited prisons and settlement houses. When a strike occurred at the Lawrence mills nearby, Professor Roman said it was not a strike but a revolution.

Mildred Scott enjoyed the fieldwork but felt that Professor Roman was a poor teacher. In December she wrote in her diary: "Dr. Roman threatened [us] in class. Told Dr. Roman many things which the other girls upheld. Next day Dr. Roman took my suggestions." Her propensity for speaking up when she thought someone was being unfair or unreasonable was growing.[17]

Several settlement house workers in addition to Vida Scudder visited the sociology class. The tie between Smith College and the settlement house movement went back to 1887, when four Smith women, including Scudder, had decided to try to do something for the urban poor and founded a College Settlement Association, enlisting the students and graduates of a number of eastern women's colleges. Two years later, College Settlement House in New York City was opened, just one week before Jane Addams and Ellen Starr opened Hull House in Chicago. Eventually, the organization supported additional settlements in Philadelphia, Baltimore, and Boston. In addition to an alumnae group devoted to fund-raising, Smith College had an undergraduate College Settlement Association. Mildred Scott joined this group and was put in charge of a project in which students dressed dolls at Christmastime for distribution to the poor families of the settlement neighborhoods.

On 5 December of this year, she turned twenty-one. Henry Scott wrote her a letter full of moral platitudes celebrating the event. "Just here let me say, always be true to your convictions. The Lord hates a coward, so do not give a rap about your enemies. 'The man that makes a character makes foes.' Keep your conscience clear, clean and conserved, and unhesitatingly follow its dictates. Have an aim in life; let it be worth while and pursue it religiously, remembering that 'Eternal Vigilance is the price of success.'"[18]

He did not, however, offer any encouragement to her to enter the law or any further help with education. Mildred had never seriously considered social work as a possible career, but she felt herself now to be in a quandary. She was sure she needed more education, but how was she to pay for it? And what should she study? Walking down the hall one day she saw a notice that the College Settlement Association was offering a fellowship for a year of postgraduate social work training to graduates of Swarthmore, Smith, Barnard, and Wellesley. Mildred decided to apply but then forgot about the whole thing. One day she rushed off to chapel, leaving her bed unmade. When she returned to the room she found a committee from the settlement association waiting to speak with her. They asked why she thought she might be interested in social work, and she told them that she had always wanted to take care of the underdog and hated people who oppressed others. The committee was evidently impressed with her answers and outlined the program. Things seemed to be going well, until one of the members mentioned that anyone who accepted the scholarship would be expected to stay in social work.

"Well, I couldn't possibly agree to do that; I don't know whether I am going to be any good at it, and I don't know whether I am going to like it," Mildred remembered telling them.[19]

In January Mildred Scott wrote a letter to the vice-president of the College Settlement Association, Eleanor Johnson, outlining her interest in the fellowship, but also her reservations. In March she received a letter asking if in fact her letter of 10 January might be considered an application. By this time it was clear to Mildred that she had no alternative. She wrote back saying yes and persuaded her Uncle William Scott and Trudy's father, E. Clinton Rhoads, to send in references.

Vida Scudder, hearing of her interest, invited her to spend the next year at Dennison House. But Mildred thought she would rather be in Philadelphia near her family and chose College Settlement, under the diminutive but formidable Anna Davies.

Social work as a profession was still new in 1912 and still very much under the control of women. Schools of philanthropy had been recently organized in New York, Chicago, and Philadelphia. For idealistic young college women, it was an exciting outlet for their energies and a welcome alternative to teaching. Many feminists chose it. Not only could women have an important voice in the establishment of social work practice, but they could believe with all the fervor of the Progressive Era that they could change society. Several of Mildred Scott's classmates entered social work after graduation and remained in the field all their lives. Mildred herself felt she had simply stumbled into social work as a poor second to studying law and eventually left the field. At the beginning she nevertheless shared some of the excitement of her friends and looked forward to the year at College Settlement.

First, though, came graduation. Mildred was involved in arrangements for Smith's traditional Ivy Day, played right wing in an exhibition hockey game, served on the committee planning the class supper, and entertained her family, her parents, Adele, and Marian, who had come to see her graduate. She walked in the parade with Norty and heard *Atlantic Monthly* editor and author Bliss Perry give the commencement address. A collation was served in the gym at noon, and there was a class supper at night. As part of her committee duties, Mildred stayed to clean up.

Several days later the women of Tyler met at Lake Winnipesaukee, New Hampshire, for two weeks of camping. The women divided the work and enjoyed canoeing, swimming, and hiking. Ruth Mellor was still mourning the loss of her father, who had died earlier that year, and she spent as much time as she could with Mildred. The two found an island that they adopted as their own and paddled around it in the moonlight. It meant a great deal to Ruth, who wrote to Mildred later in the summer:

> I want you to know how much you did for me in camp. Sometimes I feel very guilty and selfish to have come to you so much because I know a person who is unhappy and sorrowing isn't the very best company in the world but somehow I couldn't help it, although I knew I shouldn't take you away from all the fun. Your unspoken sympathy meant so much. I would come feeling so little and weak and though the ache was too big to bear you always gave me strength and made it easier for me. Aside from the love I give you, remember, I shall always be grateful.[20]

Ruth Mellor wanted Mildred Scott to visit her that summer, but Mildred was busy getting ready for a trip to Europe with Maurice and Adele. They sailed from Montreal on 2 August, stopped at Quebec the next day, and arrived at Glasgow on 11 August. The weather was cold and clear, but Mildred spent much of the trip in bed fighting seasickness. She had brought along Jane Addams's book, *Twenty Years at Hull House,* and whenever she felt able to leave her bunk she sat on the deck reading. One day she met a Hull House resident, Victor Yarros, a newspaper reporter, and was delighted to be able to ask him in person about the famous settlement house and Jane Addams, who was a hero to her.

Scotland was cold and rainy, but the three adventurers enjoyed Glasgow, took a boat ride on Loch Lomond, and visited Melrose Abbey before heading south to London. They spent a week in the city, seeing the sights and going to the theater, while Maurice transacted business for his firm. The weather continued rainy, but Adele and Mildred shopped and met American friends for lunch. Next came the continent—Brussels, Rouen, then Amiens, and finally Paris. Here Adele and Mildred met an old friend, Aunt Rhea, a childless woman who had befriended the Scott girls in their youth and had sent them glamorous presents from Paris. One gift had been a set of artist's pastels; to this Mildred attributed her lifelong interest in color. Now Aunt Rhea took them shopping and to visit Versailles and Notre Dame, while Maurice again pursued business. In the evenings they went out to dinner and the theater. All too soon it was time to catch the train for Boulogne, where their ship, the *Hamburg,* awaited them.

The crossing back was rough, and Mildred was once again confined to her stateroom. She liked being in control, and on a boat on a rough ocean she lost that sense of having a hand in directing her own destiny. But when the sea grew calm, she loved the salt breezes and spent as much time as she could on deck. She was well enough to attend the captain's dance on the last night and danced for hours. She had learned to do the new dances, the Boston and the turkey trot, and was in much demand to teach them to her partners.

Finally, on 14 September, they landed in New York. Mildred had two weeks to unpack, to see Trudy and her other friends, and to visit Adele and Maurice at Rose Valley. Then it was time to go to work at College Settlement.

3
Working Woman

C OLLEGE SETTLEMENT, the social service institution to which
Mildred Scott had been assigned, had been founded in 1892 on St.
Mary's Street and had moved in 1898 to 433 Christian Street in
South Philadelphia, a neighborhood experiencing rapid population
change as Irish, Poles, Germans, Russians, and Italians poured
into the city. Its head worker was Anna B. Davies, who had taken
the job in 1898 at the age of thirty, persuaded by her friend Jane
Addams of Hull House to enter the newly developing field of
settlement house work, in which college-trained men and women
lived among the urban poor. The settlement house workers not
only began to develop programs to alleviate some of the miseries of
their new neighbors and help them become culturally assimilated
but in some cases spearheaded social crusades against the root
causes of crime and poverty.

The College Settlement did not at first develop a crusading
bent but pioneered in cultural education. In 1908 it began a music school in which members of the Philadelphia Orchestra served
as teachers. Mary Louise Curtis Bok, wife of the editor of the
Philadelphia-based *Ladies Home Journal,* became a patron of the
settlement and helped it acquire the Christian Street property.

As new immigrants flocked into the neighborhood, College
Settlement expanded its programs to cover different nationality
groups as well as boys' clubs and activities for the elderly. The
residents tried to serve as role models to the new Americans,
teaching them not only American history but also middle-class
standards of home management and decoration. Soon new quarters

became necessary, and the settlement purchased a new house at Front and Lombard streets, near the Delaware River. An old sea captain's house, it had been beautifully equipped with mahogany doors and curving banisters, but it was situated in a declining neighborhood, opposite the sheds that lined the river. There were often drunks on the steps of the house, and the Poles and Irish who were moving into the area frequently clashed in bottle fights on the street.

It was to the Front Street house that Mildred Scott and her mother went on 1 October 1912, with her suitcase, according to instructions. They found the house locked, its aspect dirty, and the street frightening. Adele Scott was disgusted, but there was nothing to do but walk back to the Christian Street house, which was at least open. Here Mildred parted with her mother and inquired of the worker in charge what she was supposed to do now. No one seemed to be expecting the new recruit, nor was there a bed for her anywhere. She was given some work to do on a card catalog of clients, and later in the afternoon she was asked to help the members of one of the numerous clubs with the *Settlement News*. In the evening she walked back to Front Street, where Bertha Gruenberg, a resident about her age, offered to share her bed. The next day was equally chaotic, and the second night she had to sleep on the roof. Mildred had given up an invitation to visit one of her college friends in order to be on time at the settlement. She felt superfluous and unappreciated, and her quick pride was hurt.

Soon, however, she and Bertha Gruenberg were assigned an attic room in the Front Street house with the great luxury of a basin and running water. Anna Davies had the room next door and occasionally asked permission to come through Mildred and Bertha's room to wash. Mildred regarded this as a great asset. She liked Anna Davies, a short (four feet, ten inches) woman with a direct, no-nonsense manner. While other workers were intimidated by Davies's bluntness, Mildred Scott enjoyed the challenge.

Shortly after she began work, she mentioned to Anna Davies that her mother wondered if it was safe for Mildred to walk in the Front Street neighborhood at night. "That depends on you," Anna Davies said. When she subsequently asked Davies how many saloons there were in the neighborhood, Davies told her to go and find out. Mildred responded by making a neighborhood survey. Anna Davies came to like the spunky new recruit and once told her that she thought like a man—for Mildred, this was the highest compliment imaginable.[1]

A few days after she began work at the settlement, Mildred attended her first class at the Philadelphia Training School for Social Work. Organized in 1910, this school was a forerunner of the present Pennsylvania School of Social Work. It sponsored lectures by men and women who were active in pioneer social work enterprises, such as Martha Falconer, an outstanding early worker with delinquent girls, and Florence Sanville, a crusader in the field of sweatshop labor. Helen Glenn had developed an early social service department at the University of Pennsylvania Hospital and lectured on this new field. Students visited prisons, mental hospitals, training schools, and general hospitals and heard lectures on recreation, criminology, sex education, and mental hygiene. The training school's director, William Easton, worked for the YWCA and held classes there or at other locations in town. At the end of the year, each student wrote a thesis and received a certificate, not a graduate degree.

Mildred Scott found the lectures stimulating but the day-to-day work at the settlement somewhat less so. After she had been at the settlement for a few weeks Anna Davies woke her up one morning with the announcement that she was to conduct kindergarten. "But I've never even been to kindergarten," Mildred objected. "Well, you are going to find out," was the reply. Mildred did as she was told and was assigned to kindergarten on a regular basis. But she did not particularly enjoy working with the children; they often did not show up for her class, and she had to go out in the neighborhood to round up enough to make the hour worthwhile. In her diary there are entries such as "Children very bad," or "Very cross but taught them how to make paper poinsettias."[2]

In the evening, neighborhood children came to the settlement to study because there was apt to be no proper light in their homes. Mildred was often assigned to oversee this study hour. The children would be good until it was time to leave at nine o'clock.

Then sometimes the bigger boys would turn off the gas lights and open the doors of the settlement to gangs of their older brothers. The settlement workers had to bar the doors and even the transoms. Several times Mildred was alone in the Christian Street house on a Sunday night when this sort of near riot occurred. Once she remembered throwing a boy down the front steps and locking the door from the inside.

In the summer, the neighborhood children were allowed to take showers in the stalls in the backyard, each child being limited to three minutes under the water. They often wouldn't come out when told to do so, and Mildred had to go into the shower and drag children out wet. Several times gangs of small boys would try to defend their comrade, and Mildred had a small riot on her hands.

"I didn't know this was going to happen," she told Anna Davies after one of these sieges. "Well, that's your fault," Anna Davies told her. "You should know what's going to happen before it happens."[3]

In addition to the kindergarten, Mildred Scott was assigned a Bible class and a sewing class, neither of which she particularly enjoyed. She was probably too impatient and had too high standards to be an effective teacher. Besides, she found it hard to correlate the practical, service-oriented work of the settlement with the concepts of social change she was learning at the training school. At twenty-one she was more eager to get at the root of the problem than to be part of programs that she regarded as mere social palliatives.

Part of her discomfort with the settlement was her problem with other residents. Except for Anna Davies and Bertha Gruenberg she found them much more conservative than she had expected, repeating her Smith College experience. She perceived them as rigid for the most part, concerned with keeping the rules and the structure of the settlement programs going rather than with discussing the content and issues. As usual, she had little use for rules if she did not agree with them. But she was determined to be fair. "It must be my fault that I dislike the settlement workers," she wrote in her diary.[4]

In fact, Mildred Scott was often in conflict with her fellow workers over her schedule. While she slept at Front Street on weeknights, attended the training school classes, and met her obligations at the settlement, she was all over the city that year, spending long weekends with her family at 4708 Springfield, her sister at Rose Valley, or Trudy in Germantown, and squeezing into the work week a host of fittings, luncheons, and bridge parties. Many of her Smith friends were spending the year at home, involved in providing their mothers with companionship, and coming out in local society, going to teas, dances, and bridge parties. Mildred felt guilty about living apart from her family at the settlement and tried to combine the duties of daughter-at-home with those of a working woman. A typical diary entry for two days in November gives a sense of her pace:

> Tuesday: Took Margaret Lavelle to hospital then went out to West Phila and had hair washed & waved! Stopped home—got last picture and back to the settlement for lunch. Hung picture, dressed etc. and hurried to tailors—[suit] not ready. Classes then till dinner with Cyrena. Hear Jane Addams at U.P. then reception and all night with Cyrena. Wednesday: Left Martins' right after breakfast and went home to be fitted. Decided to go to A's luncheon with Mother. Helen Dalms and Katie Butler there too. Had to leave at 2 p.m. to get to Christian Street at 3:30 Study hour and play hour at 5:30.[5]

Not surprisingly she was sometimes a bit late for her groups at the settlement and not always able to accommodate the other workers when they wanted to shift hours. By March she was in trouble. Anna Davies talked to her at length about keeping to her schedule, and a few days later an older worker spent an hour supervising Mildred's sewing class. Mildred felt she was "in the wrong" but did not change her habits. The day after her session with Anna Davies she went to a costume luncheon, then on to Germantown for a bridge party, and barely made it back to the settlement for dinner and an evening of study hall.

At home, too, things were not going well. Mildred's parents were having more frequent battles than usual. It was about this time that Henry Scott became seriously involved with another

7. Mildred Scott driving a sulky, ca. 1912. *Courtesy of Olmsted Papers.*

woman, although Mildred did not know about this until some years later. Adele Scott was not well and was worried about Marian who was having learning problems and also needed an operation for tonsils and adenoids. Adele Saul visited her mother as much as possible, but she was busy with her household in Rose Valley and was pregnant with her first child. While Mildred still did not feel close to her mother, she felt responsible for her and for keeping peace in the family, and she spent as much time at home as she could. Her cousin Dorothy Biddle was getting married in April, and this occasioned many companionable sessions of sewing and fitting dresses for the wedding.

Throughout the year she kept up a lively correspondence with her Smith friends from Tyler House. Helen Wright was at the Chicago School of Philanthropy. Gwen Lowe, who had not married her older boyfriend after all, was teaching in Briarcliff Manor. Ruth Mellor was home with her mother, trying to be good humored at all times. Mildred Norton was playing the role of society woman at home in Buffalo. Several were married and expecting babies.

Mildred looked forward to June and reunion at Smith, followed by a repetition of last summer's camping trip. First, though, she wanted to march in the big suffrage parade that was scheduled in Philadelphia for early May. She had joined the College Club in the fall and through this institution learned of the plans for college women to march under the banner of their various schools. Contingents from Wellesley, Radcliffe, Swarthmore, and, of course, Smith were marching.

When she announced to her family on Friday night that she was going to join the parade, Henry Scott forbade it, saying that no daughter of his walked the streets. Mildred thought it over and told her father the next day that it was a matter of conscience and she was going to march anyway. "Then you need not come home tonight. I will not have a daughter who does not do what I say," Henry Scott told her.

Frightened but defiant, Mildred Scott joined the parade. It was a huge affair. The college women all wore their caps and gowns over white dresses. Other women were dressed in white with gold and purple banners. Bands played. They paraded up Broad Street to City Hall, passing the corner where Henry Scott had his office. Mildred saw her father in the crowd but turned her face away. At the next corner she saw her mother and sister Adele. Adele leaned out and plucked at her sleeve. "Come home tonight," she said.

Henry Scott never said a further word to Mildred about the episode. Mildred asked her mother what had happened. "It wasn't as bad as he feared," was the reply.[6]

Mildred's year at the settlement ended on 1 August. Several of her fellow students at the training school had accepted jobs for the next year. Mildred was elated in the middle of July to receive an offer to be the head worker of Friends Neighborhood Guild in Philadelphia but decided that she was too young and inexperienced for such a position. Besides, she was not sure that settlement work was her vocation.

Instead, she spent August and September vacationing, first with her parents and Marian at a farm near Quakertown, then with Ruth Mellor in Plymouth, Massachusetts, and finally with her Aunt Laura in Wilkes-Barre. She was at home in September, spending time with her sister Adele and her new nephew, Bobbie, born in June. Adele invited Mildred to help give Bobbie his bath and told Mildred that she hoped she would raise him if anything ever happened to her. But Mildred found babies uninteresting, little tyrants who lacked personality, and although she tried to hide these feelings, Adele later accused her of not being very fond of Bobbie.

Someone from College Settlement called Mildred Scott in the fall, wanting her to return to work there and take full charge of the women's club, but Mildred Scott said it did not appeal to her and went off to visit her old roommate Gwen Lowe in Newton, Massachusetts, and then Mildred Norton in Buffalo, where she attended the wedding of another member of her class. It was December before she was back in Philadelphia and ready to settle down. She put in a couple of weeks off and on at the College Settlement and then was hired by William B. Buck of the Seybert Institution, a Philadelphia foundation concentrating on youth programs, to do a survey of children with emotional, mental, or physical handicaps in the Philadelphia area.

This was her first independent job, and she wanted to do well at it. She spent several weeks in careful organization, then sent out a letter to hospital social service departments, schools, settlement houses, orphanages, church missions, and the like, asking for information about handicapped children under their care. Since few of the agencies answered the letter, she followed up by telephone calls and personal visits. By the end of three months she could report response from sixteen agencies covering 565 boys and girls in the categories under study. She had also learned to protect her independence. "Find the best way to manage Mr. Buck is to decide first and then report," she wrote in her diary.[7]

Meanwhile she found she had extra time to volunteer at the College Settlement, and also to work in the suffrage tearoom. She was asked in February of 1914 to organize Smith College Day at this tearoom, run by Philadelphia suffragists at their headquarters at 1724 Chestnut Street. By offering an attractive luncheon at reasonable cost, Philadelphia suffragists hoped to win a more favorable image in the business community. The tearoom was hung with suffrage banners and furnished with suffrage literature, and different college groups took over supplying waitresses for a day. Mildred decided to stay on after Smith Day as a regular volunteer but soon found that she was learning far more about how to be a waitress than about how to influence public opinion for suffrage. In 1937 she retold the story as a cautionary tale of how not to treat volunteers. "The only work they ever gave me to do was waiting on table in the suffrage tearoom and so in due time I went back to my social work and left suffrage to those already in it."[8]

It was shortly after this that Mildred Scott joined the Philadelphia Women's Trade Union League and began to work with the League of Girls' Clubs, organizing young working women to provide them with educational and recreational opportunities. She sponsored a club of her own, the Belmont Club, and often brought the members to her parent's house on Springfield Avenue to dance to records played on the new "keenophone," or record player, her father had purchased.

Living at home now, she was repainting and redecorating her third-floor bedroom to suit her own tastes. She stripped off layers of varnish, painted the woodwork white, and papered the walls with a black background wallpaper. She then piled puffs of blue and green silk on her bed. She had a taste for opulence in her surroundings, and her bedroom always expressed it. She had also persuaded her father to let her execute her own design for the backyard garden. She was proud to show her home to visitors.

At the end of March, she completed her job at Seybert, and she did not find regular work for some time. She nevertheless kept busy volunteering, running about to social events, and visiting her college friends, but she began to wonder just what she would do with her life. Ruth Mellor, who had become her closest confidante, wrote to her in September to encourage her flagging spirits. "Have patience for a little while, something will surely come up. Remember how guilty you felt at the settlement not being home." A few weeks later Ruth returned to the same theme.

Do you want to know how I think of you twenty years from now? When I tell you, you will know why my heart beats so fast and I get all cold as I do when there is an accident and someone is hurt. I think of you as being in a little room marked private on the door in a big building in a big city, and there I see you answering a telephone and that one sentence will change a whole big system reaching hundreds of people. Maybe a man will come to see you and in five minutes you will have mapped out for him a plan for stamping out entirely the "Black Hand" for instance, Scottie, or a scheme which will do away with slums.[9]

Finally, in January 1915, Mildred Scott found a job as field secretary for the Main Line Federation of Churches, with headquarters in Bryn Mawr. While the Main Line was an area of great wealth and beautiful estates, there were pockets of poverty and of the foreign born in each community. Mildred was hired to do casework in Villa Nova, Rosemont, Bryn Mawr, Ardmore, Wynnewood, and Narbeth. There were no other social workers in the area except for one visiting nurse, and soon ministers, teachers, doctors, and police officers were referring cases to her. Sometimes she would be called with the terse order, "Come over, a man is beating his wife." Young as she was, she had to go in and stop the beating. At first she could not always even understand what the police were talking about, but she pretended to do so. In order to look old enough for the responsibility, she took to wearing a stiff collar and a four-in-hand. She also learned to drive a car, her board presenting her with a little Model T to get around from community to community.

Anna Davies once told Mildred Scott that she was the sort of person around whom new activities developed. Rather than simply waiting for cases to be presented to her, Mildred soon was deep in a number of projects. She established a small employment bureau and a complaint bureau, made a census of part of the district, and developed a directory of resources. Her work brought her into touch with Bryn Mawr Hospital, where she discovered there was no social service department. When the Women's Committee of the hospital invited her to meet with them, she outlined the advantages of adding social services to the hospital's program. The women asked her to make a survey of the social service needs of the hospital, and when it was complete they took the survey to the doctors. The medical staff approved of the project and passed it on to the board of the hospital. This august group said they would be glad to have a social service department if the Women's Committee would finance it. The project had come full circle, and the Women's Committee agreed to take it on. At first there was little expense, since Mildred simply volunteered part of the time she was on the payroll of the federation.

Mildred Scott had studied hospital social work at the training school and had worked with hospital social workers when she was gathering material for the Seybert report. She knew that it was important to enlist the cooperation of the nurses before a social service department could be established. So she took the plan she had outlined to the superintendent of nurses and asked her to look it over. The superintendent, a large woman with a reputation as a martinet, took the plan into her office, then brought it back to Mildred Scott with every responsibility crossed out except the item that stated Mildred would sit in the clinic each day from twelve to two P.M.

For a number of days, therefore, Mildred Scott simply sat in the clinic during her lunch hour. Finally she suggested to the nurses that she would be willing to help them record the fee of fifty cents collected from each patient and also write down what the doctor had ordered. The nurses found this helpful, and soon the superintendent of nurses presented Mildred Scott with a desk in the clinic and allowed her to keep the records so that she could hand them to the nurses when the patients were called to go in to be examined.

Occasionally one of the busy doctors would look at the records on Mildred Scott's desk, and Mildred had a chance to suggest that as a social worker she could arrange to move patients to other hospitals or to nursing homes. One day the superintendent of nurses herself asked Mildred if she could get a man placed by the next day and so free up a bed. Mildred responded that she could not possibly do that in the time period allotted, but that she considered this one of her responsibilities. Shortly, she was given a desk on each of the wards and asked to begin working on transferring patients. As Mildred triumphantly said, remembering this episode, "I now had everything back from my original list."[10]

8. Ruth Mellor, Mildred's friend, ca. 1912. *Courtesy of Olmsted Papers.*

Many doctors rotated duty at the clinic. Mildred Scott soon got to know Dr. Lovett Dewees, a Quaker with a profound concern for social problems. Doctor Dewees asked Mildred if she could extend her work to cover students at the public schools, especially in areas where there was a large Italian population. Soon Mildred was helping with well-baby clinics and Little Mothers clubs. Dewees was interested in introducing the concept of birth control to the women and brought Margaret Sanger to talk with some of the mothers. Mildred Scott was present at this meeting. Margaret Sanger told the story of going into birth control work after she saw a poor woman die following the birth of her sixth child. Mildred was deeply impressed and for a while wondered whether birth control work might not be her ultimate vocation.

At about this time she was invited by some suffragists to join the Main Line Birth Control League. Because teaching birth control was actually illegal, the group met in private homes along the Main Line and was kept very quiet. One member of the group, however, whose husband was on the board of the prestigious Merion Cricket Club, decided to hold a meeting there. Word got out, and the meeting was mobbed with women who thought they were actually going to be told how to prevent pregnancy. The Main Line was scandalized, and the cricket club passed new rules that would prevent such a thing ever happening again. Socially prominent friends of Mildred's family told her that she would ruin her reputation as a young lady if she consorted with advocates of birth control. "I am not here as a young lady, I am here as a social worker," Mildred snapped.[11]

During her early days at Main Line Federation she was invited to appear before a church needlework guild to present the case for making garments for the poor families represented in her caseload. Mildred Scott continued to dread public speaking and at first wanted to turn the opportunity down. Persuaded to speak, she got to the meeting too early and had to take a walk to calm down. When she got back she was late and was being called to the front. She rushed to the platform and began talking about her families before she had a chance to tighten up. Afterwards she realized that giving a speech wasn't so bad; she had only to remember that she had information her audience needed to hear.

From then on Mildred Scott did a great deal of public speaking. She learned to dress as attractively as possible, which for Mildred always meant colorfully, then to forget about herself and concentrate on the subject. She wrote out her speeches in the beginning but then put them aside and spoke from notes. Later she simply made outlines. In her enthusiasm, she was sometimes inexact, with a tendency to exaggerate. Most audiences nevertheless warmed to her, and in time she became known for her impromptu speaking and was asked to teach courses on the subject.

Despite the many demands of her Main Line job, Mildred Scott managed to take time off in the spring of 1915 for the Smith College reunion and a houseparty with her Tyler friends at Rockport, Massachusetts. Afterwards the whole group moved on to

Plymouth for a houseparty at the home of Ruth Mellor. Ruth and Mildred had been seeing more of each other since leaving Smith and had gone on a camping trip together the previous summer, along with Ruth's mother and some other friends. During this 1914 trip Ruth's attachment to Mildred deepened. After the trip she wrote Mildred a series of sentimental letters:

> September 10 . . . I have just opened Tagore and a funny little lump that comes into my throat tells me that I love you and miss you more than I thought I would. "Jewels" how many I have, so precious I scarce dare think they are mine . . . I wonder if you have looked at the moon too.

> September 12 . . . I really am writing you all the time. This afternoon, paddling up the little brook into Billington, I wrote you volumes. Pond lilies I picked for you but they weren't very lovely . . . Scottie, tell me sometimes that you aren't drifting away beyond recall. Sweetheart!

> September 14 . . . I must write you no more. I shouldn't have written you tonight but it seems that all day all that should be and isn't has been borne in on me. You won't like this letter either. Don't worry, it will pass. [12]

Mildred at first backed away from Ruth's intensity. The Scott family was undemonstrative, and she was not used to extravagant expressions of affection. Yet she blossomed under the assurance of Ruth's love for her and did not want to lose this friend as she had lost others. She continued to correspond with Ruth and agreed to visit her again in November. At the Mellor house in Plymouth she met a slightly older divorced woman from North Carolina, Tracy, who had taken a fancy to Ruth. Tracy subsequently wrote several times to Mildred, offering to introduce her to a young matron in Philadelphia and expressing sympathy when Mildred's mother was hospitalized at Christmastime. She met Ruth and Mildred after the Tyler House reunion in June 1915 and vacationed with them later that summer in Tannersville, New York. [13]

Ruth and Mildred corresponded frequently throughout the next winter, and in the spring of 1916, Mildred, Ruth, and Adele Saul took a trip west, visiting Yellowstone Park, where Mildred and Adele had been with their father in 1907, as well as El Paso, Elephant Butte, Montana, San Francisco, and Yosemite. Adele, who was always reserved, did not care for Ruth's extravagant language or the intensity of her attachment to Mildred, but she was tactful, and the three had a fine time riding horseback and enjoying the scenery.

Mildred returned to Philadelphia and her job on the Main Line, and Ruth went south to visit Tracy on her new pecan farm, in the small town of Randall. It was during this visit that Tracy declared she was in love with Ruth, and an affair began. Ruth told Mildred about what had happened when she visited Mildred in Philadelphia during the summer, and Mildred reacted violently, as this letter from Ruth reveals.

> Scottie, Scottie, I have no words to write and yet I must or my heart will break. What have I written to make you suffer such a shock. I want you so. Dear, dear lady it isn't that you can't reach me, and haven't, you have been very close. I don't feel I have failed, not as you think. Randall has not been repeated . . . know how I want your love and sympathy. I wanted you all night . . . don't you know you are more than anything in the world to me? I know as I didn't know in Philadelphia that I am going to win. I don't want to make you suffer as I made you in Philadelphia to prove it. [14]

A few days later, Ruth wrote again.

> I have made a decision. I can't lose you, let you slip away because I am unworthy of you. The weak side of me which I have shown you wants sympathy. I have decided not to see you. I don't want our last visit repeated again . . . Randall has not been repeated. O Scottie, may you never know the hell of shame, night and day. [15]

However upset Mildred was by Ruth's revelations, she was more disturbed at the thought of losing Ruth. She felt sure that Tracy was the aggressor and Ruth the passive member of the relationship. Within a few weeks she felt that the crisis had been weathered.

Dearie, It is nice to know that time and distance haven't really separated us and made us say good-bye. It is good to feel that an ugly experience has thrown us closer together, that we can shut it up tight in the box of the past and throw it far from us while we go on secure in the realization that a real test has made our friendship only more secure. Isn't it, Ruthie?[16]

The pattern was to be repeated many times. Tracy continued to pursue Ruth, gave her an expensive ring, and dazzled her with Southern charm and attentiveness. Ruth turned to Mildred for forgiveness and moral guidance, always saying that she was unworthy of Mildred's love. Mildred was jealous of Tracy but could not bring herself to express similar emotions verbally, and she was far too controlled to do so physically.

Reflecting on these relationships as an old woman, Mildred Olmsted did not perceive Ruth Mellor as a lesbian, although she thought Ruth had several times been the passive partner in a lesbian love affair. Mildred certainly never thought of Ruth's attachment to her or of herself in such a light and was shocked when I told her that some scholars believed that Jane Addams had had a lesbian relationship with her lifelong companion, Mary Smith. "They," the lesbians, are always trying to claim people for their side, she told me.

If this seems puzzling, it is important to understand that intense relationships between women were far more common during Mildred Scott's youth than subsequently. In a society where men and women were socially segregated and where the relationships between men and women were tainted by male concepts of power and property, women turned to each other for support, love, and understanding. They wrote each other letters in extravagant and intimate language, they spent as much time as possible together, and they were often delighted to share a bed, many of them without ever considering that there might be a physical element to their feelings of closeness. In the days before Freud and his colleagues had an impact on social relations, there was little discussion of homosexuality and none of the fear of it that afflicted later generations of women and made such friendships difficult and suspect. The question that is uppermost in people's minds today—Was the relationship genital?—never crossed the minds of many of these women. (We may assume that there were probably also a percentage of lesbian relationships as we understand them today.) Passionate friendships continued after marriage, and when one friend visited another, sometimes the husband was asked to sleep elsewhere so that the friends could sleep together. As often as they could throughout their lifelong relationship, Mildred and Ruth shared a bed, in apparent innocence of the construction that might be put upon this today. I decided it was not up to me to put a name on their bonding.

Complicating the intricate relationship between Mildred and Ruth still further was the fact that Mildred had acquired a gentleman suitor. Although she liked to dress up, to dance, and to be admired, Mildred had managed to ward off any entanglements with men until she was twenty-six. When a college friend gave a journalist her address, she evaded his invitations to go out for almost a year; then she sent her loyal friend Trudy to take her place when a date was finally made. She distrusted all men, who seemed to her to have always a private agenda for getting something from her.

When therefore her friend Mally Graham Lord from Tyler House wrote her a note about Allen Olmsted, a lawyer from Buffalo recently moved to Philadelphia, Mildred Scott was prepared to dodge him as she had dodged the journalist. For months he wrote notes or left telephone messages, which she did not answer. Her mother and the maids began to tease her about her "mysterious Mr. Olmsted." Finally one night early in 1916 he showed up on her doorstep when she was home.

Mally's letter of introduction had somewhat prepared Mildred for Allen.

He has done settlement work and a lot of other interesting things besides being a great reading {sic} and very fond of music. A wild sense of humor that loves verbal practical jokes. A great longing to fly in the face of convention but a new desire to dress and act in accordance with his position in the world is causing him painful moments of transition. If he appears in overalls remember I warned you. He is a dear so I hope you like him. You certainly will like his mind and his sense of humor. [17]

Instead of overalls, Allen Olmsted wore a conservative suit and a top hat and carried a cane when he appeared. Mildred Scott was entertaining her young working women's club at the house that night, so she sent Allen to her father's library to read while she continued playing records and dancing with the women. But he must have made an impression on her in the short time she gave him, for she agreed to see him again.

Thus began a new episode in Mildred Scott's life. She found Allen's independent views refreshing and his devotion to women's rights genuine. He treated her with real respect and was willing to argue with her on equal terms. He was also, as she put it, "congenial," liking to go horseback riding and to take long hikes in the country. With him she was able to go to dances and parties without feeling compromised. Allen wrote her gay little notes in rhyme and introduced humor and wit into their conversations.

They got on so well that by spring they were having discussions about the relationships between men and women. Mildred explained to Allen her determination never to marry or have children. Theirs was to be a purely platonic relationship. Allen seemed to agree to her terms, but he kept pressing her for more dates. In June, he invited Mildred to visit the Olmsted family camp in Sardinia, near LeRoy, New York, to meet his family.

The Olmsteds were a large clan with roots in New England from the colonial period. Allen's great grandfather had moved from Williamstown, Massachusetts, to LeRoy late in the eighteenth century and had built the first house in the village. His grandfather was born and died in LeRoy. Allen's father, John Bartow Olmsted, was born in Buffalo, attended Harvard University, studied at Heidelberg, and came back to Buffalo to practice law and to marry Clara Amanda Morgan of LeRoy, one of the first graduates of Radcliffe Annex.

Clara Olmsted was evidently a woman of some ability, but she was soon immersed in motherhood. The Olmsteds had six sons with widely varying personalities. Allen and his brothers all went to private school in Buffalo before going off to Harvard, and all of them chose different professions. John Morgan went into business; Charles was an astronomer and inventor; Remington went into real estate; Harold became an artist, Allen a lawyer, and Seymour a social worker.

John Bartow's brother, Allen Seymour Olmsted, the uncle for whom Allen Olmsted was named, invented and marketed a product called Allen's Foot Ease, which made him comfortably wealthy. John himself was too interested in too many things to make much money at the law. He was a liberal, for years head of the Liberal Club in Buffalo, on the board of trustees of a number of schools, interested in the arts, and author of a book on *The Operatic Burlesque*. After some years of law practice he became a public service commissioner in the state of New York, which provided him with a steadier income. During the First World War he was a pacifist, a position that his youngest son, Seymour, or "Sims," also took.

Like his brothers before him, Allen went to Elmwood School and Lafayette Academy in Buffalo, then on to Harvard, where he received an undergraduate degree in 1909 and a law degree in 1912. He also took courses at the Harvard Business School on railroading. During his last year at law school he became president of the Harvard Men's League for Woman Suffrage. In his official capacity, he invited Jane Addams to speak at Harvard, but she was unable to promise a date.[18]

In the late fall of 1911, Allen Olmsted was asked to schedule a hall for an address by the British suffragist Emmeline Pankhurst. When he spoke to college authorities about this, he was told he could have a college hall if he invited only Harvard men, no Radcliffe Annex students and no townspeople. Allen and his league protested in vain, and finally they hired Brattle Hall so that they could invite a mixed audience. The matter became a cause célèbre, with many distinguished alumni writing to Harvard to back up Allen and his demand for free speech.[19]

In 1912 Allen was admitted to the Massachusetts bar and began practice in the legal department of the Boston and Maine Railroad. He also taught courses in English composition at Harvard that year. In 1913 he moved to New York, where he joined the firm of Cravath & Henderson and worked on anthracite coal rate cases while living at the Henry Street Settlement. Here he made friends with men and women interested in reform and new cultural trends. He entered in enthusiastically and at one point invited a group to his room to meet a poet.

It should have been a time of fulfillment for the young lawyer, but unhappily he had some difficulties with his work and was roundly criticized by a superior. This was enough to cause him to doubt his vocation in the law. He went through a period of emotional stress and depression, which manifested itself in physical symptoms about which he consulted several doctors. In January 1915 he left his job and went to California where his older brother Remington was settled, hoping to find a future direction there. But it didn't work, and after six months he came back East and accepted a job with the firm of Thomas Raeburn White in Philadelphia. It was at this time that he met Mildred Scott.

Allen Olmsted had a brilliant mind and a marvelous sense of humor and fun. He wrote witty sonnets, created bons mots, and invented games for Olmsteds to play. He had a ready ear for language and a good memory, and he drew on his classical education to find the apt quotation for every occasion. He was handsome, well-bred, and versatile; he danced and rode and played tennis with verve.

Nevertheless, he seemed to lack inner security, which caused him to doubt himself constantly and turn to others for reassurance. The others were often women. From high school on he had been involved in a series of love affairs, some slight, some not. He was deeply attracted to Grace Legat of Buffalo, but she married his older brother Harold in 1910. He then became briefly attached to her younger sister, Laura, but this was a mistake on both their parts, and Laura subsequently married Dugald Olmsted, a cousin. A third Buffalo girlfriend, Helen Heywood, ultimately turned him down to marry someone else. Although he was always able to attract women, he began to worry that he could not hold them.

When he first met Mildred Scott and found her attractive, therefore, he was determined to succeed in her courtship, and Mildred's resistance only heightened his resolve. He was intrigued by Mildred's sharp mind and forthright manner, and yet he found her extremely elusive about personal matters. She had already volunteered the information that she had no intention of ever marrying. ("Who asked you?" Allen answered.) Inviting her to Sardinia was a way of trying to get past her reserve in a place where he felt himself on firm ground.

Mildred accepted, packed a wardrobe trunk, and took a train by herself to Buffalo because her parents objected to her traveling with Allen. When she got to the camp she discovered that it was extremely rustic and that the clothes she had brought were all wrong. The Olmsteds were pleasant, but in profusion they could be intimidating. Allen himself seemed to have lost all interest in her, left her largely to her own devices, and took another girl for a walk. She departed in anger and wrote Allen a letter demanding to know why he had invited her in the first place.

Allen, who had gone to Plattsburgh for two weeks' training in the military reserve, responded with a frank letter, saying that he had invited her because he wanted to see her in a new setting, wanted to get his family's reaction, and wanted to see if she would rise to the challenge. He challenged her to be equally frank. At any rate, he told her, she owed him either a bread-and-butter letter or a birthday letter. She responded archly, and the correspondence continued. "Now that I have been here two weeks I'm beginning to get the military spirit of which an important part is the habit of bawling people out. Since I am a private I must turn to man's inferior, woman," he wrote.[20]

In early August, Adele and Maurice Saul invited Allen to dinner at Rose Valley. They liked him and became his advocates with Mildred. Later in the month, when Mildred was going through her crisis with Ruth, Allen made her his confidante. A woman he had met while at Henry Street Settlement and who had offered him emotional support while he was depressed was in love with him and had permitted him to make love to her. As Allen was not really interested in the woman, he felt he was exploiting her and giving way to his "sex urge." After he told Mildred about it he asked her to help keep him from weakly giving way to the temptation to visit Anne, as he called her.

This was just the sort of moral responsibility Mildred Scott responded to. Without perhaps realizing how much she was committing herself, she urged Allen to call upon her for support whenever he felt he was giving way to the urge to go back to New York. She told Allen that she believed the Olmsted children had not been disciplined sufficiently and therefore lacked the self-discipline to resist temptation that she had gained from her childhood. She was there to help supply that lack. Discussions of "Anne" and the other women who were to follow her became a bedrock of their growing relationship. For Mildred it satisfied the need to be turned to as the strong, important one; for Allen, the need for emotional support from a woman. It exactly paralleled the relationship between Mildred and Ruth over Tracy.

Mildred had decided that Allen was so nice that he ought to make some woman a good husband, and she suggested several of her friends to him. He dutifully looked up the women but always came back to Mildred. That fall he took a room in Bryn Mawr in order to be nearer Mildred's work, and they went riding together frequently and had dinner afterwards at a country inn. One night they lingered so long over dinner that they could not get back to Springfield Avenue in time to meet the eleven o'clock curfew still imposed by Henry Scott. When they did reach the house, it was too late for Allen to get a train back to Bryn Mawr. With her heart in her mouth, Mildred led him up to the third floor and invited him to spend the night in the guest room. He was, as Mildred told me, "a perfect gentleman," but the fact of his sleeping in an adjoining room would have compromised her in the eyes of her father. They escaped from this episode undetected, but it bonded them further. By late November Allen wrote, "I have never left you with so emphatically pleasant an atmosphere and I hardly dare speak lest the choice of a word shatter it. I have been very happy indeed all day. I have the deliberate pleasure of signing myself, love, Allen."

Some time that spring he may have asked Mildred to marry him. Mildred continued to stand firm, however. This was a friendship, not a love affair. She decided to try to interest Allen in Ruth Mellor, hoping also perhaps that for Ruth it might break the spell of Tracy. The two corresponded, and Allen sent Ruth flowers and tried to arrange to see her. But Ruth, who distrusted men even more than Mildred did, was prickly. Later in the spring Allen proposed that he join Ruth and Mildred on a camping trip.

Ruth wrote to Allen that she was game but hesitated to gamble with triangles. Mildred also made it clear that she did not think it was a good idea. Allen protested in a letter to Ruth.

> You have known Mildred longer than I, and perhaps are more fond of her than am I (though I can't imagine being quite so fond of any man as I am of her.) But I can't see why you can't make me fit into your scheme of a Mildred the same as I can you. You are one of Mildred's many fine traits, as I see her! I don't ask nearly as much for myself, only that I be considered as much a part as you are, and if you don't think me a positive blemish that is all I ask. Is this all Greek to you? Well it has seemed of late as though you saw in our triangularity a casus belli which only mutual forbearance keeps from breaking into open war. It seems silly to me, and just the contrary of my natural feelings, and perhaps my scent of the atmosphere is quite mistaken. If it is, you can do me a great favor by treating me like an ordinary person.[21]

Allen's faith that laying problems out rationally and arguing his position effectively would lead to solutions, a legacy of the Progressive Era and his own training as a lawyer, was doomed to constant disappointment in his relations with Mildred Scott and her friends. The camping trip never came off. Ruth did not cease to fear the attraction between Allen and Mildred, and for a long time Allen remained in the dark as to why this might be so.

4

The Coming of War

*W*HILE MILDRED SCOTT AND ALLEN OLMSTED pursued their friendship in the early months of 1917, war clouds gathered. Germany's declaration of total submarine warfare in February caused the United States to break off diplomatic relations with that country. In March, Germany torpedoed an American merchant ship and later in the month sank two U.S. ships, the *City of Memphis* and the *Vigilante Illinois*. President Wilson called Congress into special session and on 2 April asked for a declaration of war, saying, "The world must be made safe for democracy."

Mildred Scott always said in later years, "I believed Mr. Wilson." Although not unaware of pacifist sentiment, especially among Philadelphia Quakers, she believed at this stage in her life that war was a necessary evil, and that this war was a war to end all wars and to establish the principle of world order. Allen Olmsted felt the same way, despite the pacifism of his father and his brother. On 17 April he wrote to his congressional representative, Henry W. Watson, supporting the idea of selective conscription. "By nature I am opposed to conscription and militarism in all its forms," he said, "and write you in the belief that my views are, perhaps, typical of those of a great many other peace loving citizens, who have been brought face to face with unpleasant fact." He argued for conscription of able-bodied unmarried men, with liberal exemptions for conscientious objectors, married men, and men engaged in necessary industries. In a second letter he urged the conscription of fighting dollars and said that income tax violators should be persecuted, especially those in the higher brackets.

68

"You have called us to the colors, and we are quick to respond. But let it not be forgotten that we go in defense of democracy, and not to fight the battle of the rich."[1]

Allen did not apply for a commission, as did many of his Harvard friends, but waited to be drafted, in keeping with his concept of making the war as democratic as possible. In June, however, an invitation came to him to be a sergeant major in the First Battalion, Fourth Engineers, the Railroad Regiment. Allen enlisted and spent five weeks training at Rockingham, New Hampshire, before being shipped to France.

Like many other soldiers facing an uncertain future, Allen wanted to leave secure in his relationships at home. If Mildred would not agree to become engaged to him, which she kept making clear was out of the question, would she not come to see him in camp? And visit his mother and his favorite sister-in-law, Grace Legat Olmsted? Mildred, however, was careful to insist that this was still just a friendship. She invited Allen to join her at the Smith reunion if he would agree to also "play" with Ruth and her other friends. She wrote him news of Bryn Mawr. Allen responded for a while in kind. He arranged for one of his partners to help Mildred with legal affairs in relation to her caseload. He sent a good friend of his, a Baptist minister, Arthur Devan, to call on Mildred Scott. ("She is immensely interested in you and is gifted with a good deal more human feeling and feminine penetration than I had previously given her credit for," Arthur reported.) He tried to arrange with Isaac Sharpless, president of Haverford College, for Mildred to attend the lectures of George Herbert Palmer, the professor of philosophy at Harvard who had deeply influenced him.[2]

As the weeks passed, however, he became more and more eager to see Mildred in person. She encouraged him by saying that she missed him and would like him to be with her to read aloud a new book, *His Family,* which she subsequently sent him. She wrote that she was going to stay for a week with Ruth, who was now involved in a triangle of her own. Allen assumed this to be with two men, but in fact it was with Tracy and another woman, Ede, who was pursuing Ruth. Allen managed to get a forty-eight-hour leave, from Saturday to Monday morning, and made his way by train to Plymouth.

9. Allen S. Olmsted as a young man. *Courtesy of Olmsted Papers.*

Mildred evidently tried to make it clear in this interview that the relationship was becoming much too intense. She feared Allen was in love with her. She said that she did not expect ever to see him again and predicted he would marry a Red Cross nurse. But she agreed to write to him and to help him to remain "clean-minded," as she put it. If he felt tempted to give way to his lower self, he must turn to her. Allen found scraps of comfort in the interview. Back in camp he wrote that he thought he must be in love after all, "just as certain slanderers have been saying, and you say so too. When I begin to be unhappy because I can't marry you, perhaps I'll admit it, but not while it is strength and joy but not yearn [sic] (except to see you and hear from you)."[3]

Two days later he was on the ship *Adriatic* bound for England and looking forward to the adventure, though he knew he ought to be thinking about the submarines and the chance of death, as he wrote Mildred, and of the moral issues of the war. There were civilian women on board and a prostitute in the next cabin, so he needed to think about other things. He was reading the Bible in French in an effort to master the language and considering attending Episcopal services on shipboard.

Thus began a wartime correspondence that continued for three years. Allen wrote Mildred as often as every other day. Mildred answered somewhat less frequently but wrote quite regularly. Since their letters continually crossed in the mail they took to numbering them. By the end of 1918 Allen was writing his ninety-third letter in the series, Mildred her sixty-second.

Allen used his letters to Mildred as a sort of journal of his experiences in wartime. He described the landing in England and the attitude of the British veterans to the new American recruits and told of having to grit his teeth to keep from crying when the Yanks marched to cheering crowds in London. He shared with her the excitement of landing in Boulogne, and of coming into the war zone just south of Arras, where they were issued steel helmets and gas masks, and of hearing the roar of the cannon by night. He described the first bombed village he saw, and a trip to the Hindenburg line to see "Fritz," although he did not give her the names of any of these locations until after the armistice.

Whatever high principles had led him to want to go overseas, he was soon disillusioned. He hated army life, with its pecking order, its little tyrants, and its meaningless rules. He met a British Tommie who was fed up and thought the war could be ended immediately on the peace terms put forward by the pope. He was upset by the casual attitude toward sex of his comrades, who made frequent trips to the local brothel and talked coarsely about women, although many had wives and sweethearts back home. Most of all he disliked the constant aggressiveness, "which fills our hut with din, the office with peremptoriness, and the landscape with shell holes."[4]

Moreover, he was constantly bored. The adjutant above him did all the work and left him nothing of interest to do, and he was frequently enraged by the major, who made silly, arbitrary decisions and then would not change them. He thought of applying for a commission after all, but he was on such bad terms with the major that he was not sure it would be endorsed.

The situation brought out the worst in Allen: his tendency to depression and moods of deep resentment. Mildred wrote urging him to be aggressive, to apply for a commission, to try to make friends, to give leadership to the other men, quoting maxims of Henry J. Scott. "What you say sounds like bullying but if your mind is clear other people whose minds are blurred will look to you for guidance." And another time, "If our military system is all wrong you who see its weaknesses must get into power and change it. If you destroy yourself you remove one of the few protestants and leave the field to those who agree with it." Allen said he did not want to fit himself to army life, for then he would be unfit for anything else, and he continued to brood.[5]

Mildred tried to raise his spirits by instructing him to look at things from the other person's point of view, just as she had done:

> I used to feel that most people were too ignoble to like and each person that I met had to measure up to my standards before I accepted him. I neither expected nor desired to like everyone nor to have everyone like me. And so through school and college I was with people but not of them. I had to learn by many hurts and some pleasant surprises (to this day I am surprised to have a stranger like me and it never ceases to thrill me when I can make friends, for I've never gotten used to it,) to analyze the things people did from their own angle instead of from mine . . . like Walt Whitman, I don't believe you can hate anyone you can understand. One needs to learn to work cheerfully with those who don't understand you. To you whose early life lacked just that training (as it shows up now most awfully) I do commend it.[6]

But Allen continued to feel unhappy, and his rebellion began to center around the censorship of mail. He wrote that he hated to have his letters censored by a mere kid. One of the adjutants had been in the freshman hall for which his Harvard roommate had been responsible. Mildred wrote back to ask if the censorship was responsible for the impersonality of his letters, or if he were in a slump? She wished he could elude the censor. Finally he did so, sending several letters to her and to his law partners through the civilian mail. One letter was detected, and he was confined to camp for a month. He thought the worst was over, but a second letter was found in which he had questioned the atrocity of the Hun.

> Why don't the tommies feel this hatred of the Huns? Answer for yourself; but my answer is that it is 50-50. Over the teacups yesterday an Ausy was telling me that his officer, in detailing him to escort two prisoners to the rear, disarmed him for fear he'd bayonet them in cold blood. That certain troops never take prisoners is well known. In specific instances I know of, firing by the "Hun" on hospitals and churches has been justified (to my mind) by using of these hospitals and churches by the British for military purposes. Do you get a chance to talk to British aviators who drop bombs on undefended German cities? So let's not get too wrought up by the barbarities of the Hun.[7]

On the basis of this letter he was charged with violating General Routine Orders by criticizing the operation of Allied troops and by justifying Hun atrocities, and he was brought up for court-martial on 11 January 1918. Allen conducted his own defense and argued that he had in fact shown that letter to his commanding officer, that he still believed every statement he had made was true, and that he thought his views were consistent with the official utterances of the president of the United States, and "far more in harmony with the aims for which we entered the war than are the views, for example of those who habitually use the word 'Huns' in referring to the German people, with whom we have no quarrel."[8]

Allen's eloquence did not move the court, and he was reduced to the rank of private and fined. Now at last he would be doing the railroad work he had joined the engineers to do, he wrote Mildred, but it would be pick-and-shovel work on the rails, not office work on the legal angles of railroading. His mother, upset by the news, wrote him a critical letter, but Mildred was supportive. She said she knew what "gall and wormwood" the experience had been, and she wished she could get her letter to him quickly because he sounded as though he were left "skinned." But perhaps this experience would do him good in the long run, turning him from a man of thought and feeling to a man of action. Responding to a second letter about his ordeal she said she would not desert him; in fact she would write to him more frequently hereafter.[9]

This support in time of trouble was exactly what Allen craved, and his feeling for Mildred grew deeper. He told her about his sexual temptations and fantasies, and the one occasion when he "spooned" with a French woman, and his periods of depression. When she scolded him for these transgressions he seemed to like it and declared that "the Allen you started is not, without you, self sufficient." He even told her about the French girl, Jeanne, who sold milk to the troops and had fallen in love with him. He described his imaginary son, Richard, whom he had fantasized about for years, and asked her once more to explain to him how it could be that she never wanted children of her own.[10]

Even before the court-martial he had been alarming Mildred. He sent her a wristwatch for her birthday, which she regarded as far too expensive a present, and signed his letters, "Love to the dear source of all my happiness." She wrote to him early in January to suggest that the time had come for her to help him fall out of love with her. Although she truly believed that he was a better man with her than without her, it was too big a price to pay if it meant future unhappiness. Why did he not transfer to some place where there were lots of American and English girls who wanted husbands and homes of their own, instead of just love. "Please think about it, Allen and stop while there is still time to save us both from so much pain."[11]

But Mildred's efforts to discourage Allen's interest were always hedged by her insistence that he needed her to keep straight and that he must always turn to her whenever temptation struck. She also made it clear that she needed his love and interest, although she knew she had no right to ask for it when she had no intention of marrying him.

Allen's court-martial brought a temporary end to talk of terminating the relationship. Instead, in her concern to provide him with support, Mildred's letters grew more personal. She revealed to him her sense of being four separate selves and told of Jeremiah overcoming Joseph. (Allen responded that he was not sure that her organization of herself into squads and platoons was correct.) She explained that she wanted to love and be loved and yet not be in love entangled. She had always wanted love, but as a child it had brought her so much pain that she had thrust it from her. Now she knew she needed it from everyone and everywhere. She told him of the sense of inner wildness that she had known as a child before she was tamed, and that made her sometimes feel like Mowgli. Perhaps she ought not to send these letters to him, she wrote, and yet she continued to write in this vein. "People tell me I need love to humble my pride and break my spirit . . . I am not always strong, I want love, want it sometimes, oh far more than you have ever known or dreamed of . . . what that is is not playing with fire, it is playing with opium!"[12]

Yet despite the emphasis she put on the new, feminine Mildred that was emerging like a butterfly from its cocoon, Mildred was still ambivalent about her gender role. When Allen asked for a picture, she sent one of herself and a Smith friend dressed as men in tuxedos and high hats. "You asked for a picture of Mrs. Scott's daughter? Will you accept one of her son?" she inquired.[13]

Whoever she really was, Allen began to long to see the new Mildred who was opening herself to him in her letters. He suggested that she ought to consider coming to France to work with the Red Cross or the Smith Unit, which he had visited. He found the Smith girls in a chateau with the roof blown off. They seemed to him very chatty, very collegiate, wandering around in fur coats over plain clothes, and with no idea of military discipline. They ran a store, he discovered, and provided recreation for children while giving out clothes and materials. Mildred would have to learn French in order to do social work. France was a big country. She need not see him unless she wanted to. Meanwhile she should not miss the great experience of their lifetime.

His arguments fell on fertile ground, for Mildred was feeling restless. Ever since her return to her job at the Main Line Federation in the late summer of 1917, things had been going wrong. Her new assistant had tangled the agency up in a case they should not have taken up and run the car into a telephone pole. The chair of the social services committee at Bryn Mawr Hospital had appendicitis. Mildred was having trouble with her board, who were so averse to progressive ideas, she thought, that she had decided to initiate new projects and then inform board members, rather than seek their approval.

Ruth Mellor suggested leaving social work for newspaper work. Mildred thought about applying for the Smith Unit in France, and looked into the Red Cross and the Friends Reconstruction Unit training at Haverford College. Allen's younger brother Sims had decided to join this unit, and before going overseas he called on Mildred at Allen's request. Mildred was noncommital about Allen, he said, even refusing to send Allen a message.

While she was debating what to do, an invitation came from a social work friend, Alicia Brown, to consider becoming her assistant in working for the Girls' Protective League in the district around Camp Meade, near Laurel, Maryland. The camp had recently grown from 40,000 to 75,000 men, and young women camp followers were flocking to the area. As a result there had been some serious disappearances of young women. "I would be her assistant of course, but Alicia is far better at dealing with individual cases so most of the organizing would fall to me," Mildred wrote Allen. She wanted his advice about getting the military police to help locate new arrivals and to turn them over to her. She would have to find someone to take her place at Bryn Mawr for six months, or longer if she decided to go on to either France or Russia.[14]

In December she was asked to take charge of all Red Cross civilian relief on the Main Line and given half a dozen volunteers and a secretary. But there proved to be very few families of servicemen in need, and she was busier trying to keep the volunteers employed than in doing casework. She wrote Allen that she felt as he did that "when such great things, such epoch making forces are loose in the world, I want to be there to help mold them." When a formal invitation came to accept the job at Camp Meade she told her board that she was taking a six-month leave of absence, and she was shortly at Laurel, Maryland, taking up her new duties.[15]

At first she simply did what she had been asked to do, tried to intercept young women arriving by train, to ask them who they had come to see, and to arrange for the soldiers to meet their dates under chaperoned conditions. When girls refused to return home and proved to be sleeping around, she was supposed to pursue them to their lodgings, get in touch with their families, and in certain cases, arrange for their admission to a reformatory. She had always disliked this sort of casework, and in this situation felt herself to be acting the role of enemy. She decided without consulting anyone to try to seek more positive solutions. She began arranging dances and other recreational outlets for the soldiers and their girls, reasoning that this would help to get at the root of the problem. She found an old empty factory building, negotiated for its use, set up a decorating committee, and imported additional young women for the dances from Baltimore and Washington.

When she first moved to the area she stayed at a small inn in Laurel, Maryland. Mothers, wives, sisters, and chaperoned sweethearts of the soldiers also stayed at the inn. "We eat at long tables, and at first there were dreadful silences and then raising of eyebrows when it was found that I was not an officer's wife but a lone woman in a camp town," she wrote Allen. "All this is changed now, 'government service,' is both a cloak and a shield." Attitudes had shifted when a high-ranking officer came to consult Mildred about an upcoming social event, and thereafter the women were eager to be involved and to serve on her committees.[16]

Mildred Scott herself attended the dances and found herself the focus of male attention. One soldier wanted to kiss her, another to hold her hand. Both Ruth and Allen wrote to her urging her to unbend a little, to wear frilly blouses and allow the men to "fuss" her. She loved the dancing and the attention but kept on her guard, preferring to give amorous soldiers a short lecture on moral behavior than to compromise her own high standards. Still she thought she was on a downward path to approachableness and wrote Allen that "I am getting so soft and feminine that I fear I'll never be content with just plain hard work again."[17]

But work she did, with her usual drive and enthusiasm. In addition to planning the dances, she needed to enlist the cooperation of the local community in entertaining the soldiers. Mildred Scott began to speak at churches and other public forums about supporting the boys. She was increasingly critical of the complacency and stick-in-the-mudness of the local populace, but she evidently hid her feelings and became effective in enlisting citizens in her campaign.

None of this was exactly what she had been hired to do, but she did it well and was asked to expand her services to small encampments throughout Maryland. Soon other agencies that were supposed to be doing wartime community work protested the activities of the lively Miss Scott, who seemed to be poaching on their territory. A meeting of top-level officials was called to resolve what was being called "the Laurel situation." As a result of this summit conference, Mildred Scott was given an additional recreation worker and assigned directly to the Recreation Department. Alicia Brown was also given additional responsibility, but Mildred was subsequently transferred out of her department.

In love with Mildred though he was, Allen was sometimes surprised by her behavior. In the case of this transfer he wondered how Alicia felt about it and if Mildred would be even more ruthless if Alicia had been a stranger. Was she guided by ambition more than she realized? "Do you feel a strong desire to see Mildred Scott get along? Pride, personal ambition, what you will but not the desire to have things conducted according to your ideas, do you have much of a struggle to keep these down—not down, but away from your personal self, thus making them the driving power of your projects and your visions?"[18]

Allen felt himself to have very little ambition. To have authority over another man would always be painful to him, he felt. Yet he had finally decided to apply for a commission, in part because Mildred found it embarrassing that he was still just a private. His application was denied, and he got drunk for the first time in his life in reaction. Mildred wrote him to protest:

> On the train to Washington there was a colored man. The conductor jostled him roughly and told him to make way. I started to protest, then realized that he was drunk or half drunk. One could not respect his rights if he didn't respect

his own. And then I realized that the same was true of Allen.
Disgusting but less bestial than the other. Your desire to try
anything once is dangerous. . . . I hope the war won't end
until it has wiped out jingoism among the allies and made its
wonderful work of internationalism irrevocable and practical.[19]

Later in the summer, Allen managed to transfer to another
regiment situated near Dijon, and here he was made a sergeant
again, with a desk job to keep him occupied. Although he sometimes felt like a slacker because he was not in the thick of the
battle, he was very sure by now that he would never be able to
shoot another human being.

Back in Maryland, Mildred Scott's reaction to her own new
authority was mixed. She had been enjoying her work at Laurel for
the direct contact with the soldiers and civilians and thought of it
as a vacation from the community organization work of the Main
Line. She had grown tired of being "a moral force" and enjoyed
relaxing and acting more like a girl than she had for years. She was
dealing with group politics again. But she was glad to have the
recognition and came to enjoy traveling about Maryland. Moreover, she felt as though people liked her, which had not always
been the case on the Main Line. Sometimes she could hardly believe that she was the same person as the lonely, friendless little
girl she had once been.

Her travels for the Recreation Department meant that she
had to spend part of each week in Annapolis. Here she met a
family, the Cronmillers, who took her in. Mrs. Cronmiller was a
dowager, often nicknamed "the duchess," who entertained Mildred's friends and family when they came to visit, and who made
Mildred a part of her own extended family.

Still, Mildred longed to go overseas. In early February Allen
had gone to the Red Cross office in Paris and spoken with a college friend, Lewis Gannett, currently serving as public relations
officer with the American Red Cross, who said social workers were
needed and suggested that Mildred contact the director of civilian
relief in Washington. Allen in his eagerness cabled this information to Mildred, who promptly followed up with a trip to Washington. She introduced herself by saying that the Red Cross in

France had cabled her, which mystified the office staff. She was interviewed and told that she would normally not be considered because of her lack of fluency in French, but under the circumstances they would try to oblige their colleagues in France. What salary would she expect? Mildred told them $2,500 and worried afterwards that this was too low.

Shortly after the interview, Mildred Scott received a letter from the Red Cross, asking again who exactly had cabled her to reply. When she responded that it was not a Red Cross official, but a Mr. Olmsted, they grew cool and told her she would have to study French and apply in the regular fashion. Mildred's quick pride was affronted. She decided that she would never apply until they asked her to do so, and that she would wait until they needed her badly enough to ask.

Allen was at first taken aback. He wrote Mildred that he was amused by her saying that she had been cabled to apply, and by her asking for $2,500 when he felt he was overpaid at $399. Later, as Mildred's upset became clear, he grew alarmed. He made a special trip to Paris to explain to Lewis Gannett what had happened, and he urged Mildred to overcome her pride and submit an application in the regular manner. "We must be guided by reason," he argued. Mildred, however, remained hurt and refused to consider humbling herself in this fashion. Allen turned to urging her to consider the Smith Unit or the Friends Reconstruction Unit, working with the Red Cross, but Mildred was determined to hold out for an invitation from the Red Cross and several times asked him to hurry up the Red Cross from his end.[20]

Ruth Mellor was also interested in going overseas, mainly to be with Mildred. The two continued to correspond and see each other as much as possible. Ruth tried to get a job in war work in Washington so she could live with Mildred in Laurel but was unsuccessful. She clearly felt threatened by Mildred's growing absorption in Allen, yet she told Mildred she felt it was good for her to "play" with a man and to cultivate the feminine side of her nature a little more. Identified with Mildred, sometimes almost submerged in Mildred's strong personality, she felt at times as though she were involved in the developing romance, playing a role behind the scenes. Allen continued to ask Mildred about Ruth and to remain mystified by her attitudes, as reported to him by Mildred. What could she possibly mean about playing a role in their relationship? "She may be behind your scene but why behind my scene?" he wrote Mildred.[21]

Hearing that Ruth was again going to Randall, Allen asked if there was a man there she was seeing, and if she would someday marry. Ruth wrote Allen protesting. "I do believe you are one of those conceited men who believe that men are absolutely essential to a girl's happiness. Do you truly believe that a girl doesn't go anywhere without having a man the reason for it? Tell me. I admit they are a heap of fun, and a heap of bother and on the whole not very satisfactory, they have such a bad habit of spoiling a perfectly good friendship . . . right this minute you want to do it."[22]

Mildred Scott also wrote and visited her old friend Trudy Rhoads, who had married her brother's best friend, Ted Prichard. Prichard and Brewster Rhoads both belonged to Philadelphia's First City Troop, but the group was broken up, and Ted was sent overseas during the summer of 1918. Trudy came to see Mildred on her way to say goodbye to her young husband. Mildred thought she was Madonnalike in her dedication. After Ted left, Trudy became ill, and Mildred visited her in the hospital. In October came the news that Ted had been killed in battle. Mildred immediately cabled, "Shall I come to you or will you come to me?" She took time off to comfort her bereaved friend and was herself touched by Trudy's nobility and her determination to be sure that Ted had not died in vain.

The war seemed to be coming to an end. Mildred Scott longed for an end to the casualties but was not sure the nation was ready:

> This world brotherhood idea which we are forging so slowly, so painfully is not yet old enough or strong enough to stand, I fear. The Junkers, the Nationalists, the "eye for an eye and tooth for a tooth" men, the "bitter enders" are still in the majority. How many Old Testament followers there are in the world and how very few Christians—how very few! They openly denounce every teaching of Christ's and yet, because it

is in modern garb, they cannot see the most obvious parallel-
isms. I marvel at the things which Wilson makes them stand
for, through him, and I think it must be that they fail to
grasp what he is really saying. If only he is strong enough to
hold them to it. I fear if the reins of war pressure and sentiment are removed they will run amuck.[23]

Already, she noted, members of Philadelphia's conservative
Union League club such as her own father were calling Wilson
unreliable and personally ambitious. Perhaps he was, but so long
as his path ran with the world's advancement she hoped he would
stay in power. And it looked now as though she were going to get
the chance to keep him in power with the suffrage amendment
moving forward.

It is positively thrilling to see the way women are being
swept into every kind of work. It seems as though all the bars
are down. I am perfectly bewildered by the number of things
I should like to do. Oh to disappear like Rosalind in the fairy
tale, and come back as twelve people! It all illustrates that
economics is at the base of everything. The press has taken
up the cry and I don't believe women would be laughed at for
attempting anything. If I were a lawyer, now, for example I
think both Maurice and father would try to take me in!

Last year's ideas are as out of date as last century's. I only
hope I live to see the working out of it all! How good it is to
be young and strong![24]

After the unsatisfactory work at the suffrage tearoom in Philadelphia, Mildred Scott had taken no further part in the suffrage
struggle, but late that fall, she and a friend from Maryland went
to Washington to participate in the "Pageant of Enfranchised
Women." Mildred was dressed in the white costume of Ireland
and wore a red sash. Afterwards she and her friend were sent to a
house in the suburbs and given two cots in an attic already containing twenty occupied beds. In the morning they discovered
they were sleeping among suffragists, "most of them short haired
Jewesses on from New York and not a few of them Russian Bol-
shevists. Truly in that dim attic light they were both beautiful
and idealistic figures."[25]

On 11 November Allen was walking across a field near his camp outside Dijon. As he went out from camp he could hear the roar of battle; on his return there was a strange silence. "I heard the war end," he wrote Mildred, sharing his reactions and telling her about some of the places he had been and action he had seen that he had concealed for the sake of the censor.

War's end intensified Mildred Scott's desire to go abroad. Although stubbornly insisting that the Red Cross must send for her, she had begun to realize that this might not happen. She therefore had applied to the YMCA, as Allen had suggested. The Y personnel officers at first told Mildred that with her skills she ought to work for the Red Cross but were finally persuaded to offer her an appointment to do recreation work with the troops still in France awaiting demobilization. She would sail some time in January, she wrote Allen, and perhaps their ships would pass on the ocean. It would be just as well. The letters had gone smoothly, but if they were actually together again irritations would flare up, and they would be just Mildred and Allen once more.

Allen, however, was one of the many soldiers who were kept in France during the peacemaking process, in order to space out demobilizations. Eventually he and some of his fellow soldiers were assigned to Paris and allowed to take courses at the Sorbonne while awaiting their freedom. After all the months of boring work as a clerk and his frustrations with petty authorities, Allen was delighted to engage his mind once more. The army had intensified his devotion to personal freedom, he wrote Mildred, and his desire to fight for and to administer justice. He wanted either to go into politics or to become a judge. He was ready to make a fresh start in life at age thirty-one. Most of all he wanted to see Mildred again.

5

Over There

MILDRED SCOTT SAILED FOR FRANCE aboard the S. S. *Cretic* on 1 February. At a YMCA meeting in the United States as part of her orientation, Mildred had indicated particular interest in the college-educated troops and had suggested adult courses for them while they were still abroad. She therefore had hopes of being assigned to the unit at the Sorbonne. She had also checked with the American Friends Service Committee in Philadelphia and was told she might transfer to their reconstruction service after six months.

"You had little faith in my ability to get abroad now?" she wrote Allen triumphantly. "If you want a thing, go after it!"[1]

She was feeling successful, having been replaced by a man— "because I was doing a man's job"—at the War Camp Community Service. Allen's recent letters had been full of pessimism and his personal sense of failure, and she chose this occasion to lecture him about having a bad attitude and about his need to take control of his life, to be willing to exert leadership. He claimed that there was no relationship between efficiency and promotion in the military, but she was sure that certain personalities would triumph. Put Maurice Saul in any regiment and he would rise to the top, she said. Unselfishness and kindness did not lead to success, although they helped; as a social worker she herself chose group leaders for her ability to control them and their ability to control others. She apologized for the peppery letter and invited him to respond in kind.

One thing Mildred Scott could never learn to control was the sea. She was miserably seasick as usual on the voyage over but recovered sufficiently to enjoy dancing with the soldiers in London, where she waited for three weeks before being assigned by the Y to Paris. Although she had often said she was not sure that she and Allen should meet again, she took care to keep him informed by cable of her movements. Finally, on 1 March, they met in Paris.

Allen Olmsted would refer all his life to the joy he felt seeing Mildred on that windy March day; a joy that caused him to burst out laughing when he caught sight of her. They talked for awhile in her room while the landlady kept peeking in nervously; then they went for a walk in the Tuileries gardens, where Allen managed to snatch a few kisses. It was the beginning of a short idyll for them both. Allen was very sure now that he was in love, although Mildred's adamant attitude against marriage and children remained a serious block. Mildred was less sure, but she was young and in Paris with a handsome and devoted suitor, and she must have decided to seize the day and not to worry about the consequences. She still kept physical expression under strict bounds, but Allen was allowed to hold her hand, to kiss her, sometimes to put his arms around her. At the time it was enough for him.

Stationed in Paris and taking courses at the Sorbonne, Allen had plenty of time to plan ways to entertain Mildred. He made a long list of the best restaurants of the city as well as the principal sights in Paris and its environs, and during the four months they had together, off and on, he managed to take her almost everywhere—to the Louvre, of course, and the Eiffel Tower and Versailles, but also to the Comédie Française, to the opéra comique, and to a whole series of little tearooms and restaurants. Allen loved planning entertainments and working out transportation schedules, and he should have been in his element that spring in Paris with his lady love.

Unfortunately, he pressed his luck; within a few weeks he once more asked Mildred to marry him. She recoiled and again explained carefully that she intended never to marry and certainly never to have children. If he wanted a mother for his imaginary son, Richard, he must stop pursuing her and find someone else.

When, after several weeks in Paris, Mildred was offered temporary reassignment to Château-Thierry, she seized the opportunity to get away from Allen for a while.

At Château-Thierry a Y recreation unit was at work entertaining the remaining U.S. troops. Mildred thought the Y workers were inefficient, and she got right to work to reorganize the unit, developing a schedule for entertaining the soldiers and getting the German prisoners of war to scrub the floors. But to her chagrin her efforts were repulsed, her talent for organization went unrecognized, and she was given the job of playing the piano for the dances.

While she was at Château-Thierry, Trudy's brother, Brewster Rhoads, showed up. He had intended to go to Paris to look for Mildred and was delighted to find her. Brewster borrowed an automobile and together they visited Teddy Prichard's grave as well as the Big Bertha emplacements, had lunch in Soissons, and explored battlefields despite a driving late March snow.

Allen had applied for a weekend leave so that he could meet Mildred and take her to Reims on a Sunday. He wrote that his pass had been denied, and anyway, what was the use when he had already lost her? She was not expecting him, therefore, and was sitting at the piano pounding out dance tunes one Friday night when there he suddenly was, leaning on the piano. Mildred was not sure she could take time off, but Allen urged her to. On Sunday they would go to Reims as planned, but on Saturday they decided to explore nearby Belleau Wood, scene of a major battle between U.S. and German troops in June 1918. The day was threatening, and during the afternoon they were caught in a violent rainstorm. They were soaked through and very cold, and Allen suggested they take refuge in a half-destroyed farmhouse. A roof still stood over part of the dining room, and although the floor was littered with broken glass and crockery, Allen was able to clear a small space where they could keep out of the rain, build a fire, and begin to dry their wet clothes. They had brought a thermos of tea and some biscuits and settled themselves companionably to await the end of the storm. Allen was no longer feeling hurt by her rejection, and they agreed to live in the present and to enjoy their time together in France. At the end of the interlude

Allen took a large key from the wall. "This is as close as we are ever going to come to having a housekey of our own," he said soberly, and he put it in his knapsack.[2]

Allen went back to Paris and his studies, and Mildred continued to pound the piano. But she grew dissatisfied and after three weeks decided to return to Paris, orders or no. The Y officials did not discipline her for this but sent her to a canteen at St. Denis, just outside Paris. While there she was allowed to find lodging wherever she liked. Allen offered to find her a room and gave her a list of alternatives. She told him to choose for her, and when she was free, he showed her a lovely room in a boardinghouse at 55 rue de Vaugirard. She had a window facing the garden at the back of the house, and there were pansies in the window box.

Mildred was delighted with the room and asked if the house was near Allen's quarters. "My room is right down the hall," was his reply.[3]

Child of the Victorian age that she was, Mildred Scott felt compromised by this living arrangement and took pains to conceal it from her parents. Allen could have reassured them; Mildred's puritanical standards kept him at arm's length, although he was granted certain tantalizing intimacies: coming into her room for a goodnight chat after she was in bed, or talking to her through a crack in the closed door while she was in her bath.

Living in the same house made it possible to continue the program of sightseeing they had begun before Mildred was sent to Château-Thierry. They went to an afternoon entertainment at the Sarah Bernhardt theater and came home by way of the flower markets and pâtisserie shops and curio stores of the Latin Quarter. They went out to dinner with French friends of Allen, and Mildred was surprised and envious to hear Allen speak French fluently. She decided that she might want to take lessons after all. Allen took her to the catacombs, rollerskating in Lune Park, and to a reception at the home of the U.S. ambassador. They took a bicycle trip to Normandy and visited Mont St. Michel.

Mildred Scott had originally been assigned to the Sorbonne Unit, but the formation of that group had been held up while the Y sought a house for its headquarters. Finally the Y was given a large unfurnished house on the rue de Rivoli that had once belonged to a finance minister, and Mildred was allowed to go to work. She and the other Y workers set about furnishing the house, using secondhand furniture and improvising drapes and rugs. This was the sort of thing she especially liked to do, and the house soon had an air of elegance, she thought. Behind the house was a lovely garden, and as the weather improved, the parties the Y gave for its soldier clients spilled out of doors more and more.

Almost every night there were dances. Three nights a week the soldiers were allowed to dance with French women, under heavy chaperonage, and two nights a week with American women in uniform. American women in mufti were not allowed; once Allen Olmsted brought a former girlfriend from Buffalo to a dance and Mildred insisted that he leave the hall. "He didn't think I would insist, but I did," she remembered.[4]

There were two Quaker groups in Paris at that time, helping with civilian refugees and reconstruction. One was the American Friends Service Committee, to which Mildred had applied before leaving for France. The other was the British War Victims Relief Committee office, called the Anglo-American office because American Quakers had been volunteering to work with the British Quakers before the United States joined the war. The Anglo-American office was situated near Mildred's YMCA headquarters on the rue de Rivoli, and sometimes the conscientious objectors came to the canteen. Mildred found them fascinating to listen to and defended them when a few of the soldiers intimated that they were cowards. "They are just as brave as you are, and they are going to be treated equally here as long as I am in charge of recreation," she said in their defense. She visited their headquarters and began to think again about the possibility of transferring to a Quaker unit.[5]

She was following the Paris peace talks with great interest. "Think of my being in Paris while the epoch-making Peace Conference is meeting," she wrote her parents enthusiastically. She decided that her soldier charges ought to know something about what was going on and asked if they would be willing to devote one evening a week to lectures on the world situation. When they agreed she arranged to invite Jane Addams as the first speaker. She had read in the *Paris Herald* that Jane Addams was in the city, waiting to go to Zurich to attend a second meeting of the

10. Mildred Scott in her YMCA uniform, 1919. "I really think I don't look quite so bad as this," she wrote. *Courtesy of Olmsted Papers.*

International Congress of Women, which she had helped to found at a conference in the Hague in 1915. Jane Addams was eager to talk about the war, and when Mildred came to call she accepted Mildred Scott's invitation to speak to the soldiers. No record of what she said is available, but Mildred kept among her most precious memories the day Jane Addams met with a group of soldiers in the garden of the house on rue de Rivoli.[6]

Encouraged by the response of the soldiers, Mildred Scott next invited a Princeton professor to talk about the issue of the Shantung Peninsula then being discussed at the peace talks. The professor evidently gave a presentation slanted to the Japanese side, for the next day Mildred had an inquiry from the Chinese delegation, asking if they might be allowed to give their side of the discussion. News of this escalating interest quickly reached

Mildred Scott's superiors in the YMCA office in Paris, and she was told to her dismay to give up the political lectures and "keep the boys dancing."[7]

Between her work for the Sorbonne Unit and her life with Allen on rue de Vaugirard, it was a charmed time for Mildred Scott. She missed her family and longed for Ruth Mellor to join her, but she was happier than she had ever been. All too soon, however, the idyll came to an end. The Sorbonne courses for U.S. soldiers were terminated in the middle of June, and the students' Paris permits were canceled at the same time, bringing an end to Mildred Scott's job. Mildred inquired at YMCA headquarters about work in Germany, but she was turned down because of her lack of fluency in German. She then went to the Anglo-American Quaker headquarters and was accepted for work in Compte le Grange, in the Argonne, beginning in August. Since the Quaker work was officially under the control of the Red Cross she considered this appointment a final triumph in her personal war with the Red Cross, and she accepted. She wanted, however, to keep her YMCA uniform and battled with the Y authorities to be allowed to retain it. The Y finally made an exception in her case but told her she must not wear the uniform while working for another organization. Finally, on 27 July, her transfer papers came through.

Allen considered staying on in Paris as a civilian, but Mildred thought he ought to return to the United States and begin his postwar career. She also once more encouraged him to look elsewhere for a marriage partner, though she was willing to wear a ring he bought her. He left early in July, and their frequent correspondence began again. "Dearie, shall I tell you that I miss you," she wrote him. "I wish you were back again but I think you did wisely to go."[8]

Allen returned to Buffalo but soon took a job in Philadelphia working for the Norfolk and Western Railroad. He renewed his acquaintance with the Scotts and visited the Sauls, who began to invite him frequently to Rose Valley to play bridge or tennis or to attend one of their many parties. Mildred's aunt and mother and sister Marian had been interested in him as though he were their personal soldier all through the war, and they liked him immensely on his return. The whole family began to ask Mildred why in the world she would not marry him. He was not exactly looking for another potential wife, as he had dutifully promised Mildred he would do when he left Paris.

Alone in Paris, Mildred Scott attended a grand victory ball and went to the Bastille Day parade with her landlady, Madame Vernay, of whom both she and Allen were fond. She ran into several friends from Smith, including Clara Savage, whom she hadn't seen since college days. She remembered Clara as a demure little quiet poet. "Now she is a full fledged Greenwich Village-ite, with cigarettes and ideas about free love and immensely more attractive." Clara, a war correspondent, introduced Mildred to Charles Selden, an editor of the *New York Times*, who wanted to rent Mildred's room at 55 rue de Vaugirard. She also invited Mildred to accompany her and a captain provost, a very nice middle-aged suitor of hers, on a walking trip in Brittany. Mildred went AWOL from the Y in order to join them and had a wonderful time.

Clara Savage was the first woman in Mildred's acquaintance to talk about the ideal of combining a career and marriage. (She later married and had two children while working full time as a journalist and later as the editor of *PARENTS Magazine*.) Mildred was impressed and began to waver just a little. Back from Brittany, she wrote Allen:

> I wish you were here to talk to. . . . No, if I am strictly honest, I guess it is not to talk to but to love. I am getting the most curious ideas, and letting them grow . . . I need two lives, not consecutively, but side by side. Mere living and adventuring and experimenting would more than fill one. And really good purposeful living requires at least another. I wish all my four J.'s would come to life. Perhaps I'd really be content to dissolve them! They could each live so simply and pleasantly, and harmoniously together too. No wonder they struggle so dreadfully for, poor dears, a fourth of a life is not really enough for anybody. I have to make as many compromises and concessions and mandates as the Peace Conference.
>
> And you! Why are you way off in America when I want you here to play with? It's most unreasonable of you! To be

sure, I may have sent you to America yesterday and wish you back there again tomorrow, but today, now, I want you here and you should appear![9]

Back in Paris she went to a dance with Clara and met her roommate, a short-haired Italian woman. But Paris wasn't Paris without Allen, she had to confess. The months together had been magical, as she later wrote Allen: "As long as we both shall live they will seem like happy months to look back upon. Lights and shadows it is true but still rosy and complete and beautiful."[10] Soon it was time for her to leave Paris and go to Compte le Grange in the Argonne region to take up her work with the Friends. From headquarters in Le Grange, the Friends ran programs from a whole series of small village units, called équipes, aimed at helping the civilian refugees return to their homes and reestablish their lives. Mildred was first assigned to the village of Les Islettes for training, then to the village of Grand Pré where she was made the housekeeper—another inappropriate assignment, Mildred thought— and later put in charge of the ouvroir, the workshop where local women were paid to make trousers and vests for sale. Since Mildred had never had a brother, she had to ask her teammates to show her how men's trousers were constructed.

Once a week the goods produced by the ouvroir were loaded on a truck and taken to outlying villages. The Friends also distributed chickens and rabbits and even goats and cows to returning villagers. For those whose homes had been destroyed, and that was practically everybody, they sold at low cost "portable" or prefabricated houses that could be erected on or near the ruins of the old house.

After all her battles with bureaucracy, first with the army in Maryland and then with the Y in France, Mildred was entranced with the democratic spirit of camaraderie in the Quaker unit. She wrote to Allen about it in glowing terms:

I have yet to meet a single person who is disagreeable or even obviously selfish. Everyone is pleasant and ready to do his part and more. There is no quibbling about "whose job this is," no passing the buck, and not even any crabbing when things go wrong. Of course, people get into the dumps and of course they criticize each other but it is always so far as I have heard, done pleasantly and without personal ill-feeling. There is also a keen sentiment against wasting time or the Mission's property, so that when one job runs out people seek another of their own accord. Indeed everything seems to be of "one's own accord." We are assigned to a job and a special équipe and then left to fit into the common life and work it out together.[11]

Shortly after being assigned to Grand Pré Mildred discovered that the équipe was very low on gasoline, used for cooking and lighting, and called headquarters at Compte le Grange to ask if some might be sent immediately. Used to the army's habitual delay, she exaggerated the situation and the need a little. As a result one worker, Jim Norton, came on his bicycle a distance of some thirty kilometers, arriving at eleven o'clock that very night. Mildred was chagrined and determined to be more literal thereafter, as the Friends were.

Other members of her unit also influenced her. She was very struck by a young Englishwoman, Rachel Enid Grant, who had learned many skills, including plumbing and carpentry, and was able to repair the roof when it leaked. And she enjoyed Alec Marsh, a young Englishman who liked to read aloud to the whole unit at night, although she was sometimes put off by his insistence that they live as simply as the people they worked among. When she found shell cases in the military dumps nearby and used them for vases for wildflowers to brighten up the barracks, Alec objected and threw the flowers out. A fellow American, Emma Chandler, took care of the older children and became a friend. And after several weeks Mildred acquired a roommate, a young Dutch woman, Ada Koopmans, with whom she formed a strong bond.

Most of all, she liked the easy, brotherly relationships between men and women. Unit members were so "clean minded," she wrote, that when they went swimming it was no problem to change in the bushes, and she did not feel self-conscious in a one-piece bathing suit. In the warm weather, they carried their cots outdoors and slept as a family. She cut her hair, which made her feel more like a little boy than ever, she remarked to Allen, and went on a weekend bicycle trip with several of the fellows to visit Mainz and Cologne in nearby Germany.

The only person Mildred did not get on with well was Sarah Connah, the head of the unit. Sarah was forty-one years old, smoked cigarettes, and liked plans, according to Mildred. When she was assigned as housekeeper at Grand Pré Mildred announced that she would not do the cooking, so Sarah Connah had to continue with it, probably to her displeasure. Sarah had not wanted Mildred to go on the German trip and gave her consent only grudgingly. Mildred as usual liked to plan her own schedule and felt that most of the objections Sarah raised were unreasonable and reflected a concern for petty rules. But Mildred was so happy at first with the whole spirit of the unit that she regarded Sarah Connah as a single aberration and did not worry about her growing displeasure.

Although sewing was scarcely Mildred's favorite occupation, she liked working with the Frenchwomen who came to work in the ouvroir, and admired how their children sat docilely on stools by their side, playing with a little piece of cloth, perhaps, for as long as the mother was busy. How different from American children, she thought. Older children were assigned to a class, and when Emma Chandler, the children's worker, was sick Mildred took over the group and enjoyed taking them swimming and teaching them to make pinwheels and to work with plasticine.

Whenever she was free from duties she liked to roam the country, visiting the scenes of war and talking with the peasants. The area around Grand Pré had changed hands eight times during the war, and there was hardly one structure left standing. Returning French families camped out in bits of basements left over from the bombing. Sometimes whole hillsides had been destroyed, and peasants quarreled over the ownership of the remaining rubble. Which was now the farm on the top of the hill, and which the next one down?

Signs of the recent battles were everywhere. "German and American coats and rifles, belts and beds lay mixed together down in the dugouts and above in the sunlight," Mildred wrote Allen. "Some of the trenches and dugouts seem almost warm with the men who have been there." The skeletons of dead horses and cows, and sometimes even of hastily buried soldiers, were to be seen along each lane.[12]

She had trouble with the local patois at first, but she learned to communicate. She was deeply moved by the spirit of the people, who did not seem to hold grudges despite the devastation they had experienced. Young German soldiers from a nearby prisoner camp, wearing large P.G. (Prisonnier de Guerre) signs on their backs, were being used by the army to sweep the fields for mines and to check the poisoned wells. They were paid in scrip that could only be cashed at the local army canteen. Occasionally they also worked for the Friends. (The Friends later looked up the families of the German prisoners of war in Germany and paid them the wages the prisoners had actually earned.) Mildred was interested in the prisoners, but even more interested by the way the French accepted them and invited them to eat with them in their basement homes. "Why do you feed your enemy?" the French soldiers sometimes asked the peasant families. "Oh, we hate the Germans, but this one is a nice boy," they were told.

Some of the peasant families told Mildred of being ordered to move in twenty minutes as the frontier of the war swept close to them, of burying their belongings and putting their children on the first transportation that came along. Many families had been separated as a result, and parents were still searching for their children. Few of the peasants had any idea what the war was supposed to be about; it was simply a catastrophe visited upon them.

Mildred began to feel a personal identification with these people and a burning sense of injustice about their fate. Wars were made not by people but by their governments, who used the lure of patriotism and the false stories of atrocities to trap them into enormous sacrifices. And for what? The Treaty of Versailles with its harsh punishment of the Germans was simply an invitation to another war, while the U.S. Senate was refusing to accept the concept of a League of Nations on which so many had pinned their hopes for lasting peace.

Despite the discouraging news, Mildred continued to revel in the life of the Quaker Unit. She wrote her mother that the mission had the spirit of true brotherhood and entertained swarms of visitors. Though frugal, Sarah Connah was willing to spend money for hospitality, and Grand Pré developed a reputation for wonderful meals. Mildred encouraged Adele and Maurice Saul, who had been contemplating a trip to France, to visit her at Grand Pré. Shortly before the Sauls arrived, Ruth Fry, a representative of the London War Victims Relief Committee, made a visit, and Mildred talked to her about further foreign service after the work in the Argonne ended. On the strength of this conversation, she cabled Ruth Mellor to come over and join her in further adventures.

Ruth and Mildred's deep attachment had been strained for several years by Ruth's involvement with Tracy, and Mildred's on-again, off-again affair with Allen. Yet during the months since Mildred had left the United States they had continued to correspond regularly, and to long to be together. Both women felt it was imperative to reestablish their bonds on a firmer basis, and only a time of adventure together in Europe would do this. Mildred complained that Ruth's letters made her seem far away, and that she feared that Ruth was "becoming deadened to me and wafted away from me, the real me whom you want so much and who has been really waiting for you for years and years."[13]

Back in the United States, Allen Olmsted had come to realize that Ruth Mellor was a force to be reckoned with in his relationship to Mildred Scott. He went to see her in Plymouth, met Tracy, and surmised that there was more between the two women than he had understood. Ruth was at first cagey when he wanted to talk about Mildred, but he persisted, and on a second visit came to appreciate how profound were the ties between Mildred and Ruth. If he were ever to win Mildred, Ruth would be part of the bargain. At the same time, Ruth assured him that she was on his side. She thought he was good for Mildred, and that he ought not to marry someone else, as Mildred kept suggesting, but be willing to wait, perhaps as much as ten or twelve years, until Mildred was finally ready for marriage. "How proud I am of you for winning over Ruth. She has admitted you to the triangle," Mildred wrote when she heard about the interview.[14]

Nevertheless, when Ruth decided to join Mildred in Europe, Allen was at first opposed. Mildred's recent letters had revealed that she was no longer as happy at Grand Pré as she had been. Her best friends in the mission had left, and the remaining British members were those with whom she had the most friction, she wrote. She and Sarah Connah had had a serious disagreement about the ouvroir. Connah wanted it to cover only twelve women, while Mildred believed it should be expanded to fifty to give as many women as possible training before the mission ended. Sarah Connah told some Quakers at a conference in Switzerland that the disagreement was because of the nationality differences between them. (Interestingly, Mildred Olmsted had absolutely no recollection of Sarah Connah when she recalled for me her days in France.) There was growing friction also over economy; the British members in general and Alec Marsh in particular thought Mildred extravagant, while she believed she was working for greater efficiency. Altogether, Mildred was disillusioned, homesick, and ready to come home with Adele and Maurice.

Ruth, however, convinced Allen that Mildred needed to stay in Europe for the sake of her personal development, to discover that self-realization was as important as service. Allen felt that Ruth was better able than he to help Mildred in this quest because she was more disinterested. He swung around to supporting the idea of Mildred's staying and argued the case for it with her parents and with the Sauls.

Adele and Maurice Saul arrived in Grand Pré in a limousine one late November day, just as Mildred plowed in through the mud. She had not been expecting them, and she "went wild with joy," as she wrote Allen. They brought birthday presents from Mildred's parents, and from Allen a camera, which she had very much needed because her old one had been stolen on her trip to Brittany. (When she developed her first roll of film she found several pictures of Allen already taken.) When the first excitement was over she introduced the Sauls to Enid Grant, telling them she considered the talented Englishwoman to be "my idea of an effective modern woman." After lunch at Grand Pré the Sauls took her back to Paris and installed her in a luxury hotel room with a vase of flowers on the table. Later, they treated her to an expensive dinner. Another night it was the opera. For a week she and Adele shopped and went to museums. Mildred enjoyed it all thoroughly but wrote Allen that the Paris she and he had known was both more fun and more real than the city viewed from taxis and large hotels and expensive restaurants.

Mildred Scott took the occasion of being in Paris to stop in at the Anglo-American Mission headquarters. There she was told that Ruth could join her for only a few days, and that it might be better if Mildred decided to leave immediately for home, although they appreciated the good work she had done at Grand Pré. Since Ruth Mellor was already on her way, Mildred decided to go around to the headquarters of the American Unit, the American Friends Service Committee, and see if they had any positions open. She met the new head, Wilmer Young, who had just received a cable from the Philadelphia office advising him to hold ón to any experienced French workers. Herbert Hoover had asked the American Quakers to take over the distribution of food to starving children in Germany, and many workers would be needed. Wilmer Young could make no promises, he told Mildred, and it would be better if she and Ruth spoke German, but if she very much wanted to go to Germany it might be a good idea to delay her departure for the United States. He would cable the Philadelphia office about her and let her know the answer at once.

Mildred Scott returned to Grand Pré but kept her bags packed for a quick departure. Allen thought she might be gambling, and when he stopped by the Quaker office at 20 South Twelfth Street in Philadelphia, he was told that no cable about Mildred from Paris had been received and that she ought to make no plans until she received an official appointment from headquarters. There were many applications, and people with fluency in German were being given precedence. He persuaded Ruth Mellor, who was about to sail, to check with the Quakers also. She talked with Wilbur Thomas, the executive secretary, who told her that there was no chance for her to join the German group, but who suggested that if she went to France she might be accepted into that mission, and she would then be nearby if an opportunity to go to Germany developed later.

Although Maurice and Adele Saul had hoped to bring Mildred home with them, they finally decided to sail without her. In Philadelphia Adele gave Allen a kiss, and Maurice handed him a small package of Pears soap that Mildred had sent as a souvenir of their Paris home, but the news they brought was not encouraging to Allen's prospects. "Adele says you are going into politics. So much more exciting than marriage, and many more people to run," Allen wrote bitterly.[15]

Ruth Mellor arrived in Paris in mid-December, and Mildred met her there. When Mildred had informed Sarah Connah of the imminent arrival of her guest, she had been told that Ruth was welcome; but when the two stopped at the Anglo-American Mission they were told by Mary Moon, who was temporary head, that she had decided to transfer both young women to a larger équipe in Varennes in order to get ready for the Christmas rush. Here Ruth would be allowed to assist without being made a formal member of the mission.

The two accordingly set out for Varennes, arriving in time to help prepare a large Christmas party for the French children. There was also an English party for the unit itself, and a celebration with the German prisoners of war. The mission had given the prisoners one of its large "elephant" barracks to use for Christmas, and some food, and the Germans trimmed a Christmas tree with scraps of tinfoil, apples, and bits of cotton. They had found an old violin in a shell hole, repaired it, and put together a makeshift orchestra with which they accompanied their Christmas songs. Mildred, who was beginning to understand a little German, was deeply touched. When she noticed that some of the French guards were present, she mentioned to one of the prisoners that this was not necessary; the German boys were the guests of the Quakers for the day. "But you don't understand, the guards were homesick, we invited them," the Germans replied.[16]

On New Year's Eve the group gave a costume party and dance for the local people, and on New Year's Day Mildred and Ruth helped to deliver eight hundred presents to all persons over sixteen. But the work of the équipe was winding down, and Mildred was anxious to move on. Quaker officials from both the British and the American Friends visited Varennes and discussed options with her. Evidently appointment to Germany was becoming more and more unlikely, since the AFSC in Philadelphia had decided to give new workers from the United States first chance, the theory being to spread the opportunities for war and postwar service among the largest possible number. Mary Moon said that Ruth Mellor might be taken on in Germany because of her stenographic skills, and she suggested that the two young women take a vacation until more definite word arrived from Philadelphia. Ruth and Mildred therefore packed their belongings, visited Compte le Grange on Ruth's birthday, 15 January, and then set out for Paris and new adventures.

6

Hunger in Germany

*I*T WAS ALMOST A YEAR since Mildred Scott had sailed for France, and her vacations overseas had been short and rushed. She was ready for a real rest. She and Ruth Mellor had hardly reached Paris, however, when they learned that a cable had arrived at the AFSC headquarters from the newly established Berlin Unit saying it needed a stenographer and asking that Ruth Mellor come immediately. There was no word about Mildred's assignment, and she began to wonder whether Wilmer Young had ever cabled Philadelphia about her.

Mildred Scott went to talk to Wilmer Young about it, and he said it only confirmed his suspicions that cables were being lost. She then proposed that she accompany Ruth to Berlin in order to interview the head of mission, Alfred Scattergood, in person. Wilmer Young refused to authorize the plan, pointing out that this would place the mission in an embarrassing position because it would be hard to send Mildred back. As this in fact was the very strategy Mildred had conjured up, she continued to argue for her plan. When she asked Wilmer what he would do if he were in her place, he said that if he wanted to go to Germany as much as she did he might take his chances at the border.

Ruth and Mildred next went to the Red Cross to get papers. The officials there took it for granted that Mildred, like Ruth, was joining the Quaker mission in Berlin, although Mildred endeavored to explain that her appointment had not yet come through and she was going to Berlin only to interview Alfred Scattergood in hopes of receiving one. At any rate, the Red Cross issued papers for them both, and they took off immediately on an overnight train to Coblenz, sharing a compartment with a French officer, his wife, and two fox terriers. Their baggage was left at the border, and in Coblenz, when they finally located the headquarters of the U.S. Army of Occupation, they were told their papers were inadequate because they had not obtained a visa from the U.S. ambassador in Paris.

Having gotten this far, Mildred Scott was not to be deterred. She asked to see the captain, but when she was finally granted an interview she found this officer, though polite, equally negative. He would like to help but he could not. Mildred once more resorted to the strategy of asking the official what he would do in her position. The captain paced up and down; then he said mysteriously, "Sometimes people at the bottom don't know as much as people at the top." Mildred thanked him and, taking the hint, went downstairs to the bureau of passes. Here she once more applied for passes to proceed with their trip to Berlin. A clerk issued the necessary authorizations after barely glancing at their papers. Mildred was elated. Even if she were unsuccessful with Alfred Scattergood and had to return from Berlin, Mildred wrote her sister Adele, the adventures of the trip would have been worthwhile.[1]

They stayed on in Coblenz several days while Mildred arranged for their luggage to be forwarded and Ruth nursed a bad cold, then traveled on, passing the English lines at Cologne and the German lines at Frankfurt. En route they learned something about Germany's runaway inflation. When they entered Germany one hundred francs was worth 520 marks, but the mark was losing ground so fast that each day breakfast doubled in price.

On the morning of 26 January they arrived in Berlin. Members of the Quaker team met them at the station, took them out for breakfast, showed them their room, then invited them to visit the office. Since the unit in Germany had only been established three weeks earlier, everyone was new and welcoming. Mildred Scott realized that the rest of the team did not know she had come without an invitation, and she looked for an opportunity to speak privately to Alfred Scattergood, who was out of the office for the morning. When he arrived, however, he was introduced to her and learned about her status in front of the whole office staff. Scattergood was affable and said he thought he knew Mildred's Uncle Will Scott from Provident Life Insurance of Philadelphia, of which he was treasurer, but Mildred had a sinking feeling that this was not the sort of man to whom "high handed acts appeal." The next day, in fact, he told her that she might feel herself to be as free as air; he had no work for her at the present and hadn't made up his mind about keeping her.[2]

The Friends expected to be very busy as soon as food shipments from the United States began to arrive, but the boats were agonizingly slow. Meanwhile, more workers were being sent over from Philadelphia, all of them fluent in German. After several weeks, Alfred Scattergood told Mildred Scott that he would not have a place for her, and that he felt that appointments should go to the men and women next on the list, not to her just because she happened to be there. He seemed straightforward about it, and Mildred appreciated his candor and the respect he showed her. However, a few days later, Ruth came across the carbon of a letter he had written to Wilmer Young, saying he did not feel he had authority to order Mildred home, but he believed that she should not wear the Quaker star. When she heard this, Mildred felt betrayed. She also got a cross letter from Mary Moon in Paris, accusing her of taking advantage of the Quakers and suggesting that she leave immediately. Mary Moon herself was one of those awaiting appointment to Germany and was outraged to have Mildred attempt to supplant her.

Mildred Scott tried to take this antagonism with good grace, and to take the long view. "Of course I took things into my own hands in coming here, which probably shocked her timid soul," she wrote Allen in describing Mary Moon's letter. The Friends in Paris were upset, and Wilmer Young had written to Alfred Scattergood to say that, though Mildred had done good work, "she always put herself where she wanted to be" and was rather difficult to get along with. Mildred thought the latter remark must have come from Sarah Connah, who was herself notoriously difficult. She admitted the mission had grounds for the first accusation, Ruth having joined her in France and she joining Ruth in Germany without permission. Still, she thought she had a perfect right to remain in Germany as an ordinary tourist.[3]

Besides, she rationalized, there probably wasn't a job to her liking in the Quaker office anyway. The women members were excluded from the important staff meetings and the really interesting matters of policy, while the men scorned to do clerical work of any kind. When Mildred told Alfred Scattergood that she liked organization work and executive work but not clerking, he said dryly that he had rather imagined that. Although Mildred continued to think he was a good man, she found the American mission as a whole disappointing in comparison to the English Quakers. The American Quakers were narrow-minded, she felt, disapproved of the theater and of opera, and did not mix socially with the Germans but stayed to themselves.

In a few weeks' time, she and Ruth moved to a rooming house, and Ruth went into the Quaker office each day while Mildred took German lessons, explored the city, and tried to learn something about German social work methods. She asked the mission in France to send her the money for her return ticket, so that she could be on her own, and she received one hundred dollars from her father to keep her going. She visited the Schlossplatz, with its canal and statue of the kaiser, walked the length of Unter den Linden, roamed the parks, and took trips on the trolley. She was soon bored, however, and wrote Allen that she didn't like married life: desultory activity was demoralizing.

When Ruth got home from work, Mildred was always there to greet her, and often they went out to the theater, or to meetings of the Quaker group. Alice Solomon, the Jane Addams of Germany, entertained the Friends at the school of social work and welcomed them to the city. They went to the opera with a German woman police officer. They met at the home of a Herr Miller to discuss Quakerism and had tea with a German industrialist who felt sure that Germany would go Communist if France did not relent on reparations; others suggested the reactionaries would gain power instead.

Attending social events with members of the Quaker mission, Mildred felt that she and Ruth often became the focus of attention. "It is natural that they dislike this," she observed to Allen. Other members of the mission had never before been abroad and lacked social experience outside the Society of Friends. Alfred Scattergood did not have a very good public presence, she thought, and occasionally did undignified things in public. Once at a picnic he rolled down a grassy hill, much to her dismay. She still thought him a very good man and believed they might have gotten on well in other circumstances. One wonderful thing about Mildred, in many people's eyes, was the fact that she rarely held a grudge.[4]

The situation in Germany was bleak that winter. There were at least 80,000 unemployed, and many hungry people clustered around the food windows. With inflation raging, the food crisis was severe, with meat and bread rationed and practically unattainable. Many children suffered from rickets and other symptoms of advanced malnutrition, and tuberculosis was everywhere, attacking especially the very young and the very old. It was hard for the Quaker workers to eat with so much hunger about. Mildred and Ruth's landlady had agreed to give them three meals a day, but because they were always out to lunch she combined lunch and dinner at the evening meal. Even so, the fare was meager. Sometimes they ate in expensive restaurants where they could order anything on the menu because of the devaluation of the German mark. The food available looked and tasted good, but it was mainly ersatz and vanished from one's stomach an hour after eating.

At last the food shipments arrived, and the Quakers became busy distributing supplies to school and hospital kitchens where they were prepared for sending to other feeding stations. Sometimes chocolate soup was served, sometimes beans or oatmeal. German doctors worked with the Quakers to assure that only those children who needed the food, or were not too far gone to benefit from it, would be fed. Children brought their own containers and called the life-giving meal Quaker Speisung.

Ruth and Mildred knew about the Quaker Speisung only vicariously, for Ruth was busy in the office typing, and Mildred was roaming the streets. Everyone she talked to predicted that trouble would come that winter. On March 13 it came with the Kapp Putsch, a counterrevolutionary coup against the Weimar Republic staged by Wolfgang Kapp, a rightist backed by the army who was briefly declared chancellor and who was intent on restoring the monarchy. Mildred, caught in the middle of the battle, wrote Allen about it.

Suppose I withdraw from the revolution long enough to write you. As a matter of fact, it might be more accurate to say that the revolution has withdrawn from me, for the very bench over the way on which I sat with that intention (just within the Tier Garden, opposite the Brandenberger Tor— the big Victory arch which begins the Unter den Linden) was but a few minutes ago the very center of a crowd that had to be dispersed by the soldiers. And the usual three or four could not do it either, for others came racing through the trees, guns off their backs and under their right arms ready for use. Because the crowd seems to be getting more persistent and ugly but just baiting the soldiers stationed all about with orders to keep them moving.

Even as I write, armored cars are going through the Platz, I wonder where the trouble will be? They have put a gun I think on the Tor for I saw an officer up there directing two or three soldiers erecting what looks like a gunshield. It is possible for there, as from the Arc de Triomphe in Paris, they could sweep the streets of this section.[5]

When she awakened next morning to news that the revolution had taken place during the night, she determined to go out and see what was going on, despite the admonitions of her landlady and the maid. She had word that there was mail for her at the Red Cross, and she decided to go there, though it put her in the midst of the danger. She saw soldiers and barbed wire barriers on the street, and once found herself staring into the muzzle of a machine gun. The banks were guarded by soldiers, and the war flag had been hoisted above public buildings everywhere. Although she tried to remain quiet and inconspicuous, she stepped out into a crowded street and was knocked down by a horse and carriage. Fortunately she received only a glancing blow and managed to regain her feet (her practice in falling in basketball games coming to her rescue) and disappear into the crowd.

The Kapp regime issued orders the next day that all foreigners must leave the city, since the new administration could not be responsible for their welfare, and that a train would be put at their disposal. When Ruth and Mildred heard this news at their boardinghouse, they decided that they would not leave, but stay and carry on if necessary. They went to the mission office and discovered that all the other mission members had made the same decision.

For the next few days the city was tense and difficult. The workers responded to the coup with a general strike that brought all services to a halt. There was no electricity, no gas, no newspapers, no food delivery. The army patrolled the streets, trying to persuade the workers to return to their jobs, but the strike held, and the takeover was defeated. Years later Mildred remembered the event as the first time she experienced the power of nonviolent action.

Ruth Mellor, working long hours at the Quaker mission, seemed always tired. She had a perpetual cold and was losing weight. Mildred worried about her, but Ruth said she could scarcely work shorter hours when all the other members of the staff were under such strain. Although she had felt uncomfortable at first because of the attitude toward Mildred, she had quickly won friends and was universally liked in the office. Fellow workers were concerned also about her health and talked of transferring her to fieldwork in the spring.

Just after the Kapp putsch, Alfred Scattergood told Mildred that he had a place for her at last. Mildred responded frostily at first, telling him that "their unfriendliness had quite ruined my enthusiasm and the spirit which had made the work in France so worthwhile seemed totally lacking here and I could not do good work for people who did not trust my judgment." Alfred Scattergood evidently took this as criticism of the unit and shared it with the rest of the staff. Caroline Norment, Ruth Mellor's supervisor, who had been Mildred's most ardent critic, felt herself to have been to blame and apologized to Mildred. Mildred thought this was big of her and decided to forget her side of the grudge. When Alfred Scattergood mentioned in a group meeting that they were hoping to start a mission in Bavaria if Miss Scott and Miss Mellor would accept, Mildred said that of course they would go. The staff seemed exceptionally friendly and gave them a farewell party that surprised them both by its genuine warmth.

On a train from Berlin to Munich on 1 April, Mildred Scott exultantly wrote her mother that she was now doing what she had wanted to do two years ago. "Since you are blessed with a wandering daughter in place of a son, you must at least rejoice in the richness of her experiences and her pleasure in them," she urged. The Friends had received so much money for hunger relief that it had become possible to expand the work so that they could feed one million children. The worst months were February through July, when the harvest began. Bavaria had not been as hard hit with famine as some of the other provinces, but it had seen a great deal of political unrest. The brief Communist regime in 1918–1919 had produced a conservative backlash.[6]

The head of the mission in Munich was to be Arthur Charles, a professor at Earlham College, Indiana, who was fluent in German. He, a German social worker, Fräulein Frenzel, Ruth Mellor, and Mildred Scott comprised the mission. The Quakers were given the old royal residence for offices and were taken on a tour of all the social institutions of Munich. Child feeding began in two weeks. As in Berlin, local doctors and social workers chose the children who would most benefit from food, eliminating those for whom it was too late, and the food was cooked in local schools and distributed through churches or community centers. Mildred's job was to work in the community, visiting the cooperating institutions and enlisting the support of both community leaders and volunteers.

Bread was scarce in Bavaria that spring, and hunger was widespread. The Friends had to guard their food supplies against theft. Children were so unused to food that it was important to make sure that they ate it on the spot and did not save it for their parents. Local volunteers came forward to help, and Mildred Scott met the trainloads of chocolate or milk powder, broke the seals, and saw that the food was sent to the schools to be cooked. She loved her work, loved being with Ruth, and enjoyed her autonomy. Arthur Charles was away a great deal, either attending conferences or because of ill health. He was in any case a poor administrator, according to Ruth, unable to make decisions or to delegate authority. Mildred gradually took over most of the responsibility, as she was always apt to do. In her memory of this period, almost seventy years later, Arthur Charles had simply left, although according to AFSC records and correspondence this was not the case.[7]

Mildred Scott worked hard and efficiently and felt the job she was doing vindicated her in the eyes of the Quakers and of all who had questioned her ability. She was still angry at the Red Cross and other agencies for originally rejecting her, as she wrote to Allen.

> Tell your friend Mr. Glasgow that the young lady who called on him in Washington two years ago with a letter of introduction from Maurice and whom he rather summarily disposed of because they never used any women in the Food Distribution abroad, has been very happily and pleasantly distributing Mr. Hoover's food to some 28,000 children in Germany—just exactly where she would have told him she wished to be in that interview had he treated her more courteously.[8]

In addition to Munich, the Quakers fed children in outlying towns, including Nuremberg, Augsburg, and Furth, so Mildred Scott found herself journeying into the country and enjoying the spring flowers, the snow-covered mountains, and the charming Bavarian towns. She and a German social worker investigated some mining villages for child feeding and then climbed in the Alps and watched a woodcutters' ball. In town, she and Ruth went to the opera and were entertained by local families.

Although Mildred thought the German children were very polite, she did not like the results of Germanic upbringing in the adults. There were senseless rules and red tape everywhere, she thought. One day she took a trolley and discovered that she was headed the wrong way. When she asked the conductor to stop and let her off, he insisted that she pay her fare. She told him that she did not think she should because the trolley had not been clearly marked, and it was not her fault that she had gotten on the wrong one. The conductor insisted and threatened to call the police. Mildred told him to go ahead and do so. The conductor stopped the car and got a policeman, and Mildred was taken to the local police station.

"What was the matter?" the officer on duty asked. "Didn't you have the money?"

"I don't need money. I have free tokens," Mildred responded.

"Then why didn't you give your tokens to the conductor?" the officer asked.

"Because of the principle of the thing," Mildred told him. "I thought other travelers who couldn't afford to pay a double fare shouldn't be penalized because the directions were so poor."

Mystified by this strange American woman, the police booked her on charges of a misdemeanor but were wise enough not to try to collect a fine.[9]

Not all the Germans she met were conformists. Several families came to call at the mission to learn more about the Quakers and pacifism. Mildred Scott found it "overwhelming to be considered a representative of both America and Quakerism but it is tremendously interesting and just at this juncture when one does feel that big things in the way of international friendliness and understanding hang upon it. Ruth and I were in France so can speak for French people." The fact that people on both sides were the victims of war, and that they were taught to believe the same falsehoods about the enemy, was brought home to her when she met a peasant woman whose son had fought near Grand Pré and had heard the same rumors about the French soldiers that the French had heard about the German.[10] In addition, Mildred heard stories of American atrocities that were mirror images of stories circulated in the United States about the Germans. People everywhere were the helpless victims of war, Mildred began to see more and more clearly. War itself was the enemy, and she would never cooperate with it again.

One of the AFSC's traveling commissioners, Fred Libby, visited Munich just as Mildred Scott was becoming convinced of her own pacifism. She had also met Fred while she was in France, and the two "clicked," as Mildred put it. She told him that she intended to return to the United States and devote herself to peace, and he said he had made a similar resolution. "We'll meet on the barricades," Mildred predicted gaily.[11]

Through the child feeding, Mildred Scott and Ruth Mellor met two outstanding German women. Anita Augsburg, a physician, and Gertrude Baer, a social activist, had both participated in the International Congress of Women at the Hague, called by international suffragists under the leadership of Aletta Jacobs of

the Netherlands in 1915, with Jane Addams as chair, to seek ways
to end the war. They had also both attended its successor, a congress held Zurich in May 1919, where the name of the group was
changed to Women's International League for Peace and Freedom
(WILPF). It was this congress that Jane Addams was preparing to
attend when Mildred met her in Paris.

"What are the women of America doing for peace?" the two
asked Mildred. "Why did Carrie Chapman Catt desert us?" "Don't
you know about the women at the Hague?" Mildred knew nothing
of the organization, nor of the split within the suffrage movement
between those who had supported the war under the leadership of
Carrie Catt, and those who had opposed it through the Woman's
Peace party led by Jane Addams. The two German women described to her the work of the new group, how following the 1915
conference it had sent delegates to the heads of both belligerent
and neutral nations to seek an end to the war through continuous
negotiations, and how they were now determined to link the concern for suffrage and equality for women with the longing of all
peoples for an end to war itself. It sounded to Mildred like exactly
the sort of thing she was interested in, combining her newly
formed commitment to peace with her longtime concern for equality. She determined that as soon as she got home she would try to
find out more about the U.S. Section of the WILPF.[12]

Meanwhile, she and Ruth quickly made friends with the two
women. Anita Augsburg invited them to spend election weekend
at her tiny peasant's cottage in the mountains on the shore of a
lake, where they happily tramped in the rain, enjoying the wildflowers, then went on to the next village with Gertrude Baer who
wanted to take precautions to keep her vote secret. Gertrude had
been in the government during the brief Socialist reign and was
now under constant surveillance, she told Mildred, her mail
opened and her phone tapped. Her father was opposed to her political activism and had tried to prevent her from attending political meetings, but her mother had taken her side and left a window
open so that she could climb in at night. Mildred was somewhat
shocked when Gertrude said she was an anarchist, but she liked
Gertrude's spunk, and her fine mind, and she discovered that Gertrude was also a talented musician.

Gertrude was Jewish. Mildred had had little occasion to over-come the anti-Semitism that she had learned as a child, and that was in fact endemic to most of Protestant America at the time. But Gertrude helped her to understand some of the suffering of the Jews, and to begin the lifelong process of getting rid of these deeply rooted prejudices. (At ninety-seven, Mildred often said to me, in describing someone, "She's Jewish, you know." But I dis-covered that this was unconscious, and I came to see how much she loved and admired her Jewish colleagues.) It was through Ger-trude that Mildred came to meet a Jewish widow, "a wonderfully gentle and conservative Jewish woman who lost her husband in the war and has never recovered from the shock of writing to one of her dearest friends in Switzerland, and being told by a mutual friend that her friend had received the letter but wished never to see nor hear anything of her again as she was a German. How silly and childish it all seems."[13]

Through the WILPF, Mildred Scott and Ruth Mellor met other hardworking, thoughtful German women, many of them unmarried, making careers for themselves in medicine, teaching, or social work. Still, German women as a whole were less liberated than American women, Mildred thought. "The German girls like the French envy us our freedom. They say it shows in every mo-tion we make, and I glory in it."[14]

The work of the Quakers in Munich was beginning to gain wide recognition, and the former royal family, whose residence the unit was occupying, decided to give a supper for the unit in grati-tude. The old duchess explained that she had been brought up Catholic and had at first thought the Quakers were related to the revolutionaries. She described the revolution and red soldiers searching the palace. "We thought it was time to go, but every-one covered up," Mildred wrote describing the event. "We were thanked three times. Mr. Charles made a good speech of re-sponse."[15]

The Munich branch of the WILPF asked the Quaker mission to provide a speaker for a public meeting on 19 June. Carolena Wood, the Quaker woman who with Jane Addams had conducted the first exploratory Quaker mission to Germany and helped to set up the child feeding program, was able to come. She addressed a packed house. "She spoke wonderfully. Her audience was with her every minute, though she scolded them quite frankly for their faults," Mildred Scott wrote. Carolena Wood was followed by an English journalist, Evelyn Sharpe, who also spoke well, but following this the audience began to attack each other's political affiliations and theories. "The audience is sick, Germany is sick," Mildred's German companion said to her. Mildred, however, was stimulated by the exchange of ideas and was glad she had not missed the meeting. She was proud of Carolena Wood, who had three times managed to deflect the debate and bring the discussion back to international peace building.[16]

Originally Mildred herself had been invited to speak the night before the conference, but as a matter of courtesy she had turned the invitation over to Wilmer Young. Wilmer had transferred from the Paris headquarters to Germany and was sent to Munich to prepare to take over the responsibility for District X. With Arthur Charles close to the breaking point and Mildred in charge most of the time, this transfer meant he was apprenticed to Mildred. She tried not to gloat. "The poor man, his fiancé has died," she wrote Allen. "This is a beautiful chance for me to be magnanimous."[17]

Wilmer Young had come be Arthur Charles's assistant, as Mildred Scott and Ruth Mellor were planning to leave on 30 June. Ruth had continued to be pale and to lose weight, and several of the German doctors with whom they were working cautioned Mildred that Ruth was a candidate for tuberculosis, raging in Europe at the time. Mildred thought a six weeks' tour of Europe, which the two had been considering for some time, would provide the change of pace and relief from strain that Ruth needed. They planned to go to Austria and Italy, then spend two weeks walking in Switzerland, a few days in Holland to visit Mildred's Grand Pré roommate, then to Norway and back to Paris before sailing home from England.

Just before their departure some of their new Munich friends gave them a farewell party in the form of a raft trip down the river. The whole Quaker mission was invited, and the hosts ordered a keg of beer for the afternoon. "You'll have to drink the beer," Mildred told Ruth. The two were presented with many gifts, including beautifully framed pictures of Munich, and thanked for their work over the past three months.

Allen Olmsted was considering joining them on their travels. Mildred had continued to write frequent, affectionate letters to Allen and had taken a lively interest in his life, encouraging him to teach a course at the University of Pennsylvania and praising an article he had written for the *Nation* about the new transportation act. She worried that a girl he was seeing, Frannie, was not intellectual enough for him, and she suggested that he call on Clara Savage, back in Greenwich Village free-lancing. When he wrote that he was considering going into practice with Maurice Saul she said she thought it would be good for them both.

Allen had responded to this apparent warmth with many gifts and letters. He had sent Mildred a subscription to the *New Republic* and had insisted on giving her $200 for a luxury fund when she was unemployed in Berlin. He told her he was trying to fit his life to hers and was thinking of taking on a settlement group. He shared his grouchy moods with her. He told her about the women he was seeing, as she had urged him to do, but made it clear he was still hoping against hope that she would consent to marry him.

Ruth had also written to Allen occasionally on the basis of the understanding they had achieved before she sailed for Europe. She told him that she would never be jealous again, for Scottie needed both of them, though in a later letter she added she was still afraid of triangles. Allen thought the three of them could enjoy a trip together and investigated taking a cattle boat as a cheap way of earning his passage. But Mildred blew hot and cold over his coming. She wrote him a long letter, accusing him of giving way to his moods and his "sex interest," telling him once more that he ought to find a girl who wanted to be his wife and Richard's mother, but in the same breath indicating she thought he needed her to solve his drifting and his grouches. She mentioned the plans for the trip but said nothing about Allen joining them.

Allen was growing desperate. Earlier he had accused her of blinding herself with high motives while being selfish in holding on to him. Now her scolding letter on the eve of his departure caused an outbreak of despair:

The letter was anything but an invitation. . . . You are ten times the hardest task master I have ever known, and that is one reason why I cleave to you. . . . When you consider the conflict between the two master passions of my life, my love for you and desire to follow you in all things, on the one hand, and my desire for Richard and that you should be his mother and that you should be my wife and help me in my life on the other—a conflict which you yourself make, I could ask that you bear with me. . . .

. . . You know to what I attribute that conflict, to your unusual ideas about marriage and the apparent complete absence from your makeup of the feelings and instincts which normally attract the sexes to each other . . . I still feel your sex abnormality is in the nature of a sad perversion . . . I have thought that this *must* change in you if you fell in love with me . . . but you won't and can't fall in love because of that very abnormality, for mortal love is not a matter wholly of the soul.[18]

Mildred received Allen's cable that he wasn't coming before she received this letter, and she wrote to urge him to join them, but it was too late. She and Ruth started on their great adventure without a third member to the party. Mildred wrote Allen from Berne to say that she missed him but thought it was for the best that they parted now. They must not expect to see much of each other when she got home, but she had loved him and would always value his friendship.

The story of her trip she wrote in installments to her family. She and Ruth had loved Vienna and had gone on to Venice where they met a group of American college girls and with them traveled to Florence, which they hated to leave, and to Milan, which they found hot and modern and did not like. In Switzerland they had stayed in Geneva, gone for a boat trip to Chillon, and then started their walking trip in the Alps, climbing the Jungfrau to a pass 210 feet from the summit and ascending several lesser mountains in the rain. The food in Switzerland seemed so good to them after that of Germany that they gorged on butter and heavy cream and real chocolate. Everywhere people were kind to them, and they enjoyed meeting families on the trail. They came finally to Lucerne, where they picked up mail, and to Dresden, where they visited the Quaker mission. Then it was time to go on to Berlin where they were received warmly at the new AFSC headquarters and had lunch with a new worker, Francis Bacon, who had just arrived and was being assigned to head up the Leipzig Unit.

Mildred Scott's passport had expired, and there was a long delay about getting a new one. The American ambassador in Berlin was not very nice about it. He destroyed the old passport and scolded her for letting it run out. Regarding this as one more case of petty rules, Mildred decided to go on to Denmark without it, and to trust to her luck to talk immigration officers into letting her through. On the train to Copenhagen she and Ruth met a helpful Frenchman and an American who advised her about seeing the American ambassador as soon as she reached the city. Here she discovered it was possible to purchase a new passport. Their advisors had given them also the name of a good hotel, and they enjoyed their time in Denmark, although the food seemed almost too rich after Germany's.

Although they had planned next to take a walking trip in Norway, they felt they had to give it up because of a threatened railroad strike that might leave them stranded in some small village and unable to get back to Germany in time to take their ship home. Instead, they spent extra time in Haarlem in the Netherlands with Ada Koopmans of the Grand Pré équipe.

The long vacation together had cemented Ruth and Mildred's attachment. They had been together for almost nine months, enjoying the same things, understanding each other's moods and desires without having to ask. Ruth would remember all her life the peace and joy of that companionship. Whatever else happened to them they were now one. She could hardly bear to think of parting from her Scottie when they returned to the United States. But though Ruth was thirty-one and Mildred twenty-nine, they were both dutiful daughters. It did not seem to occur to either of them that they had any option but to return to their families, Ruth to Plymouth, and Mildred to Philadelphia.

7
Home Again

$\mathcal{T}$HE *NOORDOM*, the ship on which Mildred Scott and Ruth Mellor returned to the United States, landed in Hoboken, New Jersey, on 29 August 1920. It was nineteen months since Mildred had left the United States, and she was impatient to see home again. She did not know whether any member of her family would be able to meet her, but as the ship approached the dock she found herself straining her eyes to see if she could pick out any welcomers. Although none were in sight on the landing, on the very outermost of the posts marking the dock sat a man wearing a soldier's uniform. As they got closer Mildred thought she recognized the soldier. It was, of course, Allen.[1]

However much she had intended to avoid him, Mildred was delighted to see Allen and to have his help in getting through customs, putting Ruth on her train to Plymouth, and setting out for Philadelphia. Here her homecoming was delightful, with the whole family turning out to see the young and celebrated Miss Scott back from her overseas adventures.

Once the first excitement was over, however, Mildred was depressed by the life-style of post–World War I America. After the austerity and need in Germany, everyone here seemed to be too rich, and too bent on his or her own selfish interests. There were too many cars on the streets, too much food in the markets, too much of everything. She had no idea what she wanted to do, and Allen was an ever-present problem. She thought she might go out West for a while, where life might be simpler.[2]

Meanwhile she spent a week in the Pocono Mountains with

Trudy Pritchard, who was now going into nurse's training, and she visited Ruth in Plymouth. Ruth had been found to have a fever and was ordered to bed on an open porch. She was finding it hard to be in her mother's house again, and Tracy's visits were unsettling. Tracy wanted to resume their old relationship, but Ruth felt she had made a lifetime commitment to Mildred in Germany. Tracy was for play, Ruth thought, not to be taken seriously, and her advances must be rejected. Mildred was not to feel threatened by Tracy. Ruth wanted Mildred to come to Plymouth to be sure that all was still right between them.[3]

While Mildred Scott was traveling about visiting her best friends, a social worker named Anna Pratt had been trying to contact her. Pratt was the director of the White Williams Foundation, an old Philadelphia organization originally named the Magdalen Society that was organized to rescue prostitutes. Its focus had shifted to trying to prevent juvenile delinquency. Currently it was working with the Bureau of Compulsory Education of the public schools to keep boys and girls in school, providing them with employment help and scholarship grants and some personal counseling. It was in fact the agency that pioneered school social work, although it was still in a rudimentary stage. Mildred's friend Alicia Brown worked for White Williams and may have suggested Mildred to Anna Pratt.

As Mildred remembers the episode, Anna Pratt finally came to the house to talk to her about a job opening. "Frankly, I wouldn't be interested in any job but yours," Mildred told her, explaining that in any case she did not want to settle down in Philadelphia.[4]

Shortly thereafter, Anna Pratt wrote that she had created a new job for Mildred Scott, that of assistant director, and would that be satisfactory? The salary was generous, and Mildred did not see how she could turn it down. On 15 October she started to work at the foundation, with offices in an empty school building at 1522 Cherry Street. Anna Pratt appeared to Mildred to be giving her organizational talents full reign, and with her usual burst of energy and efficiency she set about reorganizing the operation of the foundation, which had just been through a period of rapid growth without time for consolidation.

At the time Mildred joined the staff, White Williams functioned as though it were part of the Bureau of Compulsory Education of the Philadelphia public schools and was wholly dependent upon the head of the bureau. It went into certain schools at his invitation and was subject to his pleasure. Mildred suggested that the foundation should take more control of its own destiny. Rather than going to whatever school invited its services, Mildred thought that White Williams should pick one school at each educational level and make it a model, demonstrating the results that could be obtained from careful social work methods at any level from kindergarten up. To accomplish this she urged Anna Pratt to make a shift from the Bureau of Compulsory Education to the Board of Education. She reorganized board meetings (apparently causing one board member to resign in protest) and developed streamlined office and staff procedures. She also helped to improve financing. After Mildred had been on the job just eighteen months, she claimed White Williams was known as the best-run social agency in Philadelphia.[5]

Meanwhile, Mildred Scott began to search for the WILPF, which she had met in Munich. There was no such listing in the Philadelphia phone book, and Mildred's social life then did not carry her into Quaker circles, where the Philadelphia WILPF branch was strong. At last, however, she saw an advertisement for an upcoming meeting at the Bellevue Stratford at which a woman from Germany, one from Belgium, and one from England were to speak; guessing correctly that this was indeed the WILPF, she got in touch with the sponsors. She finally found the WILPF offices in a small room off the Good Government office in the College Club. Except for a woman who came in once a week to open the mail and write news releases there was no staff; everything was done by volunteers.[6]

Delighted to have Mildred Scott as a new recruit, Pennsylvania WILPF immediately put her on the membership committee and also on a committee to work with other peace associations in the city. At the first executive board meeting she attended she reported that she had interviewed Fred Libby, whom she had met in Germany and who was now heading up a temporary group called the Friends Disarmament Council (later to become the National Council for Prevention of War), and a Mr. Plamquiest of the Philadelphia Inter-church Federation. In a few months she was placed on the WILPF nominating committee and made vice-president of the Pennsylvania WILPF board.

Mildred Scott in turn was delighted with the WILPF. She liked the women she met: Hannah Clothier Hull, the president, a Quaker and a longtime peace activist alongside her Swarthmore husband, William Hull; Lucy Biddle Lewis, also a Quaker and active with the American Friends Service Committee; Florence Sanville, a Quaker activist who had worked against sweatshops and committed civil disobedience with Alice Paul, the militant suffragist, demonstrating in front of the White House for the vote, and who had taught Mildred at the Philadelphia Training School for Social Work; Mary Winsor, a suffragist and birth control advocate whom she had known on the Main Line; Mary Scattergood, whose husband, Alfred, had headed the AFSC mission in Berlin; Lucia Stokes Adams, a distinguished suffragist. They were for the most part upper-middle-class, educated, intelligent, and willing and able to devote all their free time to the cause of peace. Mildred always believed that this was the sort of group who had the leisure and the ability to bring about social change.

Working with the WILPF meant a chance to work with Jane Addams, whom Mildred had admired since she first heard her speak at Smith and had subsequently met in Paris. The work in Hull House for which Jane Addams was famous had inspired Mildred when she went to work at College Settlement; her advocacy of peace had been a factor in Mildred's own conversion to pacifism. She had read several of Jane Addams's books and felt herself to be at one with Addams's ideas. Strong, independent, thoughtful, analytical, able to hold her own with men as well as women, Jane Addams was the sort of person Mildred most admired.

Many of the members of the WILPF had come out of the suffragist movement and had joined the Woman's Peace party organized by Jane Addams and Carrie Chapman Catt in January 1915. When Catt, as leader of the National American Woman Suffrage Association, had pledged the support of her organization to the war effort in an attempt to secure suffrage by demonstrating the patriotism of women, she lost the support of these peace-oriented suffragists, who followed Jane Addams into the Woman's Peace party and the subsequent development of the WILPF. In these early days the WILPF continued to think and act with methods left over from the suffrage struggle. The idea of trying to create a WILPF branch in every congressional district was such a residue.

Mildred Scott had not been very active in the suffrage struggle, but she felt comfortable with the women. She also liked being challenged to learn more about the political and social issues on which the WILPF worked. She learned something about U.S. relations with poorer countries when she went to hear a speech on "Haiti, the first Real U.S. Experience with Imperialism." Her experience with African Americans was broadened by attending a peace fair for "colored people." She met with members of the Women's Trade Union League when they sponsored a talk on disarmament by an English working woman. She heard about international efforts to abolish the use of poison gas, and about famine in Russia.

She attended her first WILPF national board meeting in April 1922. At this meeting a struggle that had been going on within the WILPF for some time came to a head. From the beginning there had been members who wanted to make the WILPF an absolute pacifist organization, and others who preferred it to be open to all women sincerely interested in working for peace. Mary Winsor of Radnor, one of the absolutists, put forward a pledge she wanted all WILPF members to sign. "In case our country is at war, I will not join or work for the Red Cross, nor make hospital supplies. I will not urge food conservation, I will not buy Liberty Bonds or any other similar war loans. I will not make munitions or take a man's place to enable him to go to war."[7]

Fanny Garrison Villard, daughter of William Lloyd Garrison and leader of the Women's Peace Society, spoke in support of the pledge, as did Lola Maverick Lloyd, its author. Both were committed to nonresistance. Jane Addams countered by pointing out that this pledge might damage the international WILPF, as some of the national sections would not take such a pledge. It was more important to take all women who wanted to work for peace as members, and let them learn as they worked together. The Quaker members, who were opposed to pledge taking, also objected. A report was read from international secretary Emily Greene Balch stressing the strength of unity in diversity for the WILPF. Finally the women voted overwhelmingly against the pledge. Mildred was impressed with the decision to honor individual freedom of conscience, and to depend on "pooled intelligence," as Jane Addams said, to chart WILPF's course.

The decision was the correct one if the WILPF was to survive as an international organization. But for the U.S. WILPF Section it was the source of continuing ideological struggles between those whose first priority was peace, and who believed that absolute pacifism was necessary, and those whose first priority was social justice, and whose sympathies lay with the working class, with the labor unions, and to some extent with socialist governments abroad. But in the early days of the 1920s the problem seemed minimal, and the members of the WILPF came away from the congress feeling that a difficult problem had been correctly solved. Mildred certainly felt so, and she continued to believe that WILPF had no other choice.

In addition to her job and her work for the WILPF, Mildred Scott was finding new satisfactions in her home life. Shortly after she returned home, her father had asked her how she would like to live in the country. He was no longer in the district attorney's office and therefore no longer needed to live in town, and he was looking into the purchase of a house in Rose Valley, adjacent to the place where Adele and Maurice Saul had settled. Mildred felt it was a giant reprieve from the sentence executed upon her long ago when the Scotts first moved from Glenolden to the city. She was soon happily involved in helping her father plan the landscaping for the new house. Her mother was not pleased with the impending move, preferring the sociability of city life, but this did not deter Henry Scott from pressing ahead.

Mildred had become interested in the Rose Valley community as a result of visiting Adele. The project had been started in 1901 by William Price, a talented young architect interested in reviving arts and crafts. On the land were several abandoned mills, and for a time these were used for the manufacture of furniture, for bookbinding, and for ceramics. While these enterprises failed, folk dancing, music, and theater flourished. Will Price designed several houses and helped with the conversion of others. Several artists moved to the community, including Alice Barber Stephens, a magazine illustrator, and her husband, Charles. For them Price converted an old barn to a double studio and added a wing for family living. The Stephenses called it Thunderbird Lodge. The community attracted lawyers, writers, artists, and others interested in a distinct way of life. The Sauls loved it, and by Thanksgiving the Scott family was installed in the new house.

The move to the country helped Mildred Scott get over her attack of culture shock on return to the United States. But she kept in touch with her friends in Germany, sent them food, tried to arrange for the sick niece of her former landlady in Berlin to spend time in the United States, spoke several times for the AFSC to raise money for the continuing child feeding, and arranged for a German prisoner of war whom she had met at Grand Pré to come to the United States as her father's chauffeur.

The big problem in her life was Allen Olmsted. She enjoyed his companionship and his admiration, but she remained clear that she did not want to marry him. The answer seemed to be to send him away, but that was difficult. He had become very much a part of the life of her family and in March joined Saul, Ewing, Remick and Saul, the law firm that Maurice had organized and that included his brother Walter Biddle Saul.

Besides, when she did send him away, she missed him and felt forlorn and rejected. Why must he insist on marriage and children? Why could they not go on the way they were? Ruth Mellor wrote to Allen that Scottie needed him, and that he must not quit. Why could he not just remove sex entirely from his mind? That seemed to be the root of the problem.[8]

Allen wrote back that the suggestion seemed like repression to him. But he was willing at the urging of both Ruth and Mildred to try going to a psychiatrist for a while to see if it would help with his mood swings and his periods of being angry at Mildred for the frustrations of the long-delayed decision. Meanwhile he and Ruth corresponded frequently about Mildred, her needs, and their mutual love of her. When Allen and Mildred quarreled in November, Allen went to Plymouth to consult Ruth. She helped him to achieve a reconciliation and convinced him that they might be able to share a "triangular apartment" when and if Mildred finally agreed to marry Allen. Ruth at times seemed to favor this marriage, as long as it was clearly understood that it would in no way interfere with the priority of her relationship to Mildred.

By December Mildred was wearing Allen's ring again, although she made it clear this meant no commitment. Allen gave Mildred a pedigreed police dog, Timothy, for her birthday, and a warm wool blanket for Christmas. In February Mildred was willing to visit his family in Buffalo. But the visit led to frayed nerves and more quarreling. There was another reconciliation. Allen became so hopeful that he began to plan for a June wedding and a honeymoon that would take place in the Adirondacks near the Sauls' camp on Long Lake. When Mildred discovered that he was actually making such plans, she was furious. It was a case of a man taking a woman for granted, she thought, the very sort of thing that made her hesitate so long about agreeing to marry Allen. They once more agreed to separate, and Allen planned at first to spend the summer abroad, then to go off into the woods by himself to think things over.

Mildred's father had never particularly liked Allen, but he did not understand why Mildred was hesitating so about making a decision. The problem with Mildred was that she had "an obsession with freedom," he observed. He did not understand the degree to which her childhood, and his role in it, had made Mildred fear playing the woman's role. But Mildred wanted marriage only if it excluded both intercourse and children; in other words, a companionship only. At least she wanted these to be the premarital conditions. If she gave more, it would be her free giving, not responding to a demand. These were hard terms for Allen to accept. But accept them he eventually did, somehow believing that he could talk Mildred out of both conditions once they were actually married.[9]

All through the hot summer of 1921 they were back and forth about being engaged. Allen was jealous of the time Mildred spent with Ruth, and also with a young admirer from the White Williams Foundation, Florence Pharo. "He feels like a man whose wife has been unfaithful to him," Ruth observed. Finally, in late

August and early September, Mildred took a vacation in the Poconos with Trudy and spent the time talking over the situation with her oldest friend. She enjoyed being with Allen and missed him when he went away. She did not want to alter her life to fit his, but why could she not have him as an added bonus to her own life? He said time and again he was proud of her for working and would not ever want her to stay at home. Was it not possible that with such a man as a husband she would be freer than if she remained single? Allen had tried to convince her of this time after time, but she was now coming to the conclusion on her own, away from his pressure. [10]

Returning from the Poconos, Mildred agreed to go with Allen on a short walking trip to Grand Isle on Lake Champlain. Back in Philadelphia, she wrote him a short note: "I love you, dearest, and I will marry you this fall." [11]

Allen was ecstatic. "New [Mil]Dred Scott decision handed down by Supreme Courter, held that emancipated woman leaving her free state for state of matrimony does not lose her freedom. Come and see for yourself Rose Valley October 28," he telegraphed his family. "Your lovely invitation for October 28, Looks to all the Whites and Olmsteds as if you had found your fate. Looks as if a certain Mildred had bewildered you of late. Please accept congratulations on your matrimonial state," the rhyming Olmsteds cabled back. [12]

The date 28 October was only a guess. Mildred wasn't sure she could take time away from White Williams to get married, but her office staff insisted, and the date was finally reset for 30 October. Mildred's father offered her the choice of a society wedding, such as Adele's, or a simple wedding and the money to furnish her new apartment. Mildred preferred a simple outdoor wedding in any case. Because fall colors still lingered in the Scott garden in Rose Valley, Mildred thought she ought to wear black velvet to set off the oranges and the reds and the golds. Her mother was scandalized, and Mildred said she would wear gray velvet instead. Nothing could shake her from this decision. [13]

Although time was short, the family sent out five hundred invitations, and congratulations as well as wedding presents began to roll in from near and far. The question of what sort of wedding ceremony to have was crucial. Mildred was not going to be forced to vow to "love, honor, and obey." Finally Allen and Mildred decided to ask the Swarthmore Friends Meeting to oversee the wedding "because of our sympathy with Friends ideals, especially of the marriage relationship and the marriage ceremony." Hannah Clothier Hull, whom Mildred had been getting to know through the WILPF, undertook to meet with the couple and to explain Quaker procedures.

Both Olmsteds had some objection to the simple, standard Quaker promise, which reads: "In the presence of God and these our friends I, Allen take thee, Mildred to be my wife, promising with divine assistance to be unto thee a true and a loving husband so long as we both shall live." Allen was not sure he knew what he meant by God any more and suggested a simplified version: "In the presence of these our friends assembled, I, Allen take thee, Mildred to be my wife, promising to be unto thee a loving and faithful husband, and in token of my love I give thee this ring." Mildred was not ready to make any promises at all, Friends ceremony or no. Her words were to be: "As a token of our true love, I take thy ring, and in the presence of the Lord and these our friends assembled I, Mildred take thee, Allen to be my husband." Hannah Hull gently inquired whether Mildred was not ready to say that she would *strive* to be a loving and faithful wife, but Mildred was not, and Allen backed her up.[14]

Everyone worried about the weather, but 30 October dawned clear, and the wedding went off smoothly, Mildred looking radiant in her gray velvet. Ruth, who had come to help her get ready, felt herself so much part of the ceremony that she did not feel a qualm until Allen and Mildred left for their honeymoon. Trudy was there and would remember that October afternoon as a high spot all through her life. Many Olmsteds and many college friends of Allen had come to see him married, and Adele and Maurice, whose tenth wedding anniversary it was, had special cause for celebration. After the wedding and the reception, the bride and groom and many of their friends went to the Sauls to roll up the rugs and dance.

The honeymoon did not go smoothly. Allen and Mildred had planned to spend the night in New York City, where Allen had engaged a hotel room. When it came time to leave Rose Valley and catch the train to New York, the weather broke, and the bridal couple were caught in a downpour. When they finally reached New York and the hotel, it developed that Allen had failed to specify a room for two, and they had to make do with a single. The next day, after arranging for a double room, they spent much of the day riding around in the rain in a hansom cab, while Allen pointed out his favorite haunts, including the Henry Street Settlement where he had once lived. Sometime during this brief New York interlude, they made love for the first time. Mildred did not particularly enjoy it—she told me that she felt she had always been too controlled to enjoy sex—but Allen was very gentle and patient, and it was by no means the trauma she had always feared.

On Wednesday they took a train to Long Lake in the Adirondacks, the Sauls' summer property, where the house had been left open for them. Allen had been there last summer camping in the woods, trying to get over Mildred. Now he was determined that they should camp, although the rain had continued and at this altitude was turning to snow. They hiked to Owl's Head and tried to pitch a tent, but the ground was so frozen it was impossible to get a tent peg into the earth. They gathered pine boughs and set them afire to melt the ground, dug in their stakes, and erected their tent against the wind, which had begun to blow fiercely. To make a fire protected from the wind they found a stump and cooked under its shelter, but it was hard to see the food, which came out either burned or raw.

And still the weather got worse. Allen saw some hunters at an abandoned lumber camp nearby and went to ask them what word they had of the snow. They told him that a big storm was coming and they were all seeking shelter as soon as possible. Better join them, they urged.

"Wait until I get my wife," Allen said.

"Your wife?" the hunters queried. "You don't think much of her, do you?"[15]

The lumber camp was dirty, smelly, and crowded. Mildred was used to rugged camping experiences, but it seemed to her that Allen was too ready to conclude that it was good enough for her.

The old suspicion flared: because he was a man, he was ready to take advantage of her position as his wife. Although Allen gathered pine boughs to make her a bed and tried to shield her from the hunters, not only was she cold and miserable, but she felt betrayed. It was a story to which she would return time and again in her married life.[16]

The honeymoon did not improve. When they finally left cold Long Lake and reached Buffalo, Mildred discovered that the Olmsteds and their friends had planned a series of parties for her. But Allen had not warned her (perhaps he had not known), and she had not brought along the trousseau that a proper bride ought to have in 1921. A sense of grievance, the classic sense of grievance of the new bride at that time, came home with her from the bridal trip.

As soon as they returned from Buffalo that fall they moved into their new apartment at Twenty-second and Chestnut streets, and Mildred threw herself into decorating, using her father's money and some of her own. Allen suggested that rather than pool their salaries they each take over responsibility for certain aspects of the household. Mildred could buy the furniture and linens, as well as her own clothes; he would take care of food and maintenance. They could each keep separate bank accounts and go dutch on special events, trips, or the like.

Mildred continued to love pretty things—silk draperies at the windows, colored sheets on the beds, cashmere sweaters, and suede shoes—and to believe with her father that it was never worth buying anything but the best. (It was, she would have said, the Judy side of her personality.) She loved to color coordinate her outfits. Dress, hat, sweater, shoes, and bag always matched. She even bought grosgrain straps for her watch so that these also could be changed from green to blue to red to yellow depending on her color scheme for the day. She chose bright colors—reds and purples—and sometimes added a floral hat. Her hats in time became famous. She also loved jewelry and collected it from all over the world. All of this cost money. The arrangement Allen proposed gave her free reign to indulge her tastes. When she ran out of money she went to auctions and thrift shops for both furnishings and clothing. She liked to mend clothes, a skill left over from her girlhood, and nothing pleased her more than to find a bargain that could be made usable with a touch of needle and thread.

In later years this division of financial responsibility did not work out very well; Allen's bills for food, utilities, maintenance, and salaries for the servants skyrocketed, and he was often scraping the bottom of his bank account while Mildred continued to spend freely on clothes and jewelry and extravagant presents for Ruth, and to object to his economies. Because they kept separate books she never knew precisely what his financial situation was. Mildred paid for part of her own travel, with help from Ruth, and sometimes was in debt to Allen and had to borrow from Ruth. All this complicated their already complicated relationships. But in the early days of their marriage Mildred gloried in her financial independence and was full of praise for Allen's support of this.

Cooking was another problem. Mildred had never learned to cook and perhaps never intended to. As a working woman she felt it would not be possible for her to cook for herself and Allen. In the 1920s, before the advent of supermarkets or labor-saving devices, cooking was in itself a time-consuming job. Most middle-class families had some sort of household help. Clara Savage, the Smith woman Mildred had met in Paris, was now married herself and writing a series of articles for *Good Housekeeping* about married women who pursued careers, all with the help of servants. She wrote Mildred that "I am still the same independent, individualistic, maddeningly modern person I was on that walking trip in Brittany," but being a modern person included having a cook and a maid. Mildred could not afford a cook to begin with, but she managed to arrange for their landlady to get their meals and for a woman to come in to clean the apartment. Her mother, who wished she would settle down to domesticity, gave her an electric washer for her thirty-first birthday. The Scotts had given Mildred and Allen the use of some rooms on the third floor of their house in Rose Valley, and here they often spent their weekends, out of the dirty and noisy city.[17]

As soon as she returned to Philadelphia, Mildred Scott went back to her job at the White Williams Foundation. The work of this agency had been expanding steadily during Mildred's first year on the job, and she was often asked to speak to other social agencies. In February she helped to conduct a seminar organized by the Pennsylvania School for Social Service on problems of social work in Philadelphia. Her growing fame created problems for White Williams for it cast the director, Anna Pratt, in the background. In addition, Mildred had so efficiently gathered responsibility for the day-to-day running of the agency into her own hands that Anna Pratt sometimes found little to do. Anna Pratt herself did not seem to mind, but some members of the board were upset and decided in March to ask that a study of the agency be made, to consider ways of reorganizing.

Mildred Scott was disturbed by these developments and wrote a memo to Anna Pratt, outlining the ways in which she thought she had assisted the agency. But the man hired to do the survey, Arthur Dunham, recommended that the post of assistant director be abolished, her duties divided between Anna Pratt, the supervisors, and the office managers, and her salary used to hire someone with a strong educational background to strength the school counseling program. Anna Pratt wrote a note of deep regret to Mildred and a report to the board indicating how much Mildred had accomplished in her eighteen months with the agency. But essentially Mildred was asked to resign, and it was a bitter pill for her to swallow. At ninety-seven she told me that she did not feel she had handled it very well.[18]

Typically, however, she did not brood but immediately got in touch with the Bureau of Occupations for Trained Women in Philadelphia and was told that the organization promoting the nomination of Gifford Pinchot for governor of Pennsylvania on the Republican ticket was hiring educated women as campaigners. She was given six counties in western Pennsylvania to organize and spent two weeks on the road, campaigning. She enjoyed the work—arranging for speakers, newspaper articles, and the distribution of literature—and did well. The job came to an end when Pinchot won the nomination. Mildred came back to Philadelphia and wrote a letter of application to the American Association of Social Workers, asking about "executive or organizing positions" that began the next fall. She wanted to take the summer off because she and Allen were going to Europe.[19]

The women of the WILPF, meanwhile, had learned that Mildred was looking for a job and conceived the idea of offering her the position of executive secretary of the Pennsylvania branch. The local branches were growing, the national organization was becoming more active, and they felt they ought to try a full-time executive. How to pay Mildred was a problem, as she had been receiving the high salary of $3,500 a year at White Williams. Several board members decided that they would together guarantee the salary, at least for the first six months. After that Mildred might be counted on to have developed fund raising to such an extent that money for her own salary would flow in.[20]

Mildred was interested in working for the WILPF but wondered if she ought to leave the field of social work administration in which she had come so near to succeeding. Also there was financial uncertainty with the WILPF. She decided to wait for a few weeks to reply to WILPF to see if she might get a better offer. "Tell Mrs. Pfaum of the Bureau of Occupation that I must give WILPF a definite answer by the end of the week so I am waiting anxiously to hear from her," she wrote Allen on 14 June. She had a reply from the American Association of Social Workers suggesting two possible openings, one as a recreation organizer, the other as executive for a federation of social agencies, but neither job was in Philadelphia, where her family lived. She finally told Ida Jaffe of the WILPF that she would accept the job of executive secretary in September.[21]

That June marked the tenth anniversary of her graduation from Smith, and she had gone back to Northampton with Adele, then on to the house party at Ruth Mellor's in Plymouth, which had become a regular part of reunion for the young women of Tyler. From Plymouth she wrote to Allen that after comparing experiences with other Smith women she was glad to be married to him.

> I am so proud, dearest, that I can truthfully say you believe in my freedom as much as I do and I am glad that you are close beside me in what they consider my queer standards . . . we do love unselfishly and generously and we are wholly honest in our relations. So many of the girls, I find, have had ardent love affairs and married in ecstasy and then have gone through very unhappy embittering years of adjustment before they fell in love with their husbands again. . . .

. . . On the subject of babies I have compared the experiences of many people, too and I know you would not be pleased by what I hear. Nobody seems to feel that it is practical to try to do any regular work after one has even one child. . . . Having children seemed either to have been a terrible experience, shocking to their minds and their bodies, or to have left them with physical weakness of one kind or another . . . the women in the past have just suffered this penalty without question, as they did other privations and limitations because they were women. . . .

. . . Could we but work out some simplified way of having and bringing up children that would rob it of its disadvantages as you have robbed marriage of its bondage I should like to have at least four children for the joy that they would bring us, especially as we and they grew older.[22]

While Mildred visited friends, Allen planned their trip to Norway. His legal work with railroads added to the interest of planning travel itineraries, and he loved to find out about unusual, off-the-beaten-track places to stay and to visit. For this trip, which was in the nature of a delayed honeymoon, he had planned carefully; first the sea voyage on a Norwegian ship, then a walking trip in the Norwegian mountains with overnight stops at little country inns until they reached Trondheim.

All went well until they reached Norway. Then one day while they were hiking, Allen's mood took a sudden downswing as he crossed a road. Mildred had worried about his mood swings before they were married, but this was so sudden and lasted so long that she remembered it afterwards as the beginning of her experience with the bitter moods on which she blamed all their subsequent domestic troubles.

After several days Allen recovered his good nature, and the trip continued happily. From Norway they had planned to go on to Sweden, but as they did not have visas, they had to go instead to Copenhagen where a local WILPF representative arranged for them to be admitted to the parliament. They then crossed to Germany, where one could get 650 marks to the dollar and live like kings and queens. They visited the AFSC mission and the family with whom Mildred and Ruth had boarded, met the brother of Ida

Jaffe of the WILPF, and went with him to a *Nie Wieder Krieg* demonstration that, they wrote home, would delight the heart of any pacifist. In Dresden they saw the Sistine Madonna, met old friends, and sent their bags back to Strasburg so that they could fly from Prague to Strasburg after their walking trip in the Bohemian Alps. The hike itself was a success, though they had trouble finding nice inns and once crossed the border from Germany to Czechoslovakia at night in search of a place to stay without anyone challenging their papers. Lawless Mildred had to persuade law-abiding Allen to take the chance. The flight back from Prague to Strasburg was the first air flight Mildred had ever made, and it predictably caused her to be very airsick, but she recovered quickly. In Geneva they visited the WILPF headquarters and met Emily Greene Balch, the former economics professor from Wellesley who had lost her job because of her pacifism during the war and was now serving as international secretary for WILPF. She immediately became one of Mildred's venerated heroes. It was altogether a delightful trip, Mildred wrote Ruth, and Allen had been perfectly dear most of the time.[23]

Unfortunately, in Paris they discovered that one of the suitcases supposedly forwarded from Dresden to Paris via Strasburg had been left at Dresden and would not catch up with them until they got home. Allen was philosophical, but Mildred was irate and wanted him to share her anger. It led to a quarrel that was still troubling them two weeks later. "In order to keep you contented it seems that I must aggressively resent such things," Allen wrote to Mildred, using a yellow lined legal pad. "Unless I get inwardly wrought up about them, and angry at the third persons, you get angry at me." It was when she spoke sharply to him that he became depressed and grouchy, he argued. She and Ruth claimed his bad moods had nothing to do with provocation but resulted only from some internal, probably hereditary, tendency on his part. He insisted instead that they had both learned in the past year of marriage that they reacted to one another.[24]

The letter was long, well reasoned, and well written. It had something of the tone of a legal brief and was the first of hundreds that Allen wrote to Mildred over the years, repeating one basic theme; if she would be nicer to him, he would be nicer to be with.

Both Allen and Mildred were children of the Progressive Era, the age of reason. They both believed that if their feelings could be expressed clearly enough, and frequently enough, they would somehow convince the other of the rightness of their positions. It did not make for a peaceful marriage, but it made for an interesting one. As Mildred had told her Smith friends, she and Allen tried, within the limits of their self-understanding, to be honest with one another.

8
Working for the WILPF

*W*HEN MILDRED SCOTT OLMSTED went to work for the Pennsylvania branch of the WILPF on 22 September 1922, she found her office to consist of a broken desk covered with old literature in one dark corner of the Friends Institute at 20 South Twelfth Street, Philadelphia. In the drawers were bundles of letters and a mailing list on three-by-five cards, with some sections missing. The former executive secretary, who had worked one day a week, had resigned some time before, and the headquarters had been moved from the College Club to the Friends Institute, where there was really no room for it.

Mildred always loved a challenge. She got immediately to work cleaning up, ordering supplies, and getting WILPF listed in the phone book. A prominent board member offered Mildred the services of her secretary, an African-American woman with whom she had a personality clash, specifying that she would pay the secretary's salary if this arrangement were kept secret. Mary Moon, the secretary for Friends Institute (and the woman with whom Mildred had battled over her German assignment), offered her more room in the office and a second desk. Volunteers came to update the mailing and membership lists. By the time the first monthly board meeting rolled round, the WILPF office was busy every day of the week.

Mildred was determined from the very first to build new WILPF branches. She saw no reason why there should not be a branch in every major town and city in Pennsylvania. Surely there were that many intelligent, committed women willing to work for peace. As soon as she felt things were properly in order, she took her first field trip, visiting Shamokin in the middle of the state. She went with a list of women to contact, some dating back to suffrage days, rang doorbells, made calls, organized a meeting, and left an active branch functioning. The following spring she made a longer swing through the state, visiting Scranton, Wilkes-Barre, Bedford, Altoona, Lock Haven, Bellefonte, Johnston, Greensburg, Pittsburgh, Harrisburg, Chambersburg, and Somerset. It was hard, strenuous work, she found—calling on person after person, holding meetings, writing press releases, persuading women to take responsibility for the new branch—but it was rewarding. People were almost always pleasant to her and, after the first few minutes, helpful. Often the women she contacted had thought of themselves as isolated in their desire to work for peace. Getting in touch with like-minded women through the WILPF opened new windows for them.[1]

One visit, however, was rarely enough to organize a new branch. Even when a branch was established it needed nurturing, sending stimulating speakers, consulting with the new members over problems that arose, and involving them as soon as possible in the larger family of the WILPF, the state branch, the national section, and the international body. Mildred traveled throughout the state frequently during her first years with WILPF. By 1925 she had raised enough money to hire a field secretary to help with the development of new branches.

In addition to this pioneer fieldwork, Mildred also began pushing to increase membership both locally and nationally. Some of the elder founders of the WILPF, including Jane Addams, had thought it might be a good idea to keep WILPF small and flexible, able to make decisions quickly and to do its best work by influencing other mass organizations. Jane Addams originally wanted WILPF to be composed of leaders who could keep in touch by personal correspondence, according to Mildred. Yet when Mildred asked her what WILPF offered American women Jane Addams said, "An opportunity." Mildred thought the opportunity ought to be offered to as many American women as possible and frequently tried to push Jane Addams in this direction. In her first year with the Pennsylvania branch she worked with the membership committee to increase membership from five hundred to twenty-one hundred. She also put the budget on a sounder basis and developed a system of standing committees to oversee different aspects of the work.

Most of all, she believed that the WILPF should be staffed chiefly by volunteers, providing the maximum number of women with the opportunity to work for peace. Only a small staff would be needed to serve the volunteers. She recruited women from among the board members and their friends to carry on special projects as well as to help with such day-to-day tasks as getting out mailings, writing news releases for the papers, and raising money.

In the 1920s many middle-class and upper-middle-class women had adequate household help and leisure to devote themselves to full-time volunteer work with women's organizations, which proliferated at this time. Professional women also joined these organizations, but many of these were single and able to command their own leisure time. Their choices were many. In the field of peace alone there was, in addition to the WILPF, the Women's Peace Society, founded by Fanny Garrison Villard in 1919 and supported by absolute pacifists; the Women's Committee on World Disarmament, formed in 1921; the Women's Peace Union of the Western Hemisphere, affiliated with War Resisters International; and the National Committee on the Cause and Cure of War, organized by Carrie Chapman Catt in 1925 from leaders of the major women's organizations with peace departments.

In addition to the women's peace organizations, there were such groups as the League of Women Voters, evolved from the woman's suffrage movement; the Women's Christian Temperance Union (WCTU); the National Women's party, led by Alice Paul and devoted exclusively to equal rights legislation, including the Equal Rights Amendment; the American Association of University Women; the General Federation of Business and Professional Women's Clubs; and scores of others.

In common with these organizations, WILPF offered its volunteers an exciting and challenging way to spend their days, as well as a focus for their social life. There were frequent teas and luncheons, for which the women always dressed in hats and gloves. At the national board meetings, they wore formal clothes for the evening. Their pictures appeared in the rotogravure sections of the local papers.

The number of board members and volunteers pouring into the WILPF office soon made it difficult for the Friends Institute to function. In December Mary Moon offered Mildred Olmsted the small separate office that the stenographer had previously occupied. There was no formal charge for rent, but WILPF was expected to contribute twenty dollars a month. Here they remained for almost five years, sharing space with the American Friends Service Committee. At one point Mildred Olmsted thought the AFSC ought to give the WILPF more space, as its own programs were dwindling now that the postwar emergencies were being solved, while WILPF with its commitment to political work for peace and justice was growing.[2]

In addition to her work in building the WILPF directly, Mildred Olmsted believed that it was necessary to develop coalitions with other groups to work on specific issues. She spent as much time as she could increasing contacts with the League of Women Voters, the Women's Christian Temperance Union, the Y, the Council of Jewish Women, the Greater Philadelphia Federation of Churches, teachers, and labor groups. She kept in touch with the settlements and the American Association of Social Workers, and she helped in the development of the Philadelphia Council for World Peace, a clearing house for peace work in Philadelphia. She also helped to create the Foreign Policy Association in Philadelphia, working with Francis Biddle. She continued personally to serve on the board of the Birth Control League, although birth control was not an issue on which the WILPF felt it could take a position.

In the connections she made between women in building WILPF branches, and the relationships she established with sister organizations, Mildred Olmsted revealed her commitment to and ability in networking, the forging of bonds of sisterhood between the women of the WILPF and between the WILPF and its sister organizations. The fact that the Pennsylvania WILPF remained the largest and strongest branch in the world was due to this basic and empowering work.

It helped Mildred Olmsted in coalition building that Allen too was active in Philadelphia civic affairs. Shortly after the American Civil Liberties Union was established in 1920, he began a correspondence with its executive, Roger Baldwin. Allen had joined the Willard Straight Post of the American Legion in New York City, a liberal group, and through it was trying to swing the legion toward a more progressive attitude. Roger Baldwin wrote to say he was interested "in what you are trying to do for essential Americanism with posts of the American Legion too often dominated by reactionary interests." The correspondence led to Baldwin's asking Allen to represent the ACLU in cases throughout Pennsylvania, as well as to cooperate with the independent Philadelphia Civil Liberties Committee. At Baldwin's urging Allen went to Harrisburg in the spring of 1924 to defend the right of some workers to commemorate the birth date of Lenin.[3]

Allen Olmsted was also the chair of Young Democracy, a group that held events emphasizing progressive ideals. In 1925 he became the chair of the Philadelphia Council for World Peace, which Mildred had helped to organize, and was also asked to serve on a national committee to bring the United States into the World Court. His interest in the city of Philadelphia led to his becoming the chair of the public affairs committee of the City Club, an influential group of private citizens interested in public policy. He helped draft legislation on birth control for Pennsylvania and served with Mildred on the executive committee of the Southeastern Pennsylvania Birth Control League.

But working together proved a mixed blessing for Allen and Mildred. Their methods of approach were too different. Mildred was always goal oriented; Allen liked to try to draw the will of the group out of the committee he was chairing, whether or not that will coincided with what he thought ought to happen. In making speeches, Allen was precise and lawyerlike. Mildred was imprecise and frequently exaggerated, overstating the facts, much to Allen's annoyance. She was also somewhat boastful, he thought, her own hero. They came in time to understand and accept some of these differences, but working them out in the public arena was another thing. Although Mildred had urged Allen to become chair of the Philadelphia Council for World Peace, she was too involved with it herself to let the responsibility go. There was friction between them on several occasions. Finally Allen decided to resign and put his energies elsewhere.[4]

In her work for WILPF in Philadelphia, Mildred Olmsted developed her natural flair for drama. She arranged for WILPF members to speak on street corners on Armistice Day, just as they had earlier spoken on street corners for suffrage. She planned the reading of a peace pageant written by Lydia Wentworth, and a mass meeting for Private Peat, a soldier speaking out against war. Whenever she could, she drew in prominent men and women to participate in WILPF events.

While the women of the WILPF were delighted to have Mildred Olmsted's energy and enthusiasm at work and pleased with the results that began to be manifested, they were not always pleased with Mildred herself. She had very strong ideas about what ought to be done, which did not leave room for other people's initiatives. She came to each board meeting with an agenda of what she wanted to accomplish and often with a resolution that she wanted passed. She had the capacity to make some of the soft-spoken Quaker women on the WILPF board very angry. The controlling side of her nature came to the fore in political situations. She seemed unable to trust the group to reach a right decision without her heavy-handed guidance. While in her development of networks she drew on her experience as a woman, in the political arena she modeled herself after her father. It was an expression of her divided personality that mystified all those close to her.

Certain members of the office staff also found her hard to work for in those early days. As she drove herself, she drove them, piling them with dictation to transcribe and mailings to get out, often toward the end of the day. Marian Norton, a Friend whom she had met in France, came to work as office manager and tried to straighten out some of the tangles. Let us work with you, not for you, was her constant plea. Younger staff members and volunteers were often frightened of Mildred. They complained that she issued orders like a martinet, and if she was not obeyed she had a way of fixing them with her piercing blue eyes that made them tremble in their boots.[5]

But she also had many admirers on both board and staff.

Those strong enough to stand up to her discovered that she would listen to criticism with an open mind and rather enjoyed being challenged. She was generally fair, and her energy and enthusiasm were infectious.

One of her admirers was Lucy Biddle Lewis of Lansdowne. Lucy had been a member of the Woman's Peace party, and a delegate to the first Hague conference. Now she was serving as national chair of the WILPF board, and she was eager to recruit Mildred Olmsted's talents and energies in the service of the national organization. In March 1923 Mildred attended the national board meeting in Washington and was made secretary pro tem. This was the beginning of many years of service on the national board.

Mildred and Allen had moved in December 1922 to a somewhat larger apartment at 4013 Pine Street. The house was owned by an older friend of Allen's, Marshall Smith, or Uncle Marshall as he was known, who was lonely and thought it would be nice to have the young Olmsteds sharing his house. An incentive for Mildred was that he was willing to have his housekeeper cook dinner for them all to eat together.

There would be room in the new apartment for a baby and the baby's nurse. Allen renewed his arguments for a baby in the spring of 1923. After all they were not getting any younger, he reminded Mildred. If they were to have a family at all, they must get on with it. He gave her a book that made the case for children and for full-time motherhood.

Mildred once more felt that Allen was intruding upon her freedom, breaking the fundamentals of their agreement. She was traveling for the WILPF at the time, and she wrote him a long letter outlining her position.

> I suspect I belong to the latter day feminists who revolt against being "of use" or convenience . . . serving a man's wants and needs and making him comfortable and safe. I'd rather far be a luxury for which you pay constantly and consciously. If ever I have children it will not be to satisfy your desires but because I myself have come to feel that life will be richer with them than without. You must hold me and value me for what I am myself not what I may enable you to get.[6]

She said that she thought he was entitled to children, and that she would aid and abet him in "getting them elsewhere." Allen wrote back to say that he didn't want to get them elsewhere, that he loved her and was proud of her career. She must think of the baby as her baby, and if she had a son, she must name him herself, not call him Richard to please him. Richard, Allen's dream son, was now officially dead.

Mildred was moved by this renunciation of Richard and finally, sometime that spring, relented. But she feared childbirth and wrote to her friend Trudy, now a nurse, to inquire if she could have a cesarean section, and if it would be painless. Allen meanwhile began to plan for the conception of their child as he had planned for their honeymoon and trip to Europe. It must take place in the most beautiful setting imaginable. In July they camped on the shores of Jasper Lake, so far from human habitation that they could drink from the lake and go about with no clothes on. Though Mildred did not actually become pregnant here, she conceived the next month and Jasper became to sentimental Allen a place of reverence.

The baby was due in April. Mildred Olmsted decided not to tell her board for a while and returned to the office. The WILPF was now deeply engaged with the Philadelphia Council for World Peace in a campaign to support the World Court. As part of that effort, Mildred went on a three-week organizing and speaking tour through the center of Pennsylvania. She was once more suspected of being "red" for wanting to engage the United States in the world order. The Pennsylvania Railroad and the Philadelphia *North American* both attacked the WILPF. The newspaper, in addition, went after Mildred Olmsted in person. Mildred responded briskly, then finished her tour and went on—now representing national WILPF—to speak in Detroit, Pittsburgh, and Chicago. Here she attended the national board meeting at which the decision was made to invite the WILPF's international congress and summer school to come to Washington in the spring of 1924. Mildred was put on the committee for arrangements.

Back in Philadelphia, she helped to arrange a meeting for British pacifist and philosopher Bertrand Russell, and to organize a protest against the use of war toys at Christmastime. She felt full of vigor and planned to work as long as possible. But a few days after Christmas, when she was walking down the street toward her office one morning, she was struck with a violent pain in her side. The doctor whom Allen called could offer no explanation but suggested that Mildred stay in bed and use an ice pack until the pain went away. Unfortunately, the pain lasted throughout her pregnancy and for five years thereafter. Doctors later discovered that she had a chronic kidney infection, and also a pressure on the sciatic nerve.

One can speculate that Mildred's ambivalence about motherhood and her sense that her body had been invaded by a foreign object may also have played some role in her illness. But the pain was real, and it refused to disappear. Mildred spent the remaining months of her pregnancy flat on her back on the third floor of Uncle Marshall's house. She had two cold water bottles and kept one on a string out the window, freezing, while she put the other one on her sore side.[7]

She was forced to ask for a nine-month leave of absence. Sophia Dulles, who had begun work as associate secretary in the fall, took over as executive secretary, and Mildred Olmsted's board chose to consider her request for a leave of absence as a resignation, much to her distress. Some board members believed that as a young mother Mildred should not plan to return to work. Others may have been irritated by her dominating personality. To Mildred it was one more proof that she had perhaps been unwise in allowing Allen to talk her into maternity.

But if she could not go into the office, WILPF could come to her. Members of the committee to plan the international congress in Washington met in her bedroom every Monday morning. Her doctor, who did not know about the meetings, wondered out loud why she often had a temperature elevation on Mondays. Others came too, to consult. In the spring she had a visit from Gertrude Baer, whom she had met in Munich and who was in the United States to attend the international congress and to go on tour with several other members of the international committee.

Peter Olmsted was born on 16 April, by cesarean section. Mildred's friend Trudy came to be her nurse and persuaded a friend of hers, a nurse named Mildred, to take over the care of

11. Mildred Olmsted and her son Peter at Avalon, New Jersey, September 1925. *Courtesy of Olmsted Papers.*

Peter. Both mother and baby were deathly ill for several days. Mildred had been considerably weakened by her long stay in bed, and it was now that the kidney infection reached serious proportions. Allen was so frightened that he might lose his wife and his precious new son that he decided to do some praying and joined the Unitarian church.

In a few days, Mildred improved and was able to go home, first to her sister Adele's at Rose Valley, and then to 4013 Pine Street. Although she had a full-time nurse for Peter she felt too ill, and too low in spirits, to resume her active way of life. Allen did not help. He complained that he felt too hemmed in by the city and continued to go to Rose Valley for weekends where he could walk or chop wood, leaving her alone in the apartment. This was exactly what she had feared motherhood would do to her. She had always found small babies unattractive, lacking in personality and demanding of adults. For Allen's sake she tried to take an interest in Peter, but her attitude toward him was detached and cerebral. Perhaps the long separation at the hospital had interfered with bonding. At any rate she told Allen that she did not feel as though she "possessed" Peter. And a sense of belonging never developed.

Ruth Mellor wrote to her shortly after Peter's birth urging her to breast-feed the baby, in a letter that may be a clue to Mildred's attitude toward children and perhaps more besides.

"You mustn't resent nursing him. Haven't there been enough associations to counter balance the early ones that never should have been. Can't we put them into that great big background of hurts and pains and irritations and build up whole new associations which are sweet and full of life and joy. You should feel proud to nurse your baby.[8]

This letter makes one wonder if Mildred were sexually molested as a child. If so the episode was deeply buried in Mildred's memory. When I tried to talk to her about it, she brought forward the memory of her uncle's onetime advance, nothing more.

Mildred did breast-feed Peter, but only for a short time. Allen had been gambling perhaps on the hope that motherhood would somehow change Mildred. He was alarmed by her attitude toward Peter and by her general depression. Because she could not go back to work, feeling as ill as she did, he suggested that he pay her a monthly sum equivalent to her salary so that she could continue to feel independent. But Mildred felt as though she were being bribed or paid to be a mother, and she refused the money, although she allowed Allen to pay all her bills. Allen had encroached on their original agreement by persuading her to have a baby, she felt. It was further proof that any man, even Allen, could not be trusted not to constantly attempt to place a woman at his service.[9]

Trudy Rhoads Prichard was busy nursing, and Florence Pharo,

Mildred's new admirer from White Williams, had entered Antioch College and wrote Mildred long, needful letters. In her despair, Mildred turned to Ruth for comfort. Ruth had entered the New York School of Social Work shortly after Mildred's marriage, graduated in 1923, and was now a social worker in Minneapolis. But she had managed to visit Mildred frequently and felt as identified with her as ever, speaking often of Peter as "our baby." She urged Mildred to enjoy Peter and to continue to nurse him, but she herself was desperately lonely. She wanted Mildred to visit her.

> Can't you come to Minneapolis? I wrote Allen that I felt when you began to wean Peter it usually takes a while to find a formula which will suit him, and it means a funny time. If you moved right out and let the good baby nurse or the hospital wrestle with the problem it would be the best thing that could happen and then you could get away and really and truly rest and get well and strong. About your marriage, your attitude of suspicion and feeling that everything is forced just takes the heart out of it.[10]

Ruth Mellor had just delivered a paper titled "Parental Factors in the Production of Behavior Problems." In 1924, in the heyday of behaviorism, her advice to turn weaning over to professionals was probably considered very modern.

Eventually Mildred Olmsted employed the best medicine available; she persuaded the WILPF board to let her go back to work. All spring and summer she had followed the events of WILPF with great interest. The international congress in Washington, which she had helped to plan, had been a success, with the delegates invited afterwards to a reception at the White House. When the congress was over, many of the international delegates had traveled to Chicago for the WILPF summer school aboard a train called the *Pax Special*, which made whistle-stops in a number of small towns along the way. This drew the ire of such patriotic groups as the Daughters of 1812, the Daughters of the American Revolution, and the American Legion, who were incensed by a recently published chart called *The Spider Web*. Prepared by a librarian in the Department of Chemical Warfare in the

War Department, the chart designated fifteen women's organizations and twenty-nine women leaders as subversives, who entertained Bolshevik tendencies. The WILPF and its leaders were prominently pilloried in *The Spider Web*. The War Department also sent out propaganda warning each town about WILPF, and the railroad company cooperated by spreading the scare tactics. In several towns the women could not get a hearing; in others local WILPF members were threatened if they persevered in trying to organize the whistle-stops.

Mildred was eager to get back to work to undo some of the damage of these attacks to local branches. In addition, 1924 was an election year, and it seemed important to inquire about the peace planks of the three major parties—Democratic, Republican, and Socialist—and to ask the candidates for their positions on matters of war and peace. The Pennsylvania WILPF had undertaken a study for the national WILPF on the issue of the outlawry of war; it wanted to consider ways of getting the U.S. government to declare war a crime, to call an international conference on the subject, and to negotiate treaties with other nations outlawing war.

National WILPF was looking for a new executive secretary that fall. Amy Woods, who had taken the job in 1922, had proved hard to work with, and when she asked for a leave of absence in order to visit South America, the board decided to consider the request a resignation. For several months various candidates were considered. At one point Mildred Olmsted evidently felt she could have the job if she wanted it. Allen interviewed for a job with the Department of Justice's War Transaction Section and told the lawyer who talked with him that his wife had been offered a job in Washington. In a letter he asked her when she was going to decide about the national secretaryship. Was she going to stay in peace work all her life, or return to her profession of social work? He would prefer she did the latter, perhaps concentrating on birth control. Her friend Hannah Clothier Hull had just become the national chair of WILPF, and she may have talked to Mildred informally about the secretary's job. Or Mildred, with her usual confidence, may have just assumed it was hers for the asking. Her recollection was that she didn't want to leave Philadelphia, and her ties with the Scotts and the Sauls. At any rate, as a national board member, Mildred helped to hire as new national secretary a young woman called Dorothy Detzer, with special skills in public relations and in lobbying. A family friend of Alice Hamilton, the crusading public health doctor and suffragist, Detzer had worked at Hull House and had also gone overseas for the AFSC after World War I.[11]

Mildred Olmsted had gone back to the office on 1 October, and worked through December, with time out for a long Thanksgiving holiday with Ruth at Plymouth. But she still had not gotten rid of the nagging kidney infection, or of the mysterious pain in her back. In January Allen took her to Cuba for a month's rest in the warm sun, leaving Peter at home with his nurse. They took a train to Key West, then boarded a boat to Havana. Mildred enjoyed the climate and the people of Cuba, although she worried some when she did not hear from home. The rest helped but did not effect a cure. Mildred continued to be unwell, and Allen to worry about her, for five more years.

In March the Olmsteds moved to Rose Valley, renting a portion of the Stephenses' house, Thunderbird Lodge, down the hill from the Scotts. The Stephens would continue to occupy the two studios, but the Olmsteds could have the large wing with living room, dining room, and kitchen downstairs, five bedrooms on the second floor, and space on the third. Ruth Mellor anticipated working in Philadelphia that next year and agreed to sign the lease with them in return for a room. Mildred was to have a large bedroom to herself, and Allen a small one down the hall. The triangular living arrangement was at last to be tried.

In preparation for this experiment, Mildred Olmsted suggested that she and Ruth needed to take a vacation together that summer, just the two of them. Allen not only agreed but planned and paid for Mildred's half of the trip. Ruth and Mildred spent several weeks in Sark in the Channel Islands, then visited Pont Aven in Brittany and spent a few days in Paris before proceeding to Innsbruck where Mildred was to attend the international executive committee of the WILPF. Mildred was not an official U.S. delegate but was made English-language secretary on the spot and had to attend all the meetings of "the quarreling ladies," as Ruth called them. Mildred Scott Olmsted and Lucy Biddle Lewis reported on the work of the U.S. Section on the outlawry of war and told of the successful campaign to have a bill introduced in Congress banning the use of the U.S. Army or Navy in the collection of private debts, thus helping to prevent war with Mexico. (Mildred always spoke of this campaign as one of WILPF's two most significant victories.) They also told of their efforts to protest the U.S. occupation of Haiti. [12]

On the last day of the conference Mildred's mother died of Bright's disease associated with diabetes. Allen decided not to cable Mildred but himself returned from his vacation at Sardinia to be present at the funeral. He wrote her several letters, addressed to catch up with her on her travels, reassuring her that her father seemed fine. What would the effect of this news be on her? he wondered. "Your childhood was singularly motherless. Your father was much more of a figure both for good and bad. But her affection must have soaked in. Your sprightliness and quickness you must have inherited from her and in gayer moods in childhood you must have had much in common." [13]

Not having received this news, Mildred and Ruth continued their vacation, going from Innsbruck to Italy, where they completed some of the sightseeing they had wanted to do in the summer of 1920, before sailing from Naples for home on 7 August. On this trip home, Mildred found that it was possible to slip up to the first-class deck and to enjoy all its amenities without being caught. Typically, she considered the rule against this a silly regulation. Ruth was more law-abiding, but she was entranced by Mildred's daring and was willing to follow her lead.

Back at Rose Valley, Mildred learned about her mother's death and found her father's household already settled back to normal. Her younger sister, Marian, who was limited as a result of her troubles in infancy and had tried office work unsuccessfully, was going to continue living with her father and serve as housekeeper. It was a temporary arrangement. The next year Henry J. Scott married Jesseline, who, the family subsequently learned, had been his friend for some time.

Mildred Olmsted accepted these changes in her family life with her usual stoicism and threw herself into the move to Rose

Valley. She set about furnishing the new house, haunting auctions and thrift shops for bargains. Her own bedroom was opulent, with the black furniture her father had given her as a wedding present, a mirrored dressing table, and two sets of matching bedspreads and draperies, one for the summer and one for the winter. Ruth meanwhile put her energies into starting a garden in the beautiful backyard of Thunderbird Lodge.

At the same time she was moving, Mildred was busy facing new problems for the WILPF. The office space at the Friends Institute was now unbearably crowded, and the staff and board were beginning to look around for new headquarters when the Friends suggested they use a two-story building in the back court that had been vacated by Penn Charter School when it moved to larger quarters. The building had no plumbing but was light and airy and so large that WILPF was able to share it with one of the many committees established in Philadelphia that year to celebrate the sesquicentennial of the Declaration of Independence.

Unfortunately the new arrangement lasted only one year. Mildred had been having mounting problems with the treasurer of the Pennsylvania WILPF, who tended, Mildred claimed, to keep private the information about contributors and the amount they donated. This made both fund-raising and budgeting difficult. There had been continual trouble over the payment of Mildred's salary. She had been making $3,500 a year when she left White Williams with the understanding that this would be matched. Instead, WILPF had paid her $3,000. She had frequently worked part-time because of her health and had taken extra vacation time without pay in order to relieve the budget deficit. It was never clear to her exactly when this might be necessary, nor could she depend on her salary check arriving on time.

The treasurer was a prominent Quaker and had arranged for the WILPF to have the use of the Penn Charter buildings. It finally became necessary, however, for Mildred Olmsted and sympathetic board members to bring their problems out in the open at a board meeting. Mildred brought to the meeting a letter of resignation, which the board did not accept. Instead, the treasurer announced she would resign next spring. A young housewife, Kitty Arnett, volunteered to try to raise money in order to meet Mil-

dred's salary and other expenses, although she said she knew nothing about fund-raising. At this same meeting Mildred asked that
all criticisms of office procedure come to her, as it was difficult to
operate unless it was clearly understood that the office "had but
one head."[14]

One member of Mildred's staff was loyal to the former treasurer and had been causing difficulties. Because she continued to
work for the WILPF, the office remained disturbed for six months
after the crucial board meeting until she was asked to leave. Not
long after this, the WILPF was told by the former treasurer's husband to vacate the Penn Charter buildings and look for a new
home. After quite a search they found headquarters at 1525 Locust
Street on the second floor of a building owned by the League of
Girls' Clubs. With space to spare, they began to sublet offices to
sister organizations involved with peace and justice. One of these
was the Committee on Militarism in Education headed by Raymond Wilson, who was later to become head of the Friends Committee on National Legislation and a lifelong colleague of Mildred
Olmsted's.

Mildred Olmsted was always distressed by office tensions,
without understanding how she contributed to them. She tried to
be fair, businesslike, and open, but the strength of her own drive
and sense of mission sometimes blinded her to her effect on others.
Such tensions were in any case inevitable in small reform organizations made up of strong-minded women, many of whom had no
previous experience with the use and misuse of power. They modeled themselves after their husbands and fathers—as Mildred did
after her father—yet in the world outside their organizations they
continued to experience powerlessness. The fact that they were
working for peace pushed them to the fringes of society; many
people regarded them as lunatics or as dangerous radicals. Like any
subject people, they turned much of their aggression against each
other. Modern feminist concepts of developing new styles for
women working together based on a collegial sharing of responsibilities had not been developed. Like Mildred Olmsted, many
women active in this period thought women could achieve equality by becoming more like men, rather than by developing unique
women's methods, as some contemporary feminists now suggest.

Mildred believed that men's methods were better and more direct, and that women used indirect methods because they were denied power. These methods would disappear as they gained access to power, she thought.

As a result of these attitudes, as well as of the pressure the women were under from a generally hostile public, personality conflicts permeated the national and international WILPF as well as the Pennsylvania branch. There were ideological differences also; the absolute pacifists and the Left-leaning activists were often in conflict; isolationists differed with internationalists; feminists were suspect by younger members who believed in working with men on peace issues.

Yet despite these difficulties, the WILPF had special strengths as a women's organization with a sisterhood of shared values, and with the development of networks of support between women from community to community and from nation to nation. Many women developed a deep loyalty to the organization and shaped their lives around it. Such loyal members of WILPF at the local level did an astonishing amount of work despite their small numbers and enabled the organization, though small, to play a major role in the peace movement of the 1920s and 1930s.

That movement was made up in this period of several major peace organizations as well as minor ones. Among the former were the Fellowship of Reconciliation (FOR), also organized internationally in 1915 and made up of religious pacifists; the War Resisters League, a more radical and absolute group organized in 1924; the National Council for Prevention of War, organized by Fred Libby in 1921; Carrie Chapman Catt's National Committee on the Cause and Cure of War; and the Committee on Militarism in Education. In addition, the American Friends Service Committee, which began primarily as a relief organization, developed in 1925 a Peace Section that came to play a national leadership position in the peace movement. Although most of these other organizations had much larger budgets and greater memberships than the WILPF, they had limitations of one nature or another. The WILPF did not have a religious basis and therefore was not tax exempt; it was free to lobby and did so with great success, drawing on its committed grass-roots members. This freedom and the strength of WILPF's leadership made it a full partner in the developing peace movement.

During the 1920s, for instance, the WILPF worked with the American Friends Service Committee and the American Civil Liberties Union to protest the quota imposed against the immigration of Japanese. In 1926 the WILPF joined other peace groups in protesting the marine presence in Nicaragua and supported a peace mission to that nation made up of representatives of the AFSC and the FOR, which attempted but failed to meet with General Sandino. With the National Council for Prevention of War and other internationally minded groups the women of the WILPF also campaigned to have the United States join the World Court. They supported the concept of the outlawry of war, in coalition with several peace organizations, and became advocates of the resulting Kellogg-Briand Pact outlawing war among nations.

In some cases, the WILPF took the lead. In 1926 the organization sent a fact-finding mission to Haiti, then occupied by the U.S. Marines. Emily Greene Balch, WILPF's first international secretary, participated in the mission and published a book, *Occupied Haiti*, that focused public attention on the problem and helped to spark an investigation leading to an end to the American occupation. This sequence of events was regarded by the peace movement as a major contribution.

In Pennsylvania the WILPF worked with Raymond Wilson and the Committee on Militarism in Education to get compulsory military training out of the schools, developed a series of radio forums on foreign affairs, and supported a committee headed by Rachel Davis Dubois to work with different nationality groups in developing an interracial program for the public schools. Later the Pennsylvania WILPF hired its own African-American outreach worker, Henrietta Mousserone, who helped to organize an interracial junior WILPF. Mildred Olmsted campaigned for the WILPF to refuse to hold its meetings in hotels where African Americans were excluded and worked with Mary Church Terrell, a founding WILPF member, on literature addressed specifically to the African-American community. She urged the WILPF to cooperate with the NAACP on national antilynching campaigns and corresponded with W. E. B. DuBois about the latter's interest in devoting an issue of the *Crisis* to the relationships between war and race prejudice. [15]

The women of the WILPF were breaking new ground among the general run of women's organizations in attempting interracial work in the 1920s. Their spiritual ancestors in the women's suffrage movement had drifted away from a nineteenth-century antebellum commitment to racial inclusiveness, and active African-American women had been forced to battle for the right to be heard at suffrage gatherings. Even Jane Addams sometimes had been blind to racial issues in and around Hull House. Contemporary women's groups were equally deaf to pleas to take a stand against lynching. The National Women's party attempted to be inclusive but felt that the race issue was a divisive one in an organization dedicated to the single issue of women's rights and the passage of the Equal Rights Amendment. The International Council of Women bowed to local custom and allowed segregated seating at its 1925 convention in Washington.

Several of the major peace organizations were also beginning to experiment. The AFSC developed an Interracial Section in 1925 and sent a Japanese Friend around the country to interpret the Japanese view in light of the Asian Exclusion Act, and an African-American woman to explain the impact of prejudice on her community. Later the Peace Section established an interracial peace program designed to recruit African Americans to the cause of peace. But AFSC, like WILPF, had not yet perceived the real linkage between peace and racial justice. Mildred Olmsted's letters from the time reveal a sometimes condescending attitude toward African Americans. It was her agenda—to recruit new members for WILPF—rather than their agenda in which she was interested. In discussing special peace literature to be addressed to them, she urged simple language. She was nevertheless far ahead of most women of her class and time.

Throughout the 1920s the WILPF had been forced to continue to devote time to refuting charges of radicalism. Following the attack on the *Pax Special* in 1924, several of the more centrist women's groups made a point of distancing themselves from the WILPF. The Women's Joint Congressional Committee responded to *The Spider Web* by correcting the impression that the WILPF had ever been a member of its organization. The National Council of Women was pressured by its right-wing members, such as the Daughters of the American Revolution, to ask the WILPF to resign. While the WILPF board at first refused to do so, Jane Addams suggested it ought to comply as a magnanimous gesture. In early 1925 when Carrie Chapman Catt organized the first conference of the National Committee on the Cause and Cure of War, calling together 450 delegates representing some five million women, she did not invite the WILPF to be one of the sponsoring organizations. In a letter to Hannah Hull, Catt explained that she thought WILPF attracted too many from the "lunatic fringe," and though the organization had a real value as a trailblazing group, conservatives would have to build the peace.[16]

Mildred Olmsted gladly embraced the concept of WILPF as the pioneering organization, but she was dismayed that her hero, Jane Addams, had not been invited to address Catt's gathering. At a national board meeting in 1927 she suggested that Jane Addams put out a special call to all the women of the United States to join the WILPF if they wanted to work for peace, as the National Committee on the Cause and Cure of War had organizations rather than individuals as members, and as other membership organizations, such as the Fellowship of Reconciliation, were religious in nature and therefore excluded some women. Jane Addams fixed Mildred with a cold stare and said, "I wouldn't dream of it." Emily Balch, ever the reconciler, suggested that WILPF advertise for new members and appoint a committee to that end.[17]

Mildred Olmsted felt that Jane Addams ought to represent WILPF wherever she went, as a way of building membership and prestige, and was disappointed when Addams sometimes came to Philadelphia and did not even let WILPF know. But as Addams once crisply pointed out to Mildred, whom she described as "that brash young woman from Philadelphia," she was the president of several other organizations, such as the National Federation of Settlements, and owed them an equal debt of loyalty.[18] But despite occasional sharp differences, Jane Addams served as a role model and mentor to Mildred Olmsted for many years. Mildred always called her Miss Addams, with a reverent tone, and turned to her for help and advice in many situations. Jane Addams in turn came to rely on Mildred Olmsted's willingness to execute any mission given her, and on her judgment about the women who worked for the WILPF.

As the hysteria of the 1920s against radicals and foreigners mounted, the WILPF often found itself campaigning for civil liberties, as in the case of some West Chester Normal teachers dismissed for attending a meeting. The WILPF women had followed the Sacco-Vanzetti case through its numerous appeals and had appointed one of their number to serve on a committee urging clemency. This woman was the only female to appear at a rally called by "the King of the Hoboes" and his army of unemployed. At the rally, the participants adopted a resolution calling for a stay of execution for the two convicted anarchists. Reading of this gathering, Mildred's brother-in-law Maurice Saul wrote her a caustic note. "It appears to me that the enclosed article from the *Philadelphia Record* discloses the reason why your Association is not favored by some people."[19]

Mildred thought the increasing attacks on WILPF were a sign of its growing strength and influence. The whole field of peace was expanding rapidly, becoming a reform movement similar to those of the past. In her annual report to her board in April 1928 she made the comparison.

> In general I should say that the peace field is growing rapidly and becoming more specialized. It is no longer sufficient to have a general wish for peace because the country is aroused. Both attackers and supporters are becoming more vehement. It is a similar course to that of the movement for the abolition of slavery and for woman suffrage and means, I trust, that we shall have the same ultimate success, if we can show the same endurance, the same willingness to sink individual feelings in this common cause, the same patient solving of hard problems, the same self-sacrifice, that characterized our grandmothers and mothers who won those causes for their descendants and the betterment of the world.[20]

One of the groups to attack the WILPF was the American Legion. As a patriotic child, Mildred had learned to believe that the army and the navy had no place in trying to influence public policy. Indeed her Uncle John Barton, an admiral, had told her so many times. But in the post–World War I period it seemed as though the armed forces had reversed themselves and were trying to control public opinion. One method was to make the American Legion, which was organized after World War I with the worthy goal of taking care of veterans, a channel for the expression of military viewpoints. All of this violated Mildred's deep belief in the functioning of American democracy. It was up to the citizenry, she thought, to wrest control back into civilian hands.

Allen Olmsted came under American Legion attack in 1927. The preceding year he had appeared before the House Committee on Immigration and Naturalization to argue against the deportation of aliens solely on the grounds of affiliation with the Communist party. Several members of Congress had become angry with him, and one had charged him with being a Communist. When word of this ruckus reached the papers, the West Chester Post of the American Legion mounted a campaign to have him expelled from that organization. Finally legion headquarters ordered the Howard McCall Post to which he belonged to conduct a trial of his patriotism. Allen spoke several times to the legionnaires about his concepts of foreign policy, and when the actual trial was held, the verdict was in his favor: guilty, 38; not guilty, 71. Allen often referred to this as his second court-martial, and was grateful to Mildred for sticking by him through the ordeal, as she had when he was court-martialed in France.

The marriage was continuing to be full of stresses and strains. Mildred's sharp tongue and imperious manner, her Henry J. Scott manner, as Allen called it, were manifested at home as well as at the office. She frequently scolded Allen for failure to execute an errand she had asked him to do, or to meet her at the time arranged, or to share her indignation with people who displeased her. Such failures were proof to her that he did not really love and value her but was taking advantage of her role as his wife. When Allen grew resentful or depressed as the result of these scoldings, she complained about his violent mood changes and their effect on the marriage. Allen in turn was sometimes intimidated by her and continually, and rather forlornly, searching for proof that she really loved him, despite her frequent criticisms and her prolonged absences from home. Each fresh tiff, minor in itself, rubbed both of them raw.

Complicating their relationship still further was Mildred's attachment to Ruth Mellor. Ruth had continued to live with the Olmsteds in Rose Valley until 1927, although she kept an apartment in the city nearer her work. Mildred remembered very little of that early experiment in triangularity, and there are only a few references to it in the voluminous Allen-Mildred-Ruth correspondence. Those references suggest trouble: Mildred had problems sharing Allen with Ruth; Allen often wounded Ruth with caustic remarks; the three went separately and together to see psychiatrists about their complex relationships.

Despite their rivalry, Ruth and Allen found ways to be supportive of each other. Allen felt strongly that Ruth ought to know the love of a man, as well as the love of women, and helped Ruth to feel that she was attractive to the opposite sex. Ruth often said later that he had been a wise teacher. It was Allen who encouraged Ruth to go on a boat trip in search of an unattached male. Ruth did find a Welsh man with whom she corresponded; they eventually met for a weekend in Canada. Jack was a disconsolate widower, and nothing came of this episode, but it was the beginning for Ruth of other experiments with men.

Ruth in turn became Allen's confidante when Mildred seemed to be cold, judgmental, and distant. The two had been conspiring for years to encourage Mildred to develop a more human side. Ruth often gave Mildred advice about her relationship with Allen, urging her to be less suspicious, less demanding, more supportive. She pointed out that Allen was sometimes actually afraid of Mildred and that this was no basis for a sound relationship. She took a keen interest in the baby, Peter, and this was a bond with Allen, who adored his little son. Both of them wanted Mildred to relax the high standards she set for the child, and to enjoy him more.

But living together put strains on the bonds between Ruth and Mildred. Ruth was still deeply involved with Tracy and still in touch with another female suitor, Ede. Mildred had been upset and jealous about these relationships for years, but having Ruth in the house with her made them more vivid. She continually felt threatened by the loss of Ruth, whom she needed paradoxically even more because of the pain in her marriage to Allen. In a letter written to Ruth from Cleveland, where she went to attend a WILPF board meeting in 1927, she regretted the "recurring fogs" between them and blamed the trouble on the excesses of these other relationships: "My Puritan and religious background which demand that I should not do myself what I disapproved of in others would I think have allowed a complete and equal devotion between us, as between Damon and Pythias to whom we delighted to liken ourselves, but it could not, somehow, include a miscellany of emotion or face the possibility that physical attraction was a dominant rather than a subordinate part of our friendship.[21]

Ruth finally suggested that she and Mildred go to Dr. Otto Rank, a psychoanalyst known for his use of the concepts of time and focus in his therapy, to see if he could help them straighten out their relationship. They had met Rank in Munich in 1920 and liked him. He was in Philadelphia that fall, consulting with the Pennsylvania School of Social Work. Ruth went to him for ten sessions, Mildred for nine, with Ruth paying for both of them. In Mildred's case there was no transference, as she recalled it, and the sessions ended when Rank had to go back to Europe. He told her that it was just as well; "You wouldn't have liked yourself." Mildred thought the experience probably helped her to avoid becoming too attached to people. Ruth may have changed more. She reported that Dr. Rank had asked her why she needed two mothers. Not long after these sessions she developed the courage to leave Mildred and take a job in Connecticut. Whether as a result of the sessions with Rank or not, she began to feel at this time that she ought to turn aside the advances of women and to seek relationships with men.[22]

Despite all the turmoil in his unusual marriage, Allen continued to want more children. Mildred was quite sure that she would put her life at risk if she tried another pregnancy, but she was willing to consider adoption. Having a nurse for Peter had worked well, she thought, and as Peter had grown older it was possible for the nurse to undertake more of the responsibilities of a housekeeper. Perhaps with additional household help, a second child would not make life more complicated. She was particularly encouraged when in the fall of 1926 she found a young English woman, Diane Gibson, to come as housekeeper. "Gibby" was efficient and self-confident; she took over the complete care of Peter as well as planning and cooking the meals.

Little boys available for adoption were easier to find than little girls in 1927, but finally a New York adoption agency located a girl for Mildred and Allen to consider. Using assumed names, they went to call on the mother, who was living with her brother, who was a musician, and his wife. The Olmsteds liked the tone of the home and the appearance of the baby. Gibby felt she could not take on the care of another child without help, so while they searched for a nurse, they supported the baby financially. Finally in November 1927 they adopted their daughter, whom Mildred called Enid after the British woman, Rachel Enid Grant, whom she had so admired in the Quaker équipe in France.

Perhaps because there had been no birth trauma to overcome, Mildred related in some ways more quickly to this little girl than she had to Peter. Her letters to WILPF associates speak of the new baby, how cute she is, how good, and how dimpled. She watched her thrive with interest and wrote to her mother-in-law that Enid was "the best baby I ever saw, grateful for any attention that is given her."[23]

The summer after the Olmsteds adopted Enid, Mildred was interviewed for a study on household management to be published by the Federal Women's Bureau. The resulting study listed the staff as consisting of Gibby as housekeeper, a trained nurse ("colored"), and a woman who came in two days a week to do the washing and heavy cleaning. The interviewer spoke admiringly about the arrangement.

> Mr. and Mrs. X have a partnership conception of their functions in the home. Mr. X assumes responsibility for the money end of the enterprise, checks and pays all bills, is responsible for the fire, coal and lawn also. Mrs. X is responsible for the household purchasing other than food, the children, the gardens and employs the workers. To the housekeeper is delegated the responsibility for management while Mr. and Mrs. X are away. She is expected to do exactly what

the homemakers would do if they were at home—to carry responsibility and meet emergencies.[24]

Mildred's neighbors and some members of the family were very critical of her for continuing to work, and especially for being away from home so frequently and leaving her children to servants. But Mildred had the backing of many child care experts of the day, who taught that babies should be fed by the clock rather than on demand, and who suggested that trained professionals were often better at handling children than were the parents. Ruth Mellor, who was becoming something of an authority in the field of child guidance, supported Mildred's version of parenting on the whole, although she urged her to be more tender with her children. On the other hand, she often begged Mildred to leave the children in order to visit her.

With a new baby in place and a smoothly functioning home, Mildred felt she could devote even more time to the WILPF. In 1928 the organization was mounting a campaign against the administration's efforts to build a bigger navy, planning a conference of women from both sides of the Mexican border, and continuing their efforts to get the marines out of Nicaragua. Freedom needed fighters around the world, and Mildred heard the call to arms, nonviolent though hers must be.

9

On the Road

$\mathcal{M}$ILDRED OLMSTED'S first international assignment for the WILPF was to organize a conference of American and Mexican women along the Mexican border. Having participated with other peace groups in putting pressure on the U.S. State Department to avert war with Mexico over the use of American troops to collect money owed private American businesses, the women of WILPF were eager to see what women from both nations working together might accomplish. As a first step, Mildred decided to visit Mexico on her summer vacation in 1928. She and Allen took the long overland train to Mexico, stopping by the wayside to get food and drink. It was very hot but increasingly interesting as they got further south of the border.[1]

In Mexico City they had arranged to attend a seminar on Mexican affairs run by a man called Hubert Herring. Mildred Olmsted had discovered that a Smith graduate, Elizabeth Curtis, was working for the YWCA in Mexico City, and through her was able to arrange a meeting with Mexican women. About thirty attended the first gathering. They asked if the WILPF supported free love, and Mildred realized that they were afraid of being involved in anything that went against their religion. When she was able to reassure them, they became enthusiastic about organizing for peace. Mildred held several subsequent meetings and left feeling she had developed a potential WILPF section. The women were interested in participating in the border conference, she found, but suggested that WILPF wait until they were a little better organized and could pick their own delegates.[2]

162

The Olmsteds also managed to take time for some sightseeing, visiting ruins and going to the folklorica. They saw the controversial painting by Diego Rivera on the staircase in city hall and liked it very much. Later they were delighted to meet the artist. They also discovered a distant branch of the Olmsted family living in the city and became well acquainted with these relatives in the course of the summer.[3]

When they returned to Philadelphia, Mildred Olmsted urged that a representative of the WILPF be sent to Mexico to help the women develop their section. Sybil Ann Moore of California was selected, and Ruth Mellor volunteered to go, as her job in Philadelphia was coming to an end in March 1929. Ruth had been serving as secretary of the Pennsylvania WILPF, something she did to please Mildred, although she was sometimes bored with the "quarreling ladies." Sybil Moore left in late February, but Ruth, who was to sail on 7 March, was turned back by the steamship company because of the unsettled conditions in Mexico. Shortly thereafter she took a job in Connecticut, making a survey of existing psychiatric care.

Mildred Olmsted felt responsible for Sybil Moore and wrote to her frequently. At the WILPF annual meeting in Detroit that spring she arranged to have a conference with Henry Ford about support for the border program. Mildred was at the time suffering from sciatica, a new development in the back pain that had dogged her since she was pregnant with Peter, and she was lying down in a hotel room when Henry Ford came to see her. They discussed many things, Mildred remembered, but she talked about the idea of a WILPF summer school in Mexico, and he promised his cooperation in finding and supporting women from the countries bordering the Caribbean.[4]

Mildred Olmsted retained a lively interest in the group she had helped to form. After Sybil Moore left, Kathleen Lowrie went to Mexico to work on the conference, which finally took place in 1930 with 150 women from Mexico, 25 from the United States, and 5 from Cuba. At the Sixth International Conference of WILPF in Prague, which Mildred attended in August 1929, she reported on the new group and suggested that the conference send its greetings. Emily Greene Balch thought greetings should go to all new sections, and Mildred was placed on a committee to draft these messages.[5]

At this international congress, the first that Mildred Olmsted attended, Jane Addams resigned as international president, urging WILPF to continue to work for a warless world. The women debated how to make a reality of the Kellogg-Briand Pact to outlaw war, signed in Paris the previous year, and discussed changing their constitution to give the consultative members voting rights on the executive committee. Executive committee members were chosen without reference to their national sections, while the consultative members came as representatives. Behind the debate was growing tension between the British Section, which was dominated by absolute pacifists, and the European sections (especially the French) which leaned toward the Left and were interested in looking at the economic causes of war. The British distrusted the executive committee and felt the national sections should be consulted in major policy decisions. At this session a compromise was reached in which the executive committee membership was increased from nine to twelve, but consultative members were not given the vote.[6]

On the strength of a large bonus Allen had received from the law firm, Allen and Mildred had come to Europe together three weeks before the congress and had traveled in France and along the Dalmatian coast. Then Ruth had joined them for a walking trip in the Pyrenees, Allen going off by himself part of the time so that Ruth and Mildred could be alone together. Mildred was now committed to dividing her vacation time three ways; time for Allen, time for Ruth, and time for the children.

Her vacations with her children were spent at Avalon on the New Jersey shore, where they could dig in the sand and wade in the surf when they got a little older. Mildred felt it was an opportunity to get really close to them, and to make up for her frequent absences. At the shore she took care of the children by herself, although she found somewhere to stay where meals were provided. Frequently either Ruth or Allen joined her. At home in Rose Valley Gibby continued to be her mainstay, managing the children and the household. Gibby had married a sailor, Norman Purinion, in the summer of 1927, and when he was home from his ship he

12. Enid, Anthony, and Peter Olmsted, ca. 1932, at Rose Valley. *Courtesy of Olmsted Papers.*

lived with the Olmsteds. Feeling secure in her household help, Mildred felt ready to take on another child. This time it was she and not Allen who was enthusiastic about expanding the family. In December 1930, the Olmsteds adopted a second son, Anthony. On first arrival the new baby was so charming that Mildred's sister Adele Saul asked if she might borrow him for six months. Allen however said he was getting to like a three child-family, and the Olmsteds declined. Ultimately the Sauls adopted a baby boy also.[7]

Peter was now six and going to school. In 1929 the Olmsteds had joined the Sauls and four other Rose Valley couples in incorporating the School in Rose Valley. All of the couples had young children and were interested in the new ideas of child rearing that were being widely discussed. During the winter of 1928–1929 they had attended a course in child development given by the

Philadelphia Parents Council, and this had led them to search for a school for their children devoted to the principles of progressive education. When they discussed their interest with Professor W. Carson Ryan, head of the Department of Education of Swarthmore College, he suggested that they start their own school, with his help. The school opened in a makeshift cottage lent to the enterprise rent free in the fall of 1929 with twenty-nine children, aged three to nine, and a staff of five hired by Professor Ryan. One of the five was Grace Rotzel, the director, who came from teaching in Oak Lane Country Day School, Philadelphia. Later the school moved to property owned by Adele Saul, which she rented to the board for one red rose each year.[8]

The concepts of child development promoted by the School in Rose Valley were debated by the Olmsteds. Mildred Olmsted was accustomed to feel that children needed discipline, just as her father had disciplined her as a child. Allen was much more permissive and inclined to take the childrens' side in disputes with their mother. Gibby, who ruled the household in their absence, had an English nanny's approach to the children. She introduced the concept of a nightly "children's hour" in which the parents played with the children; at other times she thought they should be restricted to the nursery, where they had "tiffin" alone until they became old enough to join their parents at dinner.

In time these conflicting approaches to child care would produce problems in the Olmsted children, but in the early days of her motherhood Mildred Olmsted felt she had solved the career versus housewife dilemma, and she was very proud of her growing family.

She was also proud of the garden that Ruth Mellor had started and that was she developing behind the house in Rose Valley. Whatever stresses and strains her work produced in her she could work off by digging in the dirt or pulling up weeds. She sent for catalogues and each spring experimented with planting new flowers. She worked with her gardener and with Allen in digging new beds and planting oriental bushes. She liked to bring plants from the homes of her friends and to see if they would adapt to her soil. Her home was her refuge; getting off the train at the Moylan station she felt she shed one persona and put on another.

13. Disarmament Caravan, summer 1931. *Left to right:* Mildred Olmsted, Hannah Clothier Hull, Katherine Devereaux Blake, Mabel Vernon, director (unknown), and Louise Wier. *Courtesy of Swarthmore College Peace Collection.*

Yet they did not own the house, and Mildred Olmsted longed to be so firmly tied to the country that she could never be dislodged as she had been at age eight by her father. Driving further out in Delaware County one day she fell in love with a beautiful farmhouse with a stream and a barn. She asked Allen to look at it with her, and at her prompting Allen made inquiries and discovered it was for sale. Allen told her that he would buy it if she really wanted it, but he pointed out to her that if she did not give up her job she was going to have many problems getting household help so far from the city and taking the children to school and other appointments. He was tactful and kind about it, and Mildred finally decided on her own that it would be better to stay in Rose Valley and to look for a house nearer by.

Meanwhile, there were plenty of tensions in the WILPF office to be dealt with in the fall of 1929. The owner of the building at Locust Street had become concerned about all the radical organizations WILPF had invited to share its space and had asked that they all leave but WILPF, putting the latter on a month-to-month basis. As this arrangement was untenable, in October the WILPF moved to offices at 1924 Chestnut Street, where they were to remain for some years.

There were upheavals in the secretarial staff too, as there often were because of the low pay and long hours WILPF work demanded. A new secretary, a young African-American woman named Marian Smith, joined WILPF that fall and became one of the longtime pillars of the organization, managing the bookkeeping as well as the office. Some of the people I interviewed felt Mildred Olmsted had been hard on Marian, driving her to work overtime and to meet deadlines. Marian herself, however, had nothing but fond memories of her days with WILPF and with Mildred.[9]

The Pennsylvania WILPF had grown under Mildred Olmsted's leadership until its membership made up about one-third that of the whole U.S. Section, and its budget equaled that of the national organization. There were many new programs, including a series of immensely popular and sometimes lucrative children's plays and a peace thrift shop. The WILPF conceived the idea of celebrating Peace Heroes Day on Memorial Day, bringing to attention those police officers, fire fighters, and nurses who had shown valor in the line of duty during the past year, and sold the idea to the city of Philadelphia. Today these heroes are still celebrated, though the word *peace* has been dropped. Violet Oakley, an artist, prepared WILPF's annual Christmas card. Such well-known women as Eva le Gallienne, Edna St. Vincent Millay, and Kathleen Norris came to speak at fund-raising luncheons. Leopold Stokowski and his wife, Evangeline, were supporters. Leopold Stokowski often dedicated his Armistice Day concerts to peace, and Evangeline was the patron of an exhibit of nonmilitary toys. In 1933 the Philadelphia Orchestra under Stokowski performed the first concert written by an African-American composer. The WILPF wrote to congratulate him and to ask him if for this special occasion "Negroes might sit in the main body of the Academy." Stokowski agreed.[10]

The Pennsylvania WILPF had also developed into a powerful lobbying group. In conjunction with the national office, it lobbied against the concept of a big navy and for U.S. concessions at the London Naval Conference. During that conference it produced a series of radio talks on the issues involved. Looking forward to the Geneva Disarmament Conference of 1932, it urged that Jane Addams, Judge Florence Allen, or Grace Abbott be appointed as an official delegate. In Pennsylvania it continued to work with other organizations to get military training out of the schools, and it inquired of the *Public Ledger* whether it had a policy against employing African Americans.

The national WILPF board, which Hannah Clothier Hull continued to chair, was eager to duplicate the success of the Pennsylvania branch in other parts of the country. It was easy to see that Mildred Olmsted's methods of developing networks and encouraging volunteers were working. In 1930 the board set up a Committee on Organization and asked Mildred Olmsted to be its chair. At the same time they hired Mabel Vernon, who had been the secretary of the National Women's party, as national finance and campaign secretary.

Although many members of the WILPF were also members of the National Women's party (NWP), relations between the two groups were uneasy. Many women in the WILPF objected to NWP's exclusive concentration on legislation for equal rights, and its failure as an organization to cooperate with other women's groups on joint projects. The rift had begun when Jane Addams, Florence Kelley, Grace Abbott, and other early members of WILPF who came out of the Hull House group and were committed to social change for women opposed the Equal Rights Amendment because it threatened the legislation protecting women and children at the workplace, which they had worked hard to see enacted. At first Alice Paul had made some effort to reach a compromise, adding to the ERA some qualifying clauses that would have protected that legislation, but she soon came to feel that this was impractical. Alice Paul believed that her organization should take on no causes other than equal rights, though her members could participate in other organizations, including the WILPF, of which she herself was in fact was a member. From the point of view of Dorothy Detzer and of Mildred Olmsted, this translated into the view that Alice Paul was willing to use the WILPF to suit her purposes but to offer nothing in return.

Dorothy Detzer had in addition had a bad experience with

the National Women's Party when she first moved to Washington to become executive secretary for the WILPF. She had barely settled into her new office when the receptionist announced that three women were waiting to see her. Ushered in, they told her they had come to welcome her to Washington and to ask her to join the NWP. Dorothy Detzer hesitated, saying she thought she ought to consult the board members of the WILPF about their policy in regard to her joining other organizations. Whom would she consult, she was asked. "Oh, probably Miss Addams or Mrs. Hull or Alice Hamilton," was the reply. "Not those old fogies," her callers said. When Dorothy expressed indignation, the NWP members said that these women were passé, finished, and if she followed their leadership, she too would be finished. "You, like every secretary of a woman's organization, are going to become a member of the NWP or we'll wreck your career," she said she was told.[11]

Dorothy Detzer's response was to vow that she would never become a member of the NWP. Thereafter, she told an interviewer, NWP indeed attempted to fulfill their threat. "For the next twenty-two years some member of the NWP who was also a member of the WILPF would introduce a motion at every annual meeting calling on the national board to fire Dorothy Detzer." Frequently the board member who rose to suggest that Detzer be fired was Anne Martin, a politician from Nevada, an NWP member, and at one time an intimate friend of Mabel Vernon's.[12]

In addition, Dorothy Detzer perceived NWP as standing for the feminism of an earlier era. Dorothy had rejected that feminism; she liked working with men, and as her book *Appointment on the Hill* reveals, she believed that using feminine appeal in her lobbying was an appropriate strategy. She took great care of her own appearance and that of her staff, and although unmarried she had several love affairs, according to Mildred Olmsted. In the early 1970s she had little use for "women's lib," although she somewhat changed her mind when she found herself to be an object of admiration and study by the new feminist historians.

Mabel Vernon had come out of the suffrage movement, as Dorothy Detzer had not, and had joined the NWP, serving for a time on the staff as secretary, a job she left temporarily in 1920 to become campaign manager for Anne Martin when the latter ran as an Independent for the U.S. Senate from Nevada. But Mabel Vernon also joined WILPF, and in 1930 she left NWP in dispute with Paul. She continued to be a militant feminist and spent most of her life with a long-term female companion.

Dorothy Detzer therefore felt that the appointment of Mabel Vernon, to which she had not agreed, was a challenge to her leadership, and she wrote to Mildred Olmsted in protest:

> Confidential, please destroy. Miss Balch has organizer and finance worker mixed up. She wrote to ask what I thought of Mabel Vernon for either place. I think it would be fatal if MV came in. We would lose all cooperation with other women's groups. Can't afford to have someone who has been secy of the Woman's party. I am applying for International. Miss Balch told me to write you confidentially about my concern. I am afraid Miss Woods would go after national office, and make this an old woman's organization, made up of tired people who belong to a feminist age which is past—conflict with men, and looking as unattractive as possible—just is past. Either we put some younger women in, and wait till we get the right one—or we are going to lose ground.[13]

Dorothy Detzer was dissuaded from resigning, and some effort was made to keep the two women apart by asking Mabel Vernon to work on finances from the Philadelphia office. This she refused to do, but she soon became interested in organizing a giant disarmament caravan for the summer of 1931, asking women to go from state to state to get signatures on a petition calling for total disarmament, to be presented at the Disarmament Conference in Geneva in 1932. This campaign kept her out of the Washington office for stretches of time and reduced tensions. But there was still occasional dissension, and Mildred Olmsted often found herself in the role of mediator.

The disarmament campaign was launched from California in the summer of 1931. Mildred Olmsted got permission from her board to take several months off work and went out West to attend the opening conference. At the close of the meetings, just at sunset, the women released a bevy of white doves to carry their peace message east ahead of the caravaners. Mildred took time off to go with Allen and Ruth for some hiking under Sierra Club auspices in Yosemite National Park, then rejoined the caravan and traveled with it as far as Milwaukee, where she left to return to the Philadelphia office to prepare for the caravan's reception in that city on October 6. She loved the whistle-stopping, the extemporaneous speeches, the newspaper interviews, even the challenges from hecklers, and her enthusiasm was a source of inspiration to others. When the caravan arrived in Philadelphia, Mildred Olmsted and her whole staff went up Broad Street to meet the cars and conducted Mabel Vernon and her triumphant caravaners to a luncheon at the Bellevue Stratford.

The WILPF campaign, planned by Mabel Vernon, was a significant contribution to the peace movement of the day. It made front-page news in each of the 125 cities it visited. It also established embryonic peace councils, which were strengthened when the caravans were repeated a second year. By the time the 1931 caravan reached Washington it had grown to about 150 cars. Here it was met by 60 more and proceeded to the White House under police escort, led by the Navy band. The women presented President Herbert Hoover with a petition bearing 150,000 signatures. Later the petition was augmented to 400,000 and sent to the Geneva Disarmament Conference in February. In other countries WILPF had obtained more signatures on less radical petitions, so that altogether six million were gathered worldwide.

The WILPF's pleasure in this accomplishment was augmented when word came in December that their beloved founder, Jane Addams, was to receive the Nobel Peace Prize, along with Nicolas Murray Butler. Addams used her share of the prize, $10,000, as a gift to help support the always tottering international office of WILPF in Geneva.

But the late fall of 1931 was shadowed for peace-minded Americans by the Japanese intrusion into Manchuria, a challenge to the Kellogg-Briand Pact. Mildred Olmsted's instincts to support the underdog and challenge the bully were called into play. Was the League of Nations in fact going to do nothing to halt this act of aggression? She wrote Dorothy Detzer that "I am nearly wild about the Manchurian news and our weak kneed policy of saying what can we do about it? Can't we galvanize peace groups into action?" She thought the least the United States could do was to join in an economic boycott.

> It seems to me as it probably does to you perfectly intolerable that countries like the United States and England should refuse to follow up their diplomatic disapproval of Japan by economic pressure because that touches our pocketbooks. . . . I am not in favor of a popular boycott against the Japanese goods because of the feeling that would stir up among the little people but I think it most desirable that we have an official embargo on trade other than foodstuffs in cooperation with other countries.[14]

Most American pacifists shared Mildred Olmsted's dismay, and many at first joined with her in advocating sanctions. The religious pacifists, however, and the supporters of nonresistance, including the Quakers, were concerned about the use of coercion in the international arena. The WILPF as an organization did not support the boycott, although Dorothy Detzer personally commended such measures to the State Department. As time went on the debate within the peace movement quickened, with the majority beginning to waver in regard to the concept of collective security, and to turn more and more to neutrality and, in some cases, to isolationism. Mildred Olmsted's commitment to a world governed by the rule of law was profound; it would take her in a different direction than many of her colleagues in WILPF and in the peace movement at large.

In the spring of 1932 she was planning to go abroad as a delegate to the Seventh International WILPF Congress, to be held in Grenoble, France. The WILPF board asked her if she would head up a peace tour of Russia, under the sponsorship of an organization called the Open Road, following the congress. The Open Road told Mildred Olmsted she could have an assistant, and she chose Allen, who immediately plunged into a lengthy correspondence with the Open Road over travel arrangements. Plans for the trip called for a minimum of twenty, but ultimately only six persons joined the tour—the two Olmsteds, Ruth Mellor, Ellen Starr Brinton of the WILPF office, and two delegates to the Grenoble congress, Mary Kutchin and Olivia Fay. The Open Road in consequence would not pay Allen's way. He went anyway, as an ordinary tourist. Ruth and Mildred shared a stateroom, and he had a bunk elsewhere on the ship. This pattern was repeated in their subsequent travels together as a threesome.

The Grenoble congress, held in May, was addressed by Professor Mary Woolley, who had ultimately been made a member of the U.S. delegation to the Disarmament Conference. That conference was already hopelessly bogged down. Both Germany and Russia had pleaded initially for general disarmament, but the major powers were clearly not interested in coming up with any tangible program, and as a result of this setback Germany's Chancellor Bruning was toppled by the far more reactionary Von Papen, a decisive step leading to the rise of Hitler. The WILPF women had been disappointed that Professor Woolley had not spoken up in the American delegation, but they listened to her politely, then wrote a manifesto to be delivered to Arthur Henderson, president of the conference, calling once more for universal disarmament, urging the nations to take the profits out of munitions making, and arguing against the creation of an international armed force to keep the peace. They had little hope for the conference now and were not surprised when it disbanded in July without much accomplished, ignoring even President Herbert Hoover's last minute call for a one-third reduction of arms across the board.[15]

Following the Grenoble congress, the Olmsteds set out on their tour. They visited Bulgaria and Turkey, where Mildred Olmsted made some contacts for the international WILPF, writing to Camille Drevet to ask that they be followed up. (They never were, much to her annoyance.) In Turkey they were supposed to be met by their Russian guides for a trip across the Black Sea. But the ship was detained, and the local Soviet representative offered them cabins on a freighter instead. Their Turkish hosts advised against taking the freighter, suggesting that they could take a regular Italian cruise ship that would land them in Novorossiysk in the Ukraine. This they did, becoming the first foreign visitors to arrive at this port since the revolution. Mildred Olmsted thought that the Russian Intourist service was not pleased. Nevertheless their Russian hosts hurried to clean up a hotel just in time for the Olmsted party's arrival.[16]

They spent several days in Novorossiysk, visiting a cement factory and a state vineyard and joining the Russians in nude swimming in the Black Sea, then went on to Yalta, to Sevastopol, to Kharkov, and finally to Moscow and Leningrad. People were friendly and seemed open to them, and Allen was allowed to visit the courts of justice, while Mildred inquired into social welfare programs. When they said they would like to attend a meeting of the Young Communists, however, they were told this would not be permitted. Mildred talked to the women guides about peace and came away with the impression that the Russian people wanted peace as ardently as she and her colleagues did. She was also impressed with the idea that the state put the welfare of the people first, not last, on its agenda.[17]

Mildred Olmsted was home in time to spend several months in the WILPF office. There was as always much to do. The economic depression was beginning to cut heavily into revenues, and it was necessary to reduce office staff just as the volume of work escalated. The national office had asked the Pennsylvania branch to serve as national headquarters for literature. As another economy move, it requested that each branch take a turn in getting out the national newsletter, the *Dovetail,* an experiment that was doomed to failure and that caused the *Dovetail* to lapse for some years. Mildred Olmsted was particularly concerned with the dictatorship in Cuba, where some WILPF members had been jailed. WILPF was sponsoring a Cuban-American Institute in Washington in December, and Mildred was working on the committee. WILPF was also lobbying against a pending law in Harrisburg demanding that teachers sign a loyalty oath, and it was cooperating with the ACLU on a test case on the use of Reyburn Plaza, across from city hall, for free speech, with Allen Olmsted as counsel. Since it was an election year, WILPF women were calling on all three presidential candidates. Mildred Olmsted led the delegation to see Franklin Roosevelt, who promised to keep in close touch with WILPF if he were elected.

She was planning to spend the last of August and the first of September as usual at Avalon with the children. Just before leaving she made the discovery that Allen had been carrying on an affair with Mary, a young woman boarder at their house. Her immediate reaction was typically controlled; she asked Mary to persuade Allen to spend the weekend in Buffalo with his family while she got her feelings in order. She did not want him to know she was going through any turmoil. "My attitude is my business." When she spoke to him she had herself so much in hand that he wrote her, "You are an amazing woman. You wish me luck and are as cheerful and loving as though I were starting out on a case."[18]

Allen's affair had many roots. For years he had been upset by Mildred's frequent long absences, her cold responses to his ardor whenever she agreed to sleep with him, and her habit of scolding him for misdemeanors. Having agreed to separate vacations, he used the time to try various experiments to satisfy his unmet needs. For several years he thought going to nudist colonies helped and urged Mildred and Ruth to join him. He spent as much time as he could at Sardinia, where the Olmsted family gave him the emotional support he craved. But he was always lonely away from Mildred. To compensate he had a number of minor flirtations, all of which he had dutifully reported to his wife. He continued to correspond with Jeanne, the Frenchwoman who had fallen in love with him, though he did not go to see her when he was abroad, as they both believed it was better to leave the past alone. It was his understanding that Mildred, who had demanded complete freedom in entering into the marriage, expected him to be free.

Mildred, however, was unprepared for the shock and pain of unfaithfulness. It fulfilled all her worst fears about men; they made themselves important to you, and then they abandoned you. Allen was turning out to be like her father, despite their obvious differences. She could not even let Ruth know how hurt she was. But she wrote to Hannah Hull, offering to go to work in the Geneva office as Dorothy Detzer had suggested, or to cover the Washington office while Dorothy stayed in Geneva.[19]

Mildred at first insisted upon separation, but the plan of moving to Geneva did not work out. After many unhappy letters and interviews back and forth, Allen agreed to tell Mary to move out of the Rose Valley house, and Mildred eventually moved back in. The Olmsteds worked out a reconciliation of sorts and went on with their busy lives.

But a fresh shock for Mildred Olmsted was coming. On 3

October Henry Scott suddenly collapsed in court in the middle of arguing a case and was pronounced dead by the attending physician. Mildred found herself involved with helping her stepmother, Jesseline, with funeral arrangements while she dealt with her own pain and grief. Her father had been the strongest influence in her life, both for good and for evil, and as Ruth said, "There must be a changing order for you when one of the big bulwarks crashes along with the other crashes. Dear little soul, with all your perspective and willingness to see situations as they really are free from sentiment and all I know you well enough to know that you will grieve frightfully."[20]

Allen helped Mildred with settling her father's affairs and tried to make amends throughout the fall. For Christmas he gave her something she had wanted for a long time, the deed to Thunderbird Lodge. The Stephens had left and were now willing to sell the house, as their son had built a house of his own. Now the Olmsteds could rent out the two studios as well as a room in the large wing and thus help to cover mortgage payments.

But they continued to be edgy with each other, and to fall easily into quarreling over petty matters. In February they fought over a small errand Mildred had asked Allen to do at work. Allen wrote a long letter about the incident, noting that peace-minded people ought to be able to live together more amicably. "On the train I read your name in the paper on a peace petition. Why do we, who are intelligent, who try to guide whole nations to settle their differences, get into such ruckusses? and then spend so much time, nervous energy, and good will in arguing over the right and wrong of such matters as this? Why do we?"[21]

By summertime Allen was seeing Mary again, and Mildred was considering divorce. She spent a week in Allentown with Ruth, who had a short-term job at the Allentown State Hospital while she waited to go to Louisville, Kentucky, as executive director of the mental hygiene clinic attached to the University of Louisville's School of Medicine. Ruth urged her to hold on to her marriage and defended Allen, pointing out that he and Mildred had always discussed the need to have perfect freedom in their relationship. To heal the immediate hurt, she suggested that Mildred ought to try a fling with another man. Ruth, who had been having a series of brief affairs with men, was now involved in a long-term relationship with a prominent married man. Mildred disapproved of this affair and felt that Ruth had deserted her when she needed her most. She even threatened to find a new friend to spend vacations with.

Ruth, however, felt that their friendship was on a healthier basis: "No woman could ever have loved a husband more intensely and completely than I loved you for years and years—the complete concentration of all the libido onto you is not so complete now, because some of it has gone to men where I have always believed it was natural for it to be. Sorry to have you suffer but I won't be apologetic."[22] Ruth returned to this theme over and over. A few years later she wrote, "Don't you remember telling me to go to Rank to get free of Tracy? I remember Dr. Rank saying I wonder why you want two mothers. We always talked about freedom, just as you and Allen did, and when he took you at your words we decided it was a good idea which didn't work very well, and now that I really have won my freedom you have no faith in the love I give you and reject any idea of friendship."[23]

But she vacillated, feeling sometimes that men were not satisfactory and that Mildred and Tracy had been the two real loves of her life. "You should have been a man, Scottie," she once wrote, "and we should have married and how happy our lives together would have been."[24]

The Olmsteds' private unhappiness seemed mirrored in the world about them. The year 1933 saw unemployment at a new high, as the Great American Depression deepened. In Germany Adolf Hitler was named chancellor, and the first concentration camp was opened in Dachau. The Japanese, still at war in Manchuria, walked out of the League of Nations; Mussolini invaded the Balkans; in Spain a revolution began, the nationalists challenging the socialist regime of the Loyalists. The hopes of the world for peace, which had seemed bright only a few years ago, were shattered.

Mildred Olmsted, as usual, found challenge in all this public adversity. WILPF was losing money and had to operate on a skeleton budget. In the office she was forced to rent part of her space, and to cut her staff to the bone; herself and Marian Smith on full-time and the field worker and literature chair on half-time. To supplement, she arranged through private and state employment offices for unemployed office workers to work for the WILPF in return for lunch and carfare. She stopped using first-class postage, sending out the newsletters, and keeping an advance supply of peace literature. And she appealed to her erstwhile supporters not to abandon the WILPF, and to put their money into programs that she felt offered prevention of such catastrophes as the depression, rather than relief from them.

The plight of the millions of unemployed was on the minds of the WILPF women. They had opposed a bill to establish a Citizens Military Training Corps, thus putting the unemployed into the army, but they applauded the development of the Civilian Conservation Corps along the lines of a plan that they had recommended years earlier. They also called on President Roosevelt to release additional aid for the unemployed.

The women of the WILPF had not forgotten that international armament makers had been busy during the Geneva conference, neutralizing their efforts. At the December 1933 board meeting of the U.S. Section it had been proposed to lobby for a congressional committee to investigate the profits of munition makers. When Congress reconvened Dorothy Detzer consulted George Norris, who suggested Gerald Nye of North Dakota as a senator to handle the issue. Once the Nye committee was convened, Dorothy Detzer, along with Fredrick Libby and Jeannette Rankin of the National Council for Prevention of War, Nevin Sayre of the Fellowship of Reconciliation, and Estelle Sternburger of World Peaceways (a small organization founded in 1931 to work for peace primarily through the media) worked closely with it, providing it with materials, lobbying for it in Congress, and publicizing its findings. Dorothy Detzer suggested Stephen Raushenbush, a young economics instructor at Dartmouth, as chief investigator, and she supported him when he was under attack.

The Nye committee developed legislation on the taxing of war profits, the regulation of war industries, and neutrality provisions for commerce abroad during wartime. It revealed the role that private armament makers had played in stimulating arms races between countries, and in wrecking the various peace conferences. Its findings created a national sensation and led to the publication of a popular book, *Merchants of Death*. Although other peace groups had worked with them in this project, the women of WILPF and Dorothy Detzer were perceived as deserving chief credit for this major accomplishment in the cause of peace.[25]

Meanwhile, news that the lives of WILPF members in Germany were in danger galvanized the women to send a memorial to Congress and the Department of Labor asking that the quotas be relaxed for the immigration of German Jews. They also wrote a protest to the German government and delivered it to the German embassy. The Swiss government had decided to deport the WILPF international secretary, Camille Drevet, because of her supposed radical tendencies, and the women wrote from all national sections of WILPF to protest this high-handed measure. Fortunately, at the last minute, the order to leave was recalled. (Ironically the next spring WILPF had to let Drevet go as an economy measure.) Altogether, it was a time when the purpose and strength of the international network of women was clear.

"It is an exciting and thrilling business being a pioneer pacifist in these times," Mildred Olmsted wrote in her annual report to her Pennsylvania board. "And the nearer one is to the heart of it, the more thrilling it becomes. . . . Comradeship in a great cause is a precious thing."[26]

In May 1934 the WILPF held its national meeting in Milwaukee. Jane Addams wrote to Mildred Olmsted, asking her to stop and see her in Chicago on the way out. Quarreling between Mabel Vernon and Dorothy Detzer was destroying the national office, Jane Addams told Mildred Olmsted at this interview. In addition, there were many complaints that Dorothy Detzer never answered her mail. Anne Martin from Nevada, still a close friend of Mabel Vernon's, in particular brought this charge. Should Dorothy be fired as executive secretary?

"Oh, Dorothy answers her mail, all right," Mildred Olmsted told Jane Addams. "She just doesn't say what Anne Martin wants to hear."[27]

Jane Addams then asked Mildred Olmsted if she would be willing to work in the national office as one of three secretaries on an equal basis—Dorothy Detzer, Mabel Vernon, and herself—and try to keep the peace between the two warring women. Mildred Olmsted, who was always willing to do anything Jane Addams asked of her, agreed. Jane Addams then suggested that the national headquarters ought to be moved to Philadelphia where she had always believed it should be. Mildred Olmsted said she thought it was unlikely that Dorothy Detzer would agree to such a move.

On the floor of the national conference itself the proposal for three coordinate secretaries was presented and accepted. Dorothy Detzer was to be called national secretary; Mildred Olmsted, organization secretary; and Mabel Vernon, finance secretary. Dorothy Detzer was not pleased at what she perceived as a demotion and announced once more that she intended to resign. By fall she had relented, but the struggle continued and preoccupied the WILPF executive committee for several years.

The proposition was that Mildred Olmsted spend half-time in Washington and half-time in Philadelphia, starting in January 1935. The board of Pennsylvania WILPF was reluctant to release her for this amount of time but had to face the fact that they really could not pay her full-time in any case. Mildred Olmsted accepted the prospect of commuting stoically. It may even have been that because her home life was especially unhappy at this time, she looked forward to being away from Rose Valley.

The International WILPF continued to be plagued by tensions of its own with constant friction between the pacifist British and Scandinavian sections, on the one hand, and on the other the European sections, which were becoming more and more anti-Fascist as the noose of Hitler tightened. In March 1934 the British Section proposed that in view of the international situation the international executive committee should not pass political resolutions without consulting the national sections. This would effectively undo the compromise reached at Grenoble, and it was decided to call a special conference at Zurich in late August to iron out the difficulties.

Jane Addams was too ill to go, and Emily Greene Balch was temporarily filling the post of international secretary in Geneva and would not be able to represent the U.S. Section on the floor of the conference. Hannah Clothier Hull wrote to Mildred Olmsted asking her to go and try to lead the U.S. delegation in suggesting a compromise. Mildred Olmsted had been away a good deal already that summer, attending the twenty-fifth reunion of Allen's Harvard Class of 1909, hiking in the Adirondacks with Ruth, and vacationing in Maine with Allen and the children. She hated to take more time, and she was not sure she would do a good job. She wrote Hannah Hull that she did not share the confidence that Jane Addams and others had expressed in her ability to make a difference, but that if she were really needed she would be a good servant of the group and follow orders. It was up to the younger members of WILPF like herself to carry out the policy suggested to them by their leaders.[28]

The U.S. delegation would be made up of Katherine Blake and Lola Lloyd, longtime WILPF members, as well as Alice Paul, who was going primarily to get WILPF to endorse an international equal rights treaty. Mildred Olmsted did not feel she could persuade any of these women to follow her lead at Zurich and wrote to Jane Addams for guidance. Addams outlined the difficulty between the British/Scandinavian and the French/German alignment and suggested a possible way out. "I think a compromise might be affected if a rule were passed prohibiting any action involving a nation in which WIL has a section without a representative of that section being present and stating the point of view of her home group. She would have to abide by the majority vote of the committee, of course, but might be able to modify the situation by the fact that the statement had been made."[29]

Dorothy Detzer had been refusing to make the trip because of the expense, but she changed her mind when Mildred Olmsted was able to raise the money. Ruth Mellor came too in order to spend a few days traveling with Mildred before the conference. After Ruth left, Dorothy and Mildred moved into a Christian working girls' residence in Zurich, attended the executive committee meetings preceding the conference, and had dinner with Gertrude Baer who had just escaped from Nazi Germany with all the WILPF papers on her person and was planning to come soon to the United States. Mildred wrote Allen that the Danish delegates wanted her to become international secretary. "DD, who is

14. Mildred Scott Olmsted, 1932. *Courtesy of Swarthmore College Peace Collection.*

my great friend now, says I would be good, but I have a husband and children. Now I am on a committee to find one."[30]

At the conference itself Mildred Olmsted spoke often and eloquently for compromise. "We are not as far apart as we seem, since the British section can accept the idea of a strike, and the French section renounces bloodshed." She pointed out that the history of the U.S. Constitution spoke to the foresight of the founders in providing for some elasticity. Finally the conference agreed to a statement of aims, and to a constitutional provision along the lines Jane Addams had outlined to Mildred Olmsted: that, when practical, the executive committee should consult the national sections regarding affairs in their own countries.[31]

Early in the sessions, Alice Paul brought forward her equal rights for women resolution, pledging each section to work for an equal rights treaty, and it was unanimously accepted. Dorothy Detzer, and perhaps other members of the U.S. WILPF team, were always suspicious of Alice Paul's efforts to recruit them to serve the agenda of the National Women's party, especially since they felt she was always unwilling to reciprocate. When the next day the Americans made an effort to recall the vote on the resolution, this was ruled out of order. Later Mildred Olmsted startled some of those present by proposing that WILPF consider changing its name and admitting men on an equal footing. In the 1934 National WILPF Conference in Milwaukee, membership had been changed to apply to both men and women, and local branches had been given the option of changing the name of the organization. This move reflected the trouble WILPF was having in some communities in recruiting members, and the challenge of other peace organizations such as the National Council for Prevention of War, which wanted a grass-roots organization to involve men. There was sentiment too among some of the younger women, such as Dorothy Detzer, that feminism was old-fashioned, and that it was important to treat men not as enemies but comrades and equals.[32]

Mildred Olmsted's resolution was turned down by this conference because there was not enough time to debate it. In private, European women told Mildred that it would be impossible: if they admitted men, the men would simply take over the organization and the women would be forced out. Although the proposition came up several times again in the United States, it was never seriously considered internationally, and WILPF preserved its uniqueness as an international organization of women. In time Mildred came to feel very glad that this was so.

The conference also voted to send a delegation into Germany to inquire after WILPF members. One in particular, Elsa Steinfurth, was in jail and had been ill. Gertrude Baer feared it might be tuberculosis. Camile Drevet, Mildred Olmsted, and Catherine Marshall were chosen for this dangerous mission, but in the end only Mildred Olmsted was able to go. Gertrude Baer briefed her. She was to memorize the names and addresses of the women she was to see, destroy all the directions before she crossed the border, and always leave her hotel room to make it appear she was an ordinary tourist. Under no circumstances was she ever to identify herself as a member of WILPF, for it was important that the Nazis believe the organization had ceased to exist.[33]

Mildred Olmsted's first object in Berlin was to visit Elsa Steinfurth in jail and find out the state of her health. Through a German official she had met at Allen's Harvard reunion, she obtained an interview with the secret police, or *Geheim Politzei*. Posing as an interested individual, she handed the official a list of names of persons whom friends of hers in the United States had asked about. She was given back the list and told to send it in writing to the proper official. As far as Frau Steinfurth was concerned, Mildred Olmsted was informed that she had been moved to the Moabit Prison. She found the jail, went upstairs, and discovered her way blocked by a big iron partition with a curtain. There didn't seem to be anyone about, so Mildred stuck her arm through the curtain, and the guard came along in a few minutes to see what this was all about. When she made herself understood, the guard took Mildred to see the woman's lawyer, a Herr Rahse, who was in the jail to investigate the case. He took Mildred Olmsted into his office but said he could not speak freely. He sent for Elsa Steinfurth, however, who was brought to the office to speak to Mildred in his presence. Steinfurth told her that she had been in the hospital because of back problems but did not have tuberculosis, and Mildred thought she looked well nourished, though somewhat pale. The German woman was hopeful that her case would come up soon, and that she would be released.[34]

This errand completed, Mildred Olmsted next got in touch with a woman in an antique shop she had been told to contact. She told the woman that she had greetings from her friend, Helene, and the woman said she would talk with her in a few minutes. Mildred walked about admiring the antiques until the woman joined her and pointed out that a German guard was often watching, and that she had to be very careful. Mildred gave her news of her former colleagues, including Gertrude Baer, and the woman gave her the names of other women to contact.

One of these women lived far out in the suburbs. On a public pay phone, Mildred Olmsted was given directions to take three different trolley cars and then wait under a bridge. She did not have long to wait before a woman came to pick her up and take her to her destination. This turned out to be the home of a woman doctor. In the parlor the doctor had a number of books on feminine hygiene laid out on the table. There were a small number of German WILPF members present, and Mildred told them the news. Whenever anyone was heard approaching the door she stopped speaking so that no one would detect her foreign accent, and the doctor took over, lecturing as though she were conducting a class in women's health problems.

In addition to running these secret missions for the WILPF, Mildred tried to see as much as she could of what was going on in Germany. She attended public gatherings; at one of these she heard Adolf Hitler speak, and she was not overwhelmed. She walked the streets, watching and listening.[35]

Sometime during this week, perhaps when she first went to inquire about the prison, she acquired an admirer in the form of a policeman. Although she knew he was a Nazi, he seemed a pleasant enough person, and his interest in her as a woman was flattering. Both Allen and Ruth had been urging her to have a fling with a man as a way of compensating for the hurt of Allen's affair. Mildred suddenly thought, "Well, why not?" The night she spent with her *polizei* was not particularly thrilling, she remembered, but it was interesting.[36]

She left Germany safely at the end of the week and wrote a report on her experiences—except the night with the *polizei*—to Gertrude Baer. When Allen met her in New York, she told him that first night about her Berlin fling. Allen was enchanted. That she could be so human as to give way to an impulse made her suddenly as desirable to him as she had been when he was courting her. All the tensions disappeared from the Olmsted marriage for many months, and they were very happy together again. Allen even suggested that Mildred might try to have another baby, and although she was forty-five, Mildred agreed to consult Dr. Lovett Dewees, who tactfully advised against it.[37]

Mildred Olmsted had been moved by her week in Germany to a fresh horror of nazism. She spoke extensively on her experiences, got in touch with the Committee for the Victims of German Fascism, and wrote to Roscoe Pound at Harvard Law School, asking him to intervene in the freeing of Elsa Steinfurth. She corresponded with Gertrude Baer and other international WILPF leaders about the desirability of sending a WILPF mission to Germany to follow up on her work, and to inquire about women in the new concentration camps. The women she had talked with in Berlin had asked that nothing be done in the name of the WILPF that might expose them, and this consideration led to dismissing the idea of a mission.

As Mildred wrote to Allen on the eve of her trip into Germany, "I am moving up in the WILPF world." Her mission had been adventurous and had impressed many people. She was even invited to become the international secretary of the organization. Though she had to turn this invitation down because of family obligations, it made her feel that she had come of age in the world of WILPF.

10

"Peace Must Be Organized"

*I*N DECEMBER 1934 Mildred Scott Olmsted took up her new
duties as organization secretary for WILPF, spending three days a
week at national headquarters in Washington. She tried to arrange
her schedule so that she was away from home only two nights a
week, but there were many exceptions. Her Rose Valley neighbors
did not approve, but they had never approved of her working full-
time, and sometimes made fun of her to her face. Adele Saul told
Mildred that they were jealous. Despite the Olmsteds' domestic
troubles Allen remained supportive, insisting that he was proud of
a wife who worked.

Allen was home more often than Mildred. He was covering
all the legal work of Saul, Ewing, Remick and Saul in Delaware
County and had been admitted to the Delaware County bar in
1930, after a legal battle overturning a statute that prohibited
members of a Philadelphia firm from practicing in the county. In
Media, the county seat, he had associated himself with another
lawyer, Joseph Calhoun, and had an office near the courthouse.
But he also did legal work for federal agencies such as the Inter-
state Commerce Commission and the Federal Deposit Insurance
Corporation, as well as for private businesses such as Stetson Hat.
Along with ACLU cases, this work frequently forced him to
travel. When home, he took a lively interest in his three children
and their welfare and spent time at the School in Rose Valley,
watching them in their plays and sports and talking with their
teachers.

The Olmsted children had the usual childhood diseases—

188

measles, chicken pox, whooping cough, bronchitis, ear infections. Peter was very ill with a mastoid infection several times, and twice with pneumonia. When the children were sick, either Mildred or Allen would stay home with them, depending on whose schedule allowed this. Sometimes, of course, they were both away, and the care of the children fell to the housekeeper.

While the Olmsteds liked the permissive environment of the School in Rose Valley, they discovered that Peter did not seem to be learning to read. The head of the school, Grace Rotzel, assured them that he would read when he was ready, but after a few more years of waiting they took him to a reading specialist and found that he had dyslexia, and that it was necessary for him to have tutoring. Eventually he caught up and was able to enter Westtown School, where he did well, but the years of not being able to read had lowered his self-esteem, which was already shaky. Mildred had been a critical parent, he said in later life, always demanding a great deal of him without being able to show him affection. Allen was warmer, but he too expected great things of his son. This combination of expectations was hard on Peter.

The other two children began to manifest problems too. Enid was a charming child, but her mother found her passive and evasive, and she did not seem much interested in school. Mildred liked to dress her up in expensive dresses, tied large satin bows in her hair, and insisted that she wear sturdy shoes at all times. Enid thought the dresses old-fashioned and the shoes ugly. There was silent warfare between them about such issues as wearing rubbers on a rainy day. Enid would put them on in Mildred's presence, then quietly remove them on the way to school.

Tony began to have behavior problems. Mildred thought he might be suffering from the fact that Allen appeared to her more invested in Peter than in him and tried to compensate, but Tony continued to be troubled. She took him for a while for counseling to the Delaware County Child Guidance Clinic, but Mildred did not like her interviews with the social worker, who often kept her waiting and did not seem to understand the importance of her various peace meetings, as Allen said rather sarcastically. She also responded to Mildred's questions by turning them back upon her. Ruth explained that this was done to help Mildred gain insight, but Mildred did not like it and could not see that the sessions were doing Tony much good, so she terminated them. Although the School in Rose Valley managed to keep him from year to year, during his first year at Westtown the staff told the Olmsteds that he needed more specialized education and suggested several private schools.

All through these years, as Mildred and Allen discussed their children's problems and worried over them, they never seemed to consider that their own marital discord might be having an effect on them. Despite their continuing bitter quarrels and occasional separations, they never considered marriage counseling.

When they were little, the Olmsted children liked to dress up and pretend they were going to a peace meeting. At first they accepted Mildred's frequent absences, and it was only when they got to school and discovered that their friends' mothers did not work or, if they worked, were teachers or nurses who came home every night, that they began to question her being away from home so frequently and for such prolonged periods. The fact that she never came to school plays or other events began to hurt. Although her absences were often on WILPF business, they were sometimes occasioned by lengthy vacations with Ruth. Yet the children never resented Ruth, for when she came to visit she was always warm and kind to them.

As adults looking back on their childhood, the Olmsted off-spring came to feel that there was very little affection for any of them in the household, and that they fought for scraps, each with different tools: Peter with health and reading problems, Enid with withdrawal, Tony by acting out. Even when Mildred was home she seemed more interested in controlling how they dressed or behaved than in sympathizing with them. Her lifelong habit of disciplining herself to show no emotion resulted in their feeling she was incapable of revealing love toward them. Allen was the warmer parent. As a result the children turned toward him, and Mildred often felt that the other four were in league against her, another form of Allen's disloyalty.

Aside from these continuing problems, the smooth day-to-day operating of the Olmsted household depended to a large extent on the housekeeper. Gibby left at the end of 1933 to make a home for her husband, Norman, and an adopted son, and the Olmsteds managed with a series of women until Hilda Osborne came and stayed for six years. Peter had been close to Gibby, but Enid came to think of Hilda Osborne as a second mother. Unfortunately Hilda and Tony did not get along, as both Ruth and Allen pointed out to Mildred. She was so satisfactory in other ways that Mildred found it hard to let her go.

There were changes in the Saul family up the hill. After twenty years of devoted wifehood and motherhood, Adele Saul decided that she needed to stretch her wings. In the fall of 1931 she went to France to join an atelier and study art. On her return she rented a studio apartment in New York City where she could go occasionally to get away from the social demands of being Maurice Saul's wife and paint in peace and quiet. The neighbors, who had been scandalized by Mildred for years, now had Adele also to gossip about.

Mildred Olmsted learned to put the concerns of the household at Rose Valley out of her mind when she stepped on the train, and to begin to think about the demands of the day. The opportunity to be national organization secretary for the WILPF was exactly suited to her. More than fifty years later she told me she regarded this as the high point of her career in WILPF. She had always believed that WILPF could grow to take in 50,000 women if properly organized; here was her chance to achieve this goal. Earlier, as chair of the organization committee, she had developed a plan of dividing the country into six regions, and having a fieldworker for each region, doing the careful community-by-community work that she had done in Pennsylvania. There were no funds for a field-worker in 1935, but she was authorized to hire one in January 1936.

Meanwhile she set to work with the help of an assistant to bring order out of the chaotic U.S. membership lists, and to work on the lists of international members, those women who elected to help maintain the international office by subscribing to the publications coming out of Geneva, including *Pax et Libertas.*

The Washington office was busy during those first months getting ready for the WILPF's twentieth anniversary with a gala celebration 2–5 May in Washington, D.C., in honor of its founder, Jane Addams. Although Addams was ill that spring, the event came off as planned. Eleanor Roosevelt entertained Jane Addams and her colleagues at the White House, and the National Broadcasting Company arranged a worldwide radio broadcast from the League of Nations headquarters in Geneva, featuring Jane Addams and leading diplomats from Tokyo, Moscow, London, Paris, and Geneva. It was to be the last time the women of WILPF saw their beloved leader. Two weeks later, on 21 May, Jane Addams died of cancer.

Despite Mildred Olmsted's best efforts, conflict still raged in the office between Dorothy Detzer and Mabel Vernon. Dorothy's chief agenda was to persuade WILPF branches to support the sort of lobbying she was doing in the capitol, such as her work to publicize the Nye committee. Mabel was far more interested in organizing large numbers of women to sign petitions and to organize local peace councils. In 1935 she became the director of the People's Mandate to End War, a project of the international executive committee, working out of U.S. WILPF headquarters. This effort removed her still further from supporting Dorothy's work. The philosophical differences between the two women were inflamed by personality conflicts and by Dorothy's indignation that Mabel was not asked to work under her. At the board meeting the three coequal secretaries were asked to retire while the board discussed the situation; they were then told that Dorothy's title had been changed to national executive secretary, and that Mabel was being encouraged to move to different headquarters. This did not satisfy Dorothy, and she once more resigned and decided to spend the summer working for International WILPF. She wrote Mildred about it from aboard the SS *Normandie*. "You say you hope I won't resign. But I have. The board has assumed for so long that I make all the compromises and you don't even take this seriously. Board reminds me of government. They vote me a cute title, I am to approve all personnel—privately tell me I have been working in a viper's nest and it will all be cleaned out if only I'll agree to keep things as they are until Oct."[1]

Mildred Olmsted predicted that Dorothy Detzer would relent once more, and in the late fall she did, returning to take up her duties in the Washington office. Mildred was told by President

Hannah Hull that she must now work under Dorothy, but Mildred had no intention of abandoning her liberty of action and continued to act on the basis of coequality. It was the root of future conflict between Dorothy and Mildred. Tired after five years of battle, Mabel Vernon finally decided to leave the WILPF in January 1936, making her new organization the People's Mandate to Governments to End War, Committee for the Western Hemisphere, into an independent organization, although working closely with WILPF.

Mildred Olmsted's refusal to play a subordinate role was characteristic. She had revealed it in her work with the Girls' Protective League in Maryland, in her troubles with the American Friends Service Committee in Germany, and at the White Williams Foundation. Once, in an angry moment, Allen had written her that she was in favor of liberty for herself and law and order for others. There was some truth in the observation. She subjected herself to a steel discipline and expected it of others, yet the discipline must come from within, never without. It was part of the obsession with freedom her father had observed. She was willing to follow the orders of someone she admired, like Jane Addams or Hannah Hull, but her obedience had to be a free and not a coerced gift. She was also willing to obey the will of WILPF if she felt it was democratically arrived at. But she realized that Dorothy Detzer did not share her view of the importance of building WILPF, and she was afraid that unless she guarded her independence she would find herself working for a WILPF with a much narrower mission: that of supporting the lobbying and public relations work that Dorothy Detzer excelled in.

While Dorothy Detzer was away in the summer of 1935 Mildred Olmsted stayed home to mind the office and to vacation with her children at the Jersey shore. She traveled in late August and September, visiting WILPF branches and helping to set up new ones in Chicago, Dubuque, Minneapolis, Lincoln, Kansas City, St. Louis, Cincinnati, Pittsburgh, and Canton, Ohio. In November she was on the road again in New York and New England. In early 1936 she traveled to Nashville, New Orleans, Louisville, Dallas, Fort Worth, Waco, San Antonio, Little Rock, Memphis, Knoxville, Charlotte and Greensboro in North Carolina, and Petersburg, Virginia. Membership statistics had begun to rise by this time and funds to increase. In January she had been able to hire a field secretary, a young graduate of Smith college named Eleanor Eaton.

Eleanor Eaton had resolve, stamina, and a sense of humor, and for three years she worked with Mildred. Together the two increased WILPF membership from less than 10,000 to 14,000. In the beginning Mildred explained to her the rationale of the work:

> . . . the WIL has so long been strong at the top and weak at the bottom that it has been like a building without a foundation or proper underpinnings, or, to change the simile, it has been very strong in the head but had a starved body so that no matter how excellent the policies adopted in Washington and Geneva, they have had nothing like an adequate response through the country because we have had no roads over which to send them out. . . .
>
> I believe that if you take twenty-five people interested in peace in almost any community and leave them to work out their own ideas, they will be nothing like as far along in their thinking and acting as if those same twenty-five people were a branch of the WIL with the stimulus and direction that comes from the thinking that is done by the National and the International and with a program which will make them see the interrelationship of peace and economic and legislative problems.[2]

As she began work, Eleanor Eaton moved rapidly from city to city. Mildred Olmsted suggested that she must stay longer in each place and arrange somehow for follow-up. Board members should be encouraged to visit each branch in their area to augment the work of the field staff, and to stop off to make visits when en route to national board meetings. Mildred conceived of the new branches as a series of stepping stones placed strategically between older established branches, so that it might be possible for a WILPF member to go across the country from branch to branch.

Some of the branches had been organized during the Disarmament Caravan, when Mabel Vernon sent field-workers into an area to contact WILPF members and other interested women, and to do advance publicity. But where that work had not been followed up, the branch languished. For this reason, there were a number of isolated branches in Portland, Seattle, Salt Lake City, New Orleans, Colorado, and the Hawaiian Islands that were hard to link up to others. It was, however, important to keep every branch alive, if possible, rather than to concentrate on a more compact geographic grouping.

In addition to nurturing old branches and organizing new ones, Mildred Olmsted felt that all branches would benefit from standardization. Each branch should have a constitution modeled after one developed in the WILPF headquarters, and there should be a membership quota for developing both state and local branches. Dues should be uniform, and branches should be encouraged to elect members to the national board. Annual board meetings should be held in different cities in order to strength the organization in each.

Older branches that seemed to be falling apart needed nurturing too. In November 1936 Mildred Olmsted sent Eleanor Eaton to New Orleans, suggesting that she bring members up-to-date and help the branch acquire newer members and work more closely with the national program. It would be good if a WILPF board member followed up on Eleanor's visit, she wrote, and if the national board would agree to meet in New Orleans.[3]

To back up the travels of Eleanor Eaton and herself, Mildred Olmsted distributed a handbook listing WILPF leaders and committees, encouraged membership drives, developed local how-to literature, began to send out regular organization letters, and encouraged each local branch to undertake a project of its own, so that members might see some immediate results more tangible than the elusive goal of world peace. She also worked to rationalize the election procedures to improve the quality of leadership on the national board. She had her eye out for leadership potential wherever she traveled and frequently participated informally in the nominating process, writing the chair of the nominating committee with her suggestions.

Because she was still executive secretary of the Pennsylvania branch, she also kept up her travels in the counties of Pennsylvania, although she usually had a Pennsylvania field secretary to help cover the areas. It sometimes seemed to the field secretaries that Mildred Olmsted could not leave the job to them but was impelled to follow up on their efforts. Yet despite all this travel she managed to keep up a correspondence with branch leaders all over the country, encouraging, cajoling, gently correcting them. She urged daughters to take on the jobs of their mothers, and young women to leave their children with babysitters to attend WILPF gatherings. In June 1936, for example, she wrote to Minnie Allen of Ames, Iowa, asking her to represent WILPF at an Institute of International Relations sponsored by the American Friends Service Committee and took time to ask about the health of her children. At about the same time she was in correspondence with Rebecca Krupp of Louisville about scheduling a WILPF speaker on the Tennessee Valley Authority, and with Virginia Fisher of McPherson, Kansas, about becoming national membership chair.[4]

Many of the letters Mildred Olmsted wrote were designed to reassure local WILPF leaders that WILPF was not Communist. The old charges of the 1920s, which had never died down, were revived in the 1930s as individual WILPF members began to express sympathy for Loyalist Spain or concern for the victims of Hitler, or to oppose Mussolini's Abyssinian adventure. A segment of the American public could not understand that to be for peace was not subversive, and all peace organizations were similarly attacked. The fact that in the 1930s many American Communists entered into coalitions opposing war gave added ammunition to the right wing. A Hearst ad appeared in the *Philadelphia Inquirer* attacking "Red Pacifists" and mentioning the WILPF.

Mildred Olmsted fought back. She circulated a letter by Hamilton Fish of the House Committee Investigating Communism that cleared the WILPF of such charges, along with a similar letter by Carrie Chapman Catt. The Pennsylvania board sent Mary Scattergood to talk with top *Inquirer* officials and get their promise to print nothing that might be interpreted as propaganda. And Mildred continued to argue that the women of WILPF were peace pioneers, on the forefront of the battle for peace, as their foremothers had been on the battles against slavery or for suffrage.

Mildred Olmsted herself frequently encountered the charge of being a Communist. Visiting Johnstown, Pennsylvania, in May

1938 she was met on arrival by a member of the local committee that had invited her, suggesting that she not stop but go on back to Philadelphia because the American Legion had been saying they were going to tar and feather her if she spoke. Mildred said she would prefer to stay—she had never been tarred and feathered and would like to see what happened. At a Lion's Club luncheon she found the men seated on either side of her were frosty. When it came time for her to speak, she announced she had changed the topic from world peace to the WILPF. The program chair objected, but Mildred said she had heard that there were false rumors in the town, and she had a right to straighten them out. She then told about the origins of the WILPF, comparing the pioneer women of the organization to the American pioneers. She spoke of her own early American ancestors, her service with the War Department, and her membership in the Women's Overseas Service League. She made the point that democracy demanded a loyal opposition, and that the WILPF was playing an essential role in making democracy work.

Her talk was well received, but she was told she had better not stay for the meeting that night at the high school, where the legion was supposed to be out in force. Mildred Olmsted, however, insisted on going through with the speech and again gave her comparison of WILPF with early American patriots. When she finished there was applause, and a peaceable question-and-answer time. Later some of the legionnaires told the local committee that they had been warned about Mildred, but that she had not said anything of which they disapproved. In fact, they invited her back.[5]

Though the fears of individual communities could be abated, the charges persisted. Like many other peace organizations, WILPF tended to lean to the Left during the early 1930s, seeking alliances with labor unions and left-wing organizations, and discussing the class struggle and whether it could be conducted by nonviolent means. As the threat of fascism deepened, the women of the WILPF sought allies with other groups opposed to Hitler. For a time they considered attending the World Congress Against War held in Amsterdam in 1932 to established a united front against fascism, and when the American League Against War and

Fascism (later called the American League for Peace and Democracy) was organized in 1933, they as well as the Fellowship of Reconciliation and other prominent pacifist groups at first were willing to affiliate and only withdrew when the rigid methods of the American Communist party began to be manifest.

Mildred Olmsted attended the organizing meeting of the ALAWF in New York. Also on the program was J. P. Matthews of the Fellowship of Reconciliation, who later became an informant for the House Un-American Activities Committee, and still later worked for Senator Joseph McCarthy. She arrived late in an already crowded hall and struggled to make her way to the platform. She had received for Christmas a little red traveling bag of which she was very fond, and she held it up high in order to get some attention. The bag worked miracles, and she was soon at the podium. Only later did she wonder if the color red had somehow helped.[6]

But the WILPF also had other allies. It had long cooperated with the National Council for Prevention of War, headed by Fred Libby, which was always careful not to affiliate with any group suspected of leftist leanings. In 1932 a second coalition, the National Peace Conference, was organized, and in 1936 Mildred attended a meeting called by Ray Newton of the American Friends Service Committee to organize a third group, the Emergency Peace Campaign, a coalition dominated by the pacifist FOR, the AFSC, and WILPF. Mildred was active with all these coalitions, bringing to them her skills in organizing and recognizing leadership potential. These networking skills were a major contribution of the WILPF to the peace movement of the day.

Working with the new coalitions, however, Mildred Olmsted also found it necessary to watch for incursions on WILPF's territory. Both the Emergency Peace Campaign and the National Peace Conference showed an inclination to organize local councils, and to draw WILPF members into them. Mildred suggested a "gentlemen's agreement": the local councils should be made up of representatives of local peace organizations, not of individuals. Enthusiastic local staff members, however, were constantly violating this agreement. In 1937, after the Emergency Peace Campaign came to an end, the National Council for Prevention of War became more aggressive in Pennsylvania under the leadership of Ray Newton. When Mildred wrote to Fred Libby to complain that Ray was recruiting individual members in her territory, who ought to be left to her, Libby answered that he thought "the people of Pennsylvania may think they ought to be consulted before so drastic a solution is agreed upon by the dictators."[7]

One obvious solution was that WILPF drop *women's* from its name, so that men wishing to join in the Emergency Peace Campaign could affiliate with local branches. Ray Newton suggested to Mildred that WILPF ought either to make that change or to resign themselves to being a sort of ladies' auxiliary to the larger peace movement. Mildred was of two minds. Some local branches had already admitted men, but her experience was that when men took the leadership, the branch promptly died out. The European women continued to oppose the idea, and the international connections were what gave WILPF its uniqueness and strength. On the other hand, younger WILPF workers, such as Philip and Betty Jacob of Swarthmore, insisted that feminism was old-fashioned and urged the change. Betty, who worked as a field secretary for the Pennsylvania WILPF, set about organizing local branches of both men and women. Philip brought a proposal to the national board meeting in 1939 that the organization drop the word *Women's*. Emily Greene Balch commented that "we must always realize that men just assume that women were nonexistent." A committee was appointed to study dropping the word. At the December executive committee meeting the committee reported on a poll of members: 244 for changing the name, another 121 for changing it in some way, 883 opposed. Pennsylvania had not yet reported, and Mildred spoke for the change, saying that "older leaders have a sentimental attachment to being a women's organization, but younger and newer members, particularly those in touch with other organizations think there is a need for an organization of men and women working together and they want WILPF to be it, rather than see a competing organization set up which might draw off some of our most promising younger people." But at the next annual meeting, in April 1940, the change was voted down.[8]

In 1938 a new organization, Keep America Out of War, was

formed, with Fred Libby as chair. Once more Mildred perceived a potential threat. She wrote to the executive secretary, Lyn Smith, suggesting that KAOW concentrate primarily on labor and youth groups and leave the general field to WILPF. Lyn replied that they were organizing men and professional women who could only come to meetings at night, but that they were carefully avoiding competing with existing WILPF branches. She knew WILPF well, having been the secretary of the New York state branch.[9]

The best way to defend WILPF from the incursions of other organizations, of course, was to keep it growing. In 1937 Mildred acquired a second field secretary, Helen Hart, and persuaded Gertrude Baer, who came to the United States that spring on a visit, to travel through the Midwest, speaking to WILPF branches. The brilliant Gertrude Baer was known throughout WILPF for her writings, and branches in Chicago, St. Louis, Fort Wayne, Minneapolis, Detroit, and Buffalo all wanted her. She set out in early May, speaking in Washington and in Swarthmore, but by the time she got as far as Pittsburgh she collapsed; she told Mildred that she had had a heart attack, that her nerves were in bad condition, and that she must go home. Mildred was distraught. Believing that Gertrude's problem was not physical but a lack of will, she gave Gertrude a spirited talking to on the phone. Gertrude wrote that "I am quite sure, dear Mildred, that you do know what you said today and in which tone you said it." She was adamant about not continuing, and Mildred and her secretary were left with the problem of finding substitutes. Gertrude rested at Awbury, a Quaker community in Germantown, while this was going on. Mildred finally tried to make amends for her anger, inviting Gertrude to visit her in Rose Valley, but Gertrude seemed intensely suspicious the whole time she was at Mildred's house, constantly changing her chair around when they were sitting in the garden so that she could watch all approaches. Mildred concluded that she was a "mental case," although she continued to respect her brilliant mind, and to champion her internationalist ideas in WILPF.[10]

To offset the disastrous Gertrude Baer trip, Mildred Olmsted kept urging Eleanor Eaton and board members to increase their branch visits in 1937, while she herself was often on the road. As the world crisis deepened, she felt it important to reach out to as many people as possible with a message of peace. She had arranged for WILPF news to be published in *Fellowship* magazine during the year, in return for a subscription going to each member. In the January 1938 issue she published an article called "Peace Must be Organized." She argued that leadership in social change came from private associations of like-minded voters who seek to educate the community.

Whether it be the abolition of slavery, woman suffrage, prohibition, or the repeal of prohibition, it was an organization of those who believed in the cause strongly enough to spend time, money, and energy working to bring it about who did bring it about, impressing office holders and office seekers with their steady persistence and willingness to subordinate other interests to this particular one. Throughout our history it is the voluntary organizations which have done the necessary research and educational work in the community to show people what they need to do to get their ideas translated into legislative action. Until the sentiment is organized, it has little effect.[11]

The WILPF, she announced, was setting out to organize a branch in each congressional district, an enterprise in which the group needed the help of every member.

Despite her hard work and cheerful reports, Mildred Olmsted did not always feel she had the support of the WILPF national board for her organizing. The women of WILPF were primarily intellectuals, and they preferred to debate policy issues rather than the nuts and bolts of organization building. At board meetings, Mildred was never given time for the discussion of organization matters and had begun to have a series of breakfasts at which she invited local branches to meet to exchange how-to-do-it tips. In time the breakfast meetings became so popular that they began to interfere with the regular program, and Mildred was finally asked to hold her organization meetings as a regular part of the agenda.

In October 1937 a new finance secretary had been hired by Dorothy Detzer with the consent of the board to replace Mabel Vernon. Catherine Fitzgibbon put her energies into trying to increase the authority and the financial support of the national office, while making economies in its budget. Concerned that Mildred had never accepted Dorothy Detzer's supervision, she tried to persuade Dorothy to make an issue of this. Dorothy had been content to let Mildred go her own way, but now she began to listen to Catherine Fitzgibbon and to feel threatened by Mildred's continued independence. The new finance secretary also believed that the national office had too large a staff. At a special meeting of the board in March 1938 she proposed that Mildred be cut to one-fourth time as organization secretary, that Eleanor Eaton be used as her assistant and the present assistant fired, and that each region be asked to hire its own field secretary.

Mildred Olmsted fought these proposals vigorously at the annual meeting held in May in Minneapolis. She countered with a proposition that WILPF raise individual dues and that the national office receive more money from the unorganized states in order to support field-workers. Membership was at an all-time high of 14,073; this was no time to cut back. More fieldwork and more members were what was needed to meet the economic crisis, she argued. With the support of the chair of the organization committee, Kathleen Hendrie, she won a narrow majority of support on the subcommittee appointed to consider the problem. But Kathleen decided the next day that this was not a good decision-making process in WILPF, which always strove for "pooled intelligence," as Jane Addams called it, and consensus rather than majority rule. She withdrew her support, and the changes were reluctantly accepted. [12]

Emily Greene Balch wrote after the executive committee meeting in March and the Minneapolis meeting in May to say how sorry she was that Mildred's splendid work was being curtailed, and that she felt she had mismanaged the affair and had not spoken forth in Mildred's behalf. "Please don't have the feeling that we do not appreciate what you do and can do in the future. I am sure that I do though you may think I do not do so as fully as I really do . . . o dear me, this money business." [13]

Mildred Olmsted did not believe that "this money business" was the cause of her troubles. Whatever the reasons leading up to it, Dorothy Detzer was now determined to undermine Mildred's growing power in the organization. She had come to feel that Mildred's difficult personality and her insistence on autonomy were hurting the WILPF and ultimately keeping it from growing. Mildred understood that there was a power struggle at work. All through 1938 she continued to argue for a reversal of the decision to cut back fieldwork. She pointed to the fact that membership was now at its peak in the history of WILPF and argued that this was the time to increase, not decrease, fieldwork. When Eleanor Eaton began working in the office, Mildred hired a younger woman at less pay to do some fieldwork. But the decision had been made, and Dorothy Detzer was determined to make it stick. When Gertrude Bussey of Goucher College became president of U.S. WILPF in 1939, she reinforced Dorothy Detzer. Mildred Olmsted was forced to cut back, and membership began to slip downward again.

Mildred Olmsted also found herself in disagreement with Dorothy Detzer on the question of neutrality. A large number of American pacifists and peace seekers believed in mandatory neutrality, saying that the president should be compelled to embargo all shipments to both sides in a conflict. Only by remaining entirely neutral could the United States play a mediating role in international conflicts, those who advocated this position believed. War itself was so evil that it quickly overwhelmed the differences between the aggressor and the victim. Although accused of selfishness and isolationism in wanting to keep the United States out of war, the advocates of mandatory neutrality insisted that theirs was an internationalist point of view.

The advocates of discretionary neutrality, on the other hand, believed that the United States should denounce the aggressor and use sanctions against that nation. They looked to the League of Nations to rouse itself from its stupor, and to advance the cause of collective security by nonviolent means. Pacifists who advocated this position talked about boycotts as a stage in nonviolent struggle and began to study the works of Gandhi for concepts of using moral force to oppose evil.

Mildred Olmsted believed strongly in the concept of collective security. Ever since the Japanese invasion of Manchuria she had been waiting for the nations of the world to punish the Japanese aggressor. World law, she thought, was the only hope for a peaceful world, and sanctions were one tool that nations could use to enforce world opinion. In a letter to Gertrude Baer she expressed her thoughts.

> I feel that the future of the world lies in the development of international law, and that that in itself means that there must be joint action, first to remove the causes of war and secondly, to punish those who transgress the law or the accepted standards of international morality. I know this is not the viewpoint of the Quakers who believe in no sort of coercion or compulsion. I am a pacifist because I believe that wars are wrong, stupid, cruel, and unnecessary and that practically no progress will be made in human history until they are eliminated. But I do believe the history of the world since the World War has shown that failure to accept a common definition of what is aggression and common action in the event of aggression has led the world backward. I believe there is a slowly rising world conscience or standard of international morality, just as there is of personal morality, and that these standards must be recognized and strengthened by giving definite force to the public protest against action which transcends such protest even before it is crystallized into definite laws.[14]

She believed that the United States was particularly to blame for refusing to enter the World Court or the League of Nations, but that public conscience in the United States objected to the invasion of China, Ethiopia, and Spain and should be led in the direction of international law. Not a popular boycott, but sanctions by government were the best tool against the aggressor.

Emily Greene Balch shared this view with Mildred and with the international executive committee of WILPF, which had tried for some time to get the organization to go on record as supporting sanctions against the aggressor. Hannah Hull, president of the U.S. WILPF, opposed such selective, or discretionary, sanctions, and so did Dorothy Detzer, although Mildred claimed that Dorothy wobbled and was more internationally minded when she was abroad. The matter was continually debated at WILPF national board meetings, with the group favoring mandatory, or indiscriminate, sanctions invariably proving themselves to be in the majority.

Neutrality was also discussed at the international gatherings. Mildred attended the Ninth International Congress of WILPF, at Luhacovice, Czechoslovakia, in 1937, present as a consultative member with Gertrude Bussey. Bertha McNeill, an African-American WILPF member, traveled with her. Delegates heard about conditions in Spain, in India, and in China and passed a resolution condemning the execution of the Scottsboro boys. Dorothy Detzer tried to interpret the U.S. position on neutrality, which some of the impassioned European women called "saving your own skin." Finally the group hammered out a statement that called for a ban on arms sales to anyone.

> Though the Women's International League for Peace and Freedom believes it is unethical and unjust to treat both aggressor and victim alike and stands always for solidarity as against isolation, it does reiterate its firm and uncompromising stand against arming or financing either side, that is, against the shipments of munitions anywhere, at any time, to any state, but rather urges that every moral, diplomatic, political and economic means—except a food blockade—be applied to the aggressor.[15]

At this meeting Mildred Olmsted was chosen as a member of the international executive committee and placed on the committee for standards for national sections, and also on a committee to oversee the Maison Internationale, the lovely old house that served as headquarters of international WILPF in Geneva. She attended her first meeting of this group the following year.

By the time of the conference in Luhacovice, Hitler had moved into Austria and Czechoslovakia and Franco was triumphing in Spain. Mildred Olmsted was overwhelmed by the spirit of the women, many of whom had already lost everything they owned and would go home to face further loss or imprisonment. "Yet not one said she was in favor of military methods. The whole five days of discussion centered around peaceful means of fighting oppression, righting injustices." She came away more convinced than ever in the rightness of the international approach.[16]

Allen had been unable to accompany Mildred to Czechoslovakia in the summer of 1937, having decided to try to fulfill the ambition of a lifetime by running for judge on the Democratic ticket in Delaware County. (As Republicans outnumbered Democrats about ten to one, and the county was in the control of a corrupt Republican machine, he had little chance of winning. It was in fact remarkable that he lost by only forty-eight votes.) Ruth Mellor had come instead. In 1938, however, Allen accompanied Mildred abroad when she attended the international executive committee meetings in Geneva. Before attending the conference they had traveled together in Germany, taking a boat trip up the Rhine and walking in the Black Forest, then had crossed over to Austria.

The purpose of the trip was to make one more effort to get their marriage back on an even keel. They had quarreled throughout the spring. In April Mildred wrote to Allen to apologize for jumping all over him, and to say she was sorry when this happened. Yet a few weeks later she wrote him a letter so critical that he felt justified in a trip to Baltimore to visit Mary, with whom he had still not managed to break completely. Heartbroken, Mildred wrote to him that she was removing her ring. "Mary has been running through our lives for so many years I am persuaded that you will never give her up." Ruth said that she hated to see Mildred so limp and numb and once more advocated that Mildred try to forgive Allen and rebuild their marriage. A trip abroad for the traveling Olmsteds always helped.[17]

In addition, this time there was an exciting adventure to share. In Austria they had a mission. Mildred Olmsted had met the president's mother, Sarah Delano Roosevelt, when she visited Hyde Park to interview Franklin Roosevelt about his views on peace before the 1936 election. (She found his attitudes "much improved" from those of her 1932 interview.) Sarah Roosevelt had met the previous year an Austrian, Franz Rehrl, former governor of Salzburg, who had been imprisoned right after the Anschluss. He was said to be diabetic and in danger of dying in prison. Clara Ragaz, of International WILPF, learned about his situation and at Mildred's suggestion wrote Mrs. Roosevelt to say that a note from her could save his life. Given such a note by Sarah Roosevelt, Mildred and Allen were able to use it to see the prisoner. He did not look well to the Olmsteds. Later they learned that their visit had led to his release, but it was too late, and he died shortly after gaining his freedom.[18]

Outside Vienna they visited Yella Hertza, head of an agricultural school for delinquent girls. Yella was a WILPF stalwart who was determined to stay on in Austria despite the fact that she was Jewish. She sent a telegram to the international headquarters urging courage. "We were pioneers when we began our work, let us continue to be pioneers." Mildred brought back the names of several families Yella wanted placed in the United States. Later they heard that Yella herself had finally been forced to flee to England, where she spent the war.

While they were abroad, the Olmsteds learned that Allen's father had died, and Allen had to hurry back to Buffalo to look after his affairs. Mildred went on to the international executive committee meeting in Geneva, a gathering shadowed by the women's growing fear that Hitler really meant to go to war. The old Maison Internationale in which they met seemed to Mildred "an island of peace, intelligence, dignity and tolerance in a crazy world of violence." The women parted somberly, knowing that some of them would never meet again. Back in the United States Mildred plunged into work but took time out to record her impressions of the Geneva meeting for *Fellowship* magazine. She also gave a speech at the Philadelphia Council for World Peace on her reactions to the Munich settlement of 29 September. The agreement had resulted from the widespread pressure for a settlement of the crisis other than by war, she said.

> So this pressure for peaceful settlement cut, as it were, a new and worse channel. It created extra-legal and irresponsible international machinery at Munich which has set back standards of national and international behavior and illustrated the successful use of threats of violence. . . . The world needs international machinery which will work and the United States needs to take its share in developing that international machinery.[19]

The United States should cease harboring the illusion that it can be isolated, she said, and should define aggression and its actions toward the aggressor, whether unilateral or in cooperation with other nations. She suggested a mandatory wartime embargo on secondary munitions, providing for distinction between the aggressor and the victim, along with support for the World Court, the League of Nations, or its successor.

Her talk was published by the *American Friend* and reprinted by the Friends Peace Committee. She did not sign her name as organization secretary of WILPF, but as a private individual. The National Peace Conference asked if they could mail out the reprint as a moderate policy position. WILPF leadership may not have been too happy about this, but they were accustomed to Mildred's assertions of autonomy, and they did not try to stop her.

The issue of mandatory versus discretionary neutrality continued to plague the WILPF. The Bronx branch resigned as a body when it learned that certain members of the Chicago branch were advocating military sanctions against the aggressor. The Massachusetts branch issued its own statement advocating discretionary sanctions, as did the California branch. Individual WILPF members, many of them not pacifists, began to resign. Among these were a number of Jewish members who were becoming convinced that only force could stop Hitler's mistreatment of the Jewish people. The coalition that the WILPF had endeavored to establish between pacifists and women committed to peace for other reasons was beginning to unravel. Other peace organizations lost members too, as those who had considered themselves pacifists began to rethink the position as they endeavored to imagine nonviolent means of stopping the threat of Hitler. Because WILPF had never espoused a pacifist philosophy as such, it was vulnerable.[20]

Mildred Olmsted was by this time sure she was a pacifist. In the early days of the Spanish civil war she and Dorothy Detzer had debated what they would do in case of the outbreak of world war and a draft. Dorothy, who had a brother who had served in the armed services, said she was not quite sure what she would do when the moment of decision came. Mildred on the other hand declared that she would never fight; she would go to jail if necessary. At the same time she understood and could sympathize with Jewish members of WILPF who felt differently.[21]

At the national board meeting in January 1939 it was decided to conduct a national poll of WILPF opinion. The national office was to send out packets of materials, including two short statements by Emily Balch and Gertrude Bussey and two longer ones by Mildred Olmsted and Dorothy Detzer, presenting the "internationalist" and the "pro-neutrality" positions respectively. Local branches were supposed to discuss the materials and hold discussions before a vote was taken. A national committee was chosen to study the results.

In the paper that she prepared for the poll, Mildred Olmsted stressed the need for international machinery to substitute law for war. She compared the conduct of Italy in 1923, when its shelling of Corfu brought world opinion and the machinery of the League of Nations into play against it, and when it backed down and paid damages, to its unrestrained attack on Ethiopia in 1935, when it knew international machinery was not powerful enough to make a difference.

Many pacifists, Dorothy Detzer among them, were arguing that the differences between the violence practiced by Germany, Italy, and Japan against the Jews and subject peoples, and that practiced by Great Britain and France against their colonies, such as India and Indochina, were matters of degree, not kind, and that the United States ought to hold itself aloof from the Allies. They continued to press for mandatory neutrality, especially in the Far East.

Mildred argued that this point of view overlooked the need to establishing law as a prerequisite of justice. Saying that no nation without a clean record should take part in restraining another also overlooked the possibility of progress. "If one reasoned always from the past, there could be no progress in the world. There was always slavery, polygamy, dueling etc., etc., until public conscience, grounded in a changing social system, rose against it."

And public conscience now is slowly but surely rising against the method of war and the more flagrant forms of international violence. . . . To stop this impulse, to tell people they must be completely neutral as between Italy and Ethiopia, Germany and Czechoslovakia, Japan and China, and to urge

their governments to be completely neutral because this does
not concern them . . . is to suppress—instead of to encourage—this growing social conscience and awareness of evolving standards of behavior in international conduct.[22]

Another argument used by many pacifists at this time was
that if the United States joined the war, it would undoubtedly
become fascist itself. The book by Sinclair Lewis, *It Can't Happen
Here*, describing how the United States might become a total-
itarian state, was widely read and quoted. Mildred argued that it
was possible to dethrone fascism and preserve democracy by employing the methods that Gandhi had developed in the struggle
for Indian independence, using nonviolence and noncooperation as
potent methods to fight fascism abroad, and fascist-type regimes if
they arose in this country. This point of view, a forerunner of the
concept of nonviolent civil defense, was just beginning to be discussed by a small circle of pioneer pacifists. Mildred Olmsted,
who was at the time the chair of a Freedom for India committee in
Philadelphia, was far ahead of her time.

The poll results were reported to the national board meeting
in May in Washington. Those for mandatory neutrality won, 714
to 244. Mildred, who believed passionately in the WILPF concept
of "pooled intelligence," took the defeat with grace, although she
urged that the international conference be held in the United
States in 1940, believing that her countrywomen were out of
touch with the feelings of the European members of WILPF. The
results reflected the dominant U.S. pacifist position at the time,
and she may have felt that her fellow American pacifists would
also benefit from a visit from colleagues abroad.

The signing of the Ribbentrop-Molotov Treaty between Germany and Russia in August and the subsequent seizure of Danzig
by the Nazis brought the Allies to a declaration of war on 3 September. Ten days later the WILPF executive board met in an
emergency session. Mildred, with her usual back-to-the-wall optimism, said she saw challenge in the coming of war and made a
long list of things that peacemakers might do to turn adversity
into opportunity: study war propaganda, promote tolerance, expand civil liberties, bring war refugees to this country, protest war

profiteering, support conscientious objectors, and talk in neighborhood meetings about the need for a new kind of world government. She also wrote to the National Peace Conference that the coming of war in Europe had increased her determination to work for peace.

> I'm just back from vacation deep in the Canadian woods and what a world awaits me! Isn't it horrible? . . . It seems as though the outbreak of war might give a new slant and a greater urgency toward harmony. It has rather changed my point of view about accepting the chairmanship of the NPC Field Committee. My first impulse was to say, no, that I was too involved but under the changed circumstances, I feel I must accept.[23]

In the peace movement in general the coming of war to Europe increased the frenzy to keep America uninvolved, and some of the pacifist organizations were not above working with the isolationists in this cause. Mildred, however, kept to her point of view that the achievement of international law demanded international action, even though it was becoming increasingly hard to see what form such action could take, short of military measures. Although she had the backing of Emily Greene Balch, she felt isolated in her position. As she wrote Gertrude Baer in November 1939, she believed that Dorothy Detzer was taking advantage of the situation to reduce Mildred's authority in WILPF.

> I think you have heard something of how difficult she has been this past winter; and in the spring with the retirement of Mrs. Hull and the coming in of Dr. Bussey, who leaves everything to her, she saw an opportunity to have entire control of the WIL. When the majority vote of the Annual Meeting supported her position on neutrality as against mine, which was that of the International, she tried to have it clearly established that all my work was to be made subordinate to her. In fact, I think she tried very hard indeed to make me symbolize to the whole WIL that viewpoint, and therefore the large vote in favor of neutrality position by the United States Section a vindication for her and a defeat for her (*sic*) . . . of course I offered my resignation and stood pat

on that because I would not lose my complete liberty of action . . . she decided to drop her position and let everything go on "as before."[24]

Mildred Olmsted said that Dorothy Detzer always responded strongly to human appeal, and that as Dorothy was going to be at the Geneva meetings she hoped that Gertrude Baer would see that she met as many of the delegates from wartorn countries as possible, and that she had a chance to understand their situation; Mildred hoped that this would bring Dorothy to a more internationalist point of view.

Dorothy Detzer, however, did not change her view, and the rift between the two women widened. Mildred had no luck in reversing the decision of the board to cut her down to one-fourth time and no longer to support any fieldwork on the national level. She decided to use the money she had been paid to commute to hire a part-time secretary, and she moved her national organization work back to her Philadelphia office in the spring of 1940. An interested board member, Grace Rhoads, volunteered to serve as her unpaid assistant. Now more than ever WILPF needed to build organization, Mildred thought, as the war clouds darkened.

Yet in the midst of all this turmoil, she was still able to inspire the women of WILPF with a vision of their mission in war as well as in peace. She spoke especially eloquently at the annual meeting in May 1940:

> Our role is to offer leadership based on the welfare of all human beings . . . for those who are pushed about against their will, who are always victims of war and victims of peace—that is the meaning of our name Peace *and* Freedom. That work is ours whether this country goes to war or not. The same impulse which gave us birth in a period of war, should carry us through this period of war again. The need is not less because of the war, but greater. It is a fundamental cause in which we work—we are the heirs of the spiritual pioneers of all ages past. It is we who must keep their work for minorities, for political freedom, growing and transmit it a little larger to those who come after us. This is the cause which may be dimmed but cannot fail if civilization is to progress. The year ahead may offer terrific obstacles, but

those who have courage and vision and yearning for a better world, will keep on working harder than before, seeing in this failure of the world to avoid this fresh war, the truth of the rightness and the practical worth of their ideals. We must go on—we cannot give up.[25]

11

Peace Work in Wartime

*A*s the war in Europe heated up in the spring of 1940
and Germany invaded Belgium, the Netherlands, and Norway,
Mildred Olmsted's heart sank. She wanted Hitler stopped, but
stopped by nonviolent means, by the use of sanctions and the
outcry of world opinion. She had little sympathy with the American isolationists who declared that the United States had no quarrel with Germany and must protect itself from entanglements
abroad at all costs. Yet she shared with fellow pacifists the conviction that if the United States became a belligerent, it would run
the risk of losing its freedoms and of becoming a fascist state
itself. Bad means could not produce good ends, and militarism
itself would be the victor.

In April 1940 a group of avowed isolationists, including
Charles Lindbergh and Robert McCormick of the Chicago *Tribune,*
formed the America First committee, a nationwide coalition determined to protest, picket, and parade for their cause. Pacifists were
divided about cooperating with America First, which did not share
their aversion to all war and which included some fascist sympa-
thizers and anti-Semites, including the notorious Detroit priest,
Father Charles Coughlin. Fred Libby of the National Council for
Prevention of War argued that Coughlin did not convert people to
anti-Semitism but simply served as their voice, and that many
people opposed the war from a variety of strong prejudices. Other
pacifists were more squeamish. While both Mildred Olmsted and
Dorothy Detzer were eager that Lindbergh's ideas get a hearing,
Mildred worried that the Philadelphia branch of America First was

under poor leadership, and that cooperating with the isolationists would dilute the pacifist message.

The WILPF had been lobbying the U.S. State Department since 1938 to expedite the immigration of Jewish refugees from Hitler. The processing of individual refugees in U.S. consulates abroad was maddeningly slow, and yet the WILPF knew that the State Department had turned down an offer from the American Friends Service Committee of volunteers fluent in German to help expedite the backlog of applications. Some people believed that the State Department was dragging its feet in part because of the waves of anti-Semitism enveloping the country.

The U.S. WILPF now developed a national committee to combat anti-Semitism as well as to help expedite the placement of individual Jewish refugees in the United States. Gertrude Baer worked on refugee problems from Geneva until June 1940, when she came to the United States for the duration of the war to represent the international WILPF at the Economic Section of the League of Nations, now in Princeton. Emily Greene Balch also put major effort into the placement of refugees, and a staff person, Eva Wigelmesser, herself a refugee, was hired by the national office to help with the placements. Allen Olmsted provided legal back-up for this work, and the Olmsteds themselves agreed to sponsor two families, the Unterleitners and the Brings, both of whom came to the United States in the fall of 1939 and stayed with the Olmsteds in Rose Valley before settling elsewhere.[1]

Gertrude Baer also stayed in Rose Valley, but despite Mildred Olmsted's best efforts, she remained suspicious of Mildred. She had not forgotten Mildred's telephone call when she suffered a breakdown in Pittsburgh while traveling in the United States in 1937, and she had unfortunately seen a letter that Mildred had written to Emily Greene Balch, mentioning that Mildred considered Gertrude to be difficult. Mildred Olmsted, as a member of the international executive committee, was appointed to an advisory council to help Gertrude Baer carry on the work of international WILPF during the war, but this relationship led to further friction. Mildred was critical of the way Gertrude managed funds, and Gertrude felt that Mildred's office invariably failed to forward her mail or to mail out her materials. When Mildred sent Gertrude a housecoat as a Christmas present in 1941, Gertrude sent it back because it was too small and because she felt that it was wrong to "manifest signs of friendship until we smoke our personal peace pipe." She was returning it, she said, until "old age has brought slimming and peace, the polishing of our edges of conviction."[2]

In addition to placing as many refugees as possible and combating anti-Semitism, WILPF was concerned with the growing erosion of civil liberties in the months following the outbreak of the war in Europe. A wave of superpatriotism and preparations for a compulsory military draft were tightening the noose around freedom of expression. Mildred's ties to ACLU through Allen, plus her own deep personal concerns about liberty, led her to urge the Pennsylvania branch of WILPF to take a strong stand in support of Jehovah's Witnesses who were being prosecuted throughout the country because of their religious objection to saluting the flag. Parents of children refusing to salute at school were jailed in this period, and the Witnesses also suffered mob violence. She was concerned as well about the passage of the Alien Registration or Smith Act, in June 1940, making it unlawful for any person to advocate or teach the overthrow of the government in the United States by the use of force, an act designed to persecute so-called subversives.

Mildred Olmsted found herself involved in a civil liberties problem of her own. She had been appointed in early 1940 to the board of the Pennsylvania state branch of the National Youth Administration, one of Roosevelt's New Deal efforts. Mildred was interested in making sure that NYA not be used to train youth for national defense and expressed herself frequently on this matter. She made several trips to visit NYA centers and as a routine matter submitted her travel expenses to the NYA office.

It was then she learned that she had to sign both an oath of allegiance and a citizenship affidavit form in order to be eligible to receive recompense for her travels. Mildred Olmsted wrote back that she was delighted to sign the citizenship affidavit, as both her ancestors and Allen's were prerevolutionary, but that she had conscientious scruples against signing the oath, "as I consider all such procedures a step away from our democratic conditions." She suggested she be sent the modified oath issued by the State Department for conscientious objectors.[3]

Officials at NYA could find no such provision for exemption, and Mildred Olmsted, always delighted to fight, wrote to Carroll Miller, a Democrat who was state chair of the NYA, saying she was prepared to carry the issue to the courts if necessary. Roger Baldwin told her that she was probably out of luck, but she persisted and next wrote about her problem to Emma Guffey Miller, a Pennsylvania representative at the Democratic National Convention. Emma Miller talked to Aubrey Williams, the executive director of NYA, who found a loophole in the law under which Mildred Olmsted might be exempted from the oath. Mildred continued to serve on the state board, as well as that of one local center, for another year, and she liked to say she had made the case for refusing to take the oath.

Those concerned about civil liberties in 1940 were discussing provisions for conscientious objectors if war came. Many of the men and women of Mildred Olmsted's acquaintance had suffered from the violations of the rights of objectors during World War I, and some had joined in developing the ACLU as a result. They were determined to prepare for better treatment of objectors should a second world war come. Shortly after the war in Europe began in the fall of 1939 WILPF set up a committee to advise conscientious objectors of their rights in the event of war. Working with the ACLU they published a pamphlet addressed to the potential problems of COs. After the passage of the conscription act in 1940, they began to offer counseling to COs and were involved in the case of two young ministers, Lloyd Schear and Jim Bristol, who had refused to register on conscientious grounds.

Just as the women of WILPF had feared, the idea of a universal military draft began to be discussed in the spring of 1940, and by the summer the Burke-Wadsworth bill was being debated in Congress. To Mildred Olmsted, the concept of conscription was anathema. Even if she were not a pacifist, she would have opposed the idea of the government's taking possession of a person's liberty. From conscription, she was sure, it would be only a small step to the totalitarianism rampant in Europe. She went to the hearing of the Senate Military Affairs Committee when it was debating Burke-Wadsworth in July, and she urged Dorothy Hommel, a New York WILPF member, to get into the anticonscription fight. "I am amazed at the inability of peace people to see that the passing of a conscription bill would do away with those fundamentals of our democratic government which keep us from becoming a kind of totalitarianism. So many of them are muddled on the question of service and training and American defense that they do not see that it would shut up those who actively criticize the government."[4]

She also could not understand why ordinary people were willing to accept conscription so supinely. "I have often wondered why it is that a family which would make a great protest if the government took away their automobile or even their dog, says nothing when the government takes away their sons."[5]

Her colleague Emily Greene Balch was reported to be wavering on the question of supporting conscription. Some of the international officers of WILPF were coming to the conclusion that only force could stop Hitler, and Emily Balch found herself deeply torn between pacifism and her loyalties to internationalism. When Mildred wrote to inquire about Emily's position on the Burke-Wadsworth bill, Emily wrote a tortured letter saying that it would be a serious responsibility not to have men trained when war came, "as every one of us would prefer not to see the United States defeated." Although personally opposed to conscription to military service, she said, she felt "a hesitation in agitating against requiring men of military age to undergo training" and added that she thought it was quite possible for Hitler to invade the United States. Yet she was really against the draft.[6]

Mildred Olmsted's opposition to conscription was absolute and colored her attitudes toward politics in the summer of 1940. The fact that Franklin Roosevelt, whom she had twice interviewed, whose wife she knew well, who had been at Harvard at the same time as Allen, was now leading the country into closer and closer ties with the Allies and was promoting conscription was more than she could forgive. He had betrayed her, as her father had betrayed her so many years ago, and as Allen seemed to her to betray her when he was not "loyal," when he did not support her or manifested an interest in someone else. When Wendell Wilkie was nominated to the presidency on the Republican party ticket and began to talk about his One World ideas, she determined to vote for him.

Allen had meanwhile entered Delaware County Democratic politics, during his unsuccessful run for judgeship, and was elected as a delegate to the Democratic National Convention in Chicago. Moreover he had persuaded Mildred's sister, Adele Saul, who had been active in Democratic politics since her year in France, to run for Congress in the 1940 fall election on the Democratic ticket. Mildred's decision to support Wilkie was incomprehensible to him. If she could not support Roosevelt out of family solidarity, then why didn't she vote for their old friend Norman Thomas?

The disagreement surfaced on their way home from Wyoming, where they had gone with Peter and Enid on a camping trip, leaving Tony in a summer camp. Why should they both not discuss these matters together before making up their minds? Allen suggested. They might disagree, but at least they would understand each other's reasons. But she wanted to shut him out from her reasoning process, he charged. "If you should become a numerologist or vote for Wilkie because he was born under Aries that would be within your rights and a freedom of action which I concede, but I would lose my respect for you and your political views, and would have to reconstruct my whole attitude toward you, consider you a child, or just another silly woman."[7]

In this same conversation on the train home, Mildred had spoken of her determination not to sign the loyalty oath, and to go to jail if necessary because of her opposition to conscription. Allen pointed out that this decision would affect him and the children and ought to be approached jointly. "The prospect of parting company with so many friends, of taking the gaff, of losing position, work opportunity, as father did, is hard enough in any event, facing it without you is terrifying."[8]

The quarrel lingered on. Mildred wrote Allen from the Jersey shore, where she went with Peter and Enid, to accuse him of being bored with her work and of not being able to sense her needs as Ruth did, "which made our honeymoon camping so unsatisfactory." She was traveling for WILPF in October, and Allen sent her a telegram on the anniversary of their engagement. She wrote back

15. Mildred Scott Olmsted, 1950. *Courtesy of Olmsted Papers.*

to say she still thought they were fortunate. "Why do we let petty friction separate us? I feel frightened when I try to picture life without you. I am glad I made my decision, except when you treat me indifferently, stand me up, ignore me or try to bully me." On their wedding anniversary Allen wrote to lament their inability to get along. "I spend my time trying to settle disputes between citizens according to rules and reason, and I cannot settle disputes in my own family. You devote yourself to peace among nations and races and cannot keep the peace in your own home."[9] Finally they achieved an uneasy peace.

Mildred Olmsted was not very well at this time. Climbing in Wyoming she had suddenly become dizzy and out of breath. Her doctor suspected it might be her heart, but the diagnosis at this point was inconclusive. She was also suffering with stomach pains that might be the product of an ulcer. But she was determined to return to the fight against conscription, and she was back at her desk in the middle of August, corresponding with the national office as well as with the branches about keeping up the pressure on Congress. In early September she spent some days in Washington, lobbying against the Burke-Wadsworth bill.

It was soon evident, however, that the campaign was in vain. The bill was signed into law on 16 September, and a national draft lottery begun on 29 October. At the October meeting of the Pennsylvania executive board, Mildred Olmsted announced days of mourning for the passage of conscription but said she felt the WILPF should be prepared to do battle against the extension of the draft to any other group in the population. When one member suggested that women be added to draft boards, she argued that this would defeat WILPF's whole position opposing conscription. Instead, women who shared the conscientious objection sentiments of their brothers or fathers or husbands should be allowed, if they wished, to *volunteer* for alternative service. WILPF set up a camp at High Acres Farm in West Chester in the summer of 1941 and recruited young women for community service in West Chester and Media.

As young men began to be called up for the draft, a few prominent women argued that women ought to be drafted too. One of these was WILPF's old friend, Eleanor Roosevelt. Dorothy Robinson, a board member, wrote her expressing WILPF's opposition and asking for an opportunity to meet with her. Eleanor Roosevelt responded that she was too busy to meet, and she suggested that WILPF look at the NYA as a good example of communities providing job training for youth. Mildred Olmsted hastened to draft a response, praising NYA but pointing out that its success came from its voluntary nature. "After all, those who go into community work unwillingly learn little and contribute less to their fellow men, indeed may even spread resentment to other youth and to their own families and friends. If we are to prepare young people to become good citizens and to make democracy their way of life, conscription is an inappropriate starting point and a poor substitute for willing service."[10]

The specter of women being drafted began to haunt Mildred Olmsted. The thought of men exercising authority over women, telling them either that they must go to work in war industry or that they must stay home with their small children, was a frightening one to her, and she continually raised it at WILPF board meetings. Dorothy Detzer did not share this fear, thinking that the chances of women actually being drafted were minimal; she was slow, Mildred Olmsted felt, to watch for opportunities to lobby against this possible extension of conscription. It was one of many causes for the growing distance between them.

The WILPF itself was torn by dissent in 1941. In January Drew Pearson published an item in the "Washington Merry-Go-Round" claiming that Emily Greene Balch was resigning from WILPF because of Dorothy Detzer's isolationist stand. The WILPF promptly corrected the statement. Balch had not resigned but only offered to, if WILPF felt her desire to aid Britain was an embarrassment to the organization. "We said no indeed because the WILPF is certainly big enough to have many viewpoints on all questions except our objectives," Mildred Olmsted wrote to explain the situation to a branch member.[11]

But there were many members like Emily Greene Balch who felt themselves emotionally drawn into the struggle on the side of the Allies. The German attack on the USSR in June 1941 caused many of the more politically radical members to support the war effort. Others were annoyed that WILPF could not unite on a more forceful antiwar position. The lack of the singleness of purpose that had been one of the strengths of WILPF proved now a weakness. "We are divided by those who support the war in their hearts and those who disapprove," Mildred Olmsted wrote to Dorothy Robinson. "I'm afraid WIL will not take a strong stand."[12]

The attack of the Japanese on the American ships at Pearl Harbor on 7 December 1941, and the consequent declaration of war by the United States, aggravated the situation within the WILPF. Although the board immediately met in an emergency session, its members could not agree on a strong statement. Some WILPF members who were not pacifists could not understand why WILPF would not now support the war; others, in agreement with Mildred Olmsted, felt that the war called on them for additional efforts to safeguard civil liberties and work against the inroads of militarism.

Mildred Olmsted was outraged by the compromising statement WIL issued. She wrote to a WIL friend that she thought it ought to be submitted to every member of the national executive committee. "Too many peace organizations' statements are distressingly weak. With our grand record behind us, I cannot bear to have us issue something unworthy in this crisis."[13]

Indeed the large peace organizations were folding fast. Pearl Harbor brought an end to Keep America Out of War and to America First. Norman Thomas led a small group of interventionists in giving "highly critical support to the war" and establishing a Post War World Council to look toward a durable peace. Only the genuinely pacifist groups—the American Friends Service Committee, the Fellowship of Reconciliation, and the War Resisters International—actually gained membership, support, or both during the war years.

With its divided views on the war, the WILPF did not fare well. Members resigned and branches collapsed all over the organization. Mildred Olmsted's organization report at the annual meetings gave a picture of a dramatically shrinking organization; in 1941 she announced that of fourteen organized states five were in danger of collapsing and of 118 local groups in Pennsylvania, 30 were all but folded. By 1943 she was willing to admit that sixty branches had folded, and in 1944 that membership had shrunk from 14,000 to 4,708 members. The following year it had fallen still further, to 3,789. Only Mildred Olmsted could give these reports and still radiate enthusiasm for the future. In 1941 she spoke of the inspiration of faithful members. "The thing that gives me courage to go on is the large number of our members who, in spite of all difficulties, are showing the courage, self sacrifice, endurance and ingenuity to carry on at any cost. To my mind they are more heroic than any military heroine and we must support them and hold them together no matter what."[14] And in 1943 she praised the faithful few who came to meetings, "even if the baby has the measles, there is a leak in the roof or their husband has a business trip or their child has a cough or the house needs cleaning. (The most frequent reason given—and they believe it is a reason—is a son in camp or in the army.) With members like these, in the end we cannot fail."[15]

Privately however, Mildred Olmsted continued to feel that the decline in members was at least partly to be blamed on the attitude of Dorothy Detzer and Catherine Fitzgibbon (who had since left the organization), and of those members of the board who sided with them in cutting Mildred's work out of the budget and sending her back to Pennsylvania. She felt aggrieved and misunderstood, particularly by Gertrude Bussey, who served as president from May 1939 to May 1941 and as first vice-president thereafter. In June 1942 Mildred wrote to Dorothy Robinson, the new president, responding to a request that she take a month's vacation at her own expense again this year. She had done this frequently of her own free will before, but she felt that it was unfair to expect it of her, especially since WILPF owed her a great deal of money on her expense account. Also WILPF had given a salary raise to Eva Wigelmesser, who did not have the experience or the background Mildred did, while Mildred herself was still being paid only $100 a year more than when she had first come to WILPF in 1922.

Dorothy Robinson passed Mildred Olmsted's letter on to Gertrude Bussey, who wrote defensively, apologizing for her inability as finance chair to raise enough money to pay Mildred's expense account or to raise her salary. On the other hand, she pointed out, Mildred's was the highest salary that WILPF paid (Dorothy Detzer's salary was entirely paid by one wealthy donor), and other employees also deserved raises.

Mildred Olmsted felt the letter reflected the fact that Gertrude Bussey and others did not appreciate the contribution she had made to WILPF.

> I suppose I should not be so constantly surprised and hurt as
> I am that you and other new people in the WIL value so little
> what I have done for it. After all, how could you even know,

not having seen me struggle through one crisis after another—against the disintegrating forces that would have destroyed it entirely. How could you who know it only in its
present pattern realize how greatly that pattern is my creation. That is the price, I suppose, of having worked indi-
rectly and inconspicuously, even though constantly. You new
ones cannot realize the value that comes to WIL from having
at least one person on the staff who has served intimately on
WIL local, state, national and international inner circles and
helped to steady it and protect it from the weaknesses produced by too brilliant personalities, too different tempera-
ments. You have not lived through the efforts I made to save
Dorothy for the WIL when her opponents rallied to throw
her out and very nearly succeeded, and also to save the WIL
from the effects of her foolishness and egotism. . . .

. . . The WIL would have been dead before this if it had
not been for my work (And perhaps the time has come when
it could get along without me, but I think, being as imper-
sonal as possible, the time is not yet.)[16]

At a conference of top WILPF executives at Bryn Mawr, Mildred Olmsted's grievances were addressed, and an uneasy truce was
achieved between the Washington and Philadelphia offices. But
there was a lot of petty bickering between the two groups, and
board members became divided into a Detzer camp, with strong
support from the Baltimore branch, and an Olmsted camp, with
support in Philadelphia and New York. (As WILPF permitted
staff members to serve on the board, both Mildred and Dorothy
were members.) Staff members also lined up, and one of Mildred's
assistants moved to Washington in order to work for Dorothy Detzer. Mildred Olmsted's outspoken pacifism and efforts to influence
WILPF policy in the direction of taking a strong antiwar stand
were believed by some to be a factor in the split. Gertrude Bussey
in particular did not share her views and thought that WILPF
should be open to a range of beliefs on the peace issue. In the
organization letter Mildred Olmsted wrote to branches, she frequently expressed herself on policy issues or she attached statements on the war with which she happened to agree, including
one by Allen Olmsted. Some WILPF members saw these practices

as ways of her using her position to seek to exert undue influence on the policies of the organization.

Mildred Olmsted had an ally at this time in Elsie Elfenbein of the New Jersey WILPF, who was the chair of the organization committee as well as a strong pacifist. Elsie was the president of the National Council of Jewish Women and could speak on the issues of war and peace without being thought anti-Semitic. She worked briefly for the WILPF in Washington, then went to work for Norman Thomas's Post War World Council. The two corresponded about WILPF's internal problems, as well as their growing concern for the warlike attitudes of the country.

Perhaps to give Mildred Olmsted a sense that she was appreciated, Pennsylvania WILPF gave her a birthday luncheon in December to honor her twenty years of service. Hannah Hull, who was too ill to attend, wrote a note of regret, praising Mildred for her enthusiasm and for her role as comforter and gentle leader as well as "the *driver* when the occasion calls for it. But she is not always meek and mild, oh no—not in Board meetings when she has a vision of her own which the rest of us have not seen . . . but one of the very nicest things about Mildred is that no matter how difficult a thing she asks of us, she never asks us to do one thing she would not willingly do herself twice as difficult . . . that is why we love her so, and enjoy working for her."[17]

Bessie Kind, a longtime Pennsylvania board member, wrote for the occasion a fanciful send-up of Mildred Olmsted's typical report to the board in which she captured Mildred's fondness for exaggeration and her imperial manner. "I addressed the Alliance Française, which had become quite militaristic and nationalistic until I explained *La Ligue Pour La Paix et La Liberte*. I had the most wonderful conference with the young Poles. They don't understand English but they were all stimulated." Mildred laughed as heartily as the others.[18]

Throughout 1942 there were rumors that legislation to demand registration of workers and of women was being considered, and by late fall of 1942 such legislation was being drafted. The resulting Austin-Wadsworth bill, introduced into Congress in early 1943, called for the registration of every man between the ages of 18 and 65 and of every woman between the ages of 18 and

16. National Board Meeting, U.S. Section, WILPF, Milwaukee, 1941.
Left to right: Gertrude Bussey, Mildred Scott Olmsted, Dorothy Robinson, Annalee Stewart. *Courtesy of Swarthmore College Peace Collection.*

50, with the understanding that, except for those women with children under twelve, all might be directed to war work.

The leaders of the WILPF, A. J. Muste of the Fellowship of Reconciliation, and representatives of other peace organizations thought it might be possible to bring the targeted groups into a campaign against the extension of conscription, whether they were pacifists or indeed objected to conscription as such. Women seemed the most likely group to respond. In December 1942 the WILPF convened a planning group at the old Broadway Tabernacle in New York City, scene of some of the riotous women's rights gatherings in the nineteenth century. As a result, in January 1943, a group of women church leaders, as well as many from WILPF, gathered at the tabernacle to organize the Committee to Oppose the Conscription of Women (COCW). Frances Knight

Chalmers and Katherine Pierce were made cochairs; A. J. Muste, treasurer; and Grace Rhoads, secretary. Mildred Olmsted was to serve as director, fitting her job into her other duties for national and Pennsylvania WILPF, with a full-time assistant, Marjorie Littel Himes. When Himes became ill, the wife of a CO, Eleanor Garst, became Mildred's trusted assistant.

The COCW set to work immediately, developing literature and circulating to many religious and women's organizations an appeal to join. They also sent Betty Jacob, Mildred Olmsted's old associate, as a lobbyist to Washington to oppose Austin-Wadsworth. Mildred called Dorothy's office to announce Betty's coming and also to ask that the national WILPF office mail out the first COCW mailing to its membership, just as the FOR was doing. On reaching Washington, however, Betty Jacob was told by Dorothy Detzer and two other peace lobbyists that she ought to leave the work to them, and that if COCW wanted to make a mailing to the WILPF list, they should pay for it.

Mildred Olmsted wrote to Dorothy Robinson to protest, reminding her that she had been reluctant to take the job of director of COCW, as the WILPF executive committee had suggested at the December meeting, because she feared this sort of conflict with Dorothy Detzer. Dorothy Robinson had told Mildred to go ahead, and she would back her up. Mildred thought the time for the backing up had come.[19]

Dorothy Robinson supported Mildred Olmsted as she had promised, and Mildred proceeded to arrange for a series of women to appear before the Senate Military Affairs Committee, including representatives of the Student Christian Movement, the Methodist church, the Presbyterian church, and the International Ladies' Garment Workers Union as well as WILPF members. Dorothy Detzer did not like this lobbying without her imput, and at the June executive committee she brought forward a motion that no WILPF members ought to lobby in Washington except through her. The secretary taking the minutes wrote that this had been agreed to, although in fact no resolution was reached. Dorothy Robinson sent out a correction to the minutes on this important issue but said that Dorothy Detzer intended to bring it up in September. Mildred Olmsted was angry.

I'm not surprised she wanted to bring it up again in September. I think I know and understand Dorothy personally better than any other member of the Board, and I believe we are kidding ourselves if we take that to mean that it is not going to come up again and again and again in one form or another. She is really out to gag or eliminate me as she did Mabel. And she will only bide her time until a propitious moment appears.

The real reason is that she feels that my activity is a threat to her because it shows up the things she does not do; and therefore it gives her a feeling of guilt which she wants to get rid of. She does not have to be afraid of me. I am personally fond of her and do not want her job. She believed that until Catherine Fitzgibbon started her on the other idea. Now when any recognition is given me by other groups, instead of taking it as a compliment to the WIL as a whole, she takes it as a reflection on her authority.[20]

Despite Mildred Olmsted's dire predictions, Dorothy evidently backed down, for the COCW continued to lobby in Washington throughout the war. After the Austin-Wadsworth bill was withdrawn, the committee opposed the Gurney-Wadsworth bill, which called for peacetime conscription, and the May bill, which advocated a year of compulsory military service after the war. Because neither of these bills specified the drafting of women, COCW changed its name to the Women's Committee to Oppose Conscription in the fall of 1944.

WCOC's longest and most successful campaign was against the bill to draft nurses, introduced into Congress in March 1945. Annalee Stewart, a Methodist minister, lobbied for the committee in Washington before the House and Senate Military Affairs Committee and joined with nurses' organizations in circulating petitions. With the help of a representative of the WCTU she was able to compile accurate figures from the nurses showing that African-American nurses were underused and that 56,500 nurses were already in service, very close to the 60,000 that the army said it needed. Mildred Olmsted joined in the final round of lobbying, taking with her a young neighbor who was the wife of a serviceman, as well as a letter her nurse friend Trudy Rhoads Prichard had written. The bill was defeated, and credit was given to the WILPF for its prompt and accurate presentation of the figures. Years afterwards Mildred Olmsted would say that the defeat of the nurses' draft ranked with WILPF's work in the 1920s when it joined with other peace groups in preventing war with Mexico as one of U.S. WILPF's two most significant victories.

Throughout the lifetime of the WCOC, the women used publicity as a potent tool. Georgia Harkness of the Garrett Biblical Institute in Chicago wrote an article that appeared in the *Christian Advocate* and that was widely reprinted. Frances Witherspoon and Tracy Mygatt, two veteran suffragists and founders of the War Resisters League, wrote pamphlets, as did Betty Jacob. Mildred Olmsted herself wrote a response to an editorial by Max Lerner in *PM* calling for the draft of women. She also wrote an article for *Four Lights,* the newly initiated periodical of WILPF, and appeared on "Town Meeting of the Air" in February 1944 to respond to the question, "Should women be drafted for service with the armed forces?"

In her reply to Max Lerner, which she drafted while on a bicycle trip of Nantucket and Martha's Vineyard with Ruth Mellor, Mildred Olmsted expressed her own deeply held belief in personal freedom for women.

> Your telegram has finally caught up with me appropriately enough in Nantucket, where the movement for the abolition of slavery began. Women have not fought for and won their right to be free from the dictation of their fathers and husbands as to when and where and how they may work only to turn it over to their neighbors. I regret to learn that Mr. Lerner, who is often a liberal, has joined hands with those reactionaries who would require all women with children to remain at home and allow no women without children to do so. Labels do not create causes but they often confuse them. Women cannot be persuaded that labeling such legislation "equality" will alter the fact that it is a return by an indirect route to the old bondage from which they have so recently freed themselves. Nor will the statement that they would have to accept it from Hitler make them welcome it from Roosevelt. This war for freedom is being fought on two

fronts, domestic and foreign. Women are peculiarly responsible for the home front. Married or unmarried they must be free to choose where they will serve.[21]

In her prepared remarks for "Town Meeting of the Air" the following February, Mildred Olmsted repeated her statement that women had fought for years against the domination of men and were not likely now to accept it, when so many traditional barriers to their advancement were breaking down. Women did not like regimentation, she said, and were enjoying their present opportunities to become economically independent and to take jobs previously held by men. Yet she also argued, somewhat in contradiction, that women were the homemakers, who played their part by keeping the home fires burning, and were needed to hold their communities together and to prevent juvenile delinquency.[22]

Not all WILPF members had been unanimous in their support of WCOC. Katherine Blake, a suffragist and WILPF founder, thought working for exemption for women violated the feminism of the organization's foremothers. Several other women wrote to Mildred Olmsted to express the view that concentrating on women's own role was selfish. Mildred argued that women should seek no special treatment as women, but that the extension of conscription to another group was the issue at stake. WCOC sometimes slipped into using antifeminist language, however, in their efforts to entice more conservative members, and particularly officials of the Catholic church, into backing their crusade.

This strategy led to their receiving support at first from some very right-wing elements. One potential donor was a rabid Roosevelt hater and America Firster; and Dorothy Day, of the *Catholic Worker,* who worked closely with the committee, reported that an audience she had been invited to address turned out to be virulently anti-Semitic. Mildred Olmsted and her colleagues were uncomfortable with such bedfellows and glad when the change of name brought the emphasis back to opposition to conscription. On the other hand, they believed they would still be able to get support from some religious groups by emphasizing a traditional view of woman's role. This may account for the fact that Mildred Olmsted mixed her arguments, and that some of the early literature of the committee, such as the pamphlet put out by veteran suffragist and feminist Tracy Mygatt, "Keep the Home Fires Burning," played on a conservative view of women's role that Mygatt herself had long ago rejected.

WCOC continued to meet irregularly after the war, concerned with the threat of peacetime conscription. It held its final meeting in February 1947, although Annalee Stewart lobbied in its name against a peacetime draft in 1948.

WCOC was only one of the committees on which Mildred Olmsted served during the war years. In April 1943 she resigned from four of the eleven affiliated organizations with which she worked as WILPF's representative, but she continued with the National Peace Conference; the United Peace Chest, a united fund approach to raising money for peace in Philadelphia; the Post War World Council; the Peace Strategy Board; the Council for Civilian Service; the Philadelphia Council for World Peace; and the Pacifist Research Bureau. The latter was an organization she had helped to form in 1942 to do scholarly research on peace subjects. Harrop Freeman, a young lawyer, was its staff, with office space in the same building as WILPF. Harrop and his wife, Ruth, and their children spent their first summer in the Philadelphia area living in a building of the School in Rose Valley, and they became fast friends with the Olmsteds.

On all these committees, Mildred Olmsted was known as a clear thinker and keen strategist. In groups made up of pacifists and nonpacifists, she was always at work to strengthen the pacifist component. A. J. Muste in particular cherished her long-range vision. In 1945 he wrote that he was distressed that she could not attend a planning meeting of the Joint Peace Board. "Mildred is always exceptionally useful in helping us to plan activities." Her ability to set aside her own agenda and to think for the group was remarkable, he thought. It was Mildred at her best, bringing to the national arena the skills of networking and of building loyalty, skills developed in herself and others by the long years of working with women for peace—WILPF's special contribution to the peace movement.[23]

She was still executive secretary for Pennsylvania WILPF throughout the war years. A major commitment of time for this group went into the operation of a hostel for Japanese Americans being relocated from the concentration camps of the West to eastern cities. WILPF had protested their confinement originally and had suggested that all branches develop programs that helped with relocation. The Pennsylvania WILPF had met with a group of concerned people, including representatives of the AFSC, about setting up a hostel in the Philadelphia area. The group formed a concerned citizens committee. AFSC said it would undertake the hostel as soon as enough Japanese Americans arrived to make it feasible, but as time went by and nothing was done, a woman working for the War Relocation Authority who had previously worked for the WILPF urged that organization to find a home for them. At first there was some question about the WRA's willingness to work with a radical organization such as WILPF, but these problems were ironed out, and WILPF found a house for the Nisei, near the University of Pennsylvania, that had a capacity of twenty-five, but that sometimes accommodated as many as forty. WILPF members opened their attics and basements to furnish the hostel and entertained the Nisei in their homes.[24]

Mildred Olmsted continued to use the house in Rose Valley as a place to entertain WILPF visitors, singly and in numbers. Dorothy Day was one of the visitors who came to spend the night during this time. Jean Wilcox, a board member, wrote to thank Mildred and to say that having seen "your lovely home I understand better now how you always have such an abundant fund of energy for your work."[25]

Whatever troubles the Olmsteds had in private, they presented a united front as charming cohosts to their guests. When Mildred brought women home from a board meeting, Allen often had a late supper ready for them, and a fund of witty small talk to take their minds off their troubles. If the guests stayed over, there was sometimes breakfast in bed, and in the spring, summer, and fall, Mildred's beautiful garden to wander in. Every spring Mildred ordered more unusual plants for her garden and garnered others from cuttings from friends. Her lilies, iris, and tulips were spectacular. Working in the garden remained her chief delight, and the results showed it.

The appearance of serenity was achieved at great price. Like other American families, the Olmsteds struggled with wartime rationing and with shortages. Hilda Osborne left in 1941, and they made do with a series of makeshift housekeepers. At the end of the war, Mildred Olmsted found two wives of conscientious objectors who together ran the household in return for room and board.

Early in the war Mildred Olmsted was asked to be a civil defense warden, and when she refused, she felt that she and Allen were viewed with increasing suspicion in the wider community. Word got about at one point that the Olmsteds were hoarding, and some wardens came to check the springhouse, where they found only a couple of watermelons cooling. Since Mildred refused to put up blackout curtains, she was under surveillance by the wardens. One night she was entertaining her cousin Forrester, sitting in the dark before an open fire. The warden came in to check and was surprised to see that Forrester wore the uniform of an officer in the army air force.[26]

Adele and Maurice Saul were sympathetic with Mildred's position on the war, but they were not themselves pacifists, and their son Bobby enlisted and was killed in battle overseas, leaving a widow and two small children behind. Adele suffered stoically as Scotts always did. Mildred wrote to her sister, "You and I have always suffered more because we are not demonstrative and can't talk, just grow hard and tighter inside. We have to work it out in our own way. It just hurts more when others try to talk along to us about it. My spirit is with you in this even though you do not see more for I know no one can help really. I wish I could."[27]

The Olmsted children were growing up. In June 1942, Peter Olmsted graduated from Westtown. He was one of the commencement speakers and his topic was "To Be or Not to Be a Pacifist." He did not tell his parents what the outcome was going to be. Mildred Olmsted had to miss a vital WILPF executive board meeting in order to attend graduation, but she felt for once that her family demands came first. Peter advanced all the arguments for going into the army, then all those for becoming a conscientious objector, and announced that he chose the latter course. It was, of course, a proud day for Mildred and Allen.

Peter decided that in light of his new decision he would like to join the Religious Society of Friends, although not until he had received his draft status as 4E, conscientious objector. Mildred and Allen had long considered the possibility of joining the Society, which they liked and respected. Mildred had left formal religious belief behind long ago and was sure she would never return to a belief in God or in an afterlife, but she wanted to stand with the Friends in their testimonies for peace, the equality of women, and justice. For almost fifty years she remained a member of Providence Meeting, always urging members to take stronger stands politically, and helping the meeting solve pressing problems without becoming much involved in its spiritual life. Allen was of a more mystical turn and found deep inspiration in the silent worship of the Friends. Tony, now a student at the Anderson School on the Hudson River in New York State, a school specializing in helping boys and girls with learning problems, also joined the Society of Friends, but Enid did not. She was having her problems at Westtown School, having been twice expelled for smoking, and was feeling rebellious against her parents whose constant talk about peace and justice issues she found boring, and whom she accused of being intellectual snobs.

Allen had hoped that Peter might follow him to Harvard, and Peter had done well enough at Westtown so that this was a possibility. He chose Haverford, however, thinking it would be more congenial to be in a Quaker environment during wartime. He was only able to complete his first year, for the following spring he was drafted and sent to a Civilian Public Service camp run by the Quakers in Gatlinburg, Tennessee. From here he wrote home a series of long weekly letters, telling about his experiences. The community about the camp was sometimes hostile to the COs and on one occasion when he was hitchhiking to town, he was thrown from the car and beaten up for announcing that he was a conscientious objector. Ruth Mellor wrote that she was shocked and upset by the incident, but Mildred was not. Her son, like her, was going to learn to fight for unpopular causes, even if his weapons must be nonviolent. Later Peter was transferred to a CPS unit in Minneapolis where research into human hunger was being conducted with the COs as guinea pigs. Several of Mildred's friends, including Ruth, were worried about Peter, but Mildred once more assumed that he would be brave and would come out all right. She was clearly proud of him during this period, mentioning him frequently in her WILPF correspondence, and taking the opportunity to go out to see him when WILPF travels took her to the Midwest.[28]

The extra pressure of the war years was hard on Mildred Olmsted's always rather precarious state of health. She continued to have confusing symptoms and was told to take thyroid because of a low metabolism. She had a series of nose and throat infections, culminating in having her tonsils out at the age of fifty-five. And in 1944 she was finally diagnosed as having a heart condition. The doctor told her that she had evidently inherited the tendency toward heart trouble from her father, and that she would have to slow down and choose between home and job if she did not want to die early, as her father had done. Mildred remembers telling the doctor that she would rather have a short interesting life than a long boring one, and that she had no intention of giving up her job. But she decided to try to take more vacations, adding a winter holiday to the rather complicated summer schedule she had evolved.

In the summer of 1941 Ruth Mellor had joined Mildred and Allen and the children for a trip to Mexico. The triangle didn't work over such a long period of time; Allen felt left out by Mildred and Ruth's intimacy and was sometimes cross with Ruth. Having the children along added to the problems. They resolved to go back to their old schedule, in which Mildred spent some time with Ruth alone, and some with Allen alone. Now that the children were old enough to go to summer camp, there was less necessity for her to take them to the Jersey shore, although she still tried to fit it in when possible.

Shortly after she had been diagnosed as having a heart ailment in the summer of 1944, Mildred went with Ruth to Monhegan Island in Maine for a short vacation; Allen stayed in Rose Valley with Tony and Enid, who at age seventeen was serving as paid housekeeper for the family that summer. Enid hadn't been feeling particularly well and developed appendicitis. Allen considered wiring Mildred to come home, but he decided not to disturb her period of rest and took care of checking Enid into the hospital and of staying with her until she recovered. Only then did he send a cablegram saying all was well. Dorothy Robinson was deeply impressed by this act of husbandly and fatherly support.

The next summer Allen took Tony on a camping trip west, while Mildred recovered from her tonsillectomy. Then, in August, Mildred and Ruth went to Banff in the Canadian Rockies. It was there, beside beautiful Lake Louise, that they heard that atomic bombs had been dropped on Nagasaki and Hiroshima, that the Japanese were willing to surrender, and that the world was forever changed.

12
One World

$\mathcal{F}$OR MANY OF THE WOMEN OF WILPF, the dropping of the atomic bomb meant the end of the world as they had known it. As Lydia Wentworth, an old-time WILPF activist, wrote Mildred Olmsted, "The coming of the bomb changes everything and makes military preparedness a negligible factor since no amount of military training will prevent destruction of cities and entire nations unless men put an end to warfare altogether. I wonder if they will have sense enough."[1]

The older reformers had shared the faith of the Progressive Era that progress toward human betterment was inevitable, if men and women of good faith were only obedient to their vision. Even the hearts and minds of the venal could be reached eventually, if one appealed to enlightened self-interest. The coming of the bomb presented humankind with the possibility that not only was progress not inevitable but life on the planet could hereafter be wiped out by the push of a button. Some of the women who had been pioneers in the peace movement grew discouraged enough to turn their remaining energies to other things.

Mildred Olmsted never shared this pessimistic view. She continued to believe firmly that history was on the side of the causes she supported. When she looked back and saw the progress apparent in her lifetime—in suffrage and advancement for women, in civil liberties and civil rights, in the number of groups ready to work for peace—she saw vindication for her views. One must always take the long view, she insisted.

One cause for optimism, Mildred Olmsted thought, was the

238

fact that the United States was willing to participate in the United Nations, though it had renounced the League of Nations. Like many peace people, she had watched the development of the charter for the United Nations, at Dumbarton Oaks in 1944 and at San Francisco in 1945, with keen interest. Dorothy Detzer, who represented the WILPF at the San Francisco conference in May, reported on what she could find out about the new charter. Mildred Olmsted worried that the Big Five were holding on to power, and that the proceedings were blanketed in secrecy. But she still felt that the organization of the world body was a step in the right direction, toward the rule of world law. With others she rejoiced when the charter was signed on 24 October 1945.

The WILPF itself needed peace badly. Mildred Olmsted and Dorothy Detzer had had another major blow-up in May, when Mildred was busy arranging for the thirtieth anniversary of WILPF at Haverford, an occasion that she hoped would restore the morale of the WILPF and start an upward trend in membership. She herself made a tour of Midwest cities in February, trying to revive dying branches and to create enthusiasm for the anniversary meeting. She was horrified to find on her return a memo from Dorothy Detzer to the membership saying that the anniversary meeting would be necessarily small, and that she, Dorothy, would not attend, as she planned to be in San Francisco.

"What possible use is there working to build up an organization which is so consistently torn down from above?" Mildred wrote to Dorothy Robinson. "You know as well as I that Dorothy is not and never has been an executive secretary, yet we continue to call her such and to let her go off on tangents on the particular thing that interests her rather than the things which strengthen the organization as a whole."[2]

Dorothy Detzer also became angry when Grace Rhoads wrote to her with instructions about sending out the agenda for the national board, a job Dorothy had done for twenty years. It was clear that the divided headquarters were causing increasing difficulty. Dorothy wanted to consolidate the office in Washington and to have Mildred Olmsted report to her. When she learned that the Pennsylvania WILPF had been offered the chance to own its own headquarters, thanks to the generosity of a member, Helen Rea, whose husband was willing to purchase a building and rent it to the WILPF, Dorothy realized that there was no longer much hope of such a consolidation taking place. As Mildred remembered the incident, she broke down and cried.[3]

In January 1946 Dorothy Detzer submitted her resignation. She said she had been with the organization for twenty years (actually, it had been twenty-three) and that for both the WILPF and herself it was time for a change, that she needed a more secure and better-paying job, and that she objected to the double national office. "This criticism is not based *in any sense whatever* on any personalities involved."[4]

The resignation was accepted with regret, and Dorothy Detzer left her post in the late spring. Following her retirement, she first wrote a book about her experiences in the WILPF called *Appointment on the Hill*, then went to work for Norman Thomas's Post War World Council. But as Mildred Olmsted perceived it, the two strong personalities clashed, and Dorothy Detzer soon left the job and went to live with her aging parents in Indiana. A longtime newspaper friend, Ludwell Denny, who had recently lost his wife, looked her up, and eventually they married and were very happy. According to Mildred there was an understanding between them that Dorothy would not be active in the WILPF or other peace organizations. Dorothy continued to contribute to the WILPF, and to entertain WILPF members in her Washington apartment, but she kept clear of responsibilities of any sort.[5]

The real cause of Dorothy Detzer's resignation in 1946 was debated for many years. Mildred Olmsted, who despite their troubles had always admired Dorothy's brilliant mind and creative ideas, felt she had gone "dead" on the job. Asked about the cause of resignation years later, Dorothy Robinson remembered that Dorothy had become "touchy, jumpy and dominating," and that "the feelings about her in the organization were pretty violent— violent for her and violent against her." Dorothy Detzer herself recalled in 1975 that the job had become too routine, and that "after 23 years of struggle I could not get the Board to agree to the kind of executive set up which I felt essential. A divided office, with organization of branches and membership in Philadelphia— separated from the political arena seemed to be inefficient and wasteful. I could not see that the effective work of the WIL should hinge on where some person lived."[6]

The struggle that had developed between Dorothy Detzer and Mildred Olmsted was a tragedy for the WILPF. Both women possessed strong and complementary talents. Had they been able to work together more harmoniously, it is possible that WILPF might have become a much larger and stronger organization during the prewar height of the peace movement. But they saw that movement very differently in the crucial years before World War II. Dorothy's thinking was much more in line with the mainstream pacifist thought of the time. Mildred, with her concept of coupling internationalism with the use of nonviolence, foreshadowed developments in pacifist thought that obtained in the 1960s and onward.

In addition they were both strong personalities, addicted to power, and sharing it only grudgingly. Neither had a concept of sisterhood, and neither was woman identified. Mildred, for all her personal distrust of men, had modeled herself after her father and admired men's ways of thinking and acting. Dorothy had never been a feminist and enjoyed working with men. Although in the early years of their collaboration they had enjoyed each other, they had no tools with which to analyze or help to resolve their differences. The second wave of American feminism, born in the 1960s and 1970s, provides women today with a theoretical basis for ridding themselves of patriarchal attitudes and learning to work collegially, as the present feminist leadership in the WILPF is now doing. But Dorothy Detzer and Mildred Olmsted came into their own at a time when American feminism was in its doldrums; they had no feminist analysis to help them and would at any rate have probably rejected it. Their story was repeated in other arenas of the WILPF, as well as in other women's organizations of the time.

The conflict left deep fault lines in the WILPF that remained with the organization for many years after Dorothy Detzer resigned. Loyalties forged during this period persisted long after their original cause was lost sight of. Mildred came away from the struggle with loyal followers but also with opposers who stayed with the WILPF and made her role difficult for many years.

At the time Mildred Olmsted felt that Dorothy Detzer's resignation solved the problem of divided headquarters. It seemed to her self-evident that now she should be named executive secretary, and that the headquarters should be in Philadelphia, just as Jane Addams had told her she thought they ought to be many years ago. The Pennsylvania WILPF was by far the strongest in the nation, and Philadelphia itself was a national center of peace activity, because of the presence of the American Friends Service Committee and other Quaker-related peace groups. The new and beautiful Jane Addams House at 2006 Walnut Street was able to accommodate many smaller peace organizations and permitted WILPF to play a nurturing role to the peace movement as it recovered from the stress of war.

But some members of the national board saw Dorothy Detzer's resignation as one more piece of evidence that Mildred Olmsted wanted absolute control over WILPF, and they were determined to deny it to her. Persistent reports that she was very hard to work with and was in fact a poor administrator, unable to delegate responsibility, were also a factor in the board's thinking. Some staff members were passionately loyal to Mildred, but others could not adjust to what they saw as her high-handed ways. Several wrote to the board at the time of their resignations to say they felt Mildred Olmsted was the source of all the difficulties the WILPF was experiencing.

At an executive committee meeting in February, Mildred Olmsted announced that she thought she should be named executive secretary. The group could not agree, and the meeting was a nightmare, according to Gladys Walser, a Smith classmate of Mildred's who was doing some fieldwork for the WILPF and was a member of the executive committee. At the next meeting Gladys Walser proposed again that the headquarters remain in Philadelphia and that, as a replacement for Dorothy Detzer, a legislative secretary be chosen for the Washington office who would report to Mildred. Some of the old-timers, especially Gertrude Bussey and Dorothy Robinson, could not agree to this. Mildred's title was finally made national administrative secretary in November 1946, and so it remained until 1963. A young woman, Katherine Marshall, was hired as legislative secretary and was to be supervised by a new policy committee with Baltimore headquarters.[7]

Mildred Olmsted resented her new title and felt hampered by having always to consult the policy committee. She sent all letters in regard to policy to the chair of that committee, stating that she wasn't herself allowed to answer them. She was, however, glad that board meetings were much calmer now that the factional battles had ceased and she had a clear field to start to rebuild the war-shattered organization. She began publishing the monthly branch letters that had been written by the executive director and mailed to all WILPF branches since 1922. With the help of Gladys Walser she tried to straighten out a longtime tangle of problems plaguing the Chicago branch, to strengthen the faltering New York State organization and to help the Massachusetts branch reorganize. As much time as she could afford to be away from the office, she spent in traveling from branch to branch again. She listened to and tried to implement suggestions that WILPF branches be conducted differently in the postwar world, with more evening meetings, more research projects, more appeal to younger people. She returned to her stepping-stone theory, that branches should be close enough together so it would be possible and not too expensive to go from one to another.

One way to rebuild the organization was to send around good speakers. Mildred Olmsted arranged for Marie Louis Mohr of Norway, a woman who had survived wartime imprisonment in Europe, to tour the United States for the WILPF in 1948, telling her compelling story of the nonviolent resistance against Hitler in the occupied countries, especially Norway. Signe Hojer of Sweden also made a round of the branches. Women were stirred by these gatherings, and slowly new and younger leadership began to emerge, eager to work against the new threat the atomic bomb posed to their children.

To these younger women Mildred Olmsted was an exciting leader, with her striking looks, her coordinated clothes, her obvious self-confidence, and her endless enthusiasm. For women who had grown up under male domination, for women who had worked during the war but were now being told that they must leave the workplace and return to their prescribed roles as housewives and mothers, contact with this woman from the older generation was exhilarating. Many thought of her as bringing into their lives the spirit of her model and mentor, Jane Addams.

By the end of 1946 Mildred was encouraged enough to report progress to the annual meeting.

> We have had various illustrations during the past year of how old branches given the right local leadership have taken on fresh energy, developed vigorous and useful programs and expanded into new activities that stirred their warweary countries. We have examples of new branches springing up, new members thankful to have discovered a group which is truly intelligent, consistent, sustained and above the reach of propaganda that has sullied the records of most contemporaneous organizations.
>
> Here is a group that is both free and fine, unselfish and informed.[8]

WILPF International needed rebuilding too. The sections in most of the European nations had been broken up by the war, and many of the leaders imprisoned. At the first postwar congress, held in Luxembourg in August 1946, delegates were shocked to hear of their losses: leaders from Holland, Czechoslovakia, and Hungary put to death in concentration camps, others dying in exile. The brutal Nazi occupation of Holland had crushed the spirit of reform in that nation. Was it worthwhile to try to revive the organization, or had its time passed? Many people seemed to think the latter. A delegate from Holland, where the WILPF was born, proposed that the organization be laid down; the pursuit of peace and freedom was now a concern of both men and women.

Mildred Olmsted was attending the congress as a delegate, having flown across the ocean accompanied by the ever-faithful Ruth Mellor. Her family had worried that the pressure of the airplane's cabin might be bad for her high blood pressure and capricious heart, and her son Tony had begged her not to go. She had, however, a relatively smooth crossing and was looking forward to a holiday in Paris with Ruth, once the sessions were over.

Hearing the delegate from Holland counsel the dissolution of her beloved WILPF, Mildred rose to answer. She said she felt WILPF should continue because "women are more important even than before . . . peace is more important even than before . . .

work against oppression and exploitation . . . is more essential than before." The fact that two hundred delegates from twenty countries had succeeded in gathering at the meeting was a proof of WILPF's vitality, she thought; and while there were new societies springing up devoting themselves to some of the WILPF's objectives, it alone included the entire program of peace and freedom and change by nonviolent methods. She also spoke, uncharacteristically, of woman's special role as nurturer, a role she herself had rejected. "Women, although often led into support of war and violence, are by nature more concerned than men with the conservation of life and the creation of the conditions under which children may grow up safely and happily. An international organization which can bring the women of the world together to exchange information and ideas and to make plans is urgently needed."[9]

Others also spoke for continuing, but Mildred Olmsted's was felt to be the decisive voice. The motion for dissolution was overwhelmingly defeated, and the women elected officers to carry on the work. Mildred was reelected to the important international executive committee. For the next seven years she attended international meetings and worked long hours on correspondence aimed at reviving the old strength of the worldwide WILPF.

As she had felt so long and so strongly about the U.S. Section of WILPF, Mildred Olmsted believed that someone had to put time and thought into international organization. She recommended in 1947 that a woman be found to organize for the WILPF in Germany and the next year suggested that the WILPF international office add an additional secretary to "travel and knit our members more closely together." It was a theme she was to return to over and over. The WILPF should try to develop national sections in the various regions of the world, as she had tried to do in the regions of the United States, and should be prepared to send organizers out to do this work. Only thus would the WILPF grow and become affluent enough to meet its financial obligations, as well as to have the influence in the world that its pioneers and martyrs had earned for it, she believed.[10]

Mildred Olmsted was also concerned that the International WILPF not become tangled up in long discussions of policy, or immobilized by conflicting views. In an executive committee

meeting that she missed in the summer of 1948, the women voted
to support the use of force against the Arabs in order to keep the
peace in Israel. Did this mean that the constitution should be
altered and the statement that WILPF stood for change by nonviolent means only should be amended? Mildred Olmsted argued
against such a change as not only weakening the WILPF position
but opening up the whole constitutional issue, which could be
both bitter and divisive. Better to ignore the action of a single
executive committee session than to create further troubles in the
name of consistency, she wrote to Barbara Duncan-Harris, a fellow
executive committee member.[11]

The faith of Mildred Olmsted and others in the importance of
keeping WILPF alive after the war was rewarded in December
1946 when Emily Greene Balch was nominated to receive the Nobel Peace Prize, the second American woman to be so honored
and, like her predecessor, Jane Addams, a WILPF founder. Emily
was too ill to go to Oslo to receive the prize that year but finally
made a delayed trip in 1948. Meanwhile she raised everyone's
spirits by deciding to give her prize money to the international
WILPF, just as Jane Addams had done in 1931.

In granting the prize to Emily Balch, Gunnar Jahn spoke of
the 1919 congress. "I can't repeat to you all the resolutions passed
as amendments for the Peace Treaty from the Congress of 1919.
But I want to say this; it would have been wise if the statesmen of
the world had listened to the proposals from these women. But in
the men's society in which we are living, proposals from women
are not usually taken seriously."[12]

The women of the WILPF had campaigned for Balch to receive the prize. In 1942 they collected a small sum of money for a
Jane Addams Peace Fund to serve as a memorial to their former
leader. The first use of this fund was to work for the Nobel Prize
for Emily Greene Balch. Once they were successful in this venture
they decided to look into enlarging and incorporating the fund.
Because gifts to WILPF were not tax-exempt, it was thought a
purely educational fund could receive funds that WILPF could
not. Mildred became a member of the fund committee in 1947,
and Allen Olmsted served as the lawyer for the incorporation. This
meant dealing tactfully with some women connected with Hull

House in Chicago who had wanted to organize a Jane Addams Peace Association independent of WILPF. Allen was successful in these negotiations and was able to incorporate the fund, renamed the Jane Addams Peace Association, in 1948. In 1949 Art for World Friendship, an exchange of children's art from around the world that had been developed by Pennsylvania WILPF member Maude Muller, became a project of JAPA, and later the association supported a new enterprise, the Committee for World Development and World Disarmament.

At about the same time, Mildred Olmsted decided to organize a Jane Addams branch of the organization to draw in all the members too isolated to belong to a local branch. The leader of the branch forwarded Mildred's regular branch letter to her flock and added comments of her own as a way of keeping these members in touch with WILPF doings.

One important WILPF goal was to receive nongovernment (NGO) status at the United Nations. Gertrude Baer returned to the United States in 1947 as the representative of the international WILPF to the United Nations and made application for consultative status B with the Economic and Social Council. When the application came up in March 1948, the Soviet delegate rose to object. The Women's International Democratic Federation, representing the socialist countries, had charged that the League was a "reactionary and pro-Fascist organization." Gertrude Baer believed that the WIDF had somehow confused WILPF with another organization, the International Alliance of Women. WIDF in fact had worked with WILPF on several occasions, although many women in WILPF at that time felt it was better to stay clear of the socialist group, believing that it tended to use other organizations for its aims. Whatever the problem, the Soviet delegate was overruled, and WILPF received its NGO status.

The next year WILPF received NGO status with UNESCO and in 1953 with the Food and Agriculture Organization in Rome. Mildred Olmsted served as a representative to the UN Council of Non-Governmental Organizations in 1949 and urged that UNICEF be made a permanent agency for children's welfare. Other WILPF women took on this job in succeeding years, working for a covenant on human rights, for the creation of the post of high commissioner for stateless persons, and for upgrading the presence and status of women in UN posts. The past international general secretary of the WILPF, Edith Ballantyne, was twice the chair of the NGOs.

Gertrude Baer unfortunately continued to be difficult to work with, especially for Mildred Olmsted. The U.S. Section decided to appoint its own representative to NGO and chose Gladys Walser. Gertrude Baer wrote Mildred a stream of letters complaining about this duplication of effort, as she perceived it, and the poor cooperation she felt she received from the U.S. Section. At one point she found her name listed as a U.S. board member on WILPF stationery put out by the Philadelphia office, and she insisted that all the stationery bearing this error be corrected or thrown out.

Mildred Olmsted avoided doing battle over small things with Gertrude Baer and found opportunities to praise her when possible. In her branch letter she described being at the United Nations when the U.S. and USSR representatives were "glaring and hurling scathing speeches at each other from opposite ends of the table like two adolescent boys." She discovered the importance of the NGOs, she said, and was impressed by the way everyone looked to Gertrude Baer. But she wrote privately to Walser that she thought "it was intolerable that she [Baer] should dictate to the United States Section whether or not they should be represented or by whom."[13]

Mildred's interest in building the international WILPF led to her frequent travel to Europe in this period of her life. In June 1947 she attended an executive committee meeting in Geneva, again accompanied by Ruth. She was heartened by the large attendance at this meeting and by the signs of renewal. Gertrude Bussey resigned as international cochair, and her place was taken by André Jouvé of France, while Dorothy Robinson became international treasurer. After the meeting Ruth and Mildred hurried back to the United States, as they had planned a vacation together on Grand Manon Island in Canada for July.

It was a busy summer for the Olmsted family. Allen was once more running for judge and was tied by politics to Rose Valley. In August Peter Olmsted was getting married to Polly Comegys, a young woman he had met in Minneapolis while he was a CO on the hunger experiment. Although the Olmsteds had objected at first to the marriage, as Peter had completed only one year of college before being drafted, they were reassured by meeting Polly, who told them she intended to help him finish his education. The Comegys lived near Cleveland, and the entire Olmsted family went out to attend the wedding.

The Olmsted children were growing up. Enid had completed her first year of college at Simmons in Boston and was spending the summer in an AFSC work camp. Tony was doing reasonably well at the Anderson School, although it was clear he would never be a scholar. Gone were the days when Mildred and Allen had to consult to be sure that one or the other of them would be home when the children were ill. With its renters and its stream of guests, the household at Rose Valley continued to be a complicated one, but the factor of having to plan for small children was now removed.

One might think that the Olmsted marriage was becoming more serene at this juncture, but in fact it was less so. Allen was not enjoying his work with Saul, Ewing, Remick and Saul very much. He was much more radical than most of his partners, always wanting the firm to add minority lawyers and to take pro bono cases, and disagreeing on principle with some of its clients. He also did not like the intense pace at which his fellow lawyers worked. His father had practiced law in a more leisurely, if less successful, fashion, and he himself was of a reflective turn of mind. The fact that Maurice Saul, his brother-in-law, was far wealthier than he, and that the Olmsteds always bought the Sauls' cars secondhand, added to his sense of failure. He was also frustrated in his longtime ambition to be a judge. (He lost the election again in 1947 and in 1949.)

He continued to feel aggrieved by Mildred's constant absences and the incursions of the WILPF on their family life. Ruth told Mildred that she thought Allen was jealous of her professional success, comparing it to his disappointments. He resented Ruth's habit of analyzing him to Mildred and nicknamed her "Dr. Floyd." He continued to be envious of Mildred's preoccupation with Ruth, to resent his wife's frequent coldness toward him, and to feel that he had the right to seek solace elsewhere. Although he had finally given up seeing Mary, he entered into a series of flirtations with other women. He insisted on telling Mildred about these affairs and asking for her approval, which of course she never wanted to give. This led to more quarrels.

What Allen principally wanted from Mildred was the one thing she could not offer: surrender. Reviewing the high spots of their marriage, he spoke of her acceptance, first of marriage, then of motherhood. "All of them were in a sense giving in to weakness and a bowing to some force within you that did not meet with the values and purposes you consciously followed." From the very beginning of their courtship he had occasionally glimpsed the Judy, or feminine, persona in Mildred, and he continued to seek that elusive self. "I sometimes think your nature is more divided than mine," he wrote her. "Do you remember the four names you once attached to your varying personalities?"[14]

Mildred for her part grew weary of his frequent depressions and laments. If he had not achieved his goals, she told him, it was because he was basically lazy and comfort loving. She compared him unfavorably to herself, who with fewer natural gifts than he had made a greater success of her life. She resented the fact that he did not like to hear her speak because he was critical of her carelessness with the facts. Allen said he feared that they were headed for a troubled old age, and Mildred wrote from Grand Manon where she was vacationing with Ruth that as soon as Peter was married she wanted a divorce. The storm blew over before the wedding, and a troubled peace prevailed.[15]

One of Allen's forms of solace was his contact with the extended Olmsted family, who gave him love and support. This source of strength was somewhat shaken in 1948 when a nephew decided to contest the will of the wealthy Uncle Al, the Foot Ease king, who had left his money evenly divided between all the cousins of Peter's generation. According to this nephew, Enid and Tony should not receive a share because they were not "real" but adopted Olmsteds. This, of course, hurt Allen as well as his two adopted children, and he fought the case, first trying to make an appeal to the nephew, then in the courts. He lost, but a favorite nephew, Seymour's son Michael, started a move to give a portion of his share to Enid and Tony, and many of the other cousins followed suit.

Despite the troubles they sometimes had, Allen and Mildred Olmsted prided themselves on their partnership in reform work. One of their joint postwar efforts was the rebuilding of the American Civil Liberties Union in the Philadelphia area, as well as elsewhere in Pennsylvania. A test case helped. Late in 1947 a group of young people persuaded seven peace groups to mount a rally on Independence Square. When the American Legion successfully objected, Allen Olmsted carried the case for the peace groups to the federal court, where he was able to get a thirty-five-year-old city ordinance declared unconstitutional, and the Cradle of Liberty thrown open to all kinds of peaceful rallies. Mildred was proud of this accomplishment and wrote about it in her branch letter. She became a member of the Philadelphia ACLU board in 1950, and Allen of the Delaware County board.

Another joint Olmsted accomplishment in this period was the organization in 1948 of the Central Committee for Conscientious Objectors, a group prepared to counsel COs and to compile information on their status under the law. The passage of the peacetime draft in the spring of 1948, over the strenuous objections of the peace community, made the committee a necessity. Although the draft was shortly suspended, many young men refused to register and were imprisoned in this period. Mildred thought of the committee as a direct outgrowth of the small group set up in 1939 by WILPF, and she was part of a small planning meeting to develop the new organization. Elizabeth Rhoads was currently the chair of WILPF's continuing CO committee and was invited to join the new group, and Allen was made treasurer. Mildred was not a founding member but went on the board shortly thereafter. CCCO, as it was familiarly called, rented office space in the Jane Addams House at 2006 Walnut and remained there for many years.

Mildred Olmsted continued her postwar travels in the summer of 1949 when she went abroad to attend the Eleventh International Congress of WILPF in Copenhagen in August, accompanied once more by Ruth. Allen stayed behind to campaign once more for a judgeship. Mildred had to leave in a hurry and left him a note. "Frantic to leave without saying goodbye especially since we have not been so happy in the last couple of months. If we are going to separate permanently I want it to be in some high and fine way, like our coming together."[16]

Ruth and Mildred saved money by flying with a youth travel group and landed first in London, then flew to Brussels where they met some WILPF delegates. Mildred had time to explore Bruges; she found the city beautiful, and in a letter to her family commented that she felt that, perhaps more even than a political education, Americans needed to develop an appreciation of beautiful things and of the importance of preserving them. "If we created more beautiful cities in America (not just convenient ones) we might be more reluctant to destroy those built up through the centuries in Europe and elsewhere."[17]

The two companions were determined to visit Germany on this trip but found it difficult. They spent a night in Cologne and had to get up at 5:00 A.M. to catch a train going up the Rhine that connected with a boat going down. They returned to Cologne and spent the night in the hotel lobby in order to catch a 3:00 A.M. train to Berlin. On the crowded train, they were told they would have to get off because they did not have Russian permits to pass through the Russian zone. They complied and managed to get their bags off the train, only to be told by the Russians they might go after all. Although a Russian officer accompanied them to the next checkpoint, the Americans said they could not give the two a "movement order." Finally they gave up and went back to Hanover, very tired and frustrated. The next day they went on to Hamburg, where they met a member of the newly revived WILPF. This German woman wanted them to drop everything and go on a speaking tour of German branches, but Mildred and Ruth had planned to go on to Sweden and did not want to change their plans.

The congress in Denmark was held at Christiansborg Castle, the seat of the Danish parliament. Here Gertrude Bussey was elected international cochair, along with Marie Louis Mohr of Norway and Agnes Stapleton of Great Britain, and Mildred Olmsted was re-elected to the executive committee. The congress decided to revive its publication *Pax International,* last published in 1940, and to press for a convention against the crime of genocide.[18]

Winston Churchill's speech in Missouri in March 1946, declaring that an "iron curtain" had descended across the continent, had marked the beginning of the cold war. By the Copenhagen congress it had hardened into reality with the Truman Doctrine, the Marshall Plan, the Soviet blockade of Berlin, and the U.S. airlift, and finally, in April, the formation of the North Atlantic Treaty Organization, or NATO. The women of WILPF protested NATO in their countries and at their congress. Instead of the creation of this military alliance, the WILPF suggested, the nations of Europe ought to work toward world disarmament and world development through the United Nations.

To combat the cold war, the WILPF felt the need to reach out to women in Eastern bloc and third world countries. At Copenhagen, WILPF established a new sections committee to assist in the development of groups that had arisen in Palestine, Iceland, and Italy and to begin work on reviving the section in Japan. This was very much in line with Mildred Olmsted's thinking, and she had many suggestions for the committee.

In her branch letter describing the congress, Mildred Olmsted mentioned her joy in the number of new young members who had been present. She was surprised to find herself one of the older leaders, both abroad and at home. She did not tell her age, fearing that people discounted the elderly, but her staff knew her birthday and decided to fete her on 5 December, when she became fifty-nine. They called the event a celebration of twenty-five years of peace work. (As Mildred started in 1922, it was actually twenty-seven.) At a luncheon in her honor, tributes were read from WILPF old-timers such as Lucy Biddle Lewis, Bertha McNeill, Dorothy Detzer, and Ellen Winsor, as well as WILPF leaders abroad. One of these, Lola Hanoskova of Czechoslovakia wrote of the inspiration that Mildred always gave her. "I am breathing quieter, since I may believe that women like you exist who do not lose their courage, who never abandon their work for the maintenance of peace, however threatening and black the world may look."[19] Roger Baldwin echoed the same theme when he said that "pacifists ought to be a discouraged lot these days but Mildred Olmsted is one of the eternally undefeated."[20]

Mildred Olmsted's own talk was a celebration of hope. She spoke of the many changes she had seen, from the day when people were shocked at the idea of pacifism to the present proliferation of peace organizations; from the United States spurning the League of Nations to its membership in the United Nations; from the women of the WILPF being called dangerous radicals for espousing a good neighbor policy toward Latin America to their being in the mainstream; from being called fomenters of trouble for insisting on holding meetings where all were welcome to the day when the national Democratic party had an African-American vice-president; from being a voice in the wilderness crying against conscription to being joined by many other groups in the fight to defeat peacetime conscription. Someday, she predicted, the WILPF's call for international disarmament would be widely supported. All one had to do was to take the long view. "History is pounding on our doors," she said in summation. "One dare not shirk responsibility by wrapping oneself in soft and pleasant surroundings and leave undone what even one small person can do."[21]

What one small person could do, if that person was Mildred Olmsted, continued to amaze onlookers. In March she attended a special State Department conference, briefing prominent citizens on atomic energy and conventional armament. When she arrived it was suggested to her that she get together all the peace people present at the conference at the lunchtime break. She had to do this by word of mouth, as it was not possible to make a general announcement, but she managed to collect twenty-three people representing both church and peace groups. She heard later that the State Department was surprised and impressed with the turnout.

In May Mildred and Annalee Stewart went to a conference on the church and war in Cleveland, Ohio, Mildred representing the Friends Peace Committee of Philadelphia Yearly Meeting and Annalee the Methodists, and together they were a powerful team. Annalee had returned to Washington and was now serving as legislative secretary for the WILPF. She and Mildred got along very well, which considerably reduced friction between Washington and Philadelphia.

The WILPF annual meeting for 1950 was to be held June 18–24 at Cazenovia, New York, but Mildred announced that for perhaps the first time since joining WILPF she could not attend.

Anthony was graduating from the Anderson School, and Enid, who had just graduated from Leslie College in Cambridge, Massachusetts, having transferred from Simmons, was marrying William Burke on 2 July in the Olmsted garden. Mildred would only have time to pick up after the wedding, plus attend to some final work in the office, before once more flying to Europe on 15 July to attend the international executive committee meetings in Liverpool.

The wedding went off smoothly. Enid had organized every detail, and the garden was at its loveliest. For the assembled guests there was only one surprise. Asked by the minister "Who gives this woman?" Allen Olmsted had answered, "Her mother and I give this woman." Both of the Olmsteds must have been thinking of their own wedding, held nearby twenty-nine years ago, and of their unusual vows.

At the international executive committee meetings in Liverpool, WILPF members wrestled with the outbreak of war in Korea. On 25 June the North Koreans had crossed the thirty-eighth parallel, and the Security Council of the UN, meeting without the USSR, had agreed to undertake a "police action." WILPF was, of course, opposed to this basically unilateral approach, and the committee meeting at Liverpool developed a statement calling for an immediate cease-fire under the supervision of the UN, and for the seating of the People's Republic of China at the United Nations.

The Korean conflict reminded everyone of how easily war could break out when nations were armed to the teeth. Mildred Olmsted had been thinking a great deal about disarmament as a major WILPF objective, and at the Liverpool meetings she presented a resolution to be made public by the WILPF calling for an immediate truce on the expansion of armaments, the calling of a conference by the UN to consider ways to reduce armaments, and the development of alternative constructive ways of employing displaced labor and material.[22]

Another concern of Mildred Olmsted's was, of course, growth. She complained that WILPF was not considering the development of its work around the world seriously enough and feared the organization was growing weaker at a time it should grow stronger. Why not try to organize regionally, as the AFSC had done in the United States, with committees all over the world reporting back to a central committee? And why not ask the committee on national sections to keep in touch with all traveling WILPF members, so that their trips might be made useful for the expansion of WILPF? When asked if she would serve on this committee, Mildred somewhat uncharacteristically said no. She believed that too many American women were taking responsibility for international WILPF, and that if it was to survive the European women must play a larger role.[23]

Following the meetings Ruth Mellor and Mildred Olmsted vacationed in southern France and on the Spanish island of Mallorca in the Balearics, then went on to San Remo, Italy, to the conference called by the One World Award committee, 22–27 August. Originally this group had sought to honor Emily Greene Balch; when she was unable to come, the committee began to correspond with Mildred Olmsted about sending other WILPF leaders. The committee spoke at first of paying the transportation of some members, but in the end it was not able to do so. Gertrude Baer thought WILPF ought to be disassociated from the enterprise, but Mildred had promised to go and believed it would not be fair to pull out. She found the conference something of a flop but met a young Italian woman who seemed interested in starting a branch of the WILPF.

Returning to the United States was always something of a culture shock. In the fall of 1950 Americans were preoccupied with the Korean War and the fear of communism, greatly inflated by the pronouncements of Senator Joseph McCarthy. "The world is having a hard time growing up," Mildred wrote in her September branch letter. "It continues to act like an adolescent." The United States and the USSR should have used the Korean situation as an opportunity to develop new machinery for peaceful settlement, she thought. "In such times it is a joy to have a sane, intelligent group of people like WIL to turn to. I am proud to have Emily Greene Balch as honorary international president, who has not been afraid to sign statements in which she believed no matter how they are labeled nor how misused."[24]

The statement about Emily Greene Balch's courage may have been prompted by a letter she had just received from her old friend

Norman Thomas, asking her to make sure his name was not listed as sponsoring WILPF. Although he had been honored to work with WILPF on many issues, he had decided that these were not times to have his "name appear officially as the sponsor of any organization whose immediate policies I have no part in shaping. This general principle is made more important to me because I have not always agreed with your analysis of communism or with your suggestions as to what might reasonably have been done in Korea."[25]

While Mildred Olmsted had the greatest respect for Norman Thomas, it saddened her to have him sounding as though he were becoming fearful of former allies, as were so many people at this time. As Mildred often said, fear brings out the very worst in people. She was thankful that, like Emily Greene Balch, she remained unafraid to speak her mind.

The WILPF celebrated its thirty-fifth anniversary with a gala meeting at Hull House that fall. The ranks of the first pioneers were growing thin, but Mildred Olmsted's work on organization was at last beginning to show results. A new generation of leaders was coming into the organization, many of them young mothers determined to do something to make the world their children had been born into a less dangerous place to live. Mildred Olmsted had started out in WILPF as one of the young ones. Now she provided continuity with the early days of the organization. And although she would be sixty in December, she had no plans to retire.

13
Survival in the Fifties

$\mathcal{T}$o MILDRED SCOTT OLMSTED it seemed self-evident that world disarmament was the great need of the 1950s. The pictures in the daily papers showing Korean waifs sleeping in ditches in the bitter cold, and American soldiers burning the houses of suspected collaborators, made her angry. So did the news from Ellenton, South Carolina, where a group of poor farmers and sharecroppers had been dispossessed of their land to make way for a hydrogen bomb plant. "What we should have is some real moral indignation that our beloved country is so often represented at its worst instead of its best, that we as exponents of democracy show so little understanding and sympathy for the human problems which are at the root of this world upheaval," she wrote.[1]

The WILPF now had a new Committee for World Development and World Disarmament (CWDWD), established at the Chicago board meeting, to gather material on these subjects, put on national workshops, conferences and seminars, and help local groups to do the same. Because this work was educational rather than lobbying, it could be financed by the tax-exempt Jane Addams Peace Association. It began work in Philadelphia but moved to Connecticut and then to New York, to be near the United Nations. Its first director was Robert Folwell, but soon Agnes Morley took over the organization and her great friend, Jo Pomerance, provided the money through JAPA. Late in 1952 Emily Parker Simon of Baltimore became the director. Ruth Chalmers, a young Smith graduate hired by Mildred to raise money for the program, later became the head of JAPA and has so remained until the present.

258

Mildred Olmsted was a great booster of the work of CWDWD, urging local branches to build their programs around a thorough study of disarmament in particular. She had always felt that WILPF should provide its members with an education, as Jane Addams had once said, and the materials produced by the CWDWD seemed to offer an opportunity for such studies. In the same vein, the board decided to hold a CWDWD institute at the time of the annual board meeting, in Cazenovia, New York.

Mildred Olmsted was not going to the international executive committee meeting in Geneva that summer. In a frightening episode with high blood pressure on her way to Florida, she had to be taken off the train. Her doctor had once more ordered her to cut back on her schedule. Gertrude Bussey went instead, and after the meetings in Cazenovia, Mildred and Allen and Ruth set out on an adventure in the Yucatan and Guatemala. As usual they did not stay in the obvious tourist places but arranged to go horseback riding on a *finca*, a farm, and to take a long trip on the Rio Dulce.

Allen wanted Mildred to rest throughout this vacation, but once they were back in Guatemala City, Mildred insisted on calling on the women whose names she had received from Heloise Brainerd, for many years WILPF's coordinator for relations with Latin America. A Señora de Holst took her to see Señora Arbens, wife of the Guatemalan president. Mildred found her "to be something of an Eleanor Roosevelt, with her own secretaries, offices, and appointment list. When we did get in we were charmed by her." She met that evening with a group of Guatamalan women, who all expressed interest in joining the WILPF. Many of them had known Heloise Brainerd, about whom they felt as Mildred Olmsted had felt about Jane Addams.[2]

Mildred Olmsted was increasingly aware that the older generation on whom she had depended for inspiration and guidance was slipping away. Emily Greene Balch was eighty-five on 8 January 1952. Mildred attended the banquet given in her honor and chaired by Henry Cadbury, at which Pearl Buck spoke and many old companions paid tribute. Mildred talked of Balch's capacities as a reconciler. "How often have I seen you at an international congress or executive [committee] made chairman of a committee composed of those with strong but opposing ideas which threatened to split the meeting, and then return hours or days later with a unanimous recommendation. No one else could have that amazing reconciling effect but our own Emily Greene Balch."[3]

Privately, however, she wrote Gertrude Baer that Emily Balch seemed "sadly old and unsure of herself." These days Emily Balch often wrote to Mildred Olmsted for advice on how to deal with some of the tangles of the International WILPF (especially problems with Gertrude Baer herself) and often seemed to change her mind. In Mildred's view, Emily Balch was not the tower she had once been.[4]

Feeling better in health and responsible for International WILPF, Mildred Olmsted agreed to attend the international executive committee meetings in Geneva in August of that year. Annalee Stewart traveled with her aboard the Holland American Line. The two decided that on a Dutch ship they ought to capitalize on the fact that Aletta Jacobs of the Netherlands had been the initiator of the 1915 meeting of women at The Hague, by doing some shipboard educating. They persuaded the steward to post notices that Annalee Stewart, who had attended both the Democratic and Republican conventions for WILPF, would speak. To their surprise, 75 showed up for the first session, and 125 for a second session in which they arranged for nine people to present a panel on their views of disarmament. A third session was hastily arranged, at which an English doctor spoke on socialized medicine and announced that she had agreed to join WILPF as soon as she got home.[5]

One of the problems to be addressed at Geneva was that of administration. Gertrude Baer had returned to Geneva from New York in 1950 and taken over the international office, which had been run for thirty years by Louisa Jacques. This arrangement resulted in a great deal of friction, and members felt Gertrude was trying to force Louisa out. In April Mildred Olmsted had written to her colleagues on the committee, urging that they work together to clarify the nature of the job that the international office was expected to do, regardless of personalities. As a result of this preplanning, the sessions were not as tense as many had feared. Although several loyal colleagues voted for her, Gertrude Baer was not reelected vice-president but instead was asked to represent WILPF at the international UN offices in Geneva, as well as to edit *Pax International*. Meanwhile it was decided that one of the newly elected vice-presidents, Agnes Stapleton of England, would supervise office administration.[6]

While she had served as administrator, many felt, Gertrude Baer had blocked anyone trying to organize new sections of WILPF without working through her. This had made the task of the new sections committee difficult. At the meetings, Mildred insisted that adequate time be given to the report on new sections and repeated her plea that this work be given high priority.

While Mildred struggled with these problems in Geneva, Allen was on a walking trip with his old friend Jeanne, whom he had not seen since 1919. Apparently they enjoyed each other, but no new sparks flew. He joined Mildred as soon as she was free, and together they vacationed in France and Italy along with Mildred's WILPF friend Helen Rea.

Returning to the United States, the Olmsteds were aware of a heightening of the anti-Communist hysteria that seemed to be seizing the nation. It is hard for those who did not live through those years to understand the degree to which fear of subversion, or of being called a subversive, spread. Even liberals were not exempt, and many liberal organizations conducted purges of their suspect members that today most of them would rather forget.

In this climate, several of the WILPF branches were worried about how to deal with the possibility of being taken over by Communist infiltrators, while others deplored the attitude of suspicion behind such an accusation. The WILPF began to watch very carefully that it did not endorse Communist-dominated gatherings, such as they perceived the Vienna congress of 1952 to be; at the same time they did not want to join the witch-hunters.

Many members of the WILPF urged that the organization make a statement about the Rosenbergs, awaiting execution at Sing Sing that fall after being found guilty of violating the Espionage Act by supplying secret information to Russia. Some WILPF leaders thought that there was evidence of guilt, although several lawyers pointed out defects in the trial. Rather than trying to settle that issue, however, the women preferred to address themselves to asking for clemency, as they were opposed to capital punishment and believed the sentence excessive in any event. "May the day never come when the WILPF refuses or fails to state openly and for all to hear its fundamental support of freedom and civil liberties," the board said in a policy statement.[7]

This statement probably did not satisfy WILPF's critics from the Right or from the Left. By January 1953 some of the branches were pressing the WILPF to take a strong and unequivocal stand against communism and Communist members. Instead, the WILPF prepared a packet of materials for branches suffering from real or threatened infiltration and appointed a special committee on branch problems with veteran WILPF member Bertha McNeill as chair. In March Mildred wrote an article for *Four Lights* that she called "United We Stand Strong."

This was not the first time that the WILPF had been under attack as either pro-Communist or pro-Nazi, she said. The year after the Russian revolution the WILPF had gotten up a mass meeting, with Senator William Borah as chief speaker, to call for the recognition of the new government.

> I have no doubt that then, as now, we probably had some Communist or near-Communist members. (General Bedell Smith says he has some even in the Central Intelligence Agency! . . .) Whenever there is a hue and cry against any group so that they dare not organize or work openly, they are likely to turn to joining other organizations whose program includes *some* of their objectives. Because the Communists or the Nazis or some other undesirable group whose methods are different from ours, choose to support some of the same objectives we do, those objectives, do not, ipso facto, become undesirable. . . . We cannot disavow them because others, possibly for ignoble reasons, choose to support them too. But the important thing, the essential thing—then as now—is that our leadership always remained clearly in the hands of the genuine pacifists. Those who thought to infiltrate us had either to content themselves with *working within our framework* and putting their energy into promoting *our* program, or they got out. Eternal vigilance and hard work ourselves,

not ejection and timidity, are the price of peace within our organization.[8]

Despite these brave words, some members were beginning to fear that the WILPF was infiltrated by Communists. In Chicago in particular a group of women became so upset about what they perceived as the WILPF's failure to make a clear statement against communism that they withdrew, issuing a press statement about their fear that the WILPF was infiltrated, and they influenced some of the board members of Hull House to disassociate themselves from the WILPF. Ruth Freeman, Mildred's old friend and now president of U.S. WILPF, made a special trip to Chicago to see if she could not get to the bottom of the trouble; she came back discouraged, having found the leader adamant. The Chicago women not only went through with their threats but circulated to all WILPF branches a letter from a former president of the Denver branch, making the same charges.[9]

Whether sparked by this letter or not, the Denver branch also was soon in trouble. A member of the War Resisters League, who published a paper containing the news of all peace groups in Denver, came out with an attack on the WILPF, saying it was infiltrated by Communists and mentioning by name two or three of the most active members. His story was picked up by the Denver papers, with the result that the husband of the chair of the WILPF branch was fired from his government job, and she resigned.[10]

Mildred Olmsted asked a WILPF member to inquire of the War Resisters League about the author of the charge, and also to ask the Fellowship of Reconciliation about similar charges being made against WILPF by one of their West Coast representatives while visiting Denver. The answer that came back was that, though the editor had acted "oddly," the Denver WILPF was not adequately facing the problem of infiltration and ought to concentrate on that. Meanwhile the husband of another WILPF member lost his job because of his wife's affiliations. Mildred decided unilaterally, without consulting the committee on branch problems, to send her friend and coworker Kitty Arnett to Denver as her personal envoy to see if she could get to the bottom of the problem, but Kitty had little success and came home wanting only to get help for the victims.[11]

Finally, at the end of the year, one Denver member wrote Mildred Olmsted that the FBI had been to see her three times, and that the problem seemed to stem from the fact that some of the husbands of WILPF members had belonged to a union that was thought to be Communist led. The member whose husband had lost his job wrote to say that the charges against her husband stemmed from the fact that they subscribed to the *National Guardian* and from allegations that she had joined WILPF although she knew it was infiltrated.[12]

Like an infectious disease, the troubles began to spread from branch to branch. In Louisville, Kentucky, where a new branch had recently come into being, a particularly nasty situation arose over an interracial matter. In Shively, a suburb of Louisville, Carl Braden, a white man and an employee of the *Courier Post*, bought a house for an African-American family, the Wades, using his own name for the purchase. When this came to light, someone fired shots into the Wade home, burned a cross on the lawn, and lobbed a bomb onto the porch. The local WILPF, thinking to calm the situation, wrote a letter addressed to "Dear Shively Resident," pointing out that property values had not fallen in other suburbs where African-American families had moved, and arguing somewhat naïvely that Shively residents of German and Irish extraction, whose own immediate ancestors had known discrimination, should understand the need of the African-American families to live decently.[13]

Rather than soothing the situation, the letter sounded like proof to some people that the WILPF was behind the move and that the Wades had been placed in their neighborhood as part of a giant Communist plot. The state attorney claimed that the house had been bombed by the Bradens and others as a deliberate effort to create ill will between the races, and called for a grand jury investigation. Carl Braden, his wife, and others were called for questioning, including Louise Gilbert, the president of the Louisville branch of WILPF.

To have Louise appear before the grand jury was a shock to WILPF, whose members could not see the connection to the Wade case. In the course of the hearings it came out that the printer who published the WILPF's letter to Shively residents also published a small local magazine, in one issue of which Carl Braden had explained why he had bought the house for the Wades. Called before the grand jury, the printer was eager to cooperate with the government and gave Louise's name and address to the court as the person who had delivered the Shively letter to him. This seemed to be the extent of the attorney general's case against Louise Gilbert, but in the overheated atmosphere it created ripples. One member of the Louisville WILPF resigned, and another suggested disbanding. More seriously, because of the resulting publicity Louise was fired from her social work job.[14]

The ACLU provided a lawyer who appeared before the grand jury to argue the constitutional issues of the case, and Mildred corresponded with the national office, urging yet more efforts in the defendants' behalf. But the grand jury indicted six of those called, including Louise Gilbert, and each faced a civil trial on the charge of conspiracy. The first to be tried was Carl Braden, who was found guilty and sentenced to fifteen years in prison. Frightened, Louise Gilbert and her lawyer were glad to have an offer of help from the Emergency Civil Liberties Union, a group organized by Corliss Lamont to deal specifically with the McCarthyite cases. Later Louise agreed to speak about her case at a series of public meetings the ECLU was conducting.

By this time, with her civil case still pending, Louise Gilbert had gone to work for the WILPF in Philadelphia as an assistant to the indefatigable Kitty Arnett. When she began to speak for ECLU, therefore, WILPF received a number of complaints from more conservative members who feared that the ECLU had leftist leanings. One group to become upset was the Providence branch of the WILPF, where Louise Gilbert spoke early in 1955. The speech disturbed an older member of the Providence branch, and the president, who was regarded by some as too liberal, asked Mildred Olmsted to come and speak to them about the issues involved. Mildred did so and felt that she had answered their questions, but several members thought she had leaned too far on the side of witch-hunting. One wrote, "I was disturbed by your oversimplification of 'how to be aware of communist followers,' which I believe gives a green light to those among us who are already imbued with suspicious minds. How can honest, decent, forthright members work to carry forward our splendid program without spending all our energies looking under the beds for reds? That is the crux of the problem."[15]

The liberal president, moving to California in May, wrote to Mildred Olmsted that she would not rejoin WILPF because she could not "be part of any group which encourages its members to go to other members and ask their political affiliation."[16]

Still other branches were disturbed. The Drexel Hill branch was on the point of being admitted to the Delaware County Federation of Women's Clubs when a member of the federation objected because she had heard that WILPF was a subversive organization. The source of the allegation was an admiral who had spoken on civilian defense at the Media Women's Club and had distributed a pamphlet containing a list of "Known Communist Organizations in the United States." When someone said the WILPF was not on the list, he countered by saying that the organization frequently went under other names. *His* source of information in turn was the president of the Llanarch Women's Club, who was convinced that the WILPF was subversive and took material to all the Delaware County papers to prove it. The material did not support her allegations, and the charges were eventually dropped.

The Miami branch also was shaken when a charge that the local Unitarian church was a hotbed of Communist activity led to a grand jury investigation of communism, which resulted in several members being subpoenaed and one jailed after taking the Fifth Amendment. Several WILPF members had in fact joined an organization called Women for Peace, which Mildred Olmsted believed at the time to be Communist led. The WILPF persuaded the ACLU to take the case and gave what moral support it could. As a result of the whole experience Miami became a stronger WILPF chapter, Mildred felt.[17]

In Massachusetts another problem developed, with one of the officers of the state board openly declaring herself to be a Communist. Should she be asked to resign from the WILPF? After a long and painful period of wrestling with the question, the group decided that no officer of the organization could be a declared Communist. Many of the Massachusetts members felt that the packet on infiltration developed by U.S. WILPF did not speak to their problem, and that the national office was not helpful to them during their period of struggle. Mildred Olmsted went to hear their criticisms and relay them to the various committees that were wrestling with branch problems.[18]

Listening to criticism from both sides became one of her roles during this trying period. Some women continued to feel she was gullible. In response to these objections the committee on problems rewrote a section of one of her reports. "We thought you had not had dealings with an infiltrator whose methodology is more subtle and devious and not so forthright as a Communist who says he is a Communist and is openly so," the chair wrote to explain.[19]

Mildred Olmsted's own support of those caught in the trap of McCarthyite accusations made more timid members suspicious. Mildred was a member of the Committee to Repeal the McCarran Act, legislation that made it illegal for a person who had ever advocated violence to become an American citizen, and she had signed an open letter to that effect in 1952. She urged Governor John S. Fine of Pennsylvania to release Steve Nelson, a man who had been arrested in Pittsburgh for supposed violations of the Smith Act, and in 1959 she signed a letter to the attorney general asking that further prosecutions in Denver under the Smith Act be dismissed. She also appealed for the dismissal of charges against Carl Braden in Louisville. In Philadelphia, she urged organizations such as Americans for Democratic Action to avoid purging members suspected of being leftist. As Robert Folwell said, she refused to look for Communists under the bed, much to the annoyance of some ADA members. Despite her record, a few more radical members felt that Mildred Olmsted was compromising on civil liberties and encouraging members to spy on one another.[20]

She was also criticized for her tendency to take matters into her own hands by going herself to trouble spots or by sending a trusted colleague, as in the case of Kitty Arnett's going to Denver, without consultation with the committee on branch problems. This was an old pattern. However thoroughly Mildred Olmsted thought she believed in group process, it was hard for her to hold herself back when her beloved WILPF seemed threatened, and

17. Mildred and Allen Olmsted at WILPF conference in New Delhi, summer 1955. *Courtesy of Olmsted Papers.*

when it was clear to her that she was needed to straighten things out. This gave her a reputation for not abiding by the rules she established for others. She also began to feel that to avoid problems she ought to see every public statement made in the name of WILPF. Other peace organizations were forced to adopt the same rule in this trying time, but in the WILPF it heightened Mildred's reputation for being arbitrary and controlling. The fact that with growing age she found it more and more difficult to delegate responsibility added to the legend that her leadership was autocratic and idiosyncratic.[21]

How many members WILPF lost during this period is difficult to judge, but many resigned in anger and some as the result of fear. Edith Simester, the president of the Jane Addams branch, wrote to Mildred to share a letter from a WILPF member who was proud of Louise Gilbert but fearful that the investigators would find WILPF literature in her own possession and would regard it as subversive. She wrote, however, "I do not want to take any action and above all things do not wish my name or this letter to be used." "Such is the result of the withering influence of a climate of fear and suspicion on everybody," Edith Simester wrote.[22]

Mildred herself frequently wrote and spoke during this period of the dangers of the climate of fear. At the height of the problems in Denver she made a speech there entitled "The Role of Fear in the Modern World." "Fear is the most destructive of human emotions and produces the least intelligent action," she said.[23]

Even old friends became uneasy and fearful of guilt by association with the WILPF. In June 1954, the WILPF legislative office in Washington moved from F Street, where it had been for eight years, to the annex of Belmont House on Second Street, home of the National Women's party. The staff was barely settled in when Alice Paul, executive director of the NWP, received a letter written by an Ohio member who noted that WILPF was calling for the seating of the People's Republic of China and said she had been told that the organization was a "successor to some 'League Against Communism' 1936–1939, a definite Red-Front Organization."

Alice Paul wrote back that she had been a member of WILPF from the beginning and "have always had the highest respect for their ideals and their work. I have never heard it suggested before that the WILPF is a 'Red Front Organization' and I do not believe this to be the case. However, if such should turn out to be the case, or if there is any opposition to our renting rooms to the organization, the rental can be ended at any time. We rented the rooms with the explicit understanding that the rental could be terminated on 30 days' notice by either side."[24]

The year 1953 witnessed the high tide of McCarthyism within WILPF. It was also a hard year for Mildred and Allen. Mildred's stepmother, Jesseline Scott, had died, leaving Henry Scott's remaining land to his three daughters. Adele Saul, who was executor, wanted to sell several acres near Mildred's house in Rose Valley, but Mildred was afraid that someone would build on the lot and ruin her sense of privacy. She decided to try to buy a piece of land from Adele and from some neighbors, the Harrisons, and asked Allen to act for her and to help her finance the purchase. Allen negotiated with the Sauls and the Harrisons and in the process, Mildred felt, gave away five feet of her land.

She was extremely angry and told him that he didn't know what loyalty meant and never had. Allen pointed out that her attachment to land was irrational, based on the wound she had suffered when her father had moved her from the country to the city, and that he was really a far better pacifist than she. The quarrel was conducted by mail, as so many of the Olmsted quarrels were, and lasted for several months, while Mildred was going from city to city, ironically enough trying to make peace between the quarreling WILPF women.[25]

Reading at the age of ninety-eight some of her own letters about this and similar troubles, Mildred said with a deep sigh that she now realized that Allen had never really meant to be disloyal, and that she had been pretty hard on him. For a woman of her pride and temperament, it was a painful admission.[26]

After the long winter and spring of problems at home and abroad, Mildred Olmsted was glad to get away to attend the Twelfth International WILPF Congress in Paris in the summer of 1953. In 1951 Emily Greene Balch had suggested that a study of governmental noncooperation based on Gandhian principles be made to determine whether this would be a feasible strategy for governments in place of war. A committee was appointed to study nonviolent techniques, especially to investigate wartime resistance in Denmark and Norway during World War II.

At the Paris congress this committee made its report, and Else Zeuthen of Denmark delivered a keynote speech emphasizing the necessity of popular understanding and embracing of nonviolent principles: the fact that violence breeds violence; the necessity of truth seeking; the importance of equal rights; and the need to seek nonmaterialistic goals. Mildred Olmsted felt this emphasis on nonviolence came at just the right time, when WILPF was "under enormous pressure to prove that we are not under Communist influence."[27]

Mildred Olmsted herself addressed the congress, giving a survey of U.S. attitudes in world affairs. She described the popular confusion about the war in Korea, which most Americans viewed as a police action taken to support the United Nations; the resentment of European criticism of the United States despite the bounties of the Marshall Plan; factors behind the election of President Eisenhower; and the rise of McCarthyism, which she confidently assured her listeners would soon be defeated. "The history of these movements is that after they have sprung up and grown big enough, the better elements in the communities or the nation become aroused to action. Sometimes the leaders are imprisoned because of dishonesty or other law breaking, sometimes just sufficient exposure causes their followers to melt away and they are reduced to insignificance."[28]

An armistice agreement had been arranged in Korea a few days before the congress opened, but Korea was in shambles, with 10 million of its 21 million people refugees, 125,000 abandoned children, and 15,000 vagrant adolescents. The WILPF pointed out that the seating of the People's Republic of China was essential before this peace could become permanent.

Mildred Olmsted attended the executive committee meeting prior to the congress but decided to remove her name from the list of those nominated to serve again. She had been a member for fourteen years; it was time for other women to have a turn, and it was important not to have too many Americans on the committee. She was, however, glad to accept appointment to the international education committee at this congress.

It was a relief the next summer not to have to go abroad on WILPF business. Instead she and Allen visited Tony in Mexico, where he was at work on a two-year assignment in an American Friends Service Committee project working to improve water and agricultural methods in a Mexican village. Like his brother Peter, Tony was a conscientious objector, and this work was his alternative service. At the camp Mildred Olmsted was asked to talk about her work, and several of the young women came up to her afterwards and said they would like to work for the WILPF. She came home elated, planning to find more ways to reach young people in colleges with the WILPF message.[29]

Some of the internal troubles WILPF had had during the

height of the McCarthy period were a result, in Mildred Olmsted's view, of problems of unclear assignments and overlapping committees. In the spring of 1954 she had proposed that a survey be made of the WILPF organization, and in the fall of that year she persuaded her old friend Arthur Dunham to do such a survey for $500. The Dunham report, which was released in the spring of 1955, suggested that the board was far too large, that there were too many overlapping committees, and that the administration be centralized in the Philadelphia office, putting Mildred in charge of the Washington program. He also recommended that staff members should no longer serve as voting members of the board of directors, and that attention be given to strengthening branches. Mildred Olmsted was not sure that WILPF could function with the drastically reduced board Dunham suggested, but she liked the rest of his ideas and set to work putting them into action. She was now effectively executive secretary, although she was not given that title for another eight years.

While she still did not tell her age, members of the inner WILPF circle realized that Mildred Olmsted would be sixty-five in 1955. There were some on the board who began a campaign to persuade her to resign, although they did not come right out and say it to her face. Mildred herself had considered resigning in order to run for president of the U.S. Section, and Allen and her friend Helen Rea both encouraged her in this plan. In the long run, however, the thought of getting along without the WILPF, which was her life, was too hard to face. Since 1922, the WILPF had met her needs for influence, for recognition, and for the integration of her whole self into a struggle she could believe in; to contemplate giving it up was too hard. Any thought of resigning was put on hold.

She did, however, finally agree to Allen's proposition that they at least take time for a lifetime dream, a trip around the world, taking the money from his savings. At first she wondered if they could afford it, and she talked it over with Ruth Mellor, who feared that Allen was not putting money aside for his and Mildred's old age because of his depression. Allen wrote to Ruth to refute this charge, and to say that Mildred would have at least $100,000 when he died. Ruth responded by apologizing, saying that they must go. "If I die I will leave money to Mildred, and if we both live I'll move to Rose Valley and we'll spend it."[30]

For Ruth Mellor was going to accompany them. The tensions of the triangle had at last eased, and the three were knit into a relationship in which each had a role. Ruth was confidante and supporter to Allen, helping him to get over his hurt feelings when Mildred snapped at him, and trying to aid him in understanding why Mildred was the way she was. "Ruth keeps saying that it is an inherent and immutable part of your character and integral part of what we both love in you that you cannot admit fault and must blame others for what is as much your responsibility as theirs," Allen once wrote to Mildred when he was hurt and angry.[31]

In return for soothing support, Allen helped Ruth to continue to feel confidence in herself as a woman and liked to take her on side adventures when Mildred was too preoccupied with the WILPF to have time for either of them.

Mildred was the apex of the triangle, needing the admiration and love of the other two. She was not to be possessed. She wanted and needed love without demands. She was, as Ruth once said, insatiable. After Ruth had spent a Christmas with the Olmsteds and had found it hard to be just a part of the family, she had written to Mildred, "I need you. You are a precious person. Strong & unselfish—able and willing to carry burdens. They pile up and you take them on. Vivid—alive—insatiable little thing—you really want everything out of life and are not afraid to go after it."[32]

The trio flew to Hawaii in July 1955 from California, after Mildred Olmsted attended a WILPF annual meeting in Oakland, and they spent a couple of days at Waikiki Beach before going on to the quieter island of Kauai. Arriving in Tokyo after a seventeen-hour flight from Honolulu, Mildred was met by a delegation of Japanese women who presented her with a bouquet and a specially made kimono. That afternoon another delegation arrived at the Imperial Hotel, where the Olmsteds were staying, to invite Mildred to speak in Hiroshima on 6 August at an international meeting in observance of the tenth anniversary of the first atom bombing. She was also asked to attend a conference of leaders of different religious faiths, and to meet with women members of the Diet.

The Japanese section of WILPF was under the leadership of Tano Jodai and Fuji Nomiyama, both connected with the Japan Women's University (Tano Jodai later became president) and both of whom had visited Mildred in Rose Valley. The group was strong and had established branches throughout the country. While the Olmsteds were in Tokyo, the Japanese WILPF arranged a whole series of events and entertainments for them, including dinner at a tempura restaurant and an evening of Kabuki theater. The Olmsteds were glad to spend a few quiet days in a Kyoto inn before going on to Hiroshima for the 6 August observance.

Their reception in Hiroshima was overwhelming. When their train pulled in, they were met by a horde of newspaper reporters and photographers, as well as singing school children and flag-waving crowds. Mildred was invited by the mayor's committee to lay a wreath at the memorial arch. They were escorted to the best rooms in the new hotel and given seats of honor at the auditorium.

Mildred Olmsted's speech was short and powerful. She spoke of the development of the WILPF and of its many years of struggle to make the world aware of the common interests of all persons, as neighbors.

And all the world has become our neighborhood! The invention of the airplane and the telephone, radios and television has done that, so I can leave America one day and be here the next. But most of all the development of atomic energy has made us neighbors because we all stand together in fear of it. It can destroy us all or it can save us all. It is the people of the world who will determine which.

I said that I am here as an international representative of an international organization for women for peace and freedom, but I cannot forget that I am also an American. I am sorry that my country ever used its knowledge of atomic energy to destroy life for us all and to the people of Hiroshima I want to express my regret. . . .

. . . Ideas are more powerful than swords and they spread even further than atomic dust. Today as we stand in Hiroshima, ten years after that first terrible blast, we who are here know that war must be wiped out forever and more intelligent methods substituted for settling the disputes that will ever arise among men. We know and we are determined that atomic energy and human energy alike must be devoted exclusively to promoting the welfare of all men everywhere. If only we work hard enough, ten years from now when our children meet together, the idea of national armaments in any country may sound as ridiculous and as incredible as the idea that the earth is flat and not round. A whole new world is opening to us all![33]

This speech was met with uproarious applause, and Mildred Olmsted's picture and words appeared in all the Japanese newspapers the next day. It was one of the high points in her life.

After Japan, the Olmsteds and Ruth Mellor visited Hong Kong, Thailand, and India, staying in out-of-the-way guest houses, exploring the jungle, and riding on elephants.

"You can imagine that Allen's exploring mind has shown us many things not on the ordinary tourist plan," Mildred wrote Adele. "Each country we have been in has been both interesting and enjoyable, some cities, some countryside, swimming, hiking, travel by boat, plane, electric line, sleeping car, auto, bus, rickshaw and even sedan chair. We have stayed in native hotels and eaten a wide range of foods, natural to the country, as well as fine old chilly British colonial hotels with modern air-cooled rooms, wide open air dining rooms, excellent service, delicious eight course meals and private porches. We have left each country with regret that we couldn't stay longer and see more."[34]

In India, Mildred Olmsted met with a WILPF branch in New Delhi. An Indian WILPF Section had been organized by Madame Pandit and was now led by Sushila Nayar, speaker of the Delhi State Assembly. Mildred made a speech, stressing her experiences in Japan where so many of the women she met longed for peace and "are hungry to join with women from other countries in any action that will keep them free from another armaments race, provided they are not committed to either a pro-communist or an anti-communist organization."[35]

For Mildred Olmsted, it was clear that the answer to the need of the Indian women was WILPF. Gone was the day when she thought the organization should not belong exclusively to women, for it was clear to her now that the women of the world had common interests and longed to work together for peace. If only the WILPF had the resources to respond to these openings!

After India, the travelers went on to Egypt, where they saw the pyramids and took a camel ride into the desert. Although Allen and Ruth were sixty-seven and Mildred almost sixty-five, the three companions seemed to thrive on their life of adventure and returned home in September determined to see even more of the world.

Back in the United States the Olmsteds caught up with their extended family. Peter and Polly now had two sons, Eric and Kenny, and had recently moved to the University of Pittsburgh where Peter was teaching biochemistry, having received his doctorate from Harvard in 1954. Enid and Bill and their son, Stuart, were living in Springfield, Massachusetts. Tony had returned from his two years in Mexico, more self-confident than he had ever been as the result of his engagement to Isabel Gaster, a beautiful girl he had met in Mexico. It was clear that Tony was not going to college, but he had a good job in an automobile shop and was saving for his marriage. Mildred's sister Marian, who had broken her ankle and been diagnosed as diabetic while Mildred was away, was out of the hospital and back living in a nearby boarding house.

Mildred Olmsted had scarcely unpacked her bags before she was busy answering requests from organizations who wanted to hear her reactions to her around-the-world trip. She spoke to several branches of the WILPF, to a Fellowship of Reconciliation meeting, to the Friends, to the Delaware County Evening Group, and to a YWCA public affairs forum. Her trip had shown her, she said, that Americans were quite unaware of how they were viewed by the developing nations. "Rightly or wrongly, they believe that we want to bind them to us so as to use their land for military bases and their people to fight our battles, or that we are more concerned about exploiting their raw materials for our purposes, than we are about the welfare of their people."[36]

Mildred Olmsted's deep-seated patriotism was affronted by the view of the United States she had experienced abroad, and yet she had to admit that in its present state, America had earned its bad marks. The solution, she thought, was to get to work to influence the Congress and the administration to give up the dangerous dogma that all nations must join the country's military alliances, and to begin to offer the kind of disinterested aid to the developing world that would help to create widespread conditions for peace and freedom.

14
Time of Troubles

*I*N JANUARY 1955 Rosa Parks refused to move to the back of a bus in Montgomery, Alabama, and began a nonviolent movement for civil rights. In February 1956 a federal court ruled that the University of Alabama must accept its first African-American student, Autherine Lucy. The cold war was heating up, and American school children were crouching under their desks in preparation for atomic attacks. Britain gave up its rule of the Suez Canal, but with France tried to regain possession of this vital waterway after Egypt seized it. Revolutions began that year in Algeria, in Hungary, in Kenya, and in Cuba.

To some it was a terrifying year, but to Mildred Scott Olmsted, who gloried in change, it was a time of challenge and hopefulness. In her speeches during this period she liked to say that the world was in the midst of four revolutions.

> 1. a social revolution which will change basic patterns of human relationship, within families and communities as well as between stronger and weaker groups and between nations, 2. an economic revolution which would make prosperity and poverty dependent upon conditions outside the control of any one country or group of countries, 3. a political revolution which created more than a score of new countries and encouraged the growth of both nationalism, regionalism, and internationalism simultaneously, and 4. a scientific revolution which has carried us below the seas, above the air and around at such incredible speeds that it makes the whole earth very tiny indeed and vulnerable to annihilation in numerous ways.[1]

Mildred Olmsted planned the 1957 annual board meeting, held in Miami, which had as its theme, "Nonviolent Paths to Peace." Delegates from seventeen states, some 25 percent African American, attended. Mildred arranged as far as possible that African-American and white women traveled together to Miami. At the conference the women heard reports about violence against African Americans and whites who supported integration, including an eyewitness account by Clarence Jordan on the attack on Koinonia, an integrated community in Georgia, and they resolved to send a certificate of honor to each African-American child who had faced mob violence to enter an integrated school.

After this conference the WILPF began organizing in the South in earnest, first in Atlanta and then in Tuskegee. A branch in Durham–Chapel Hill decided to run an interracial preschool group. In April 1958, Mildred Olmsted visited Montgomery, where she interviewed Irene West, one of the organizers of the bus boycott, who told her that northerners should look to the practice of integration in northern cities. Mildred agreed and persuaded her to come to the WILPF annual meeting in Wisconsin. She also stopped in Atlanta, where the integrated group was having leadership problems, and recruited more women for the Wisconsin meeting. A carload of four women from Montgomery and Atlanta drove to Appleton and participated in the meeting. Tragically, on the way back they had a serious car accident, and all but Irene West were killed. The WILPF mourned their loss and determined to set up a special fund for integration work in their memory.

In March 1959 the WILPF held a special conference entitled "Civil Rights in the South" in Atlanta for women from seven southern states, with attendance equally divided between whites and African Americans. Mildred Olmsted drove to the conference with three women from Tuskegee Institute and learned something about segregation firsthand en route. When the women grew hungry, they could not find a place willing even to sell them sandwiches to eat in the car, despite the many eating establishments advertising along the way for business. "What an eye-opener it is to anyone to work in the South and how thrilling to see the courage which our members are showing when faced with Nazi-like actions!" Mildred commented in her branch letter.[2]

At the conference Mildred Olmsted spoke of the role non-violence was playing in the struggle for justice in the South. "It is becoming more accepted as a method of getting change made in the world," she said. "It is a technique requiring skill, patience and courage, but it has already been proved effective."[3]

As a follow-up for the conference, Mildred Olmsted hired a special fieldworker for part-time work in the region and planned a second conference on the same subject for 1960. In late 1959 Virginia Durr, a WILPF member who had moved to Montgomery, Alabama, especially to work on civil rights, urged Mildred to plan this conference around the issue of disarmament, since she said African-American women were tired of discussing race relations and would prefer to work with their white sisters on common problems. In 1960, however, the civil rights movement began to heat up, with members of the Student Nonviolent Coordinating Committee starting their lunchroom sit-ins, and WILPF members became involved in supporting these efforts. The conference, postponed to 1961, concentrated on civil rights in the South.[4]

In 1960 the WILPF celebrated the one hundredth anniversary of Jane Addams's birth with a special centennial committee working to raise money. Mildred believed that the money collected in the United States for the celebration ought to go to support work for integration and set herself a goal of $20,000 for that purpose. There was also an international committee collecting for the fund with the goal of underwriting a Jane Addams Memorial Home for Refugees in Spittal, Austria. The contributions of U.S. WILPF members therefore supported both goals.

Not all integration problems were in the South. In the course of an ugly explosion of racial hatred in Levittown, New Jersey, a young minister lost his job for taking a courageous stand in support of an African-American family and was forced to move to Philadelphia. Mildred looked up the wife of the minister and offered her a job as the WILPF literature secretary.

But the WILPF's mandate to work for both peace and freedom, and Mildred's own commitment to peace, did not allow her to concentrate exclusively on the civil rights movement in the late 1950s. The growing concern about the proliferation of the atom bomb and the dangers of atmospheric testing were bringing many new people into the peace field. Mildred would have liked them all to join the WILPF, which was slow to recover its membership after the effects of the war and the McCarthy period, but instead, they formed new peace groups. Following the policy "If you can't lick 'em, join 'em," Mildred became active herself in many of these organizations.

In the spring of 1957 Clarence Pickett, executive director emeritus of the American Friends Service Committee, Norman Cousins of the *Saturday Review*, and Homer Jack of the Unitarian Service Committee held the first of a series of meetings at the Jane Addams House in Philadelphia, which resulted in the fall of 1957 in the development of a National Committee for a Sane Nuclear Policy, or SANE, as it came to be called. In November, SANE invited WILPF and other organizations to send members to participate in a vigil against nuclear bomb tests before the White House, and in December ran a series of ads in the *New York Times* and elsewhere. Mildred urged the WILPF branches to place the ads in their local papers, but to be sure to use the WILPF name.

Nobel Prize–winner Linus Pauling, who had circulated a petition signed by some 11,000 scientists asking for a cessation of nuclear testing, took part in the White House vigil along with Clarence Pickett and afterwards visited Haverford College, where Mildred Olmsted met him and his wife, Ava, who was persuaded to become an active WILPF member. Six months later Mildred Olmsted helped the Pennsylvania branch of WILPF arrange a public meeting at the Philadelphia public library at which three Nobel Prize–winners, Dr. Pauling, Pearl Buck, and Clarence Pickett (the AFSC won the prize under his leadership), spoke to a standing-room-only crowd.

An action-oriented group, the Committee for Nonviolent Action Against Nuclear Weapons, that had formed in the summer of 1957 to protest bomb testing in Nevada, moved into the Jane Addams House, and WILPF became the sponsor of several of its projects. One was the sailing of a vessel, the *Golden Rule*, into atomic test waters in the Pacific in the summer of 1958. When the crew of the *Golden Rule* was stopped and jailed in Hawaii, another ship, the *Phoenix*, sailed by Earle Reynolds, his wife, Barbara, and their daughter, took up the mission. Mildred loved the courage and adventurousness of the mission.

In 1959 a group of peace activists under the leadership of

A. J. Muste of the Fellowship of Reconciliation decided to establish a vigil around Fort Deitrich, in Maryland, to protest the continued manufacture of weapons of biological warfare. The WILPF had a special day to stand in vigil, and Mildred Olmsted took her turn. Vigiling was not the sort of thing the WILPF did in the old days, but times were changing, and Mildred was delighted to change with them.

Even the Quakers were holding vigil. In November 1960 Peter and Polly Olmsted joined Mildred and hundreds of other Friends in a vigil for peace in Washington, D.C., to commemorate the first statement made by the Quakers against war in 1661. For Mildred it was a proud day.

Peter and Polly had recently moved to the Philadelphia area, where Peter had a position teaching at Temple University. They chose a house in Rydal, on the other side of the city from Rose Valley. Mildred thought that they were trying to be as far from her as they possibly could, fearing her interference. It was, she thought, a false fear; she had made up her mind not to be involved in the lives of her children once they were married. All three children, however, saw it differently. Peter complained privately that when he went to see his mother, he was always given a list of things to do. Relations between Enid and Mildred were proper on the surface but never really close: Enid had never been much interested in Mildred's various campaigns; Mildred joked that her daughter did not approve of her. Underneath seemed to be unresolved differences that reached back into Enid's early childhood. Tony kept his distance; having found Isabel, he was able to move away from his parents. Mildred accepted this situation with stoicism and kept herself too busy to be hurt.

There continued to be new developments in the peace movement to occupy her. The continuation of atmospheric testing was frightening to mothers of young children, who were learning more and more about the dangers of radiation poisoning appearing in the milk and vegetables their children ate. In the fall of 1961 a group of housewives in Washington, D.C., organized a Women's Strike for Peace. In the Philadelphia area, a WILPF member, Ethel Taylor, took the leadership in bringing together a large number of women to participate. The organizers of WSP planned to keep the group loosely structured and spontaneous. Some women who were tired of what they perceived to be the increasing bureaucracy of the WILPF decided to put their energies in WSP instead. Mildred Olmsted, however, looked on WSP as an offshoot of the WILPF and took pride in its accomplishments. This was the beginning of the role the WILPF was to play in nurturing new women's peace groups into being.

Another new peace group to organize in the fall of 1961 was Turn Toward Peace, a coalition of major churches and organizations such Americans for Democratic Action, the American Veterans Committee, and the United Auto Workers, as well as such stalwarts as the Fellowship of Reconciliation, the American Friends Service Committee, Consultative Peace Conference (as the name implies, a group of peace organization leaders who consulted together on strategy), and the WILPF. Norman Thomas was the leader, and Sanford Gottleib and Robert Pickus were to direct the organization.

Mildred Olmsted greeted this new activism with enthusiasm. "Here in the United States the peace movement is no longer content to stay indoors," she wrote in an editorial in *Four Lights*. "Like the anti-slavery movement and the suffrage movement it has spent years studying, educating, collecting signatures, sending delegations, persuading. Now it is turning to marches, to picketing, to demonstrations and it is getting the attention of the press!"[5]

At the same time she worried that such groups as Turn Toward Peace might attempt to persuade some of her WILPF members to put their energies into the new organization. It was the same old conflict. On the one hand she recognized that different groups brought in differing constituencies, and therefore a larger number of workers overall for the peace movement; Jane Addams had always insisted the more peace groups the better. On the other hand Mildred hated to see energy and money going to other organizations when it might be spent building up her beloved WILPF. She found it particularly hard to watch WILPF members raising money for other groups. She felt that WILPF had initiated many of the ideas for which others got the credit, and that WILPF had a shrinking-violet mentality about advertising itself. In one of her branch letters she quoted a former branch chair.

I cannot agree with some of my friends who say that they will work in other groups for peace and freedom. On the contrary, I am keenly aware of the small number of organizations and the very small number of leaders who are working directly on disarmament, world development, alternatives to violence, against the encroachment of the military upon civilian life. I know WILPF is a small organization, but I would rather work on a valid cause in a small organization that fails than to work on lesser programs in organizations that seemingly succeed by virtue of funds and members.[6]

Mildred Olmsted sometimes envied organizations such as the Fellowship of Reconciliation or the American Friends Service Committee that seemed to grow and to raise money almost effortlessly. But they were tied to religious groups and had to worry about their tax-exempt status. "Not being tied to any religion or party we are *free*," she declared with joy. She urged her friends and colleagues to give their money to the cause least secure, the cause farthest out. In most cases, she thought, WILPF was that cause.[7]

She remained determined to do what she could to rebuild WILPF's membership. Despite her increasing age and her family's concern about her heart, she kept up a rugged schedule of traveling. In March 1956 she visited branch meetings in Minnesota, Wisconsin, Illinois, Missouri, and Kentucky. In July she flew to Birmingham, England, for the international congress, then visited Spain and Portugal with Allen. The Olmsteds made a quick trip to Mexico for Tony and Isabel's wedding in early 1957, and later that spring Mildred traveled through the South on her way to the board meeting in Miami. In early 1958 she visited branches in Miami, Montgomery, Atlanta, Dayton, Cincinnati, Columbus, and Richmond and spent her vacation horseback riding in Montana. In the spring of 1959, she traveled in the South, winding up at the Atlanta conference, then in New England, where the annual meeting was held in June in Massachusetts.

At the time of the 1959 annual meeting the WILPF family was shocked by a tragedy. Jack Arnett, the younger son of their beloved finance secretary, Kitty Arnett, had finished medical school and was living in Pittsburgh. For no reason that anyone could understand, he committed suicide. Kitty was devastated and took

18. Ruth Mellor, Allen Olmsted, Diana Olmsted, Remington Olmsted, Samuel Olmsted, and Mildred Olmsted in Remington Olmsted's restaurant, Da Meo Patacca, in Rome, ca. 1962. *Courtesy of Olmsted Papers.*

a leave of absence to recover. Mildred, who was very close to Kitty, suffered with her, although with Scott stoicism she suffered in silence.

Following the annual meeting, Allen, Mildred, and Ruth Mellor had planned an adventure in Iceland, a ten-day pony-trekking trip exploring the ice fields, glaciers, and geysers of this northern land. The three companions, joined by a young teacher from Scotland, had to travel overland by jeep to join the group riding ponies. At some places they were forced to get out and climb so that the jeep could make it up the hill, or wade so that it could make it across a river. But there were compensations—

lovely pools of water heated by volcanic action to bathe in, and fish ready to take Allen's hook whenever he had a moment to drop it into a pool. It was the kind of adventure Mildred had loved since she was a small girl, and she rejoiced that she was still able to keep up with the other riders.[8]

From Iceland, Mildred and Ruth went on to the WILPF International Congress in Stockholm, where the delegates heard reports from twenty national sections, listened to a keynote speech by Linus Pauling, and advocated the creation of a research institute under the United Nations to study the causes and solutions of world tensions. Individual visitors were present from Russia, Poland, and East Germany, but there were no WILPF sections from behind the iron curtain.[9]

Traveling as private individuals rather than WILPF members, however, Ruth and Mildred were able to visit East Germany after the conference was over. In West Berlin they were met at their hotel by members of the German Women's Council, and asked what they most wanted to see. Mildred said they wanted to see East Berlin, a part of the city where they had lived in 1920, as well as the badly bombed city of Dresden. The women of the organization arranged for both of these trips. In East Berlin they met with women who told them that East Germany was here to stay, that they intended to keep Berlin as their capital, but that they were eager to work with other women to stamp out war.

While Mildred and Ruth journeyed in Europe, Allen hurried home to a job he loved, judge of the Court of Common Pleas of Delaware County. After years of running for judge, Allen had finally been chosen by Governor George Leader to fill an unexpired term on the bench. He was sworn in on 5 December 1958 and spent eleven of the happiest months of his life on the Delaware County bench. Writing to Adele and Maurice Saul in their winter home in Key West in February 1959, he described some of his pleasure. "They said, don't you wish you were going to Key West? And I had to be honest and say nothing in Key West is as much fun as what I am doing in Media. I like telling the jury what the law is. I can't say why I enjoy this so much more than making decisions in the office. I got through five weeks of jury trials with no slips."[10] And writing Mildred a few weeks later:

In the afternoon I went to the Parole Board at the new State building at Broad and Spring Garden. Surprising to me how surprised and pleased everyone was to have a judge come and visit them. It seems to me the most natural thing in the world, but apparently few judges do it. . . .

. . . Writing "sentences" today which I am going to distribute to the newspaper. I am trying to write sentences of which the Prophet Micah would approve.[11]

The joy was not to last. Although Allen won the respect of his Republican peers as well as that of many independent lawyers, he was unable to defeat his Republican opponent in the 1959 elections and had to return to the practice of law. Mildred, who had enjoyed Allen's surge of good spirits during the judgeship, shared his disappointment. "I am no Republican," she wrote in her branch letter of December 1959. "My husband has just been defeated by a corrupt and entrenched Republican machine." People pointed out to the Olmsteds that a dead Republican had once defeated a live Democrat in the county, and that the Republican machine continued to infiltrate and control the regular Democratic party (Allen had always run as a Reform Democrat), but it remained a bitter pill for Mildred and Allen to swallow.[12]

To get over this blow, and to prepare Mildred for the year of centennial celebration of Jane Addams's birth, the Olmsteds spent the month of January 1960 in the Caribbean, visiting Cuba, where the revolution had recently taken place. Having seen Cuba a number of times under a corrupt dictatorship, Mildred was pleased with some of the changes she saw, though she was aware that freedom of speech was curtailed as it had been under President Batista.

The centennial year was a full one. In May the Pennsylvania branch gave a banquet for seven hundred, with Linus Pauling and Helen Gahagan Douglas, now active with the Committee for World Development and World Disarmament, as principal speakers. National WILPF put on a second major dinner in Washington in June with Philip Noel-Baker, British pacifist, and Agnes Meyer, noted journalist, speaking. In her speech, Agnes Meyer suggested that perhaps the time had come for personal diplomacy between

19. Ruth Mellor, ca. 1960. *Courtesy of Olmsted Papers.*

American women and those behind the iron curtain. After the banquet the WILPF followed up on her idea and developed a committee to begin to plan for a little conference between U.S. and USSR women.

Mildred Olmsted was still trying to raise $20,000 to support special WILPF work in the South during this busy year and was encouraging WILPF branches to have their own centennial celebrations. Weeding her garden was a refuge from her worries. "If only WILPF branches were like strawberries," she said in a branch letter, "sending out runners." One branch had just divided itself into three, so perhaps a trend was starting.[13]

20. First WILPF-sponsored U.S.-USSR women's conference at Bryn Mawr, 1961. Mildred Olmsted is seated behind the table. *Courtesy of Swarthmore College Peace Collection.*

In August she took time out for a trip with Allen and Ruth in the wilds of northern Canada, canoeing or following trails known only to their Indian guides, surrounded by miles of silent forests and lakes. "The still and the peace were so satisfying," she wrote. "It was a shock to emerge into the strident voices, the charges and counter charges, the terrible senseless stupidities of the current world."[14]

There was at least some good news. Belmont House, the home of the National Women's party from which WILPF was currently renting office space, had been threatened by demolition in order to create a parking lot for the capitol. Annalee Stewart, the WILPF legislative secretary, and others had lobbied for it to be named as a historic building instead, and this had been accomplished. Alice Paul of the National Women's party had written a letter of appreciation to Annalee Stewart for the work she had done on Capitol Hill to save the building. (Ironically it developed a few months later that because of its new status, the Belmont House could no longer rent office space to WILPF.)[15]

Mildred Olmsted's trip behind the iron curtain to visit East Germany had intrigued her. She still remembered her 1932 visit to the USSR with much pleasure and wanted to go back. She was happy, therefore, to serve on the committee planning the little conference between Soviet and American women suggested by Agnes Meyer. She was very ill with shingles during the early months of 1961 but recovered in late spring and volunteered to be the one to negotiate the details of the exchange with the Soviet women's committee.

Mildred Olmsted's proposed trip to the Soviet Union interested the FBI, and they began to watch her movements. The bureau had been keeping a file on her since 1932 and the trip to the USSR she had led under the sponsorship of the Open Road. Listed were Mildred's brief membership in 1938 on the advisory board of the American League for Peace and Democracy, and on a committee to support the World Youth Congress at Vassar; her work with the Committee for Freedom for India in 1945; and participation in an event to welcome the Dean of Canterbury in 1948. Her protests against the McCarran Act and against the Smith Act, which prohibited the advocacy of the violent overthrow of the government, were noted. Her participation in the National Council Against Conscription, which the House Un-American Activities Committee claimed had fellow travelers among its officers, was also cited. Mildred finally obtained this file in 1975.[16]

An FBI agent interviewed members of Mildred's staff in 1961, and found one informant who said that "Olmsted was an offensive type personality. Also an overbearing type person and not popular with her colleagues."[17]

Unaware that this investigation was going on, Mildred and Allen planned their trip, of course including Ruth. By happy coincidence Peter Olmsted had been invited to go to Moscow in the summer of 1961 to attend an international biochemists' conference, and Polly had arranged to leave their three children and accompany him. The four Olmsteds and Ruth Mellor crossed the ocean on a Holland America Line steamer, then visited Amsterdam, where they saw the house of Anna Frank, before going on to Warsaw, where they toured the museum of the Holocaust at Auschwitz and were deeply troubled. They also stopped at Krakow and

Kiev before going on to Russia. On the way home, they stopped in Vienna, then in Switzerland and France, to show Peter and Polly some of their favorite places.[18]

It should have been a joyous occasion, but it was marred for Mildred and Allen by their discovery that all was not well between Peter and Polly. They knew enough about marital discord themselves to recognize the symptoms, and Allen thought he should talk to Peter about it. Polly, with whom they discussed the situation, told them no, she would prefer to try to handle the problems herself.[19]

In Moscow, Peter and Polly went to stay at the college where the symposium on biochemistry was being held, while Allen, Mildred, and Ruth stayed at a regular tourist hotel. Allen arranged to see a case being tried in court, while Ruth went to see a special school for girls with problems. Mildred, meanwhile, took her invitation to the little conference, which was to be held at Bryn Mawr, to the Soviet women's group. The Soviet women introduced Mildred Olmsted to Madame Popova, president of the Union of Soviet Societies of Friendship and Cultural Relations with Foreign Countries, and her aides; after a formal and lengthy interview, these women told Mildred that she would receive an answer to her invitation in about a week. When Madame Popova and her assistant came to give this answer and saw the hotel where Mildred was staying, they said she ought not to be in an ordinary hotel but somewhere she could be given special treatment. Mildred said that her quarters were fine, and she went on to negotiate the details of the visit: who would interpret, what the women would do in case they disagreed, how they would handle statements in the press.[20]

The Soviets offered to pay their U.S. expenses, but Mildred insisted that they would be the guests of WILPF and hurried home to start fund-raising for the event. She also went to see Eleanor Roosevelt, and to ask if she would be willing to receive the Soviet women in her apartment in New York.[21]

The resulting conference between ten Soviet women and twelve American women was held at the Deanery at Bryn Mawr College for one week overlapping the Thanksgiving holidays. The Soviets had sent important women: one was the deputy mayor of

21. Mildred Olmsted meets Nina Khrushchev, Moscow, 1964. *Courtesy of Women's International League for Peace and Freedom.*

Moscow, another the editor of the leading women's magazine, a third the rector of the Second Moscow Medical Institute, and so forth. The American delegation had one anthropologist, one sociologist, and one lawyer, but most were generalists, hardworking members of the WILPF. The Americans were surprised to discover that the Soviet women wanted to hear their criticisms of the Soviet Union and were interested, rather than defensive, when they expressed these criticisms. The atmosphere was therefore frank and open. The women discussed "peaceful coexistence," disarmament, the future of Germany, then very much at issue, the admission of China to the United Nations, and the role of the United Nations itself. In speaking of Germany, the Soviet women each rose to recount the story of their own losses during World War II, and their consequent dread of another war, in a manner that deeply impressed the Americans.

Standing in the way of the two groups' ability to arrive at consensus was a cultural difference, according to Elise Boulding, a sociologist and active WILPF member who participated. The Soviets as a whole liked to make long-range plans and tended to feel that once an image of the future was created it was "as good as done." The American people liked to take a cautious, one-step-at-a-time approach, emphasizing what could be done right now. The Soviets therefore did not want to consider details until a broad agreement was reached, while the Americans did not want to commit themselves to a long-range goal until next steps had been worked out. Some of these differences played themselves out in modified form in the course of the conference. The two delegations were able nevertheless to agree upon a statement urging their governments to work for general and complete disarmament.[22]

Mildred Olmsted was a part of the U.S. delegation and also took responsibility for the entertainment of the visitors before and after the conference. In New York the Soviets met Marian Anderson at Mrs. Roosevelt's apartment, toured the Guggenheim Museum, visited Harlem and Macy's, and took in a musical comedy. In Philadelphia they saw an integrated housing development and school, visited Independence Hall, the Philadelphia orchestra and the art museum, and were entertained individually by American families for Thanksgiving dinner. In Washington Eunice Shriver led them through the White House, and they had a conference with Esther Peterson of the Labor Department, tea at the Russian embassy, and a special reception at the home of Agnes Meyer.[23]

After the conference was over, WILPF prepared a packet of materials on life in the United States to be sent to the Russian women. The State Department wanted some information on the United States included, and an FBI agent called on Mildred Olmsted to make this request. When she refused to comply, he told her she was no patriot and stamped out of the office.

Mildred Olmsted, however, felt the whole exchange with the Soviet women was an expression of her patriotism. She was exhausted but triumphant. It had been one of the high points of her long career. Her mentors, Hannah Clothier Hull and Emily

Greene Balch, had died in recent years; she was one of the oldest active members of the WILPF family. She could look back on the early 1920s when WILPF's advocacy of peace seemed outrageous to most people, to the days when she and her colleagues had been called red, to the long struggle to influence the United States to recognize the USSR, to the dark days of World War II, to the chilling atmosphere of the McCarthy period, and feel a genuine sense of pride in accomplishment. "I hope you can take a bit of a vacation and enjoy the triumph of your Soviet women's conference," Ruth wrote to her on her seventy-first birthday.[24]

Enid Burke had given birth to her fourth child, a girl, in late November, and was not coming to Rose Valley for Christmas. The Olmsteds contemplated a trip to London but decided on a quiet Christmas at home. Mildred spent a night with Peter and Polly and their three children in their house in Rydal during the Christmas preparations and noticed that Polly seemed extremely restless. She spoke to Peter about it when they took the train into town together the next morning, and Peter brought Polly a box of candy that night.

A women's march on Washington had been called by Women's Strike for Peace for 15 January 1962. Some WILPF members, including Kitty Arnett, went down the day before. Mildred Olmsted with others took an early train from Philadelphia that morning. When she reached Union Station in Washington she was surprised to find Kitty anxiously awaiting her train.

"I need to talk to you for a moment," Kitty said, drawing her aside. Then, as gently as possible, she told her the terrible news. Early that morning Peter Olmsted had been found dead in his laboratory at Temple. He had committed suicide.[25]

Mildred returned to Philadelphia by the next train, accompanied by Kitty Arnett, and Allen met her. Together they went to Rydal to see Polly, who was of course very upset. She told them, according to Mildred, that she had been trying in vain for years to persuade Peter to see a marriage counselor and had finally given up hope. The night before she had told Peter that she wanted a divorce and custody of the children, and that she had already consulted a lawyer. Peter left to walk the streets and eventually to go to his laboratory, where he wrote Polly a note and then took poison.

For Mildred, the next few days passed in a blur. The Olmsteds felt that under the circumstances they ought to arrange for Peter's burial, and Polly acquiesced. Peter was cremated, and they buried his ashes in a beautiful part of the garden at Rose Valley and arranged for a memorial service at Providence Meeting the following Sunday. Letters of sympathy began to pour in from all over the country and the world, along with contributions in Peter's name to the American Friends Service Committee, the School in Rose Valley, and the WILPF. Old comrades like Norman Thomas and Clarence Pickett and Nevin Sayre wrote to express their sorrow. Judges and lawyers and clients sent notes to Judge Olmsted and his wife. Gibby and Hilda Osborne wrote, and Trudy Prichard tried to arrange to come to Mildred, as Mildred had once come to her at a similar time. There were letters from all the Olmsteds, from branches of the WILPF all over the country, from men and women who had met the Olmsteds on their travels and had somehow heard the news. Classmates of Peter's from Westtown and Haverford sent condolences, as did Rose Valley neighbors.

Many of the letter writers expressed helpless outrage that Mildred and Allen, who had done so much for the world, should be asked to suffer such a blow. Some blamed Peter's suicide on the terrible state of the world. "We are living in a day almost unbearable even for the old and seasoned in the struggle for peace like you and me," Ruth Gage Colby wrote. "How then can it be borne by the young and sensitive ones. How are we to let these men who are driving us toward the precipice know that they are destroying us before any bombs are dropped? How are we to make them understand that they are making our world untenable without the holocaust?"[26]

Several of the Olmsteds' friends expressed the belief that sometimes suicide could be an act of courage and that people had the inalienable right to decide for themselves when they have had enough. Others told of suicides or other tragedies in their families and especially of the loss of loved ones. It was, as Mildred wrote in her branch letter, a great outpouring of love.

Emma Cadbury, a Quaker whom Mildred had known in Vienna, wrote to Mildred Olmsted, "I am glad thee has thy daily work which is so needed today and I hope thee finds comfort in the service thee can render at this time in the world's need." She was right; for Mildred, work was the best solace. Within a week Mildred was back in the office, plunging into WILPF work as though nothing had happened. Some found this devotion admirable, but others saw that it was a necessary part of the general denial with which Mildred met her son's death, as she met all tragedy.[27]

According to her housekeeper, Laura Jane Anderson, Mildred said that she believed that Peter had the right to do whatever he wished with his life, even end it. It was part of her creed of absolute freedom for the individual. She refused to appear crushed or to feel guilty. Twenty-five years later when I said to her in a warm moment between us that I thought a child's suicide would be the greatest tragedy a mother could suffer, she responded defensively by saying that she had never wanted to be a mother, and that having children had been a concession to Allen.[28]

Allen, on the other hand, seemed crushed by Peter's death. He wept, blamed himself, and blamed the way he and Mildred had raised Peter. All the frustrations of his years of wanting to conquer Mildred, and of wanting to be a judge, came out in a torrent of grief.

One of his confidantes in this period was Pat Olmsted, the widow of his nephew Michael Olmsted, who had died the year before of Hodgkin's disease. Pat worked at Smith College in Northampton, Massachusetts, and Allen went to see her frequently during the early months of his despair, combining a visit to Northampton with a visit to Springfield, where Enid lived. Pat would walk with him in a small city park while he wept and talked about Peter.[29]

He had felt from the start that Polly was at least partially responsible, having given Peter a shock with her ultimatum. Friends wrote to him urging him to assuage his own grief by helping Polly and her children, but Allen's sense of hurt was too acute, and he projected some of his anger on his daughter-in-law. In April, three months after the suicide, he wrote her two long and bitter letters, blaming her for the tragedy. Lawyerlike, he kept copies of the letters and showed them to Mildred.

Mildred thought the letters vindictive and designed to punish Polly, and she tried to persuade Allen to write an apology. The letter of apology, however, was grudging. Allen did not really forgive Polly, but he wrote admiringly of Mildred's ability to do so. Allen said that Mildred had a much livelier sense of Polly's frustrations with Peter and sympathized with her efforts to handle the problem.

> She is a very big personality, and has the quality of throwing out her emotions of disapproval on relatively trivial matters, such as the Pennsylvania Railroad upholstery or some public man's speech that is forgotten tomorrow. Most unreasonable and intolerant are the outbursts, whereas I try to take (and do take) a juster judgment in such things. But in deeper things that matter she is less extravagant. She used to say when we talked about divorce, sometimes in general and sometimes about the possibility of our own, she would say that we could have a friendly divorce and I said no, if it ever came to that I would be so bitter I would never want to speak to her again. Well Peter's divorce has come pretty close to being my divorce and my reaction has been as violent as I had predicted. I am glad for your sake and very proud of her that she can meet her personal tragedy in a so unselfish and constructive manner.[30]

It took years for Allen's feelings toward Polly to heal. Mildred, however, was determined to keep in close touch with Peter's wife and family, and to include them in family dinners and outings to Avalon or to Sardinia. She insisted that Polly was always welcome and shielded her as best she could from Allen's grouchy attitudes. Polly herself was strong, able to endure and turn aside Allen's occasional remarks.

Throughout those first bitter months, Ruth Mellor tried to help both the Olmsteds to come to terms with their loss, although she too was devastated by the death of Peter. She counseled Allen to stop trying to investigate the death, for all the information in the world would not bring Peter back. She praised Mildred for her strength but urged her to be less objective, and to help Allen.

Very gradually life for the Olmsteds resumed some aspects of normalcy. They spent a few weeks at Key West with the Sauls that winter, and in the summer were ready for another of their adventures, a month-long trip to Hawaii with Ruth. After Ruth and Mildred attended the Fifteenth Triennal Congress of WILPF, held in Asilomar, California, the three boarded a freighter and were met in Honolulu by WILPF women with leis. Mildred gave a speech, "Is Peace Possible?" Then, duties over, they flew to the island of Maui, where they stayed in one small inn near the mountains and another on the seashore. On a third island, Lanai, they found a beach so deserted that they could skinny dip. They had planned to visit Guam and Saipan, but Ruth had forgotten to bring her passport, so they continued to idle on Oahu until it was time to fly home.[31]

But travel helped only a little. Allen kept the memory of Peter alive, observing his birthday and thinking of him each Christmas. He never completely got over the pain of the loss of his precious son. Mildred healed slowly over the years, helped by her work and her optimistic belief that the world was bound to become a better place. Although she had never cared much about young children, she began to take an interest in Peter's three— Eric, Kenny, and especially Marcy, the youngest. Unlike other babies, she thought, Marcy had a personality from the start. It was her way of not dwelling on the past but looking to the future. And it helped.

15
The Vietnam Era

IN SENDING GREETINGS to the Fifteenth Triennial Congress of the WILPF at Asilomar, California, Norman Cousins wrote, "As a matter of dramatic irony I've always been amused by the thought that women—who are despised by the war-makers as sentimental weaklings—may finally bring the war dogs to heel."[1]

At this congress WILPF established a peace research committee, the first of its kind since the Pacifist Research Bureau and a pioneering forerunner of the peace research movement. Mildred Olmsted was enthusiastic about the new committee, always believing that peace efforts ought to be based on solid research.

But there was not always time for such research as the crises of the 1960s proliferated. Mildred felt compelled to respond to each crisis, persuading the WILPF board and membership to make a statement or a protest. It was not good for her blood pressure, but it helped to divert her from the deep hurt of Peter's death.

She had hardly settled back at her desk at the Jane Addams House in the fall of 1962 than the Cuban missile crisis began to engross national attention. For seven days in October the peoples of the world held their breath as President Kennedy and Premier Khrushchev seemed to be playing an international game of chicken. The WILPF sent telegrams to Kennedy and other officials urging restraint, and members joined picket lines in leading cities. Mildred Olmsted marched in Philadelphia on 22 November, and heard her old friend Norman Thomas speak against the bellicose attitude the United States seemed to be taking.

Once the crisis was behind them, American peace organizations began organizing missions of goodwill to the Cuban people. The Committee for Nonviolent Action developed a Quebec-to-Guantanamo Walk for Peace, and the American Friends Service Committee sent four emissaries and $50,000 worth of food after the devastating hurricane Flora hit the island. The WILPF considered such a mission, but because of its time and budget constraints it had to content itself with offering moral support to others and attending conferences on better relations in the Caribbean.

The Algerian war had ended, but the news from Vietnam was disquieting, with American advisers being shot down by soldiers of the National Liberation Front. The peace movement continued to press for an atmospheric-test-ban treaty. In April 1963, 2,000 women formed a Mothers' Lobby in Washington to demand an end to nuclear testing. The group was organized by Women's Strike for Peace and supported by WILPF. The women rejoiced in August 1963 when the United States, the USSR, and the United Kingdom signed the first test-ban treaty.

As part of its work against the atomic bomb, Women's Strike for Peace was helping to arrange a visit of five Japanese women who had been victims of the bombing, under the sponsorship of the Japan Council Against A and H Bombs, along with Kaoru Yasui, chair of the council. There were continuing allegations that part of this council was under Communist domination, and although the WILPF continued to send representatives to council meetings in Japan, it decided not to sponsor the tour. Later, Dagmar Wilson, the founder of Women Strike for Peace, and Donna Allen, the legislative chair of WILPF and a WSP member, were called before the House Un-American Activities Committee for questioning concerning their role in requesting a visa for Kaoru Yasui, a visa that the State Department ultimately decided to grant. While the WILPF pointed out that Donna Allen had acted as a member of WSP and not of the WILPF, it decided to enter an amicus curiae in the case, to be filed by Allen Olmsted.

During these tempestuous days the South continued to be rocked with violence as Governor Ross Barnett refused to admit James Meredith to the University of Mississippi, leading to a showdown with President John Kennedy, and Governor George

Wallace defied the federal government to enforce desegregation in Alabama. Martin Luther King, Jr., was leading marchers in nonviolent protests, and students were going south to aid in voter registration, conducted by the Student Nonviolent Coordinating Committee with the aid of materials prepared by another new group, Students for a Democratic Society.

"On fire at last!" Mildred wrote in the margin of her June 1963 branch letter. "Civil rights leaders are on the march and resistance is crumbling at last in the South. Peace and freedom must go together. We need to demonstrate democracy at home." She was leaving, she said, to visit new and potential branches in Indiana, Wisconsin, and Chicago on her way to the annual meeting in Estes Park, Colorado.[2]

At this annual meeting the women heard a written report from Elise Boulding, who had attended the World Congress of Women in Moscow as an observer and had spoken on changes each side might make to ease cold war problems. Her audience at first was chilly, although afterwards she had been secretly congratulated on her bravery. They also heard that the Soviets had invited the American women who attended the conference at Bryn Mawr for a return visit. Although the women of the WILPF were still cautious, they were beginning to reach behind the iron curtain.

In Estes Park, Mildred Olmsted finally was given the title for which she had yearned for many years, executive secretary. Some of those who had opposed her because of loyalties that stretched back to the Dorothy Detzer era had finally resigned from the board, and new members had been added who knew nothing of the old wars. As she was indeed acting as executive secretary, it seemed wrong to deny her the title. Although she continued to hide her age, many knew she was seventy-three, and the campaign to persuade her to resign continued.

Most WILPF members had to acknowledge that the pace Mildred Olmsted was able to maintain was that of a far younger woman. She was still capable of traveling all night, and with a brief catnap, banging her gavel with freshness and vigor the next morning. She was still criticized as a poor administrator, insisting that everything concerning the national office cross her desk, and thus creating a bottleneck, but now she was surrounded by a loving staff who found ways to get around this problem. Having waited so long for the title, she did not hide the fact that she was pleased and began immediately to use it in her correspondence.

From Colorado, Mildred Olmsted went to Washington to represent WILPF at a White House conference to organize a National Woman's Committee for Civil Rights. In August many WILPF members marched with Martin Luther King, Jr., in a giant rally for jobs and freedom and heard King give his famous "I have a dream" speech. In September they were shocked to hear about the bombing of a church in Birmingham which killed four little girls and sent letters of sympathy to their parents.

To get away from some of the pressures of the times, Mildred, with Allen and Ruth, took time off during the summer of 1963 for a seven-week tour of Africa, combining sightseeing with observation of the new nations of Africa. They flew from Athens to Addis Ababa, Ethiopia, then on to Nairobi, Kenya, where they spent a night in a hotel before going out into the bush on a big game expedition. They passed their first night out on an open platform among the tree tops, watching elephants, rhinoceroses, and baboons drifting in and out of the clearing to visit the salt lick and the water hole. It was chilly, but worth it. The next day they went out in the Landrover and saw bull buffalo, elephants, and giraffes "who run like slow motion pictures," as Mildred wrote Adele, as well as dik-diks, giant anthills, jackals, ostriches, and zebra. Although it was lion country, they saw no lions. Ruth and Mildred sat on a rock that was a favorite lion haunt and watched Allen catch a fish. Later, back at the hotel, Mildred tried riding a tame zebra.[3]

Continuing their big game trip by Landrover, they visited Kaimosi, a Friends center in Kenya, and spent a night at Kisumu on the shores of Lake Victoria, where they saw warriors in full regalia riding motorcycles. They crossed over into Tanganyika, where they visited the Serengeti National Park, saw lions in great abundance, drove through a huge brush fire, and went down into the Ngora Ngora crater.[4]

From the Serengeti Park, Allen wrote Polly to thank her again for his birthday present, obviously a peace offering on both their parts. He was still thinking constantly about Peter, and he could not refrain from telling her about it. "This morning among other things, we saw a gazelle giving birth. This reminded me of Peter and started a train of thought—the difficulties of his birth, his attitude toward the birth of your children, his courtship days with you, and ending with his strange unbelievable disappearance from the scene. I expect you have similar reveries. Ah me."[5]

From Tanganyika they crossed over to the island of Zanzibar, which they found more Arab than African, and where they sampled sugarcane, coconuts cut especially for them, and cloves just plucked from a tree. Next came Victoria Falls, in Northern Rhodesia. They walked through the rain forest opposite the falls, appreciating the African violets that grew everywhere and hearing the crashing of some big animal nearby, then later in the day took a boat trip up the Zambesi River, watching for hippopotamuses and crocodiles.

In Salisbury they stayed with Lyle and Becky Tatum, working in Southern Rhodesia for the American Friends Service Committee. Lyle was in touch with many of the African groups working for liberation in the Rhodesias and in South Africa, and he was able to brief the Olmsteds and give them the names of Africans to look up before they went on to South Africa. In Johannesburg they were taken on a tour of Soweto. Freedom-loving Mildred was quite disturbed by the climate of fear and repression in South Africa and thereafter took a more active role in working for the end of apartheid. It was a relief to get into the freer air of Nigeria, liberated in 1960, and of Ghana, liberated in 1957, before finally coming home.

Mildred Olmsted reported in the October issue of *Four Lights* on this trip, saying they had visited ten countries in seven weeks and covered over 25,000 miles. Many of the new nations had terrible economic problems, she said, and while they resisted outside interference they were torn within by religious differences and tribalism. Colonial divisions that had arbitrarily cut across tribal lines had added to the troubles. There were also divisions between educated Africans steeped in Western society and primitive societies in which polygamy was still practiced. "Women are a kind of property; however, as men become educated they often want edu-

cated wives, so things are changing," she said. "In South Africa, as
the government becomes more unpopular it gets more repressive.
We were told that individual boycotts don't help much, but that
if the United States would stop buying gold or a naval blockade
could be instituted it would be effective. South Africa, with its
racial ghettos is trying to force people back to tribalism while
other countries are trying to get away from it."[6]

The visit to Africa made a profound impression on Mildred
Olmsted. She followed the rapidly changing course of events on
the African continent with great interest and was startled but
pleased to learn of unrest and change in Tanganyika, Uganda, and
Zanzibar. "I am glad I was there and also I realize how much can
be going on below a smooth surface," she wrote in her branch
letter, "just as it has in our South for years."[7]

She also wrote to the International Red Cross the following
year, urging them to visit the prisoners in South Africa arrested
under suspicion of "subversive activities." "I was there last summer
and felt the tension was very great," she said.[8]

The Soviet women had originally scheduled the second conference with the women of the WILPF for November 1963, but it
was put off until spring. As a result Mildred Olmsted was in the
United States to experience with her fellow citizens the shock of
President Kennedy's assassination in Dallas on 22 November. She
shared the sense of disbelief and betrayal of millions of Americans
but with her usual surprising optimism was soon able to say that
perhaps this dreadful occurrence had been a catalyst for changes
that were already stirring. President Lyndon Johnson seemed to be
moving swiftly on the Civil Rights Act, and to be putting the
United States behind the United Nations.[9]

On her way to Moscow for the second Soviet-American
women's conference, Mildred Olmsted stopped off in Great Britain
to attend the annual meeting of the British WILPF Section and to
lecture on developments in the United States. The U.S. WILPF
was working hard to organize new branches in the South, she told
her British audiences. Following a regional conference in Tuskegee, Alabama, she and three other WILPF members had fanned
out to visit old and potential branches and had revived seven, she
thought. An African-American member of WILPF, Amelia Boyn-

ton, was playing a leadership role in Selma; another, Vera Foster, was a member of the delegation to the Soviets; and four WILPF members were going to spend the summer in Mississippi working on voter registration.

The women held the second Soviet-American women's conference 14–19 April 1964 in Moscow. The participants talked about recent successes—the signing of the Moscow Test Ban Treaty, the agreement not to put nuclear weapons in space, and the establishment of a hot line between Washington and Moscow—and discussed the goal of complete disarmament. There were disagreements about method, but it seemed to the American women that the Soviets listened carefully to the American point of view, especially the insistence on the importance of dissent. Mildred Olmsted had tea with Nina Khrushchev, wife of the Soviet premier, during this visit.[10]

Following the conference the American women visited Leningrad, Tashkent, and Samarkand and saw factories, farms, institutions, and homes. It was Mildred Olmsted's third visit to the Soviet Union, and she continued to be interested in the emphasis on social welfare, as passionately as she disagreed with the restrictions on free expression of ideas.[11]

On her way home she stopped in Denmark to visit Else Zeuthen, WILPF's international chair, and discussed her concern that national sections be built up, and new ones organized. U.S. WILPF was beginning to think that perhaps it ought to send observers to the conferences of the Women's International Democratic Federation, something it would not have considered a few years earlier. This possibility meant that international WILPF would have to rethink its policy on how it related to other organizations.[12]

While Mildred Olmsted traveled, Allen stayed in Rose Valley and wrote to report to her on her lovely blooming spring garden, and to express his longing for her to come home. Still devastated by the loss of Peter, he had come to depend on Mildred as never before to keep up his spirits. To pass the time, he began to plan the next trip for himself, Ruth, and Mildred, a seven-week tour of South America including one hundred miles down the Amazon.

First, though, Mildred Olmsted had five visiting Romanian women to entertain, a mortgage-burning ceremony at Jane Addams House to organize, and the 1964 annual meeting at Indianapolis to attend. This was the forty-ninth year of the WILPF, and plans had to be made both nationally and internationally for a fiftieth anniversary celebration in 1965. With participation in the civil rights struggle in the South and the new exchange program with the Soviets, it seemed almost too much for a small organization, still struggling to meet its budget, to undertake.

Mildred Olmsted could not understand why the WILPF remained so small. "It is a mystery to me why an organization with the courage and the standards, the services it provides and the record of accomplishment of the WILPF does not increase in numbers more rapidly than it does!" she wrote in her 1964 annual report.[13] The WILPF continued to work hard to reach more members, organizing workshops for leaders and for speakers as well as interesting legislative seminars in Washington. It had been asked by other peace organizations to concentrate on the United Nations, and it ran regular well-planned seminars in New York on UN issues to which it invited people from many organizations. Through the Jane Addams Peace Association the group raised money to send young women to the international summer school that the WILPF had been running for many years, as well as for internships in the various WILPF offices. They encouraged each member to bring a younger woman with her to each meeting. Mildred Olmsted as well as other WILPF leaders attended innumerable national conferences of women at the White House and elsewhere and never failed to do their best to find new WILPF members. Still, growth continued painfully slow. There were many other peace groups now competing for members, and the fact that many of the loyal WILPF members were now middle-aged or elderly created an age gap difficult to surmount. Although here and there new branches with younger members were being formed, the overall statistics did not change.

Two of the major organizations with which WILPF worked, SANE and United World Federalists, were considering combining, and WILPF was invited to join. Once more the question arose as to whether there was a use for a distinctly woman's organization. But now the first breaths of the new feminism were stirring, and Mildred Olmsted sniffed them eagerly. Forgotten were the many years she had urged WILPF to drop the word *women* from its title. In April she had reminded members to use their own names rather than their husbands'. "We are a feminist organization, growing out of the struggle of women—and it was a long hard one, where feeling ran almost as high as the present struggle of Negroes."[14]

A male supporter of WILPF sent Mildred Olmsted a series of papers that demonstrated that the hope of the world lay with women "because they are not polluted by the masculine instinct for power which, however useful in providing for isolated societies has now become a decided curse." Mildred, who herself liked to exercise power and believed that women used pretty much the same methods as men, did not agree, pointing out that men were working in the peace field too. But she was pleased when WILPF's long-range committee on future development turned down the offer to merge with SANE: "Because of our distinct international and feminist character it was important for us to preserve our identity."[15]

Finally in late July the Olmsteds and Ruth Mellor took off for their South American journey. They visited Surinam and what was then French Guiana, where they saw the infamous Devil's Island penal colony, then traveled to Chile and Argentina. In Rio de Janeiro they rode in a small plane to see a famous waterfall and had to scramble down a slippery bank into a boat. It was winter in South America, and Mildred got flu and stayed in the hotel while Allen and Ruth went sightseeing. Later the other two also caught cold, but they pressed on toward their trip up the Amazon, frustrated by the continual changes made by local travel agents in Allen's beautifully worked out schedules.[16]

The Amazon River, when they finally reached it, was hot and steamy, and they wondered what was happening in the Democratic National Convention in Chicago as they watched the jungle glide by. By chance they met a traveler who thought he had heard over the radio that Hubert Humphrey had been chosen as vice-presidential candidate, an event that pleased both Olmsteds greatly. They got home to Rose Valley the day before Labor Day, physically tired but refreshed and ready for the busy anniversary year.[17]

To gear up for that anniversary, Mildred Olmsted took a swing through the Southwest, Far West, and Northwest in the early months of 1965, rediscovering old friends and meeting new members. Some branches were so new, she discovered, that they did not know how to use all the WILPF materials. But not every branch could do everything, she concluded. The WILPF should be viewed as offering a smorgasbord from which branches could choose.

In April she had just returned from these travels when Amelia Boynton called from Selma asking that the WILPF send representatives to join the Selma-to-Montgomery march. A few days earlier WILPF members had seen Amelia beaten on television. WILPF's Dorothy Hutchinson, confined to a wheelchair by polio, was one of those who responded. James Reeb, a Unitarian minister with WILPF connections, was beaten to death, and Mildred led the WILPF to raise money in his honor to be given to the African-American Burwell Clinic, where he was medically treated after having been turned away by the white hospital.[18]

In Vietnam the marines landed, and U.S. planes began to drop napalm. The South Vietnam Women's Unit for Liberation wrote to WILPF to protest the fact that American women were being sent to train Vietnamese women to be soldiers. In Detroit a longtime WILPF member, despondent over all the bad news, immolated herself. The world indeed seemed to be exploding.

The murder of three civil rights workers in the city of Philadelphia, Mississippi, in June 1964 had shocked WILPF and led the organization to join a program called Wednesdays in Mississippi, or Women in Mississippi, in the summer of 1965. In cooperation with the National Council of Negro Women and other groups the WILPF sent two teams of four women each, two African-American and two white, from Philadelphia, Pennsylvania, to spend two weeks in Philadelphia, Mississippi, helping in community projects such as day care and discussing ways to achieve a quiet integration of the schools and community. Mildred Olmsted did not go to Mississippi herself but worked hard to recruit volunteers.[19]

For its fiftieth anniversary the WILPF was returning to The Hague, where it had held its first meeting in 1915. Allen, Mildred, Ruth, Kitty Arnett, and Kitty's husband, John Arnett, took a Holland America Line vessel to sail across the Atlantic for the event. Unfortunately it was the same ship they had taken four years earlier with Peter and Polly, and it produced sad memories. In Southampton Allen got off with John Arnett for some bachelor wanderings before rejoining the women, while Mildred, Kitty, and Ruth went on to the congress.

Women from six continents assembled for the historic meeting 26–31 July. "The Congress was notable for the new and younger women present, for the general agreement and harmony of the proceedings, for strict adherence to parliamentary procedures and for a peaceful revision of the constitution," Mildred Olmsted wrote in her September branch letter. They were taken through the Peace Palace, reminding Mildred that the United States continued to reserve the right to decide whether or not a case could be brought against it in the World Court. ("Imagine any state taking that attitude toward the Supreme Court!") A climax of the meetings was a pageant gotten up hastily for the occasion. Mildred took a leading role in a reenactment of a 1931 scene. Kitty Arnett played Jane Addams, and her husband, John Arnett, played a diplomat and stole the show, according to Allen Olmsted, who was in the audience. In the end women from various nations gathered on the stage to say, "Lovers of our own lands we are citizens of the world."[20]

"It made us realize that we are truly a movement among women," Mildred Olmsted wrote exultingly. "The possibilities of international development are almost limitless with our own Dorothy Hutchinson as new international chairman."[21]

After the congress Mildred, Ruth, and Allen traveled together in Europe, visiting Paris and Munich, where they looked up landmarks from their 1920 work for the American Friends Service Committee and had a WILPF meeting; and East and West Berlin, where the wall had been built since their last visit. They made a brief foray into Yugoslavia and Hungary, armed with introductions from Madame Frolova, the woman in the Soviet embassy in Washington with whom Mildred Olmsted had conducted negotiations for the Soviet-American women exchange. They got to Budapest two days later than they had planned, however, having missed several trains, and had little time for visiting. Mildred complained to Adele that travel behind the iron curtain was frustrating because the travel agents were inefficient and there were not enough hotel rooms or seats on the trains. Several times Ruth and Mildred were separated from Allen as a result of the train's leaving while he was still arranging for baggage or tickets, but in these predicaments people were warm and friendly and helpful, once the two women could find someone who could understand Mildred's rusty German.[22]

"In Munich, our branch was taking part in a Hiroshima Day demonstration, launching lighted paper boats in memory of the victims of the atom bomb," Mildred Olmsted wrote in *Four Lights*. "I met women in Hungary who knew of our Congress in The Hague and were disappointed they were not invited. I left some of our literature there and they have written for more. One can't help feeling that people are much the same all over the world and would draw closer together if only their governments would let them."[23]

They returned home just before Labor Day and were just getting settled when terrible news came from Enid and Bill Burke in Springfield, Massachusetts. Their two sons, Stuart, aged twelve, and Gregory, seven, had been playing on the sidewalk in front of their house on a quiet residential street when a teenage girl driving a car had tried to light a cigarette, lost control of the car, and run up on the sidewalk, killing Greg instantly and badly wounding Stuart.

With the raw wound of Peter's death just beginning to heal, it must have seemed like too much for one family to bear. It certainly did to the Olmsteds' friends who deluged them with letters of condolence. Mildred and Allen went directly to Springfield to be with Enid and Bill, and the four of them alone attended the brief funeral ceremony for Greg. Mildred and Enid had never been close, but now she tried as best she could to let Enid know she shared her grief and was proud that Enid was determined not to dwell on the accident, or to allow the children to blame the driver of the car. "In my house there will be no hate," Enid told her son, Stuart, when he was well enough to recollect what had happened.[24]

Mildred Olmsted tried to take the long view, as usual. "My beautiful grandson Gregory, not quite seven has just been killed and his older brother Stuart, twelve, sent injured to the hospital by a seventeen year old girl driver. Pure accident, but the grief is hard to take. How much worse must be the suffering of the thousands of women in Vietnam," she wrote in her September branch letter.[25]

Fortunately for Mildred Olmsted there was no time to brood. She and Allen were on a committee to give a dinner for Barrows Dunham, a professor at Temple University who had been fired during the McCarthy period for his principled refusal to give information about his associates, and who was later reinstated to his old position. It was one of many civil liberties cases the Olmsteds worked on together.

In addition, the U.S. Section of WILPF was holding its annual meeting in Philadelphia in October, and it was to be a gala affair, celebrating fifty years of the WILPF. Kay Camp, who had joined the WILPF in 1958, was chairing the event, and the final banquet was being given in honor of Mildred, as she had at last listened to the counsel of those who loved her and decided to retire from WILPF, at the age of seventy-five.

The mayor of Philadelphia sent greetings at the opening of the sessions, and Staughton Lynd made a keynote speech. Every living president of WILPF was present as well as two of the founding members. Retiring president Dorothy Hutchinson spoke on "Preparing Head and Heart for Peace and Freedom," and Mildred Olmsted gave her annual report, "Fifty Years and the Road Ahead."

In her report Mildred briefly recapitulated the history of U.S. WILPF as she had known it, stressing the special WILPF spirit of working together to resolve differences, a spirit she said was much too valuable to lose—"In fact, it may be the most important thing that we can hand on to our successors because it is a living demonstration of how people of differing backgrounds and viewpoints can work together."

She wrote of her disappointment that WILPF had never

grown beyond the high watermark of 14,000 members in 1937, but she philosophized that perhaps this had been for the best:

> Miss Addams never wanted us to be "popular" and attract a mass membership because out of her great experience she realized that if we did we should lose the ability to pioneer, be flexible and to move quickly. We who were younger and saw the attacks upon her and upon the positions we took and the actions we advocated, and then watched too how when these positions were accepted by more popular organizations, and our work to bring it about was totally ignored, could not see it! . . . It always seemed so unfair that we should carry the brunt of an unpopular proposal and then when it became acceptable, other less courageous or less farsighted organizations got the praise, the membership, the publicity, and the contributions while we continued to scrimp along. But now that I am older and wiser I see that Miss Addams was right. It has been difficult enough to hold together a smaller number of people so deeply concerned that they were willing to and able to carry on in spite of handicaps. Our strongest claim to attention today is our 50 year record of consistency and integrity.[26]

She reviewed the history of the WILPF, including her own work for the organization, and made recommendations for the future: that there be a special consultant on committees to prevent too many overlapping committees developing; that there be a consultant on representation to prevent all of WILPF's energies going to playing a role in sister organizations; that the work at the United Nations, which had sagged in recent years, be given a higher priority; that WILPF's longtime interest in Latin America be revived.

But most of all, her fifty-year report was full of the hopefulness that was so characteristic of Mildred Scott Olmsted:

> When I first came out of high school I was determined to help the poor and the weak. I had a flaming sense of the terrible things done by people in destroying trees and the natural beauty of the earth, of the cruelty to animals, the injustices and unequal opportunity for immigrants and Ne-

groes, of the subjugation of women. Later I knew Margaret Sanger and as a social worker I saw for myself the tragedy of unlimited children. That was the first unpopular cause I joined. I flouted tradition by smoking and cutting my hair, I risked a family split by marching in a suffrage parade and came under neighborhood and family censure by working when my children were small. So I sympathize with the new generation of young rebels.

And now I have lived long enough to see birth control openly taught, to see the equality of women established at least theoretically, to see the conservation of nature acquire a great following and the beautification of America receive government leadership, to see immigrants of all nations put on an equal footing, to see the Negro emerging in importance, to see the war on poverty born, and urban renewal and housing proposed for cabinet level status, to see the establishment and enormous growth of the United Nations and to hear the demand for world disarmament and an end to all war rising to a crescendo. I have seen for myself that women all over the world speak the same language and welcome us.[27]

Mildred Olmsted's speech, in which she gave the highlights of this report and told of the early days in the WILPF, was greeted with a standing ovation, as most of her speeches had been in the past. Her capacity to inspire and encourage the women of the WILPF had always been one of her outstanding gifts to the organization. As she grew older she matured in this gift and became a symbol of continuity with the glorious past.

At noon on Saturday some 250 WILPF members joined a large demonstration at city hall, part of a nationwide protest organized by the National Coordinating Committee to End the War in Vietnam. WILPF members walked two and three abreast through downtown Philadelphia, wearing yellow paper sashes in honor of their suffragist origins and carrying WILPF signs.

In the afternoon there was a tea in honor of old-timers and retiring staff. Dorothy Detzer spoke, telling amusing stories of her early days at WILPF, and of some of her exploits with Mildred Olmsted when the two were the youngsters in the WILPF family. She told of meeting Mildred first when Mildred was flat on her back directing the Philadelphia office from her bed, and of the times she and Mildred stole away from board meetings in Geneva, Philadelphia, or New York, to look for antique jewelry. "How frivolous Katherine Blake thought us; how baffled by such errands was Lucy Biddle Lewis."[28]

At the banquet that night the women at the head table wore yellow corsages, and Coretta Scott King led the huge hall in singing "We Shall Overcome." Martin Luther King, Jr., spoke, and Mildred Olmsted was presented with a red book of messages from her many friends and associates all over the world. Norman Thomas and Roger Baldwin wrote, as well as A. J. Muste, Homer Jack, Stewart Meacham of the American Friends Service Committee, and Raymond Wilson of the Friends Committee on National Legislation. Most of her original colleagues were gone, but there were a few letters from WILPF members of the earliest vintage— Tracy Mygatt, Frances Witherspoon, and Dorothy Detzer. Gertrude Baer wrote a warm letter, recalling the day she had met Mildred and Ruth in Munich in 1920, and first told them about WILPF, and praising Mildred for her lifelong devotion to the cause.

Among the themes repeated over and over in these letters was praise for her dispassion and broadmindedness. As A. J. Muste put it, "In situations where people held sharply divergent views, and this is often the case in the peace movement, Mildred Olmsted was always clear and emphatic about stating hers and tenacious in arguing for it. At the same time she seemed invariably understanding of other points of view, ready for cooperation wherever that was possible, and glad to see someone else work as hard on his or her program as she on hers."[29]

Another theme of the messages was her constant cheerfulness and ability to inspire others, with her cheery smile and the brilliant clothes and flowered hats she always wore. Kay Camp, who had served as chair of the anniversary celebration, wrote of this attribute:

> I shall never forget one dreary afternoon some years ago during the End Nuclear Testing campaign when a handful of weary walkers ambled dejectedly in the shadow of City Hall. We were callow, dispirited and intimidated by the taunting

we received. Then you arrived! Your warm smile radiating confidence, your dignified bearing, your gay floral hat, your honored reputation—your very presence changed the whole paltry procession into a parade. The pace picked up, signs straightened, morale quickened. You have had the same effect on me ever since, and I suspect, on the whole American peace movement as well.[30]

Perhaps most gratifying to Mildred Olmsted were those who wrote to praise the role she had played in keeping WILPF going all through the years of turmoil. Hannah Barshak, who had been her assistant for ten years, said that it was her sincere conviction that without Mildred's never-ending devotion to the ideals of peace, WILPF would not be still in existence. Else Zeuthen, the international chair, said she remembered Mildred from 1937, when she had spoken at the Luhacovice congress on the theme of nonviolence, words Else had remembered during the occupation of Denmark in World War II. She added praise for Mildred's contribution to international WILPF. "We in the International owe a deep debt of gratitude to Mildred, first for what she has contributed internationally but most of all for what she has done for making the U. S. Section the cornerstone of our organization."[31]

It remained for a Massachusetts branch member, Florence Selleck, to find an apt quote. "'A survey of man's progress demonstrates the truth that first must come the seer with vision, and next the educator to wing desire, and thirdly the man of action to give shape to the dream.' You have given shape to the dreams of Jane Addams, Emily Greene Balch, and those early pioneers of WILPF."[32]

Lucy Carner, a retired social worker who had joined WILPF in Chicago and was now an active member in Germantown, spoke at the banquet and later published her expanded remarks in an article in *Pax et Libertas*, the international publication of WILPF, as: "Mildred Scott Olmsted: Architect of the U. S. Section." She described Mildred's patient efforts to build WILPF branch by branch.

> Her faith and courage have been contagious. In the dark days of the Second World War when she was traveling in the interest of peace, friends used to say that Mildred's gay hats

kept up their courage and brought them hope. They followed her lead as King Henry's soldiers are said to have followed his white plume.

The challenge Mildred Olmsted brought (and still brings) was not only loyalty to the vision, but willingness to study and act on the immediate and practicable next steps to give it reality. For she was never lost in the clouds. She lived "close to the headlines," to use her own phrase, while keeping her eyes on the distant horizon of a world freed from war and developing in freedom man's capacities for brotherhood and creativity.

A younger worker in the peace movement in the United States wrote recently: "Whatever the failings and shortcoming of peace workers, there is one mission they must never betray: to be keepers of the dream—much can be forgiven, but not the abandonment of hope." Mildred Olmsted has been true to that mission.[33]

At the banquet the new executive secretary elect was introduced. She was Jo Graham from Madison, Wisconsin, a teacher, social worker, and mother of three, who had been active in the WILPF at both the local and national levels, and who was leaving a position at the Wisconsin School of Social Work to take the WILPF job. Mildred Olmsted had used her as troubleshooter, and felt she was the best possible person to take her place.

The actual transition did not take place until February 1966. Mildred Olmsted meanwhile carried on, attending a White House Conference on International Cooperation Year and continuing to protest the war in Vietnam. She had recently accepted a position on the board of Upland Institute at the Crozer Theological Seminary in Chester, organized to train young men and women in techniques of nonviolent democratic change, adding this to her long list of extracurricular activities.

In late November she appeared on the radio talk show of a Delaware County rightist, Carl McIntire, in order to answer comments made by a previous guest on the program to the effect that she and the WILPF had "Communist leanings." Although she had been promised to see the charges against her in writing before appearing on the show, this did not happen, and she was asked to explain on the air why 54 of the 111 sponsors listed on the back of a WILPF pamphlet had Communist leanings, and why her name had appeared in the *Daily Worker*. She handled herself adroitly under this questioning but felt she had not been given her day in court, and later she was part of a group bringing suit against the station, WXUR, in a fairness case before the Federal Communications Commission.[34]

At the February board meeting, Mildred Olmsted was made executive secretary emeritus and given a surprise birthday dinner, at which she was presented with a generous check, and a tray and china for breakfasts in bed. This was a less formal affair than the banquet, and Mildred was asked to reminisce. Her accounts of her early experiences, of the high blood pressure and the ulcers, brought forth not sympathy but gales of laughter.

Mildred and Allen and Ruth were celebrating the retirement in true Olmsted-Mellor style: a second African safari, including a trip up the Nile beyond the Aswan Dam and into the Sudan, where they were to be met by guides with tents and a Landrover.

Finally it came time to clean out her office, and to write her last column for *Four Lights*. She congratulated WILPF on its new leadership and on the the never-ending stream of ideas and suggestions of its members. "This terrible war goes on but the extent of the opposition to it both at home and abroad is finally getting through to the president. . . . Much political work lies ahead. There are many limitations on our growth and the greatest of these is lack of money. But never forget, we are working for the better life for all, people and animals, our lesser kin. We are working *with* the flow of history and in the end we shall overcome."[35]

And in her last branch letter she wrote: "A new world is breaking through the clouds. There is frustration, hard work and hope ahead—fifty more years for WILPF. May you all enjoy this most satisfying fray as much as I."[36]

16

Golden Years

*Y*OUR RETIREMENT is turning out just the way I thought it would be. You are working just as hard, but not being paid," Trudy Prichard wrote Mildred Olmsted in October 1966. It was true. Mildred Olmsted knew that she ought to stay as far away from WILPF as possible in order to give her successor a chance. She had, however, agreed to serve on two crucial committees, finance and policy. These jobs, along with the Upland Institute, the Friends Peace Committee, the American Friends Service Committee's Peace Education Committee, SANE, and ACLU, kept her about as busy in the months following her retirement as she had been in those preceding it.

All was not well with WILPF. One might have predicted that after many years of Mildred Olmsted's sometimes autocratic and always idiosyncratic control, any new executive secretary was going to have a very hard time. Jo Graham, whom Mildred Olmsted had handpicked for the job, lasted only two years; she was followed by Glenna Johnson, who also served only two years. The diversity that had long proved WILPF's strength was also its weakness: without the magic of Mildred Olmsted's strong hand, the pacifists and the antiwar activists collided; the old-timers quarreled with the new members; questions of regional autonomy versus centralized control again came to the fore. The countrywide crisis brought on by the war in Vietnam, the assassinations of Martin Luther King, Jr., and of Robert Kennedy, and the upsurge of the youth culture all put pressure on the WILPF, in common with other peace groups, to become more radical and to express its

318

solidarity with oppressed groups struggling for liberation. Older members feared that it might lose sight of its commitment to nonviolence as a method of social change.

In fact, in the early seventies, the appropriateness of advocating nonviolence to groups struggling against oppression became a subject of heated debate in the WILPF worldwide. At the eighteenth triennial, held in New Delhi, India, in December 1970, the women wrestled with the issue and came out with a statement.

A society that is military and exploitative generates movements for rapid change towards social justice. It is a human right to resist injustice and be neither silent witness nor passive victim of repression. Although we affirm our belief that violence creates more problems than it solves, we recognize the inevitability of violent resistance by the oppressed when other alternatives have failed.

The WILPF has a duty to study and work towards develop ing methods for the effective use of nonviolent means; to make the public aware of the problems of the oppressed and the exploited; to analyze the structure of power in society and the use made of it; to engage ourselves actively in nonviolent movements for change.[1]

This statement failed to please the advocates either of nonviolence or of solidarity with revolutionary groups in the U.S. WILPF. The struggle over nonviolence continued for many years to plague the organization. Mildred Olmsted remained an advocate for nonviolence and a nerve center for those on the board who wanted to hold close to that commitment. When Dorothy Steffens, executive secretary from 1971 to 1977, was preparing for a trip to North Vietnam in 1973 to visit the North Vietnamese Women's Union, Mildred Olmsted suggested to her that she talk about the necessity for training in effective nonviolence. Yet eventually, over the years, Mildred came to feel with the rest of the WILPF that wealthy North Americans had no right to preach nonviolence to groups involved in struggles for their own liberation. Nonviolence as a tactic in such a struggle was sometimes an expression of powerlessness. Principled nonviolence on the basis of

22. Mildred Olmsted hears a young feminist, Charlotte Bunch Weeks, speak at an American Friends Service Committee conference, "The U.S. in a Revolutionary World," held at Princeton University, April 1968. Photo by Bill Pepper. *Courtesy of American Friends Service Committee.*

religious belief such as the Quakers held belonged in a whole different category.[2]

When board members came to Mildred with their dilemmas over the growing polarization of the organization following her retirement, she told them that she was the last person able to help. True to her intentions, she kept hands off as best she could. But whenever there was an opportunity to offer objective counsel without becoming involved in the struggle, she was always available to do so. "Thank God you are near to give them your wisdom," an old-time WILPF member wrote.[3]

The Jane Addams House on Walnut Street continued to house the offices of a number of other peace groups. One of these was The Resistance, an anti-Vietnam War activist group of young people. This group began receiving threatening letters, which they did not call to the attention of the WILPF staff. In the early hours of 23 March 1970, a fire of suspicious origin broke out in the basement and rapidly spread to engulf the whole building. By the time the fire fighters came it was much too late to save the house from major damage. The central staircase was destroyed, walls and ceilings crashed, and many valuable files were lost. To redo the building would cost far more than the limited fire insurance WILPF had been carrying on the advice, Mildred Olmsted said, of the insurance company. There seemed to be no way out of the disaster. Once more U.S. WILPF was faced with the need to find a new home.

As it had often done in the past, the WILPF board now debated whether it would be better to consolidate its offices by moving to Washington, although this would be inconvenient to the United Nations and the Jane Addams Peace Association offices in New York. Mildred Olmsted once more summoned all her argumentative skill to insist that WILPF should remain in Philadelphia. She helped look for new headquarters, which the women finally found at 1213 Race Street. Here the new boardroom was dedicated to her in 1972.

During this period many social change organizations faced challenges from their junior staff to become more communal and less hierarchal in office procedures. In 1973 such reorganization was called for in the WILPF office. Mildred wrote a long letter outlining the methods she had used to give all staff members a sense of participation in the work of WILPF: weekly staff meetings with a rotating chair, encouragement to attend events and marches, and her own efforts to emphasize the interdependence of the work, and of each staff member on the other. (Some former staff members would have disagreed.) She returned to an old and favorite theme in suggesting that the use of volunteers be stressed and urged the reorganization committee not to consider setting up the staff as a commune.

> Undoubtedly some staff members will propose a "commune" type of reorganization which is so popular in the thinking right now. I serve on two reorganization committees right now besides being connected with other bodies that are going through such a phase.

A "commune" or a "cooperative" sounds very appealing to concerned young staff members who, for one reason or another, disagree with methods or decisions of their executive, but it is a slow and inefficient way of working because every staff member has to spend so much time away from his own particular task to consult about every other staff member's problems and to help decide every question that comes to the whole organization or any part of it and also to the training of each new staff member. The staff members (not all, however) like it because they tend to become the organization and have a sense of team work which makes the board almost superfluous.[4]

She went on to describe the situation with the Friends Peace Committee, on which she served, which had felt its executive to be "arbitrary" and had set up a commune with mixed results. She still believed firmly in hierarchy, holding as she had in 1925 that only one person could be the head. She did not mention and did not seem to remember that she herself had never been willing to be subordinate to Dorothy Detzer. Although she was interested in the emerging feminist movement of the time, she still retained a strong sense of the importance of power in an organization, learned many years ago from her father.

Whatever the issue, Mildred Olmsted was always willing to be consulted by the WILPF and to write a thoughtful letter of advice. Sometimes her concepts were dated, as in the case of her defense of hierarchy, but often they were surprisingly forward-looking. Frequently she reviewed policy statements and made pertinent suggestions for wording, based on her long experience. Executive after executive found her invaluable without being intrusive into the day-to-day functioning of the organization. Freed from the sense of responsibility and the concomitant need to control, she played an important role in the WILPF for almost twenty-four years after her retirement as wise elder stateswoman and as a role model for younger staff members. She had been given a lifetime place on the board of the U.S. WILPF and faithfully attended board meetings as well as regional and annual meetings. As she grew older, she learned how to refresh herself at such meetings by taking a brief nap with a handkerchief over her face, while other younger board members enjoyed a coffee break.

She also kept her interest in the international WILPF alive, combining trips to the various congresses with travel with Ruth and Allen. In 1968 she went to the seventeenth triennial congress at Nyborg, Denmark, before continuing with the other two on a trip around the world with stopovers in Iran, Kashmir (where they rented a houseboat on a beautiful lake), Singapore, Australia, New Zealand, Fiji, and Samoa. In Australia they attended a WILPF meeting at Adelaide, and Mildred Olmsted spent three weeks subsequently traveling in Australia and New Zealand, meeting with WILPF members and potential members, making speeches, and appearing on radio and television. She rested in an inn in southern New Zealand, looking out at a blue lake and glacier-covered mountains, while they waited for the road into Milford Sound to be cleared of snow from an avalanche, and Allen was able to spend some time fishing.[5]

In December 1970, the adventurous trio set out for New Delhi and the world congress held there. Here Mildred weakened in her resolve to remain detached and agreed to meet with the international executive committee and to serve on a standing committee to raise money to develop new national sections. Following the closing of the meetings, WILPF sent a delegation of four women to visit North and South Vietnam.

After the congress, the Olmsteds and Ruth flew to Bangalore and were driven by car to Mysore, where they spent several days in a game reserve, riding on an elephant and sleeping out at night in the midst of the jungle noises. Their next stop was Cochin, where they took a boat ride along the coast and watched a splendid religious ceremony. When they returned to the United States, they discovered they had been in parts of India few Philadelphians had ever seen, and Mildred was doubly proud of Allen's ability to ferret out interesting places to visit.

The next international congress was held in Birmingham, England, in July 1974. Delegates from both Lebanon and Israel were present, and tensions of the Middle East bristled, but the women were united in condemning the outbreak of violence on Cyprus. After the congress, the trio visited Scotland and the island of Barra.

Mildred Olmsted's travels to the international congresses kept alive her lifetime longing to see the WILPF grow as she felt it should. Her old friend Elise Boulding, who was serving as senior consultant to the international executive committee in 1968, and who wanted to resign in order to teach sociology, wrote her a long letter, urging her to put her energies into reforming and rebuilding the International WILPF structure. "Mildred, you are the only person I know of in the WILPF, in *any* country who sees what needs to be done and has at least the possibility of thinking about whether you ought to involve yourself in the work of doing it. . . . I would like to ask you to consider replacing me as Senior Consultant to the International. . . . I will have to resign as Consultant in any case, but I will do so with a much lighter mind and spirit if I know that you feel free to take over."[6]

Mildred Olmsted did not accept the position, and instead of resigning Elise became international president in 1968 and served for three years. But it was hard for either of them to do anything about restructuring WILPF, they felt, as so many of the international leaders at that time were elderly and set in their ways. Mildred's earlier proposal that the international hire a professional to do a survey, as the U.S. Section of WILPF had done in 1955, had met with a very angry and defensive response, and the accusation that Americans did not understand the European ways of thinking.[7]

Nevertheless, Mildred Olmsted retained her keen interest in the development of the international WILPF and corresponded with Tano Jodai in Japan, who urged her to accept the international presidency ("You are more like Jane Addams than anyone else"); with Gertrude Baer, who continued to be prickly; with Else Zeuthen; and with Phoebe Cusden and Sybil Cookson, both of the United Kingdom, the latter interested in strengthening WILPF in Africa. She kept up a lively correspondence with the women she had met in Australia and New Zealand and was happy to learn that the WILPF was growing strong in these two nations. She believed that the WILPF should develop regionally, just as U.S. WILPF was doing, and looked with particular hope to the Orient with Australia as base.[8]

Planning and arranging for travel remained one of Allen Olmsted's chief hobbies, if not passions. In between the big trips, the Olmsteds took many smaller ones during their retirement years. In January or February they generally went south, sometimes to stay with Adele and Maurice at Key West, but often to visit the various islands of the Caribbean or the countries of Central America. As often as possible they took one of their eight grandchildren along on trips. One summer they took Eric Olmsted to Alaska and camped out on the tundra with him. A few years later they took Diane Burke with them to Italy. On their trip to England in 1974, they asked Kenny Olmsted to come along as driver and found him an appreciative and pleasant companion.

There were sentimental trips too. Allen revisited the camp in Jasper, where they had gone to conceive Peter. Allen and Mildred traveled together to France to visit the battlefields of World War I, including the grave of Ted Prichard. In 1971 they celebrated their fiftieth wedding anniversary with a quiet trip to the Pocono Mountains. They traveled several times in Maine and took both boat and train trips in northern Canada, which they continued to love. They went together to Sardinia, where they were now the seniors of the family, given the best bedroom and not required to work.

On the home front, Mildred Olmsted became more and more of an activist. She had taken a lively interest in the Poor People's Campaign in the summer of 1968, following Martin Luther King, Jr.'s assassination, and in Resurrection City, the shantytown built by marchers on the Mall in Washington. As a result, she and Allen were involved during these exciting years in helping to fund a Freedom City commune in Alabama established by Ray and Cheryl Robinson, an African-American couple they had met, on land donated by Mildred's friend Amelia Boynton. In 1969 Mildred stood on a vigil line in Philadelphia to protect antiwar demonstrators from the police, and she joined other members of Providence Meeting in a witness of support when one young member turned in his draft card. In 1971 she, along with Stewart Meacham of the American Friends Service Committee Peace Education Committee and Joe Miller of SANE as well as Kay Camp of WILPF, walked into a draft board and attempted to make a citizen's arrest of an official. She turned down a similar opportunity to sit in at a draft board with a group of activists, including WILPF's own Dorothy Hutchinson. She said she did not feel drawn to it, perhaps because she had taken no role in the planning.

The stirring events of the day reached into the peace of Providence Friends Meeting, to which the Olmsteds belonged. A young draft resister asked if the meeting would provide him with "sanctuary" against arrest. The meeting agreed at first, but some members became upset when his girlfriend moved in with him. Soon factions had formed. When the young man was brought to trial for draft evasion, the meeting went on record supporting his stand but of course said nothing about his life-style. One member of the meeting, however, felt it necessary to speak to the judge and say that he himself did not support the resister and had not concurred with the minute of support. The meeting in turn minuted its disapproval of this individual action. Although the resister himself was ultimately found guilty, imprisoned, served time, and moved away, factions remained within the meeting. Mildred was asked at this crucial juncture to become clerk of the meeting and try to heal the wounds.

She felt at first that the meeting had chosen the wrong Olmsted. "I wish they had asked Allen instead of me to be clerk. He has so much more time and presides and mixes with people better than I and is less vigorous and partisan in his positions," she wrote Ruth. Besides, she sensed that he was hurt that she had been chosen instead of "the judge." But she applied herself to the problem, inviting all the former clerks of the meeting to sit with her and suggest ways out of the dilemma. Gradually she was able to air the dispute at monthly meeting in a manner that brought healing to all but one of the disaffected members. She was surprised that she was able to do so well, and she received many letters from members of the meeting expressing their appreciation for her wise and dispassionate handling of the problem.[9]

Every March when the Philadelphia Yearly Meeting was held at the old meeting house at Fourth and Arch Streets, Mildred was in attendance, sitting in the front of the meetinghouse because of her hearing. Whenever the meeting hesitated over taking some bold step in social action or in peace, Mildred rose and spoke clearly and persuasively in favor of moving forward. For example, she was successful in urging the Yearly Meeting to adopt a statement favoring civil rights for lesbians and gays in the early 1970s. She wanted the Quakers, as well as WILPF, to keep up with the movement of history.

She greeted the new women's movement with the enthusiasm of an old soldier welcoming the long-awaited arrival of young recruits. In April 1968 she attended a conference held by the Peace Education Division of the American Friends Service Committee on "The U. S. in a Revolutionary World." Charlotte Bunch Weeks of the Institute for Policy Studies was one of the speakers. Mildred greeted her joyously. "Now tell me, what are the radical young women of today thinking?" she asked. By 1973 she had become sufficiently a booster of "women's lib" to suggest turning the New Century Club, established by women who were active in the 1876 Centennial Fair in Philadelphia, into a museum of modern women's liberation.[10]

The WILPF as a whole was beginning to rediscover its feminist roots. In 1970 the board once again considered the question of endorsing the ERA. Mildred Olmsted wrote a statement entitled, "Why I Am Opposed to the Equal Rights Amendment Now." She said that as a longtime feminist she supported the Equal Rights Amendment (although she had not in the past), but that she felt that now, with the unpopular Vietnam war causing many people to consider alternatives to conscription and other ways to reduce the power of the military-industrial complex, it was "exactly the wrong moment in history to push for a constitutional amendment that at one stroke would extend that power to control at least 50% more of the population."[11]

> There is widespread repugnance in American tradition to conscripting women. So long as we can take advantage of this, women will be freer in their movements than men.
> We must first get rid of conscription itself and then push through the Equal Rights Amendment.[12]

The WILPF board considered her arguments but voted by a large majority to endorse ERA. Mildred Olmsted decided that she had been wrong, and a few years later joined in a march for ERA in Washington. In 1976, when the city of Philadelphia celebrated the bicentennial of the Declaration of Independence, she was asked to take part in the observation on 26 August of the passage of the Nineteenth Amendment. She repeated her story of marching in the 1913 suffrage parade time after time.

Her old colleague, Dorothy Detzer, was being interviewed by women historians of the "women's lib" variety, as she called them. "Don't you find it very strange to know that you are now part of history?" she wrote Mildred Olmsted. Dorothy said she had received some thirteen books in which either she was quoted or her name appeared. Gerda Lerner, whom Dorothy identified as "one of the intelligent women libbers," wrote to her about Schocken Press bringing out a new edition of *Appointment on the Hill*, although this project never came to fruition. Dorothy still felt very doubtful about feminism, but she was glad for the recognition for WILPF, she wrote Mildred in June 1977.[13]

Mildred Olmsted had written to her earlier, in 1972, but now the two began to correspond just as though all the troubles of the 1940s had never existed. Dorothy's beloved husband, Lud, had died, and Dorothy herself was struggling against cancer and losing her eyesight. "I agree with Sir Hugh Cecil that 'Age is the out patient department of Purgatory,'" she wrote. Yet her spirits apparently were good. The two exchanged letters briskly for several years, and Mildred visited Dorothy when she went to California to attend a WILPF meeting in 1978. They discussed what was to be done to augment the pension of their old comrade Gertrude Baer, who was reported to be nearly destitute in Geneva. As Gertrude had said long ago, time had brought healing.

As Mildred Olmsted grew older, more and more groups chose to honor her. In 1972 SANE made her the recipient of their annual Peace Award, and her old alma mater, Friends Central, gave her their Distinguished Alumnae Award. Mildred went back that year to Smith College for her sixtieth reunion, which she found interesting but not particularly uplifting. The same conservative women she had disliked as an eighteen-year-old were among the classmates still well enough to come to the reunion, and many of them expressed themselves as horrified by "women's lib," believing that a woman's place is in the home. Smith, however, looked on Mildred with a more kindly eye than she on her alma mater,

23. Kay Camp, Owen Lattimore, Mildred Olmsted, and Fujiko Isono of Japanese WILPF, May 1971. *Courtesy of Swarthmore College Peace Collection.*

and in 1974 they presented her with an honorary degree as doctor of humane letters.[14]

This was a great occasion in the Olmsted family. Some thirty-two Olmsteds attended, according to Allen's count. Mildred looked beautiful and spoke well. Allen was very proud of his wife and began a playful series of letters headed, "Humane Letter No. 1," "Humane Letter No. 2," and so forth.

There were honors for Allen too. In the spring of 1977 he was feted at an appreciation banquet in Media, for his work in behalf of Media Fellowship House and other interracial projects in the Media area. And the Jane Addams Peace Association, for which he had served as counsel, gave a tea in his honor that fall.

Mildred had turned eighty in 1970; Allen was two years older. Their friends and relations were dying—Marian Scott in 1969, Fred Libby in 1970, Maurice Saul in 1974. The Olmsteds were in a car accident in the fall of 1971, and both suffered lacerations and broken ribs. Allen had an emergency appendectomy in

1972, and Mildred spent four weeks in the hospital in 1973 as doctors tried to discover why she was having so much difficulty in breathing. She also had a cataract on one eye, which was removed in 1974. Both, however, kept bouncing back from these indignities of age and going on with their busy schedules. Allen still suffered from occasional grouches, and the two bickered. On a plane trip home from visiting Ruth in Louisville, Mildred felt that the snacks served for supper on the plane were inadequate, and although they had brought sandwiches that Ruth had packed for them, she protested "on principle" just as she had done about a trolley ride in Munich fifty years before. Allen was mortified and wrote to Ruth in a postcard that the snacks were indeed adequate. Mildred should not have a husband who was a lawyer. None of Allen's other clients so blatantly repudiated his advice. It was a typical Olmsted quarrel.[15]

But there were many happy times. Their children noticed that they seemed almost like honeymooners, sitting as close to each other as possible when they drove in the car, and relatives were struck that Mildred and Allen often had breakfast in bed together, inviting the occasional privileged visitors to join them in this intimate setting. Among Allen's papers was a birthday letter from Mildred that is not dated but was probably written in 1975.

> Happy birthday dear. Marriage has been a long and difficult adjustment for us both—more difficult for me than for you because of many things—but it has been a rich one. It has never been static but we have come at last to a pretty good understanding of each other—not that our foibles no longer irritate but that we are tolerant of them and don't take them too seriously. I believe in separation still but I'll be glad to be together again. We are both blessed by having lived together, and can enjoy the happy end of life for which the first was made.[16]

It was not to last. The Olmsteds and Ruth went to the WILPF congress in Japan in 1977, intending to follow up with a trip into the interior, and a stay at a mountain inn. But Allen felt unwell throughout the congress and said that he thought they had better not travel but return home. Back in Rose Valley Allen had

24. Mildred Olmsted receives an honorary degree from Smith College, June 1974. *Courtesy of Women's International League for Peace and Freedom.*

a thorough checkup, but nothing special was found to be wrong. Still he did not feel well, and he frequently sank into the depression that had never quite left him since Peter's death. He would sit in his favorite chair, staring into the fire. Mildred could not distract him, until finally his mood snapped, and he suggested that they play a game. His spirits rallied briefly in October when WILPF gave a banquet in honor of Mildred at the University Museum, and there were again tributes from old friends like Roger Baldwin. In early December his doctor put him into the hospital for a series of tests, but again there seemed to be no particular cause for alarm, and shortly before Christmas he came home again.

Both Mildred and Allen believed that it was their right to end life when it was no longer rewarding, and both had pills set aside for this eventuality. Mildred knew Allen was not feeling well and seemed depressed on December 21, and she was loath to leave him to go into town to attend a Jane Addams House committee meeting at WILPF. She was attending this meeting when she was called to the phone with the message that Allen had gone to bed for a nap, telling the housekeeper to awaken him when his long-time secretary, Helen Maag, came to take dictation; he had died in his sleep. Mildred wondered if he had taken his pills, but the rest of the family were quite sure it was a natural death, and a blessed release for a man who had been struggling valiantly to keep up his spirits for so many years. The fact that Helen Maag was en route argued for the latter interpretation. He would never have inconvenienced her if he could help it.

With typical Scott stoicism Mildred showed little emotion as she went about organizing a memorial service for Allen at Providence Meeting and a reception afterwards at Rose Valley for members of the family. She saw to it that the local papers carried fitting obituaries, mentioning his pioneer work for the ACLU and his term of office as a judge.

At the memorial service, a Delaware county lawyer praised Allen as a "transition" man, carrying the values of the past into the present and future. "At a time when compromise with corruption permeates all the world from the highest officials to the lowest common denominator, Judge Allen Olmsted never hesitated, never flinched, never compromised with corruption. He was the epitome of the frontier judge whose impeccable honesty gave heart to all struggling people."[17]

Letters of condolence flooded in. For Peter, and later for little Greg, they had been letters full of pain and hurt, but for Allen they were full of joy in a life well lived. Galia Votaw, a Quaker and family friend, recalled that someone had told her that Justice Brandeis spoke of Allen's presentation of a case before the Supreme Court as one of the best he had ever heard. Spencer Coxe of ACLU recalled that Allen had helped his wife get her citizenship after World War II when she refused to swear to "bear arms."[18]

One writer said that she thought Mildred and Allen had been

an ideal couple, "each brilliant, talented, dedicated to the best of ideas and ideals." Helen Rea, who had known them well and traveled with them, said that she regarded their marriage as one of the few truly successful ones she had known. "You were a wonderful wife and companion and Allen's pride and joy in you illuminated his face whenever his eyes fell on you. Thank God you have survived him. His life without you would have been unbearable."[19]

Ruth afterwards praised Mildred for the remarkable courage with which she had dealt with Allen's death, but it was simply her nature not to show grief and to return as quickly as she could to a life that kept her too busy to brood. When the excitement of the memorial service was over she went to Key West with Adele and Marcy Olmsted, her beloved granddaughter, for a period of rest. Then it was back to Rose Valley to pick up the threads of her life, her responsibilities to WILPF and to the other organizations, and her garden.

Of course she missed Allen, and she revealed it in wanting to be sure that his memory was honored. She was delighted when in 1980 the ACLU held a banquet honoring him posthumously, and later when the Delaware County ACLU set up an annual Allen Olmsted award. She took a keen interest in Delaware County politics, in which he had fought so valiantly, and was delighted when Bob Edgar, a Democrat, was elected to the House of Representatives, finally breaking a precedent of Republican dominance. She encouraged and backed Bob, who was also a peace advocate, and he often sought her advice.

Allen and Mildred had always kept separate books, and she was astonished to discover, when his estate was settled and the bills paid, that he had left her only $15,000. She had her Social Security check, and a small amount that Ruth Mellor had arranged for her to receive quarterly, but no other source of income. The rentals on her two apartments did not even pay for the heat. For a woman who had managed a nationwide organization such as the WILPF she was curiously naive about money. For a while after Allen's death she was quite at a loss. Fortunately a member of her meeting, Murray Hoffman, a retired financial adviser, offered to take on the job of handling her finances. At about this time she sold an acre of ground, and with this money, in addition to Allen's $15,000, Hoffman was able to build up her capital until it provided a sufficient income to maintain the big house and give her enough to live on. But the living had to be modest; she continued to frequent auctions and thrift shops and learned to defer major repairs until the end of the year.

Much of the turmoil in the Olmsted marriage had been over money. As Mildred herself came to grips with what it cost to maintain a household, she looked back with some regret that she hadn't understood Allen's reluctance to advance her money when she thought she needed it. One cannot help wondering, however, why Allen clung so tenaciously to the male role and refused to show Mildred his books.

If she had lost Allen, she still had Ruth. Ever since Ruth had moved to Louisville, she had written sad letters expressing loneliness and wishing that she could be with Mildred. For years she spoke of living with the Olmsteds as soon as she retired. But now she was too old and too tied to her home to think of moving. Instead they went on with their usual pattern, taking vacations together in the summer, Ruth spending some part of each Christmas at Rose Valley, and Mildred tying in trips to see Ruth with WILPF work in the Midwest.

Without Allen to serve as their travel agent, Ruth and Mildred limited themselves to slightly less adventurous trips than formerly. In the summer after Allen's death they visited the Trapp family lodge in Vermont; the next year Mildred attended the WILPF biennial in Santa Cruz, California, participating in a workshop on feminism and pacifism. Ruth came along, and afterwards they traveled together to their beloved Banff. In the spring of 1980, they took a cruise on the Mississippi River, and later in the summer, after attending the WILPF international congress in Hamden, Connecticut, they signed on for a whale-sighting trip on the St. Lawrence River, sponsored by the World Affairs Council. The following year they vacationed together in the mountains of Colorado. In January 1982 they went on a Caribbean cruise that included a trip through the Panama Canal. Ruth had broken a rib and felt miserable, but she mended sufficiently so that she was able to join Mildred on a raft trip over some rapids. Ruth was ninety-four and Mildred, ninety-two.[20]

Sadly, however, the travel adventures ended. Ruth was beginning to be very forgetful. Her letters to Mildred were repetitious, and her friends in Louisville wrote to Mildred saying that Ruth was beginning to need supervision in daily living. Mildred was worried about her and made several trips to Louisville to see if she could not talk Ruth into giving her lawyer power of attorney, as she had no nearby living relatives.

On one of these trips, in November 1982, Mildred Olmsted slipped on ice on Ruth's steep driveway and fell, breaking her hip. She was too far from the house to attract Ruth's attention, and she lay there for some time before some men in a passing car stopped to find out what was the matter. She was then taken to a hospital in Louisville where she remained until she was well enough to be flown back to a rehabilitation hospital in the Philadelphia area. She was finally allowed to go home in January, but she had to remain on the second floor.

She learned eventually to get around with a walker, but the hip did not heal properly and had to be reset in the fall. Soon, however, she was up and about again, often dragging her walker along behind her in her hurry to be on time to meetings. Asked to attend a peace rally on the steps of the Media Courthouse, she set her walker firmly aside when she stepped forward to address the crowd. Crossing a busy street, she saw that a truck was coming, and picking up her walker, she ran to the farther curb. She even said she thought she had learned something by breaking her hip and having to use a walker. "People are more interested in helping me than I would have thought."[21]

Ruth meanwhile continued to fail and was finally placed in a nursing home in Louisville, diagnosed as having Alzheimer's. For a while she continued to write Mildred occasional confused letters, but she soon became unable even to remember who Mildred was. Mildred wrote to her and sent her birthday and Christmas presents but was told it was no use; Ruth was interested in nothing but her three meals a day. All the longing and loneliness of Ruth's emotionally starved life ended up concentrated on food. She lived on until 1989, physically healthy but mentally unable to remember or concentrate.

Mildred still had her sister Adele, also a widow, living next door. But the two sisters had developed into such different people with such different interests that, though they were very fond of each other, they saw rather little of each other from day to day. Adele continued to spend time painting in her studio in Rose Valley. For sociability she liked to play bridge, which Mildred had deliberately decided never to learn. Mildred preferred to keep her time filled to the brim with meetings. She loved to feel that she was as busy as she had once been at the helm of the WILPF. She and Adele talked on the phone every morning, and she would frequently suggest to Adele interesting meetings that Adele might want to attend, even though Adele invariably turned her down.

Each winter Mildred spent several weeks with Adele at her home in Key West, and here they sometimes regaled each other with memories of their joint past. Interestingly enough they remembered it quite differently. And the relationship of early childhood still held true: Adele was her older sister, a person to be admired and emulated but too self-contained for the exchange of confidences. Adele's death in December 1988 left Mildred feeling more bereft than she had ever been before. Losing Adele meant a break with her childhood, and with the last of her contemporaries. Typically, however, she did not show her pain.

Enid had developed emphysema and was dependent on oxygen, and she therefore curtailed her visits to Rose Valley. Tony and Isabel still lived in West Chester, but their lives were busy, and Tony and his mother continued to have occasional differences. Barbara Sprogell Jacobson, Adele's daughter, had always had a good relationship with Mildred, whom she called "Aunt Jane"; she had been recruited by Mildred to serve as president of the Jane Addams Peace Association, but she too was very busy and often away. As she grew older Mildred became more interested in her grandchildren, especially Peter's daughter Marcy. Marcy seemed to Mildred somewhat like herself at that age. She was a rebel and an activist in the seventies, and she loved adventure, taking a trip around the world in 1980. After trying out work as a paralegal and in public health, she decided finally to become a doctor and entered medical school in 1983. Mildred was interested in her other grandchildren too; she was particularly pleased when Kenny Olmsted decided to become a lawyer like his grandfather and interned at Saul, Ewing, Remick and Saul, although he chose to enter practice on the West Coast. But Marcy was both a granddaughter and a friend.

Mildred Olmsted kept up a correspondence with the extended Olmsted family and enjoyed spending time in Sardinia, where she was given the best quarters. Gone were the early days when she came in Allen's shadow and was ignored by the Olmsted clan. Now she was the matriarch, and the center of attention. The Olmsteds found Mildred less warm than Allen, but they admired her style.

After her broken hip finally healed, Mildred Olmsted entered a spell of relative good health. Despite a second cataract operation she continued to have trouble with her eyes, she remained short of breath because of her heart, and she suffered periodically from gout, but her doctor regarded her as a phenomenon as she kept active well into her late nineties.

The housekeeper she had had with her for many years, Mrs. Anderson, had finally become incapacitated; Mildred had nursed her and had arranged for her to be placed in a nursing home. After a series of temporary helpers, she decided to offer the position to a woman from a domestic abuse center, and through social work connections she found a younger woman, Ari Breckenridge, who came to live with her with her two sons. Ari shared Mildred's love of color and decorating and was an excellent cook. She brought Mildred breakfast in bed every morning in the silver and black bedroom, served her and her frequent guests elegant lunches in the dining room of Thunderbird Lodge, and brought her dinner by the fire, where Mildred could watch the McNeil-Lehrer news program every night. In the early days of their relationship Ari found Mildred domineering, but by stating her own position clearly and strongly, she was able to work out a modus vivendi.

When she was not going out to a meeting, Mildred went to bed relatively early, taking with her papers to read and correspondence to look over. Because she had never developed the habit of throwing things out, her large bedroom was crowded with boxes and bags of old letters and reports, waiting to be sorted. On a special table by her bedside was her favorite reading matter, an article or a book on archeology. Reading about ancient civilizations was her "Tasty Cake" she said, to be enjoyed when the work of the evening was accomplished. It was another way to take a long view of social history.

As she reached her midnineties, Mildred Olmsted began to prepare for her own death. One form of preparation was to ensure the continuation of the things that mattered to her. In 1984 she addressed a letter to all her grandchildren asking which one wanted to inherit Thunderbird Lodge, which was in the process of being listed on the National Register. Both Marcy and Kenny indicated interest, but so did her son Tony, whom Mildred had not consulted, thinking him happily settled in West Chester. Mildred's final decision was to leave the house to Tony but to have it go finally to Marcy and her husband, Billy, Kenny having withdrawn. Along with the house she left a trust fund, comprising her principal, for the upkeep of the lodge. It was terribly important to her that the house and garden on which she had lavished so much love be kept in the family.

As she regaled audiences with the story of her life, everyone kept suggesting that she write her memoirs. But Mildred Olmsted, who had once wanted to be a writer, felt now that she preferred to be a woman of action. Friends and family began a search for a biographer. It was a great grandniece who first suggested Mildred to me as a subject. Once I had begun interviewing her, she began to unearth boxes of letters and documents that she had been saving for years with a biography in mind. Together we sorted many mountains of papers. At first Mildred was somewhat reluctant to have her private letters turned over to the Swarthmore College Peace Collection, but in time she came to agree that this was the best disposition for them.

A third concern on her mind was the continuation and the growth of the WILPF. In 1984 she addressed a letter to Helen Kusman who had accepted the chairmanship of the committee on the future of WILPF. The league had become top-heavy, Mildred Olmsted said, "not enough body to support the head." She recommended that a goal be set for 50,000 members by the time of the seventy-fifth anniversary. "Or should we say 75,000?" She continued with pages and pages of suggestions for better publicity, bet-

25. Jane Fonda and Mildred Olmsted at a SANE (National Committee for a Sane Nuclear Policy) dinner, 1979. *Courtesy of Swarthmore College Peace Collection.*

ter recruitment of potential leaders, better use of volunteers. She also thought WILPF headquarters should be expanded, perhaps by buying adjacent properties. Other organizations, such as SANE, had grown recently. Why not the WILPF?[22]

She continued to attend as many WILPF meetings and events as she could, and she represented WILPF at scores of conferences. She was active in WILPF's Star (Stop the Arms Race) Campaign and marched in the giant Nuclear Freeze Vigil in New York in 1982, speaking from the platform. After she broke her hip, she did not attempt to go abroad again, but in the United States she often flew to attend meetings and conferences, sometimes with Ari as her companion.

She also continued working with SANE and presented the SANE Peace Award to Jane Fonda and to Joan Baez. Although she

26. Mildred Olmsted and Joan Baez at a SANE dinner, 1983. *Courtesy of Swarthmore College Peace Collection.*

resigned from the state ACLU board, she remained on the Philadelphia board. She was honored in 1985 for her thirty-five years of service. She served as a sponsor of Jobs for Peace when it was organized in 1983 and continued on the Committee for Promoting Enduring Peace, an organization that presented the Gandhi Peace Prize to her friend and colleague Kay Camp in 1984, for her work as president of U.S. WILPF and international WILPF, as well as at the United Nations. When a group of Philadelphians organized a Valentine's Day dinner to support civil liberties for lesbians and for gay men, Mildred Olmsted was one of the sponsors.

She became a familiar sight during these years at the many banquets held in Philadelphia to raise money for liberal causes. Always dressed in full evening attire, with brilliants sparkling on her ears and on her bosom, her cheeks and lips bright with makeup, her manner regal and joyous, she made a vivid impression by her presence. Invariably introduced, she waved happily to the crowd. At demonstrations and peace marches of all kinds she was present, properly hatted, standing among the celebrities, taking her turn at the microphone to wave and say a few cheery words of encouragement. Everyone smiled and sat up a little straighter when Mildred was there. She had become, in her old age, a celebrity and a symbol of continuity.

17

A Legend in Her Own Time

*I*N THE LAST DECADE OF HER LIFE Mildred Olmsted assumed a new role. As a woman who remained alert and vigorous into her nineties, she became an important link with the past. Women historians and women activists sought her out for her memories of that past. The news media began to see her as a valued resource. Women in the WILPF turned to her for wise counsel and continuing inspiration. The fact that she had lived so long and still faced the future joyously was empowering to the men and women she encountered. Pilgrimages to the house in Rose Valley became more and more frequent.

With the growth of feminism and the development of women's studies, the history of the WILPF became of great interest to scholars. Women activists and theoreticians were exploring the links between feminism and pacifism, feminism and nonviolence. The WILPF as an organization had not always considered itself feminist; nevertheless its roots were in the feminist past, and its mission since 1915 had concerned women and peace. The widespread development of peace studies and peace research in the 1950s had stimulated the development of peace libraries. In addition to the Swarthmore College Peace Collection, which holds the bulk of WILPF's records, the University of Colorado had acquired the papers of international WILPF. Scholars worked in both libraries on WILPF-related topics, and many of them came to interview Mildred Scott Olmsted.

Among these was a teacher from Southwest Texas State University, Carrie Foster-Hayes, who interviewed Mildred Olmsted in

1980 and who earned her doctorate with a dissertation titled *The Women and the Warriors, Dorothy Detzer and the WILPF* in 1984. She is currently publishing a book on a related topic. Another was Catherine Foster, a freelance writer and peace activist, who in 1989 published a book, *Women for All Seasons,* bringing the WILPF story up to date. Amelia Fry, writing a biography of Alice Paul, interviewed Mildred Olmsted. Jacqueline Van Voris and Eleanor Flexner talked with her in regard to a proposed biography of Carrie Chapman Catt.

Frances Early, a Canadian professor of women's studies, researching the lives of Tracy Mygatt and Frances Witherspoon, talked with Mildred Olmsted in 1985 on the early days of the peace movement and published the interview in *Atlantis.* At one point she tried to pin Mildred down on the question of whether women had unique qualities that made them especially fitted to conduct the search for peace. Mildred, who had been on both sides of this question all her life, backed away from committing herself, repeating the assertion that it would have been impossible for the international WILPF to survive a change to an organization of both men and women.[1]

She had other callers. A young woman sought her advice on how to combine a career in social work with one in the peace movement. Eleanor Smeal, then president of the National Organization for Women, came to consult her on politically effective strategies. A student from Moorestown Friends School interviewed her for a class assignment.

All interviewers got the benefit of Mildred Olmsted's comments on the news of the day. To keep abreast by reading the newspaper from cover to cover and by watching television coverage seemed an important duty to Mildred Olmsted, just as it had been when she was administrative secretary for the WILPF, and it was hard for her at times to turn to answering questions about the past, when what was happening on Capitol Hill that very day claimed her attention.

She had always been interested in the media, and now she was pleased when reporters sought her out. The BBC interviewed her on camera for a series called "The Road to War," examining the origins of World War II. Mildred was the subject of an article

27. Coretta Scott King and Mildred Olmsted at WILPF's seventieth anniversary dinner, 1985. *Courtesy of Women's International League for Peace and Freedom.*

in *Modern Maturity,* reprinted in the *Washingtonian* magazine, that brought her letters from many old friends. The Philadelphia *Inquirer* and *Daily News* both did profiles, as did the Smith College *Alumni Quarterly* and the Delaware County *Daily Times.* Radio and television reporters came to the house at Rose Valley to get Mildred's opinions on a host of subjects.

In all these interviews, and in all her speeches now, she told her own life story with enthusiasm, stressing the victories. In the process she helped to build her own legend. Aspects of the story became a bit augmented in the process. It was frequently said that she was a pioneer suffragist (though she actually marched only once), that Herbert Hoover had asked her to go into Germany to help with the child feeding, that she had been handpicked and trained for her work with WILPF by Jane Addams, that she had been WILPF's executive director for forty-four years, that Allen Olmsted was one of the founders of the ACLU. At first she tried to straighten out reporters, but later she decided that it did not matter, she told me. Some of these errors found their way into *Who's Who in America,* which further confirmed the legend.

Persons I interviewed who had known Mildred Olmsted in the 1940s and the 1950s insisted that she had never been a feminist, but Mildred now believed otherwise and the media concentrated its attention on this part of the story. Younger women coming into the WILPF in the 1980s, eager to explore the links between feminism and pacifism, were delighted to discover Mildred and astonished by the youthfulness and openness of her approach. One young woman on Long Island described a meeting in which Mildred participated.

> The differing views of feminism were drawn partly along generational lines, although one of the oldest women there, Mildred Scott Olmsted (92, I think—a founding member of WILPF) had thoughts more close to the younger set than some of those in between. She chronicled for us the ongoing debates amongst WILPF and related groups, through its herstory, over whether women's rights was simply one of the struggles of equal importance, or if a feminist approach to all the issues was our special strength and should permeate all our work. This controversy, although I found it somewhat surprising and frustrating, only makes me more determined to carry on our dialogue and growth, and infuse some new healthy feminist energy into an organization which is ready to keep growing at age 65![2]

WILPF's endorsement of a women's camp at the Seneca, New York, missile site in the summer of 1983 was a source of great interest to Mildred Olmsted, as it brought many young feminists to the peace struggle. She was also pleased to meet some of the women who had created a similar camp at Greenham Common in England, who were touring the United States in 1985. In that year she participated in a lecture series at Pendle Hill on the Quaker contribution to feminism and took part in several celebrations of the centennial of Alice Paul. These occasions somewhat embarrassed her, as she and Alice Paul had never gotten along very well, but she was careful not to say anything negative and to stress the fact that Alice Paul had been a woman before her time.

28. Eleanor Smeal of NOW and Mildred Olmsted at a banquet in her honor, 1986. *Courtesy of Women's International League for Peace and Freedom.*

In 1986 a new executive director, Jane Midgley, was chosen to lead WILPF. She was a young woman who had worked in the WILPF legislative office in Washington and was an ardent feminist and author of *The Woman's Budget,* a study of the national budget from the feminist point of view. She also shared Mildred Olmsted's interest and faith in building the WILPF and she was particularly concerned to bring in younger women, and to introduce a feminist perspective to an organization made up of many women who had come of age in the 1940s and 1950s who did not always understand or agree with the philosophy of the new feminism. She supported the development of programs with a specific feminist emphasis, such as one concentrating on violence against women, and she used a collegial style, sharing power with others in the national office. Mildred Olmsted did not always understand the new methods, but she was very pleased with Jane's spirit, and the two worked well together.

Younger WILPF women rising to new positions of authority in the organization sought her out for counsel. Phyllis Rubin, WILPF's director of development, came to know her through answering calls from persons in the media who wanted to interview her. Soon Mildred discovered to her delight that Phyllis shared her eagerness to see the WILPF grow, and to receive the attention it deserved. She began to bring Phyllis interesting appeal letters from other organizations, and to call her with suggestions for things WILPF might do. Phyllis responded eagerly, finding Mildred to be absolutely right in her tips. The two worked together in planning the seventieth anniversary celebration of WILPF, as well as later events. Mildred once invited Phyllis to dinner at the house in Rose Valley and told her that she ought to look ahead to a larger field of service in WILPF. The league needed her because she was organization minded.[3]

Regene Silver, who chaired the WILPF's celebration of its sixty-fifth birthday in 1980 and served as vice-president, was a frequent lunch guest at the house in Rose Valley. She and Mildred discussed personnel problems facing WILPF in the 1980s, as well as Mildred's interest in building the organization. When Genie went to the Soviet Union in 1983 on a WILPF mission and was disturbed by the lack of liberties she observed, she talked over her feelings with Mildred, who told her that the Russian women were listening to the women of the WILPF, even though they were not always free to express themselves fully. When Genie decided to write her doctoral thesis on Jane Addams, Mildred was encouraging, but when interviewed she had few memories to contribute.[4]

Mary Zupernick, who became president of the WILPF in 1989, called Mildred Olmsted frequently on the phone. Mary, who had worked in the WILPF office in Philadelphia for a time, recalled with pleasure a time when the WILPF board meeting was to be held at a rather primitive camp site in New Jersey. Many board members called the office to inquire rather apprehensively about conditions. Mildred called and asked matter of factly if she should bring her grandson's sleeping bag.

The stories in the paper and on the air about Mildred in turn generated more stories and more honors. In 1985 Mildred received the first Sacco Vanzetti Award, developed by a liberal clergyman in Boston, and was feted by the Pennsylvania School of Social Work as the oldest living graduate of the original school, the

Philadelphia Training School for Social Work. In 1986 the WILPF gave a dinner for her at the Franklin Institute and presented her with a lifetime achievement award. There were tributes from old comrades and from WILPF members all over the globe. One of those she most prized was from a man whose civil liberties she had defended. "You and Clarence Pickett responded to my appeal for support to reverse the twenty year sentence imposed on me by the court in Pittsburgh on a charge of 'sedition.' Your unhesitating response and support during the 50's to defeat the shameful frame up ended in victory when the U.S. Supreme Court reversed the conviction and at the same time struck down the infamous sedition laws in the United States."[5]

And still the honors continued. In 1987 Swarthmore College gave her an honorary degree, and in 1988 Haverford College followed suit. In 1990 the city of Philadelphia gave her a lifetime achievement award. At all these occasions she spoke without notes, telling the story of her life and the great changes she had seen. The life story was joyous; she simply left out its dark side, as she had always done, and concentrated on the good things that had happened to her and the progress she had seen: the development of an environmental movement, the proliferation of the peace movement, the burgeoning of the women's movement, all in her lifetime. "One of the very great satisfactions in my older years is to see that more and more people are now beginning to recognize the interrelatedness of all social problems," she said.[6]

To her the future opened up endless opportunity. As she said to the graduating class of 1987 at Swarthmore when she got her honorary degree:

> You are walking into a world full of opportunity, full of excitement, full of challenge. Every direction in which you look, there is an expansion of information. . . . Nothing is the way it used to be. We need the best brains, the best skills of everybody to work on the world's problems. Population explosion, destruction of our common resources, everywhere you look disease, everywhere, any field. So you have the opportunity. You may not get rich, and maybe you won't like your jobs—they won't be easy jobs—but if you go into this exciting, new world, which is just the world that the

29. Mildred Scott Olmsted at her home in Rose Valley, 1981. *Courtesy of Olmsted Papers.*

men who drew up our Constitution had to face. They had to create new things. You will find that you have an exciting, challenging and very worthwhile world.[7]

She still believed in progress, although she told the students that if they turned aside from the challenge, it was possible that the civilization of today might be destroyed and rediscovered in some later age by an archeologist from a better civilization. "I congratulate you on having an opportunity, which is rare. I hope you take it."[8]

In the summer of 1989, Mildred had planned to go to the biennial WILPF conference in Madison, Wisconsin, in June and to the Twenty-fourth International Congress of WILPF planned for Sydney, Australia, in July. The latter was a fulfillment of a dream to Mildred, as she had long advocated regional development for WILPF, and the holding of congresses in such regions as the Pacific. But she was too ill to make either journey. In her absence the women of WILPF at Madison voted for the establishment of a

Mildred Scott Olmsted fund for fieldwork; the women at Sydney discussed the possibility of raising money for an international regional organizer. It was the greatest possible tribute they could pay to their aged mentor.

Her health continued precarious during the fall and winter of 1989, and in the early spring of 1990 she fell and injured her back. She was in and out of the hospital thereafter, and her mind became cloudy. On 2 May WILPF had planned a gala celebration of its seventy-fifth birthday, with Alice Walker as the featured speaker, and Mildred Olmsted, at almost one hundred, an honoree. Phyllis Rubin told Mildred that she must make this event, even if she had to come in a wheelchair, but when the day came this proved impossible. Mildred remembered that she had to make the party, and she felt terribly guilty that she had let WILPF down. In consequence she began to think it was necessary to establish how sick she really was. When someone from WILPF came to tell her about the event, Mildred had been sitting up reading the paper, but she asked the nurse to help her back into bed. There she lay, scarcely breathing, throughout the visit. After the woman left, she sat up and asked for her lunch.[9]

Throughout the spring and early summer she had a nurse during the day but was taken care of by Ari at night. The two had had many disagreements, but in the intimacy of the sickroom, they drew closer together. Mildred became interested in Ari's grandchildren, who were frequently about. When Ari's daughter had a new baby, Mildred held the infant in her arms, marveling at the miracle of tiny fingernails and eyebrows. She had never before held such a small infant, she confided to Ari, not having been able to hold Peter because she was too ill. To Ari and her daughter it seemed as though Mildred was at last finding a closeness and warmth she had always yearned for and never seemed able to achieve.

She still sometimes talked of ending her own life by taking pills, but insisted in the same breath that she was still enjoying life and was too busy to die, too eager to see how it all came out. She often told people who called her on the phone that she was as busy as she could possibly be, although in fact she only moved from bed to chair. For a time her mind remained cloudy and her memory fragmented, but as she grew weaker she regained clarity.

In one of those days of clarity, Phyllis Rubin brought a WILPF member to interview Mildred on videotape. In the process of the interview, Mildred told about the four personalities that had been with her for so many years: Joseph, the efficient one; Jane, the athlete; Judy, the artist; and Jeremiah or Jonathan, the visionary who took the long view. "And now there is only Jonathan left," she said with a laugh.[10]

Toward the end of June she began to resist eating and grew steadily weaker. Ari and her little granddaughter Jessie were sitting with her on the night of 2 July. She did not speak to them, but she smiled when Jessie said "Olmsted likes her purple nightgown." Shortly before ten o'clock P.M. Ari asked her if she wanted a cup of tea and went down to brew it, taking Jessie with her to be picked up by her mother. When Ari returned with the tea, Mildred Olmsted's heart, which had ticked so valiantly for so many years, had finally given out.[11]

At the time of the celebration of her ninety-fifth birthday David McReynolds of the War Resisters League had written, "The program notes state, 'a biography of Mildred Scott Olmsted reads like the history of progressive social change in the past decade.' Decade indeed! I would say the better part of a century. I have not always agreed with WILPF but I have always thought of you as a tower of strength within the broader peace community. One of those authentic rocks of this republic; one of those marvelous rocks against which tyrants occasionally run aground."[12]

Mildred Olmsted may not have changed the course of history. But she believed with rocklike stubbornness that in a democracy social change had to come from the action of private citizens who were willing to advance unpopular ideas until their time at last came. One has to ask what violations of civil liberties, what infringements of civil rights, what indignities to women, what bowing to the military-industrial complex might have come about if she had not been there, playing the role into which she had cast herself, that of loyal opposition. That some of the energy for this lifelong struggle came from a battle to preserve her own sense of self, a battle that was sometimes painful to herself and others, does not detract from the accomplishment.

That sense of self had been threatened by conflict over the stereotyped gender roles that she learned as a child, and that she simply could not accept as limitations on her personal freedom. In a way that she herself never quite understood, she was a victim of the pervasive sexism that she challenged all her life. By channeling her private pain and her personal obsession with freedom into a lifelong struggle to keep alive the original vision of the founders of WILPF in the interrelatedness of peace and of freedom, she helped to preserve a vehicle for change for almost seventy years.

In a sense the WILPF was born before its time. The concept that women may have a unique set of values and skills to contribute to the quest for peace and justice is being considered more seriously today than at any time in the history of feminist thought. Feminists of the time of Jane Addams stressed woman's maternal instincts as prompting her toward peace but believed that women must behave like men in order to obtain power and to be effective. The concept of moving both men and women away from the patriarchal view of power *over,* to one of power *sharing,* is just now being explored.

Younger women today, wanting to combine their feminism and pacifism, are discovering the WILPF with the realization that they do not need to reinvent the wheel. As the first and most important international peace group for women, with sections in thirty-one nations around the world today, WILPF is a living monument to those pioneers who first saw the vision of women working together for peace. And while they may have borrowed some of their methods from their male colleagues, they contributed many things to the peace movement of their day: skills in networking and coalition building, the development of the bonds of sisterhood and intense loyalty, a pattern of combining the struggle for peace with that for justice, the importance of an international outlook.

Today the WILPF is developing a feminist analysis and bringing into its ranks younger women who want to work on women's issues as well as on peace, and who see the correlations very well. Whether the organization itself can bend enough to change its direction and absorb these new energies is hard to assess. Perhaps in the long run the institutional life of the WILPF as such does not matter. What matters is that the history of WILPF itself is empowering to women, just as Mildred Olmsted, in her person, was always empowering.

It may be that the time has at last come when the women of the world will lead humanity in saying a final no to war. If so we all owe a debt to the valiant woman with the piercing blue eyes who kept on for so long, keeping on.

Notes
For Further Reading
Index

NOTES

1. A Troubled Childhood

1. Interview. Margaret Hope Bacon interviewing Mildred Scott Olmsted, 22 Oct. 1987. Between May 1987 and May 1990 I conducted fourteen two-hour interviews, of which the first seven were transcribed and deposited at the Swarthmore College Peace Collection (SCPC). Hereafter: Interview, date.

2. Interview. 22 Oct. 1987.

3. Interview by Sol Jacobson of Adele Saul, 8 June 1987, tape in possession of Barbara Sprogell Jacobson.

4. Interview, 22 Oct. 1987.

5. Ibid.

6. Ibid.

7. Ibid.

8. Ibid.

9. Interview, Mildred Scott Olmsted by Jacqueline Van Voris, 29 May 1972, at West Springfield, Mass. (hereafter: Interview, Van Voris), Mildred Scott Olmsted Papers, Document Group 82, Box 8, Swarthmore College Peace Collection (SCPC). Hereafter: Mildred Scott Olmsted Papers.

10. Mildred Scott, Fragment, ca. 1919? Olmsted Papers. These papers, including letters from Mildred, Ruth Mellor, Trudy Pritchard, Allen Olmsted, and many other relatives and friends, were given to me by Mildred Olmsted with permission to quote at will. After completing the biography I deposited them at SCPC. Hereafter: Olmsted Papers.

11. Interview, Van Voris.

12. *Record 1908,* Friends Central School, Philadelphia.

13. Interview, 22 Oct. 1987.

14. Mildred Scott to her mother, 24 July 1907, Olmsted Papers.

15. Adele Scott to Mildred Scott, 7 Nov. 1907, 87A, uncataloged papers, and Allen Olmsted Papers, SCPC. (At the time I was working on the biography Swarthmore had seven boxes entitled "correspondence, biographical,

personal material of Allen Olmsted, Mildred Olmsted, and various family members." These papers were subsequently integrated into the Mildred Olmsted and Allen Olmsted Papers.)

    16. Mildred Scott to Adele Scott, Nov. 1907, Olmsted Papers.

2. "Educated Gentlewomen"

    1. Adele Scott to Mildred Scott, 3 Dec. 1910, Olmsted Papers.

    2. "Woman Suffrage at Smith," Document Group U.S. 2; 1912 yearbook, Smith College; Smith College Monthly, 1910; Sophia Smith Collection, Smith College.

    3. Interview, 23 Mar. 1988.

    4. Interview, Van Voris.

    5. Mildred Scott diary (hereafter: Diary), Olmsted Papers.

    6. Mildred Scott to Gwen Lowe, ca. July 1909, Olmsted Papers.

    7. Gertrude Rhoads to Mildred Scott, 18 Apr. 1910, Olmsted Papers.

    8. Interview, Van Voris.

    9. Interview, 28 Oct. 1987.

    10. Ibid.

    11. Interview, Van Voris.

    12. Diary, 10 Feb. 1910, Olmsted Papers.

    13. Mildred Scott to Ruth Mellor, 10 Nov. 1919, Olmsted Papers.

    14. Mildred Olmsted to Ruth Mellor, 12 Jan. 1969, Olmsted Papers.

    15. Interview, 1 May 1987.

    16. N.d., Olmsted Papers. "Fusser" was the slang word for a flirt.

    17. Diary, 8 Dec. 1911, Olmsted Papers.

    18. Henry Scott to Mildred Scott, 4 Dec. 1911, Olmsted Papers.

    19. Interview, 1 May 1987.

    20. Ruth Mellor to Mildred Scott, 14 Oct. 1912, Olmsted Papers.

3. Working Woman

    1. Interview, 1 May 1987.

    2. Interview, Van Voris; Diary, 12 Dec. 1912, 29 Mar. 1913, Olmsted Papers.

    3. Interview, Van Voris.

    4. Diary, 18 Sept. 1913, Olmsted Papers.

    5. Diary, 25 and 26 Nov. 1912, Olmsted Papers.

    6. Interview, Van Voris.

    7. Diary, 8 Jan. 1914, Olmsted Papers.

    8. Mildred Olmsted Report to Pennsylvania Branch WILPF Annual Meeting, 15–16 Apr. 1937, Harrisburg, Series B3, Box 8, 1937, U.S. WILPF, Document Group 43, SCPC. Hereafter U.S. WILPF.

9. Ruth Mellor to Mildred Scott, 24 Sept. 1914, 2 Oct. 1914, Olmsted Papers.

10. Interview, 1 May 1987.

11. Ibid.

12. Ruth Mellor to Mildred Scott, 10, 12, and 14 Sept. 1914, Olmsted Papers.

13. Tracy is not the woman's real name.

14. Ruth Mellor to Mildred Scott, 25 Aug. 1916, Olmsted Papers.

15. Ruth Mellor to Mildred Scott, 28 Aug. 1916, Olmsted Papers.

16. Mildred Scott to Ruth Mellor, 23 Sept. 1916, Olmsted Papers.

17. Mally Lord to Mildred Scott, 15 Sept. 1915, Olmsted Papers.

18. Jane Addams to Allen Olmsted, 8 May 1911, Allen S. Olmsted II Papers, Document Group 95, SCPC. Hereafter: Allen S. Olmsted Papers.

19. Witter Bynner to President Lowell, 30 Oct. 1911, Henry Higginson to John Olmsted, 6 Dec. 1911, *Crimson,* 2 Nov. 1911, Allen S. Olmsted Papers.

20. Allen Olmsted to Mildred Scott, 23 July 1916, Olmsted Papers.

21. Allen Olmsted to Ruth Mellor, 6 June 1917, Olmsted Papers.

4. The Coming of War

1. Allen Olmsted to Henry W. Watson, 17 Apr. 1917, 22 May 1917, Olmsted Papers.

2. Arthur Devan to Allen Olmsted, 23 July 1917, Allen Olmsted to President Isaac Sharpless, 14 July 1917, Olmsted Papers.

3. Allen Olmsted to Mildred Scott, 24 July 1917, Olmsted Papers.

4. Allen Olmsted to Mildred Scott, 22 Sept. 1917, Olmsted Papers.

5. Mildred Scott to Allen Olmsted 9 Sept. 1917, and 11 Dec. 1917, Olmsted Papers.

6. Mildred Scott to Allen Olmsted, 17 Nov. 1917, Olmsted Papers.

7. Charge Sheet, Court Martial of Allen S. Olmsted, 12 Jan. 1918, Olmsted Papers.

8. Ibid.

9. Mildred Scott to Allen Olmsted 7 Feb. 1918, 13 Feb. 1918, Olmsted Papers.

10. Allen Olmsted to Mildred Scott, 17 Aug. 1917, Olmsted Papers.

11. Mildred Scott to Allen Olmsted, 10 Jan. 1918, Olmsted Papers.

12. Mildred Scott to Allen Olmsted, 20 Mar. 1918, Olmsted Papers.

13. Mildred Scott to Allen Olmsted, 24 Mar. 1918, Olmsted Papers.

14. Mildred Scott to Allen Olmsted, 25 Nov. 1917, Olmsted Papers.

15. Mildred Scott to Allen Olmsted, n.d. Dec. 1917, Olmsted Papers.

16. Mildred Scott to Allen Olmsted, 14 Feb. 1918, Olmsted Papers.

17. Mildred Scott to Allen Olmsted, 24 Mar. 1918, Olmsted Papers.

18. Allen Olmsted to Mildred Scott, 7 Aug. 1918, Olmsted Papers.

19. Mildred Scott to Allen Olmsted, 11 Aug. 1918, Olmsted Papers.
20. Allen Olmsted to Mildred Scott, 8 Oct. 1918, Olmsted Papers.
21. Allen Olmsted to Mildred Scott, 28 Apr. 1918, Olmsted Papers.
22. Ruth Mellor to Allen Olmsted, 14 June 1918, Olmsted Papers
23. Mildred Scott to Allen Olmsted, 14 Sept. 1918, Olmsted Papers.
24. Ibid.
25. Mildred Scott to Allen Olmsted, 15 Dec. 1918, Olmsted Papers.

5. Over There

1. Mildred Scott to Allen Olmsted, 3 Jan. 1919, Olmsted Papers.
2. Interview, 1 May 1987.
3. Ibid.
4. Ibid.
5. Ibid.
6. Mildred Scott to Dearest Mother and Father, 29 Apr. 1918, Olmsted Papers.
7. Interview, 1 May 1987.
8. Mildred Scott to Allen Olmsted, 3 Sept. 1918, Olmsted Papers.
9. Ibid.
10. Mildred Scott to Allen Olmsted, 29 Sept. 1919, Olmsted Papers.
11. Ibid.
12. Mildred Scott to Allen Olmsted, 21 Oct. 1919, Olmsted Papers.
13. Mildred Scott to Ruth Mellor, 10 Nov. 1919, Olmsted Papers.
14. Mildred Scott to Allen Olmsted, 2 Jan. 1920, Olmsted Papers.
15. Allen Olmsted to Mildred Scott, 21 Dec. 1919, Olmsted Papers.
16. Mildred Scott to Dear Family, 27 Dec. 1919, Olmsted Papers.

6. Hunger in Germany

1. Mildred Scott to Adele Saul, 23 Jan. 1920, Olmsted Papers.
2. Mildred Scott to Allen Olmsted, 24 Jan. 1920, Olmsted Papers.
3. Mildred Scott to Allen Olmsted, 7 Feb. 1920, Olmsted Papers.
4. Mildred Scott to Allen Olmsted, 24 Feb. 1920, Olmsted Papers.
5. Mildred Scott to Allen Olmsted, 13 Mar. 1920, Olmsted Papers.
6. Mildred Scott to Dearest Mother, 1 Apr. 1920, Olmsted Papers.
7. Interview, 22 Oct. 1987.
8. Mildred Scott to Allen Olmsted, 24 June 1920, Olmsted Papers.
9. Interview, 28 Oct. 1987; Record of Arrest, 20 Feb. 1920, Olmsted Papers.
10. Mildred Scott to Adele Saul, 6 June 1920, Olmsted Papers.
11. Interview, 1 May 1987.
12. Ibid.

13. Mildred Scott to Adele Saul, 6 June 1920, Olmsted Papers.
14. Mildred Scott to Allen Olmsted, 30 May 1920, Olmsted Papers.
15. Ibid.
16. Mildred Scott to Adele Saul, 6 June 1920, Olmsted Papers.
17. Mildred Scott to Allen Olmsted, 24 June 1920, Olmsted Papers.
18. Allen Olmsted to Mildred Scott, 23 June 1920, Olmsted Papers.

7. *Home Again*

1. Interview, 1 May 1987.
2. Ibid.
3. Ruth Mellor to Mildred Scott, 16 Oct. 1920, Olmsted Papers.
4. Interview, 1 May 1987.
5. Anna Pratt Report to the Board of White Williams Foundation, 19 May 1922, Olmsted Papers.
6. Interview, 1 May 1987, Series B3, Box 5, 1921, U.S. WILPF.
7. Minutes of the Annual Meeting, 1922, Reel 130.6, U.S. WILPF.
8. Ruth Mellor to Allen Olmsted, 11 Nov. 1920, Olmsted Papers.
9. Ruth Mellor to Mildred Scott, 23 Apr., 1921, 7 Sept. 1921; Mildred Olmsted to Allen Olmsted, 9 May 1923, Olmsted Papers.
10. Ruth Mellor to Mildred Scott, 11 Aug. 1921, Olmsted Papers.
11. Mildred Scott to Allen Olmsted, 20 Sept. 1921, Olmsted Papers.
12. Allen Olmsted to Whites and Olmsteds, 26 Sept. 1921; Olmsteds to Allen Olmsted, 5 Oct. 1921, Olmsted Papers.
13. Interview, 1 May 1987.
14. Allen Olmsted to Swarthmore Monthly Meeting of Friends, 19 Oct. 1921; Hannah Hull to Mildred Scott, 27 Oct. 1921, Olmsted Papers. Interview, 1 May 1987.
15. Interview, 1 May 1987.
16. Ibid.
17. Clara Savage Littledale to Mildred Scott, 26 Oct. 1921; Adele Scott to Mildred Olmsted, 3 Dec. 1921, Olmsted Papers.
18. Anna Pratt Report to the Board of White Williams, 19 May 1922; Anna Pratt to Mildred Olmsted, 10 June 1922, Olmsted Papers.
19. Pinchot Campaign to Mildred Scott Olmsted, 7 May 1922; Mildred Olmsted to American Association of Social Workers, 25 May 1922; Mildred Olmsted to Bureau of Occupations, 25 May 1922, Olmsted Papers.
20. Interview, 1 May 1987. Pennsylvania Executive Board Minutes, 29 May 1922, Series C, Box 5, U.S. WILPF.
21. Mildred Olmsted to Allen Olmsted, 14 June 1922; American Association of Social Workers to Mildred Olmsted, 15 June 1922, Olmsted Papers.
22. Mildred Olmsted to Allen Olmsted, 22 June 1922, Olmsted Papers.
23. Mildred Olmsted to Ruth Mellor, 2 Aug. 1922, Olmsted Papers.
24. Allen Olmsted to Mildred Olmsted, 9 Sept. 22, Olmsted Papers.

8. Working for the WILPF

1. Report of Pennsylvania Executive Secretary, Sept. 1922–May 1923, Series B3, Box 5, U.S. WILPF.

2. Mildred Olmsted Report to the Board, Pennsylvania Branch, Sept. 1923, Series B3, Box 5, U.S. WILPF.

3. Roger Baldwin to Allen Olmsted, 14 Dec. 1920, Allen S. Olmsted Papers.

4. Interview, 3 Nov. 1987.

5. Interviews, descendants of early Pennsylvania board members. Marian Norton to Mildred Olmsted, memo, n.d., Series B3, Box 5, U.S. WILPF.

6. Mildred Olmsted to Allen Olmsted, 10 May 1923, Olmsted Papers.

7. Interview, 11 Nov. 1987.

8. Ruth Mellor to Scottie, 11 May 1924, Olmsted Papers.

9. Allen Olmsted to Mildred Olmsted, 1 Aug. 1924, Olmsted Papers.

10. Ruth Mellor to Scottie, 4 Sept. 1924, Olmsted Papers.

11. Allen Olmsted to Mildred Olmsted, 22 Nov. 1924, Olmsted Papers. Phone interview, Mildred Olmsted, 10 Feb. 1989.

12. Proceedings, Executive Committee Meeting, Innsbruck, 10–15 July 1925, Series B2, Box 1, International WILPF, SCPC.

13. Allen Olmsted to Mildred Olmsted, 16 July 1925, Olmsted Papers.

14. Interview 17 Nov. 1987. Pennsylvania Branch Board Minutes, Sept. 1926, Series B3, Box 5, U.S. WILPF.

15. W. E. B. Dubois to Mildred Olmsted, 5 Mar. 1932, Series C, Box 17, Folder: Pennsylvania Executive Secretary, U.S. WILPF.

16. See Anne Marie Pois, "The Politics and Process of Organizing for Peace: the United States Section of the Women's International League for Peace and Freedom" (Ph.D. diss., Univ. of Colorado, 1988), 196–200.

17. 1927 Annual Meeting, Series A2, Reel 130.5, U.S. WILPF. Interview, 17 Nov. 1987.

18. Jane Addams to Mildred Olmsted, 4 Oct. 1932, Series C, Box 21, Folder: Addams, U.S. WILPF.

19. Maurice Bower Saul to Mildred Olmsted, 9 Aug. 1927, Olmsted Papers.

20. Report of Pennsylvania Executive Secretary, Apr. 1927–Apr. 1928, Series B3, Box 5, U.S. WILPF.

21. Interview, 11 Nov. 1987. Ruth Mellor to Mildred Olmsted, 8 Mar. 1937, Olmsted Papers.

22. Mildred Olmsted to Ruth Mellor, n.d. (ca. 5 May 1927), Olmsted Papers.

23. Mildred Olmsted to Dear Gramp and Grayma, 19 Nov. 1927, Series B3, Box 5, Folder: Organizational Peace Work, U.S. WILPF.

24. "Case Studies in Household Management and Household Employment," Amey E. Watson, Research Director, Philadelphia Council of Household Occupations, 26 Sept. 1930, Olmsted Papers.

9. On the Road

1. Interview, 15 Dec. 1987.
2. Mildred Olmsted to Elizabeth Curtis, 27 June 1928; Mildred Olmsted to Senorita Palacios, 2 Sept. 1928, Series B3, Box 37, Folder: Mexican Border Conference, U.S. WILPF.
3. Interview, 15 Dec. 1987.
4. Ibid. Mildred Olmsted to Sybil Moore, 4 June 1929, Series B3, Box 37, Folder: Mexican Border Conference, U.S. WILPF.
5. Proceedings, Prague Congress, Series B2, Box 1, International WILPF, SCPC.
6. Ibid.
7. Allen Olmsted to Mildred Olmsted, 6 Jan. 1931, Olmsted Papers.
8. Grace Rotzel, "The School in Rose Valley," in *A History of Rose Valley* (Rose Valley: Borough of Rose Valley, 1973).
9. Interview, Marian Smith, 21 Feb. 1988.
10. Mrs. Norman Brown to Leopold Stokowski, 30 Jan. 1933, Series B3, Box 41, Folder: Stokowski, U.S. WILPF.
11. Dorothy Detzer to Rosemary Rainbolt, n.d. (ca. 1976), comments on dissertation, page 41, Document Group 86, Box 2, Detzer Papers, SCPC.
12. Ibid.
13. Dorothy Detzer to Mildred Olmsted, n.d. 1930, Series B3, Box 28, Folder: Detzer, U.S. WILPF.
14. Mildred Olmsted to Dorothy Detzer, 23 Dec. 1931, Series C, Box 17, Folder: Pennsylvania Executive Secretary, U.S. WILPF.
15. Proceedings, Grenoble Congress, Series B2, Box 1, International WILPF, SCPC.
16. Allen Olmsted, Trip Log, 12 July 1932, Olmsted Papers; Interview, 10 Feb. 1988.
17. Allen Olmsted, Trip Log, 12 July 1932, Olmsted Papers; Interview, 10 Feb. 1988.
18. Mildred Olmsted to Mary (not her real name), 7 Aug. 1932; Allen Olmsted to Mildred Olmsted, 30 Aug. 1932, Olmsted Papers.
19. Mildred Olmsted to Hannah Hull, 2 Sept. 1932, Olmsted Papers.
20. Ruth Mellor to Mildred Olmsted, 6 Oct. 1932, Olmsted Papers.
21. Allen Olmsted to Mildred Olmsted, 6 Feb. 1933, Olmsted Papers.
22. Ruth Mellor to Mildred Olmsted, n.d. Oct. 1934, Olmsted Papers.
23. Ruth Mellor to Mildred Olmsted, 18 Apr. 1937, Olmsted Papers.
24. Ruth Mellor to Mildred Olmsted, 16 Apr. 1936, Olmsted Papers.
25. See Charles Chatfield, *For Peace and Justice: Pacifism in America, 1914–1941* (Boston: Beacon, 1973), 165–67.
26. Mildred Olmsted Report to Pennsylvania Branch WILPF Annual Meeting, 25 Apr. 1933, Reading, Series B3, Box 7, U.S. WILPF.
27. Interview, 12 Nov. 1987.

28. Mildred Olmsted to Hannah Clothier Hull, 3 Aug. 1934, Series B3, Box 33, Folder: Hull, U.S. WILPF.

29. Jane Addams to Mildred Olmsted, 13 Aug. 1934, Series C, Box 21, Folder: Addams, U.S. WILPF.

30. Mildred Olmsted to Allen Olmsted, 31 Aug. 1934, Olmsted Papers.

31. Proceedings, Zurich Conference, 1934, Series B2, Box 1, International WILPF.

32. Ibid. See also Rosemary Rainbolt, "An Inquiry into the Opposition of WILPF to the ERA," paper presented at the Berkshire Women's History Conference, 18 June 1981, SCPC.

33. Proceedings, Zurich Conference, 1934, Series B2, Box 1, International WILPF.

34. Interview, 24 Nov. 1987. Mildred Olmsted to Mary Cary, 20 Dec. 1934, Series C, Box 22, Folder C; Mildred Olmsted to Roscoe Pound, 7 Dec. 1934, Series C, Box 45, Folder P, U.S. WILPF.

35. Interview, 24 Nov. 1987.

36. Ibid. Allen Olmsted to Mildred Olmsted, 16 Nov. 1934, Olmsted Papers.

37. Dr. Lovett Dewees to Mildred Olmsted, 31 Jan. 1935, Olmsted Papers.

10. "Peace Must Be Organized"

1. Dorothy Detzer to Mildred Olmsted, 25 July 1935, Olmsted Papers.

2. Mildred Olmsted to Eleanor Eaton, 4 Nov. 1936, Series C, Box 33, Folder: Eaton, U.S. WILPF.

3. Ibid.

4. Mildred Olmsted to Minnie Allen, 5 June 1936; Mildred Olmsted to Rebecca Krupp, 21 Apr. 1936; Mildred Olmsted to Virginia Fisher, 16 Dec. 1937, Series C, Box 34, Folders: Iowa, Kansas, Kentucky, U.S. WILPF.

5. Pennsylvania Board Minutes, 17 May 1938, Series B3, Box 9, U.S. WILPF. Interview, 17 Nov. 1987.

6. Pennsylvania Board Minutes, 20 Dec. 1932, Series B3, Box 7, U.S. WILPF. Interview, 28 Oct. 1987.

7. Fred Libby to Mildred Olmsted, 29 Oct. 1938, Series C, Box 33, Folder: National Council for the Prevention of War, U.S. WILPF.

8. National Board Meeting Minutes, 4–6 May 1939; Executive Committee, 18 Dec. 1940; Executive Committee, 27–30 Apr. 1940; Annual Meeting, 27–30 Apr. 1940, Series A2, Reel 130.11, U.S. WILPF.

9. Mildred Olmsted to Lyn Smith, 30 Nov. 1939; Lyn Smith to Mildred Olmsted, 6 Dec. 1939, Series C, Box 34, Folder: Keep America out of War, U.S. WILPF.

10. Gertrude Baer to Mildred Olmsted, 20 May 1937, Series B3, Box 23, Folder: Baer, U.S. WILPF. Interview, 28 Oct. 1987.

11. Mildred Scott Olmsted, "Peace Must be Organized," *Fellowship,* Jan. 1938, 6.

12. National Board Meeting Minutes, 29 Apr.–1 May 1938, Series A2, Reel 130.9, U.S. WILPF. Interview, 17 Nov. 1987.

13. Emily Greene Balch to Mildred Olmsted, 14 Mar. 1938, Series C, Box 33, Folder: Balch, U.S. WILPF.

14. Mildred Olmsted to Gertrude Baer, 24 Dec. 1937, Series C, Box 33, Folder: International, U.S. WILPF.

15. Statement of Neutrality, Luhacovice, Czechoslovakia, Proceedings, 1937 Conference, Series B2, Box 1, International WILPF.

16. Mildred Scott Olmsted, "The International Executive Meeting of the WIL," *Fellowship,* Nov. 1938, 7–8.

17. Mildred Olmsted to Allen Olmsted, 2 Apr. 1938; Ruth Mellor to Mildred Olmsted, 18 May 1938, Olmsted Papers.

18. Clara Ragaz to Mrs. James Roosevelt, 14 Aug. 1938, Allen S. Olmsted Papers.

19. Mildred Scott Olmsted, "An American Policy after Munich," *American Friend,* 8 Dec. 1938, 524–25.

20. See Pois, "Politics and Process," 445–47.

21. Interview, 17 Nov. 1987.

22. "Poll of WIL Opinion," unsigned statement by Mildred Olmsted, Branch Letter, 5 Jan. 1939, Series E, Box 3, U.S. WILPF.

23. Mildred Olmsted to Henrietta Roeloffs, 1 Sept. 1939, Series C, Box 35, Folder: National Peace Conference 1939, U.S. WILPF.

24. Mildred Olmsted to Gertrude Baer, 24 Nov. 1939, Series C, Box 34, Folder: Baer, U.S. WILPF.

25. Mildred Scott Olmsted, Organization Report, Annual Meeting, 27–30 Apr. 1940, Series A2, Reel 130.11, U.S. WILPF.

11. Peace Work in Wartime

1. Affidavit of Allen Olmsted and Mildred Olmsted about Ernest Unterleitner wife and children, American consulate in Switzerland to Allen Olmsted, n.d.; Olmsted to Consulate re Brings family, 28 Mar. 1939, Allen S. Olmsted Papers.

2. Gertrude Baer to Mildred Olmsted, 23 Dec. 1941, Series C, Box 33, Folder: Baer, U.S. WILPF.

3. Mildred Olmsted to Walter Cowing, 21 Nov. 1940, Series B3, Box 53, Folder: NYA, U.S. WILPF.

4. Mildred Olmsted to Dorothy Hommel, 18 July 1939, Series C, Box 33, Folder: Hommel, U.S. WILPF.

5. Quoted in *Four Lights,* Feb. 1966, 2.

6. Emily Greene Balch to Mildred Olmsted, ca. July 1940, Series C, Box 33, Folder: Balch, U.S. WILPF.

7. Allen Olmsted to Mildred Olmsted, 15 Aug. 1940, Olmsted Papers.

8. Ibid.

9. Mildred Olmsted to Allen Olmsted from Avalon, n.d.; Mildred Olmsted to Allen Olmsted, 20 Sept. 1940; Allen Olmsted to Mildred Olmsted 30 Oct. 1940, Olmsted Papers.

10. Mildred Olmsted, draft of letter to Eleanor Roosevelt, 4 June 1941, Series C, Box 33, Folder: "Hamilton," U.S. WILPF.

11. Mildred Olmsted to Anna C. Ames, 11 Feb. 1941, Series C, Box 34, Folder: Illinois, U.S. WILPF.

12. Mildred Olmsted to Dorothy Robinson, 2 Feb. 1942, Series C, Box 40, Folder: Robinson, U.S. WILPF.

13. Mildred Olmsted to Elsie Elfenbein, 11 Dec. 1941, Series C, Box 35, Folder: New Jersey, U.S. WILPF.

14. Mildred Olmsted, Organization Report, National Board Minutes, Annual Meeting, 1–4 May 1941, Series A2, Reel 130.11, U.S. WILPF.

15. Mildred Olmsted, Organization Report, National Board Minutes, Annual Meeting, 29 Apr.–2 May 1943, Series A2, Reel 130.11, U.S. WILPF.

16. Mildred Olmsted to Gertrude Bussey, 26 June 1942, Series C, Box 43, Folder: Bussey, U.S. WILPF.

17. Hannah Clothier Hull to Dear Co-Workers, 2 Dec. 1942, Document Group 82, Box 10, Folder: Events/Projects, Mildred Scott Olmsted Papers.

18. Ibid.

19. Mildred Olmsted to Dorothy Robinson, 17 Feb. 1943, Series C, Box 40, Folder: Robinson, U.S. WILPF.

20. Mildred Olmsted to Dorothy Robinson, 3 Aug. 1943, Series C, Box 40, Folder: Robinson, U.S. WILPF.

21. Reprint from *PM*, 18 July 1943. Women's Committee to Oppose Conscription, Document Group 68, SCPC. Hereafter: WCOC Papers.

22. Reprint from "Town Meeting of the Air," February, 1944, WCOC Papers.

23. A. J. Muste to Eleanor Garst, 27 Aug. 1945, Box 2, Folder: F.O.R., WCOC Papers.

24. Mildred Olmsted to Dorothy Detzer, 24 Feb. 1947, Series C, Box 44, Folder: 15, U.S. WILPF.

25. Jean Wilcox to Mildred Olmsted, 13 June 1942, Series C, Box 40, Folder: Wilcox, U.S. WILPF.

26. Interview, 22 Oct. 1987.

27. Mildred Olmsted to Adele Saul, ca. 10 Sept. 1943, Olmsted Papers.

28. Ruth Mellor to Mildred Olmsted, 5 Oct. 1943, Olmsted Papers.

12. One World

1. Lydia Wentworth to Mildred Olmsted, 13 Sept. 1945, Box 4, Folder: "W," WCOC Papers.

2. Mildred Olmsted to Dorothy Robinson, 3 Aug. 1945, Series B3, Box 59, Folder: Robinson, U.S. WILPF.

3. Dorothy Detzer to Grace Rhoads, 11 Jan 1946, Series C, Box 41, Folder: Detzer, U.S. WILPF. Interview, 24 Nov. 1987. Mildred remembered that they had a meeting in the new Jane Addams House to which Dorothy came, and at which she cried; this cannot be, however, as WILPF did not move into its new headquarters until sometime after Dorothy's resignation.

4. "Miss Detzer's Statement to the Board Submitting her Resignation," 27 Jan. 1946, Branch Letter, 1946, Series E, Box 3, U.S. WILPF.

5. Interview, 24 Nov. 1987.

6. Dorothy Robinson to My dear Miss Rainbolt, 18 May 1975; Dorothy Detzer to "Dear Rosemary," 9 Sept. 1975, Detzer Papers, Document Group 86, Box 2, Folder: Rainbolt, SCPC.

7. Gladys Walser to Mildred Olmsted, 4 Mar. 1946, Series C, Box 41, Folder: Walser; Mildred Olmsted to Olive Reddick, 13 Sept. 1948, Series C, Box 45, Folder: Reddick, U.S. WILPF.

8. *Four Lights,* Jan. 1947, 2.

9. Mildred Scott Olmsted, "Shall the WILPF Continue or Dissolve?" Proceedings, Luxembourg Congress, August 1946, Series B2, Box 1, International WILPF.

10. Mildred Olmsted to Gertrude Baer, 9 June 1948; Mildred Olmsted to Emily Greene Balch, 6 Oct. 1947, Series C, Box 44, Folder: Balch, U.S. WILPF. International Executive Committee, Liverpool, 1950, Series B2, Box 1, International WILPF.

11. Mildred Olmsted to Barbara Duncan-Harris, 4 Jan. 1949, Series C, Box 44, Folder: International Executive Committee, U.S. WILPF.

12. Gertrude Bussey and Margaret Tims, *Pioneers for Peace: Women's International League for Peace and Freedom, 1915–1965* (London: Allen and Unwin, 1965; reissued 1980), 190.

13. Branch Letter, Apr. 1947, Series E, Box 3; Mildred Olmsted to Gladys Walser, 31 Mar. 1947, Series C, Box 45, Folder: Walser, U.S. WILPF.

14. Allen Olmsted to Mildred Olmsted, 31 May 1947, 22 July 1949, Allen Olmsted Papers.

15. Allen Olmsted to Mildred Olmsted, 31 May 1947, Allen Olmsted Papers. Mildred Olmsted to Allen Olmsted, n.d. July 1947, Olmsted Papers.

16. Mildred Olmsted to Allen Olmsted, n.d. 1949, Olmsted Papers.

17. Mildred Olmsted to Dear Children, 25 July 1949, Series 2, Box 7, Mildred Scott Olmsted Papers.

18. Proceedings, 11th Congress, Series B2, Box 1, International WILPF.

19. Birthday Luncheon, 1949, Series 4, Box 10, Folder: Events/Projects, Mildred Scott Olmsted Papers.

20. Ibid.

21. Ibid.

22. Proceedings, International Executive Committee, Liverpool, 15 July 1950, Series A, Box 11, International WILPF.

23. Ibid.

24. Branch Letter, 15 Sept. 1950, Series E, Box 4, U.S. WILPF.

25. Norman Thomas to Women's International League for Peace and Freedom, Dear Friends, 28 Aug. 1950, Series C, Box 52, Folder: Thomas, U.S. WILPF.

13. *Survival in the Fifties*

1. Mildred Olmsted, Branch Letter, 1950, Series E, Box 4, U.S. WILPF.

2. Mildred Olmsted to Elsie Picon, 29 Aug. 1951, Series C, Box 51, Folder: Picon, U.S. WILPF.

3. Mildred Olmsted to Emily Greene Balch, 8 Jan. 1952, Series C, Box 46, Folder: Balch, U.S. WILPF.

4. Mildred Olmsted to Gertrude Baer, 11 Jan. 1952, Series C, Box 46, Folder: Baer, U.S. WILPF.

5. Mildred Olmsted to Dear Staff, 3 Aug. 1952, Series C, Box 48, Folder: International Executive Committee, U.S. WILPF.

6. Proceedings, International Executive Committee, 1952, Series A, Box 11, International WILPF, SCPC.

7. "The Rosenberg Case," December 1952, Series C, Box 51, Folder: Policy Committee, U.S. WILPF.

8. *Four Lights,* Mar. 1953, 1.

9. Mildred Olmsted to Emily Parker Simon, 15 Jan. 1954, Series C, Box 59, Folder: Policy Committee, U.S. WILPF.

10. Mildred Olmsted to Orlie Pell, 16 Mar. 1954, Series C, Box 54, Folder: Committee on Branch Problems, U.S. WILPF.

11. Arlo Tatum to Kitty Arnett, 19 Mar. 1954; Juliet Saltman to Mildred Olmsted, 31 July 1954, Series C, Box 54, Folder: Committee on Branch Problems, U.S. WILPF.

12. Wilma Nissley to Mildred Olmsted, 25 Nov. 1954; Juliet Saltman to Mildred Olmsted, 31 July 1954, Series C, Box 54, Folder: Committee on Branch Problems, U.S. WILPF.

13. "Dear Shively Resident," 31 Aug. 1954; Series C, Box 54, Folder: Committee on Branch Problems, U.S. WILPF.

14. Maeme Brock to Mildred Olmsted, 9 Oct. 1954; Mildred Olmsted to Evelyn Johnson, 25 Apr. 1955; Beatrice Pearson to Dear Mrs. Olmstead, 11 Nov. 1954, Series C, Box 54, Folder: Committee on Branch Problems, U.S. WILPF.

15. Leah Goldstein to Mildred Olmsted, 19 Apr. 1955, Series C, Box 54, Folder: Committee on Branch Problems, U.S. WILPF.

16. Doris Mills to Mildred Olmsted, 4 June 1955, Series C, Box 54, Folder: Committee on Branch Problems, U.S. WILPF.

17. Mildred Olmsted to Mary W. Howgate, 3 May 1955, Series C, Box 55, Folder: Field Secretary, U.S. WILPF.

18. Mildred Olmsted to Jeannette Cleary, 4 Oct. 1955, Series C, Box 54, Folder: Committee on Branch Problems, U.S. WILPF.

19. Fran Hurley to Mildred Olmsted, 4 Jan. 1955, Series C, Box 54, Folder: Committee on Branch Problems, U.S. WILPF.

20. Leah Goldstein to Mildred Olmsted, 19 Apr. 1955, Series C, Box 54, Folder: Committee on Branch Problems, U.S. WILPF.

21. Bertha McNeill to Mildred Olmsted, 8 and 27 July 1954, Series C, Box 54, Folder: Committee on Branch Problems; Mildred Olmsted to Alice Woodruff, 29 Apr. 1954, Box 54, Folder: Committee on Evaluation, U.S. WILPF.

22. Edith W. Simester to Mildred Olmsted, 2 Oct. 1954, Series C, Box 54, Folder: Committee on Branch Problems, U.S. WILPF.

23. Mildred Olmsted Speech, Denver, Series 3, Box 8, Folder: Speeches, Mildred Scott Olmsted Papers.

24. Alice Paul to Mrs. Kenyon Rector, 17 June 1954, Series C, Box 60, Folder: Washington, D.C., U.S. WILPF. (The carbon of Alice Paul's letter is not signed, but Amelia Fry, Alice Paul's biographer, confirms that it is undoubtedly her letter.)

25. Allen Olmsted to Mildred Olmsted, 12 Feb. 1953, Box 1, Folder: Correspondence, Mildred Scott Olmsted Papers.

26. Interview, 11 Nov. 1987.

27. Mildred Olmsted to Agnes Stapleton, 9 Dec. 1952, Series C, Box 48, Folder: International Executive Committee, U.S. WILPF.

28. Mildred Olmsted, "The World Today: A Survey of U.S. Attitudes in World Affairs," Proceedings, 12th International Conference of the WILPF, Paris, 1953, 196–201, Series B2, Box 1, International WILPF.

29. Mildred Olmsted to Signe Hojer, 5 June 1954, Series C, Box 48, Folder: International, U.S. WILPF.

30. Ruth Mellor to Allen Olmsted, 6 June 1955, Allen Olmsted Papers. Allen Olmsted to Mildred Olmsted, 11 June 1955, Olmsted Papers.

31. Allen Olmsted to Mildred Olmsted, 6 July 1942, Olmsted Papers.

32. Ruth Mellor to Mildred Olmsted, 2 Jan. 1946, Olmsted Papers.

33. Mildred Olmsted Speech, 6 Aug. 1955, Series C, Box 58, Folder: Japan, U.S. WILPF.

34. Mildred Olmsted to Adele Saul, 18 Aug. 1955, Olmsted Papers.

35. Mildred Scott Olmsted, "Open Doors for WILPF?" Four Lights, Dec. 1955, 2.

36. Ibid.

14. Time of Troubles

1. Mildred Olmsted Report, WILPF Annual Meeting, 16–21 June 1959, Lasell College, Auburndale, Mass., Series A2, Reel 130.18, U.S. WILPF.

2. Branch Letter, Apr. 1959, Series E, Box 5, U.S. WILPF.

3. Ibid.

4. Virginia Durr to Mildred Olmsted, 1 Oct. 1959, Series C, Box 59, Folder: Alabama, U.S. WILPF.

5. Mildred Scott Olmsted, *Four Lights,* Apr. 1962, 2.

6. Branch Letter, Apr. 1957, Series E, Box 5, U.S. WILPF.

7. Branch Letter, Mar. 1961, Series E, Box 6, U.S. WILPF.

8. Ellen McGranahan to Mr. and Mrs. Olmsted (enclosing newspaper clipping), 25 July 1961, Olmsted Papers.

9. Proceedings, Stockholm Congress, 1959, Series B2, Box 2, International WILPF.

10. Allen Olmsted to Adele and Maurice, 7 Feb. 1959, Olmsted Papers.

11. Allen Olmsted to Mildred Olmsted, 17 and 18 Feb. 1959, Olmsted Papers.

12. Branch Letter, Dec. 1959. Series E, Box 5, U.S. WILPF.

13. Branch Letter, July 1960, Series E, Box 5, U.S. WILPF.

14. Branch Letter, Sept.–Oct. 1960, Series E, Box 5, U.S. WILPF.

15. Ibid.

16. FBI Records, 7 June 1961, Box 11, Mildred Scott Olmsted Papers.

17. Ibid.

18. Allen Olmsted, Trip Log, ca. 1976, Olmsted Papers.

19. Interview, 24 Nov. 1987.

20. Ibid.

21. Ibid.

22. Report, "U.S.–U.S.S.R. Women's Conference," Nov. 1961. Typescript, unpublished article by Elise Boulding; Branch Letter, n.d. 1962, Series E, Box 6, U.S. WILPF.

23. Report of 1961 Conference, Branch Letter, Dec. 1961, Series E, Box 6, U.S. WILPF.

24. Ruth Mellor to Mildred Olmsted, 2 Dec. 1961, Olmsted Papers.

25. Interview, 24 Nov. 1987.

26. Ruth Gage Colby to Mildred dear, 25 Jan. 1962, Olmsted Papers.

27. Emma Cadbury to Mildred Olmsted, n.d. Jan. 1962, Olmsted Papers.

28. Interview, 24 Nov. 1987.

29. Interview, Pat Olmsted, 9 Feb. 1989.

30. Allen Olmsted to Polly Olmsted, 16 Apr. 1962, Allen S. Olmsted Papers.

31. Mildred Olmsted to Dear Children, 27 July 1962, Olmsted Papers.

15. The Vietnam Era

1. Norman Cousins to Asilomar Congress, 6 July 1962, Series C, Box 65, Folder: Triennial Greetings, U.S. WILPF.

2. Branch Letter, June 1963, Series E, Box 6, U.S. WILPF.

3. Mildred Olmsted to Dear Family, 19 July 1963, Olmsted Papers.

4. Allen Olmsted to Isabel and Tony, 22 July 1963, Olmsted Papers.

5. Allen Olmsted to Polly Olmsted, 26 July 1963, Olmsted Papers.

6. Mildred Olmsted, "Dear Member," *Four Lights,* Oct. 1963, 2.

7. Branch Letter, Feb. 1964, Series E, Box 6, U.S. WILPF.

8. Mildred Olmsted to International Red Cross, 21 July 1964, Series C, Box 62, Folder: I, U.S. WILPF.

9. Branch Letter, Jan. 1964, Series E, Box 5, U.S. WILPF.

10. Report on U.S.–U.S.S.R. Conference, *Four Lights,* June 1964, 1.

11. Ibid.

12. Else Zeuthen to Mildred Olmsted, 1 May 1965, Series C, Box 62, Folder: International, U.S. WILPF.

13. Mildred Olmsted, Report of Executive Director, Annual Meeting, U.S. Section of WILPF, 26 June 26–1 July 1964, Series A2, Reel 130.23, U.S. WILPF.

14. Branch Letter, Apr. 1964, Series E, Box 7, U.S. WILPF.

15. Branch Letters, Jan. and Apr. 1964, Series E, Box 7, U.S. WILPF.

16. Mildred Olmsted to Adele and Maurice, 4 Aug. 1964, Document Group 87A, uncataloged papers, Mildred Scott Olmsted Papers.

17. Mildred Olmsted to Dear Folks, 14 Aug. 1964, uncataloged papers, Mildred Scott Olmsted Papers,

18. Branch Letter, Apr. 1965, Series E, Box 7, U.S. WILPF.

19. Report marked "Confidential," Philadelphia, Mississippi, and WILPF, Series C, Box 63, Folder: Mississippi, U.S. WILPF.

20. Mildred Olmsted to Adele and Maurice, 12 Aug. 1965, Olmsted Papers; Branch Packet, Sept. 1965, Series E, Box 7, U.S. WILPF.

21. Branch Letter, Sept. 1965, Series E, Box 7, U.S. WILPF.

22. Mildred Olmsted to Adele and Maurice, 12 Aug. 1965, Olmsted Papers.

23. *Four Lights,* Oct. 1965, 2.

24. Ruth Mellor to Mildred Olmsted, 30 Sept. 1965, Olmsted Papers.

25. Branch Packet, Sept. 1965, Series E, Box 7, U.S. WILPF.

26. Report of Executive Director, 13–17 Oct. 1965, Box 10, Folder: Events, Mildred Scott Olmsted Papers.

27. Annual Report, Fiftieth Annual Meeting, Branch Packet, Oct. 1965, Series E, Box 7, U.S. WILPF.

28. Dorothy Detzer to Mildred Olmsted, n.d. Sept. 1965, Box 10, Folder: Events, Mildred Scott Olmsted Papers.

29. A. J. Muste to Mildred Olmsted, 5 Oct. 1965, Box 10, Folder: Events, Mildred Scott Olmsted Papers.

30. Kay Camp to Dear Mildred, 1 Oct. 1965, Box 10, Folder: Events, Mildred Scott Olmsted Papers.

31. Else Zeuthen to Mildred Olmsted, n. d. Oct. 1965, Box 10, Folder: Events, Mildred Scott Olmsted Papers.

32. Florence Selleck to Mildred Olmsted, n.d. Oct. 1965, quoting Lloyd C. M. Hare, *The Greatest American Woman, Lucretia Mott* (New York: Historical Society, 1937), Box 10, Folder: Events, Mildred Scott Olmsted Papers.

33. Lucy Carner, "Mildred Scott Olmsted: Architect of the U. S. Section," *Pax et Libertas,* Apr.–June 1966, 20–21.

34. Transcript, FCC Hearing, Box 11, Mildred Scott Olmsted Papers.

35. *Four Lights,* Feb. 1966, 2.

36. Branch Letter, Feb. 1966, Series E, Box 7, U.S. WILPF.

16. Golden Years

1. Statement, 18th Congress, New Delhi, 1970–1971, *Congress Report* (Geneva: WILPF, 1971), 31.

2. Mildred Olmsted to Dorothy Steffens, "Random and very hurried thoughts for Dorothy Steffens, January 22, 1973," Box 5, Mildred Scott Olmsted Papers; Interview, 17 Nov. 1987.

3. Interview, 24 Nov. 1987. Ruth Freeman to Mildred Olmsted, 6 July 1976, Olmsted Papers.

4. Mildred Olmsted to Dear Joyce, Series 2, Box 5, Folder: 1973, Mildred Scott Olmsted Papers.

5. Mildred Olmsted to Dear Everybody, 3 Oct. 1968, Olmsted Papers.

6. Elise Boulding to Mildred Olmsted, 3 Jan. 1968, Series 4, Box 10, Mildred Scott Olmsted Papers.

7. Ibid.; Mildred Olmsted to Phoebe Cusden, 17 Apr. 1956; Marie Louis-Mohr to Mildred Olmsted, 14 June 1956, Series C, Box 56, Folder: International, U.S. WILPF.

8. Tano Jodai to Mildred Olmsted, 31 Mar. 1968, Series 2, Box 4, Mildred Scott Olmsted Papers.

9. Mildred Olmsted to Ruth Mellor, 15 May 1970, Olmsted Papers. Interview, 3 Nov. 1987.

10. AFSC, Peace Education Minutes, 24 Apr. 1968, AFSC Archives. Adelaide Baker to Mildred Olmsted, 23 Mar. 1973, Olmsted Papers.

11. Issues Paper in Branch Packet, Feb. 1970, Series E, Box 15, U.S. WILPF.

12. Ibid.

13. Dorothy Detzer to Mildred Olmsted, 22 June 1977, Series 3, Box 8, Mildred Scott Olmsted Papers.

14. Interview, Van Voris. Series 3, Box 8, Mildred Scott Olmsted Papers.

15. Mildred Olmsted to Ruthie Dear, 11 Mar. 1969, Olmsted Papers.

16. Mildred Olmsted to Allen Olmsted, n.d., Allen S. Olmsted Papers.

17. Statement by Mike Kessler, ca. 27 Dec. 1977, Olmsted Papers.

18. Galia Votaw to Mildred Olmsted, 2 Apr. 1978; Spencer Coxe to Mildred Olmsted, 30 Dec. 1977, Series 2, Box 5, Mildred Scott Olmsted Papers.

19. Anonymous, n.d.; Helen Rea, 27 Dec. 1977, Series 2, Box 5, Mildred Scott Olmsted Papers.

20. Mildred Olmsted to Enid and Bill, 26 Jan. 1982, Olmsted Papers.

21. Interview, 1 May 1987.

22. Mildred Olmsted to Helen, 5 Sept. 1984, uncataloged papers 87A, Box 1, Mildred Scott Olmsted Papers.

17. A Legend in Her Own Time

1. Frances Early, "An Interview with Mildred Scott Olmsted: Foremother of the Women's International League for Peace and Freedom," *Atlantis* 123, no. 1: 142–50.

2. Susan Blake to Dear Sister Activists and Friends, n.d. June 1980, Series 4, Box 10, Mildred Scott Olmsted Papers.

3. Interview, Phyllis Rubin, 16 Jan. 1991.

4. Interview, Regene Silver, 23 Jan. 1991.

5. Steve Nelson to Mildred Olmsted, 20 Sept. 1986, Olmsted Papers.

6. Interview of Mildred Olmsted by Mercedes Randall, 1972, Series 4, Box 9, Mildred Scott Olmsted Papers.

7. Transcription of charge to graduating class, Swarthmore College, 1 June 1987, Olmsted Papers.

8. Ibid.

9. Interviews, Ari Breckenridge, July 1990; Regene Silver, 23 Jan. 1991.

10. Interview, Phyllis Rubin, 16 Jan. 1991.

11. Interview, Ari Breckenridge, July 1990.

12. David McReynolds to Mildred Olmsted, 15 Oct. 1986, Series 4, Box 10, Mildred Scott Olmsted Papers.

FOR FURTHER READING

Addams, Jane. *Twenty Years at Hull House*. New York: Macmillan, 1910.

Addams, Jane; Emily Green Balch; and Alice Hamilton. *Women at the Hague—1915*. Reprint. New York: Garland, 1972.

Brown, Elizabeth Potts, and Susan Mosher Stuard. *Witnesses for Change: Quaker Women over Three Centuries*. New Brunswick, N.J.: Rutgers Univ. Press, 1989.

Bussey, Gertrude, and Margaret Tims. *Pioneers for Peace: Women's International League for Peace and Freedom 1915–1965*. London: Allen and Unwin, 1965.

Chatfield, Charles. *For Peace and Justice; Pacifism in America, 1914–1941*. Knoxville: Univ. of Tennessee Press, 1971.

Cook, Blanche Wiesen. "Female Support Networks and Political Activism: Lilian Wald, Crystal Eastman, Emma Goldman." *Chrysalis 3* (Autumn 1977): 43–61.

Cott, Nancy F. *The Grounding of Modern Feminism*. New Haven: Yale Univ. Press, 1987.

Davis, Allen F. *American Heroine: The Life and Legend of Jane Addams*. New York: Oxford Univ. Press. 1973.

DeBenedetti, Charles. *An American Ordeal: The Antiwar Movement in the Vietnam Era*. Syracuse: Syracuse Univ. Press, 1990.

Detzer, Dorothy. *Appointment on the Hill*. New York: Holt, 1948.

Faderman, Lillian. *Surpassing the Love of Men; Romantic Friendship and Love Between Women from the Renaissance to the Present*. New York: Morrow, 1981.

Foster, Catherine. *Women for All Seasons; The Story of the Women's International League for Peace and Freedom*. Athens: Univ. of Georgia Press, 1989.

Jones, Rufus. *A Service of Love in Wartime*. New York: Macmillan, 1920.

Lamson, Peggy. *Roger Baldwin: The Founder of the American Civil Liberties Union*. Boston: Houghton Mifflin, 1976.

Miller, William. *Dorothy Day: A Biography*. New York: Harper & Row, 1982.

Pickett, Clarence. *For More Than Bread*. Boston: Little, Brown, 1953.

Pois, Anne Marie. "The WILPF: 1915–1941." Ph.D. diss., Univ. of Colorado, 1988.

Rainbolt, Rosemary. "Inquiry into the Opposition of WILPF to the ERA." Paper presented at the Berkshire Women's History Conference, 18 June 1981, Swarthmore College Peace Collection.

Randall, Mercedes. *Improper Bostonian: Emily Greene Balch*. New York: Twayne, 1964.

Robinson, JoAnne. *Abraham Went Out; A Biography of A. J. Muste*. Philadelphia: Temple Univ. Press, 1981.

Silver, Regene. "Jane Addams; Peace, Justice, Gender, 1860–1918." Ph.D. diss., Univ. of Pennsylvania, 1990.

Smith-Rosenberg, Carol. "Female World of Love and Ritual." *Signs: Journal of Women in Culture and Society* 1 (Autumn 1975): 1–29.

Sochen, June. *The New Woman; Feminism in Greenwich Village, 1910–1920*. New York: Quadrangle, 1974.

Swanberg, W. A. *Norman Thomas: The Last Idealist*. New York: Scribners, 1976.

Tims, Margaret. *Jane Addams of Hull House, 1860–1935*. New York: Macmillan, 1961.

Wittner, Lawrence. *Rebels Against War: The American Peace Movement, 1933–1983*. Philadelphia: Temple Univ. Press, 1984.

Wreskin, Michael. *Oswald Garrison Villard: Pacifist at War*. Bloomington: Indiana Univ. Press, 1965.

INDEX

One Woman's Passion for Peace and Freedom

was composed in 12 on 13 Garamond No. 3 on a Mergenthaler Linotron 202
by Eastern Composition, Inc.;
printed by sheet-fed offset on 50-pound, acid-free Natural Smooth,
Smyth-sewn and bound over binder's boards in Holliston Roxite B,
and with dust jackets printed in 2 colors
by Braun-Brumfield, Inc.;
and published by
Syracuse University Press
Syracuse, New York 13244-5160

Syracuse Studies on Peace and Conflict Resolution
Harriet Hyman Alonso, Charles Chatfield, and Louis Kriesberg, *Series Editors*

A series devoted to readable books on the history of peace movements, the lives of peace advocates, and the search for ways to mitigate conflict, both domestic and international. At a time when profound and exciting political and social developments are happening around the world, this series seeks to stimulate a wider awareness and appreciation of the search for peaceful resolution to strife in all its forms and to promote linkages among theorists, practitioners, social scientists, and humanists engaged in this work throughout the world.

Other titles in the series include: